CREATING A
SOFTWARE
ENGINEERING
CULTURE

CREATING A

SOFTWARE

ENGINEERING

CULTURE

Karl E. Wiegers

Dorset House Publishing
353 West 12th Street
New York, New York 10014

Library of Congress Cataloging-in-Publication Data

Wiegers, Karl Eugene, 1953–
     Creating a software engineering culture / Karl E. Wiegers.
          p.   cm.
     Includes bibliographical references and index.
     ISBN 0-932633-33-1 (hardcover)
     1. Software engineering.   I. Title.
     QA76.758.W52 1996
     005.1'068--dc20

                                                    96-27627
                                                    CIP

Cover Design: Jeff Faville, Faville Design
Cover Photograph: Jim Newmiller

Copyright © 1996 by Karl E. Wiegers. Published by Dorset House Publishing, 353 West 12th Street, New York, NY 10014.

Distributed in the United Kingdom, Ireland, Europe, and Africa by John Wiley & Sons Ltd., Chichester, Sussex, England. Distributed in the English language in Singapore, the Philippines, and southeast Asia by Toppan Co., Ltd., Singapore; and in the English language in Japan by Toppan Co., Ltd., Tokyo, Japan.

Printed in the United States of America

Library of Congress Catalog Number: 96-27627

ISBN: 0-932633-33-1   12 11 10 9 8 7 6 5 4 3 2

To
Pretzels the Clown

Acknowledgments

The dedicated critiquing efforts of Marcelle Bicker, Tim Brown, Lynda Fleming, Anne Fruci, Kathy Getz, Lesle Hill, Trudy Howles, Kevin Jameson, Tom Lindsay, Lori Schirmer, Doris Sturzenberger, Mike Terrillion, and Nancy Willer led to countless suggestions for improvement. These reviewers caught many errors; any that remain are entirely my responsibility. I also appreciate the helpful comments provided by Linda Butler, Henrietta Foster, Beth Layman, Mark Mitchell, Carol Nichols, Tom Sweeting, and Peter Szmyt.

None of the achievements made by our Kodak software groups would have been possible without the active involvement of all team members. I am indebted to the original members of the Photographic Applications Software Team, who worked with me as we learned how to build better software from January 1990 through April 1993. We learned a lot from each other, built some useful applications, and had fun in the process. Many thanks to Ray Hitt, Tom Lindsay, Mike Malec, and Mike Terrillion. Mike Terrillion also allowed me to describe his work correlating the number of requirements in a software requirements specification with the work effort needed to deliver the application.

Thanks go as well to John Scherer and Jim Terwilliger, managers who didn't know a lot about software, but were willing to learn. They provided solid management support and encouragement during the early years of our process improvement efforts. They also understood the importance of providing recognition for the team's efforts to improve our work and to share our approaches with other software groups at Kodak. Judy Walter and Jeffrey Yu in the Kodak Research Library kept me in touch with the software literature by responding quickly to a steady stream of requests for books and articles.

I am grateful to the staff at Dorset House, particularly Wendy Eakin, David McClintock, Ben Morrison, and freelance editor Teri Monge, for their careful review and editing, insightful recommendations, and support throughout this project.

Special thanks go to Professor Stanley G. Smith of the University of Illinois at Urbana-Champaign, who taught me a lot more in graduate school than how to do physical organic chemistry.

On the home front, I wish to thank my cat, Gremlin, for keeping my lap warm whenever I try to read, and the musical genius of "Weird Al" Yankovic, for helping to put life into proper perspective. My deepest appreciation goes to my wife, Christine Zambito, for her limitless support, encouragement, listening ability, and sense of humor. Living with a clown is just slightly less peculiar than living with a computer person.

Permissions Acknowledgments

The author and publisher gratefully acknowledge the following for their permission to reprint material quoted on the cited pages.

p. 16: Material from *Yeager, An Autobiography* by Chuck Yeager and Leo Janos, p. 235, reprinted by permission of Bantam Doubleday Dell Publishing Group. Copyright © 1985. All rights reserved.

pp. 23, 45: Material from *Peopleware: Productive Projects and Teams* by Tom DeMarco and Timothy Lister, pp. 135 and 12, reprinted by permission of Dorset House Publishing. Copyright © 1987. All rights reserved.

p. 35: Material from *Managing Software Maniacs* by Ken Whitaker, p. 45. Copyright © 1994, published by John Wiley & Sons. All rights reserved.

p. 51: Material reprinted from *Communications of the ACM,* stated purpose—reprinted monthly. Material reprinted from *IEEE Computer,* stated purpose—reprinted monthly.

pp. 61, 214: Material reprinted from *Software Reliability* by Glenford J. Myers, pp. 39, 189–95. Copyright © 1976, published by John Wiley & Sons. All rights reserved.

pp. 61, 165, 313: Material reprinted from *Quality Is Free* by Philip Crosby, pp. 15, 58, 131. Copyright © 1979 McGraw-Hill. Reproduced with permission of The McGraw-Hill Companies.

pp. 63, 147, 158, 168, 170, 215: Material and data adapted from *Assessment and Control of Software Risks* by Capers Jones, pp. 29, 34, 286, 435, 436. Copyright © 1994. Reprinted by permission of Prentice-Hall, Inc., Upper Saddle River, N.J. All rights reserved.

p. 85: Figure 6.3 reprinted from IEEE Std 830-1993 IEEE Recommended Practice for Software Requirements Specifications, Copyright © 1994 by the Institute of Electrical and Electronics Engineers, Inc. The IEEE disclaims any responsibility or liability resulting from the placement and use in this publication. Information is reprinted with the permission of the IEEE.

pp. 105, 127: Material reprinted from W.S. Humphrey, *Managing the Software Process* (pages vii & 287), © 1989 Addison-Wesley Publishing Company, Inc. Reprinted by permission of Addison-Wesley Longman Publishing Company, Inc.

Contents

Figures and Tables

Preface

Rarely has a professional field evolved as rapidly as software development. The struggle to stay abreast of new technologies, to deal with accumulated development and maintenance backlogs, and to cope with people issues has become a treadmill race, as software groups work hard just to stay in place. A key goal of disciplined software engineering is to avoid the surprises that can occur when software development goes awry. Software surprises almost always lead to bad news: canceled projects, late delivery, cost overruns, dissatisfied customers, and unemployment because of outsourcing.

The culture of an organization is a critical success factor in its efforts to survive, improve, and flourish. A culture based on a commitment to quality software development and management differentiates a team that practices excellent software engineering from a gaggle of individual programmers doing their best to ship code. In a software engineering culture, the focus on quality is present at all levels—individual, project, and organization.

In this book, I share a cultural framework that was effective in improving the results obtained by several software groups at Eastman Kodak Company. Most of our projects involved small teams of one to five developers, with typical durations of six months to two years. Each part of the book discusses several guiding principles that shaped the way we chose to create software. I also describe the specific software engineering practices that we adopted to improve the quality and productivity of our work. We believe a culture based on these principles and practices has improved our effectiveness as software engineers, the relationship and reputation we have with our customers, and our level of collaborative teamwork. Many of the experiences related and suggestions offered are most relevant to workgroups of two to ten engineers. Since even large software products are often constructed by small teams of engineers working together, these technical activities are applicable in a wide variety of organizations.

With this book I hope to reach first-line software managers, project leaders, and practitioners who wish to drive progress toward an improved, quality-oriented culture in their organization. My goals are to provide practical ideas for immediately improving the way a team performs software engineering, and to show that continuous software process improvement is both possible and worthwhile. I am assuming that the reader has the ability to actually change the culture of his software group, or at least to positively influence those who can drive changes.

I present here a tool kit composed of many ideas and practices for those who wish to improve the quality of the software they develop, along with case studies of how these methods really worked. Our groups have applied all the methods described, and I have used nearly all of them personally. Every anecdote is real, although the names have been changed. While not every team member has used every good method on every project, we invariably obtained better results when we applied these solid engineering practices than when we did not.

An organization grows a quality-directed software culture by blending established approaches from many sources with locally developed solutions to specialized problems. To help point toward useful sources in the voluminous software literature, each chapter provides an annotated bibliography of references and additional reading materials. The references I feel are particularly valuable are marked with a bookshelf icon.

Each chapter contains several "Culture Builder" tips (marked with a handshake icon), which are things a manager or project leader can do to promote an attitude and environment that leads to software engineering excellence. "Culture Killers" are also described, and are marked with a skull and crossbones warning icon. Culture killers are management actions that will undermine a team devoted to superior software engineering or prevent such a culture from developing. Sadly, many of these are real examples. You can probably think of other culture killers from your own experience, as either victim or unknowing perpetrator. Although both builders and killers are written in the form of recommendations, remember that the culture killers are tongue-in-cheek. Don't rush into work next Monday with an agenda of action items selected from the culture killers!

Some of the experiences of our software groups at Kodak were published originally in the following articles; material is included here with permission from the publishers:

Wiegers, Karl E. "Creating a Software Engineering Culture," *Software Development*, Vol. 2, No. 7 (July 1994), pp. 59-66.

———. "Effective Quality Practices in a Small Software Group," *The Software QA Quarterly*, Vol. 1, No. 2 (Spring 1994), pp. 14-26.

———. "Implementing Software Engineering in a Small Software Group," *Computer Language*, Vol. 10, No. 6 (June 1993), pp. 55-64.

———. "Improving Quality Through Software Inspections," *Software Development,* Vol. 3, No. 4 (April 1995), pp. 55-64.

———. "Lessons from Software Work Effort Metrics," *Software Development,* Vol. 2, No. 10 (October 1994), pp. 36-47.

———. "In Search of Excellent Requirements," *Journal of the Quality Assurance Institute,* Vol. 9, No. 1 (January 1995), pp. 23-32.

CREATING A SOFTWARE ENGINEERING CULTURE

Part I

A Software Engineering Culture

very organization has a culture of its own—a set of shared beliefs, goals, and values that characterize its priorities and actions. The culture of a group that performs software development has a major impact on the quality of its products, the productivity of its developers, and the teamwork among its members. A software group committed to quality has a "software engineering culture" focused on the belief that certain technical and managerial practices are more conducive than others to creating quality products in a positive environment. A software engineering culture is a fusion of quality-oriented attitudes, human interactions, and technical processes. The culture is based on a set of precepts, often unspoken, that guide the behaviors of the people in the organization.

This book is divided into six parts. Part I describes the elements of a software engineering culture and addresses three cultural premises that shape the way people in an organization devoted to excellence in software engineering might choose to behave. Parts II through V present technical practices that can be used to help an organization evolve toward a quality-driven culture, and the impact these practices have had on some small software groups at Eastman Kodak Company. Part VI identifies top-priority action items that software managers and developers should consider undertaking as they start on the path to a software engineering culture.

The cultural precepts addressed in Part I are

✔ Never let your boss or your customer talk you into doing a bad job.

✔ People need to feel the work they do is appreciated.

✔ Ongoing education is every team member's responsibility.

Chapter 1

Software Culture Concepts

*With a little artistic license and stretching of the imagina-
tion, we could imagine computer programmers as having a
culture—a shared set of beliefs and activities which shape
their day-to-day activities.*

—Gerald M. Weinberg, *The Psychology of Computer Programming*

In their classic book *Peopleware*, Tom DeMarco and Timothy Lister report a range
of performance among the best and worst individual computer programmers
who participated in their Coding War Games of about ten to one [DeMarco,
1987]. Other studies have shown variations of up to twenty to one in programmer
productivity and quality [Weinberg, 1992]. DeMarco and Lister also describe an
eleven to one productivity range among the ninety-two software development
organizations in their study. We can conclude that not all software groups are created, or perform, equal.

Imagine the impact of a ten to one range of productivity or quality in other
professions: assembly line workers, airline pilots, physicians, race car drivers, or
secretaries. Most businesses could not tolerate such huge differences in the capabilities of individual employees, but this is a reality in the software world.
Software managers must find ways to deal with such a wide range of individual
performance.

Culture Defined

A significant factor in this performance variability is the culture of a software
development organization. *The American Heritage Dictionary* defines "culture" as
"the totality of socially transmitted behavior patterns, arts, beliefs, institutions, and
all other products of human work and thought characteristic of a community or
population." Culture includes a set of shared values, goals, and principles that

guide the behaviors, activities, priorities, and decisions of a group of people working toward a common objective. Cultural cohesion is not necessarily constructive or forward-thinking. The nineteenth century British workmen known as Luddites had a common culture, which was to oppose the labor-saving textile machinery that they feared would eliminate their jobs. Some cultures are characterized by a divergence of opinions and behaviors rather than by shared values. But when coworkers align along common, uplifting beliefs, it is easier to induce changes that will increase the group's effectiveness and its likelihood of survival. A shared culture is one difference between a team and a "bunch of bozos on a bus" (to paraphrase Larry Constantine).

The ability to implement any specific change in the techniques or tools used by an organization depends on the prevailing cultural attitudes. A development staff with a commitment to excellence in software engineering is more receptive to trying new approaches that might help it reach this objective. In contrast, an attitude of "just bang out the code because we haven't got time to think about the problem before trying to solve it" will make it difficult for a manager to encourage process improvements or behavioral changes.

Every organization has its own culture, but some are more uplifting than others. When I refer to a software engineering culture, I'm talking about the quality-focused group, not the code crankers. I often call this a "healthy" software engineering culture, because it includes three essential components:

- personal commitment by each developer to create quality products by systematically applying effective software engineering practices

- organizational commitment by managers at all levels to provide an environment in which software quality (in its many dimensions) is a fundamental success driver, and which enables each developer to achieve this goal

- commitment by all team members to continuously improve the processes they use, thereby continuously improving the products they create

Figure 1.1 illustrates how a software engineering culture relates to the goals, actions, priorities, and technical practices of an organization. The values and beliefs held by the team members define quality and productivity goals, which imply the practices that are adopted to achieve those goals. The consistent application of these practices, and the ability to demonstrate that you are achieving the desired results, reinforces the culture devoted to software engineering. Similarly, the culture provides a foundation for decisions and actions, the consistent application of which further reinforces the cultural values. The culture also helps the organization's managers set their priorities. Consistent priorities communicated by managers send the message that all levels of the organization share a commitment to software quality. These reinforcing feedback loops are needed to sustain the evolution of the software culture to ever-improving performance.

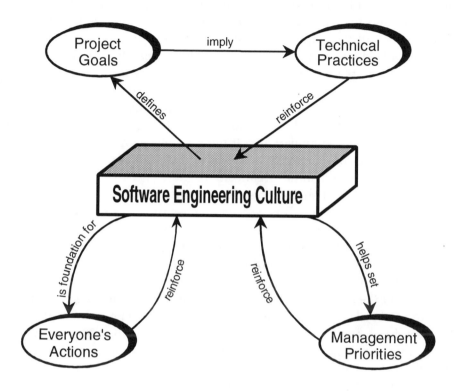

Figure 1.1: A software engineering culture.

People working in a culture oriented toward software engineering realize there is much more to application development than hacking out a computer program. The tasks of project planning and management, problem domain analysis, requirements specification, architecture and program design, validation, and documentation far outweigh the effort that goes into the actual programming step. These other activities lay the foundation for the solid code that will deliver what the customer needs. Software engineering focuses on developing useful applications by using a variety of tools and techniques that cover a range of application problems, not simply writing programs.

As software organizations throughout the world strive to improve their processes and products, those organizations that develop a culture that effectively implements sound engineering practices ultimately will beat out the competition. This is true for software groups that support the internal operations of a corporation, as well as for those that sell in the commercial or embedded systems markets. Corporate software groups that deliver quality products on schedule and budget are more likely to survive the ever-present threat of outsourcing.

Growing Your Own Culture

You can't buy a culture in shrink-wrap; you must grow your own. Every software team works in a different context of technologies, application domains, customer expectations, and management pressures. While the trade-offs made in different environments will vary, quality-focused attitudes and the sound engineering processes that lead to quality products are applicable nearly everywhere.

There is no simple recipe or checklist for creating a software engineering culture. There is only a set of technical practices that are known to facilitate the building of quality software products, the individual discipline to apply these practices, and leadership behaviors that nurture the budding quality-focused culture. Cultivating a software engineering culture is a long path with many steps. Each step will contribute constructively to the culture as well as to improving the products created by the people in the organization.

In a group without a shared objective of software excellence, not every member feels the need to change. It is easy to dismiss process improvement efforts as just the latest management blathering. Therein lies the seeds of conflict, as some members of a team embrace new ways of working, while others grumble their resistance. This conflict is not a requirement: If all goes well, a nucleus of improvement enthusiasts will serve as role models for those more skeptical about the need for change and the anticipated benefits. As most of the team forges ahead toward the future world of software engineering, those who don't embrace the new culture will probably complain for a while, and then leave. Alternatively, the resisters may attempt to drag the group back to their own comfort level, if permitted to do so by their management and peers.

The process of agreeing on principles and values provides many opportunities for improving the work environment and the work results. Aligning the group members toward common improvement activities is best performed through group brainstorming exercises or formal process assessments. Small teams composed of representatives from the group can then work together to identify better ways to perform the group's software tasks. The software manager cannot simply decree the changes that need to be made and expect anything constructive to happen. His job is to steer the team toward working on the key improvement areas that constitute the next step toward the software engineering culture.

A shared culture is a necessary foundation for progressing through the software process maturity sequence, to the discipline of repeatable and measurable development processes. As an organization systematically and thoughtfully works to improve its procedures and processes, a common culture is a natural by-product. A quality-oriented culture enables all team members to contribute their full capabilities to building excellent products through both individual achievements and effective teamwork. People working in such a culture recognize that employing defined processes for developing software does not inhibit their creativity; instead, it lets them shift their creative energies to other aspects of the development life cycle, such as requirements engineering and software design.

Once the improved processes are under control and have become part of the normal way of doing business, more focus can be placed on the product itself. Companies and development organizations don't produce processes—they create *products* intended to delight their customers. When the culture supports process improvement as a matter of course, people will not waste energy resisting beneficial changes; instead, they can concentrate their creativity on building new and better software products, using improved techniques.

Even though aspects of an organization's culture may be documented in writing, the real culture is revealed through the behaviors of everyone in the group. Writing mission statements, visions, values, and principles are the latest rage. Mission statements can help everyone in the group understand his or her role in the grand scheme of the corporation, and having the team agree on a vision describing long-range objectives that transcend individual projects also provides a focus for sustained achievements. The culture can indeed be shaped through this sort of practical and meaningful documentation of shared philosophies, provided it offers working tools rather than just the output of one-time exercises in group-think.

Too often, though, missions, visions, and the rest simply contain platitudes. "We value honesty, integrity, and respect for others." "We will be a world-class software supplier." "We will produce zero-defect products." Few can disagree with such lofty goals. But are they realistic? Can they be measured? Do they have any impact on the way the people in the group work and act? Do the leaders practice what the slogans on the wall preach?

Sometimes, the official behavioral expectations of a group are documented in a shelf full of software development standards. But are they followed and enforced? Do they add value to the development process and its products, or are they a standing joke among the development staff? The official party line expressed in this kind of written documentation may be at odds with the underlying, unwritten culture of the group. Standards and methodologies may represent what the managers claim they want from people, or what they think they are *supposed* to want. The unwritten culture, though, is shaped by the degree of trust and mutual respect among all members of the organization. It is reflected in the consistency, or congruence, between what is said and what is done by managers and team members [Weinberg, 1994]. In short, culture is "how things are really done around here."

The first-line manager or project leader has a tremendous influence on the ability of a software group to evolve constructively. The manager must shape the culture by gentle persuasion, leading by example, providing positive and negative reinforcement, and supplying the resources necessary to make change happen. For example, a manager who declares that 5 percent of each engineer's time should be devoted to process improvement activities but then does not adjust project responsibilities to make this time available will likely harm the culture, not help it. The manager is sending mixed signals, and the action of always succumbing to project pressures speaks louder than the words "process improvement."

The path to a software engineering culture involves changing the behaviors of team members so they follow proven practices that lead to superior software. By moving toward an environment in which every team member can effectively apply the best available software engineering methods, the group will enjoy improved quality and productivity. When your developers have truly internalized the concepts of software engineering, those concepts define *the* way software is built in your group, not *a* way someone might choose to build software. A developer interested in software engineering practices may use them if it is convenient, but a developer committed to software engineering will stick to a disciplined approach even if it is inconvenient at times.

A Healthy Software Culture

The culture of a software group is revealed through the behaviors of individuals, teams, and managers, and in the characteristics of the organization as a whole. A group having a true commitment to excellence in software engineering and enlightened management is likely to exhibit many of the following characteristics.

Individual Behaviors

- Each individual explicitly strives to perform some aspect of each project better than on the previous project, reflecting an individual dedication to continuous improvement.

- An egoless attitude encourages team members to submit work products for review by their peers, and to be receptive to finding mistakes in their work and learning from those mistakes.

- Individuals spend some personal time reading software books and periodicals to keep abreast of new technologies, and they continually look for ways to apply superior techniques to appropriate problems.

Team Behaviors

- Mutual respect among the developers permits vigorous technical discussions without fights or put-downs.

- Newer team members benefit from effective and nonjudgmental mentoring by those who have more experience.

- Team members use common engineering procedures and tools to collaborate effectively on projects. Teamwork is the rule, not the exception.

- Existing work products, including code, are extensively reused, because of an attitude that the greatest productivity comes from not doing work that has already been done.

- The team shares an attitude of getting it right the first time. The quality emphasis is on preventing defects, not just fixing them when the customer or tester complains.

- Data on the team's software products and processes is collected and analyzed to find ways to do even better on the next project.

- Customers of the software being created are at the center of the requirements specification and design efforts.

Management Behaviors

- Management and the company provide support for ongoing education through conferences and seminars, tuition reimbursement for college studies, and purchase of technical books and periodicals.

- Management provides the money and time for appropriate tools, training, and support for new technologies. Training needs are factored into project schedules.

- Senior non-software managers recognize the alignment of sound software engineering practices with the desired business results of the company.

- The actions managers take are consistent with their words. They understand the premises of software engineering, and they reward those staff members who consistently practice it well.

Organizational Characteristics

- An ongoing effort is devoted to process improvement. All team members participate in improvement activities as part of their regular job responsibilities.

- Overarching business and information technology strategies provide a framework for the evolution of the organization, making decisions, and setting priorities.

- Written software development procedures of manageable size have been adopted by the team members and are regularly followed.

The software utopia described here probably doesn't really exist. Approaching it is hard work, demanding visionary leadership and sustained teamwork over a long period of time. The more of these characteristics that can be found in your environment, the more attractive it will be to prospective employees who want to work in a quality-driven culture.

A Less Healthy Software Culture

Other groups have cultures based on informal, unstructured, and undocumented ways of building software. The results obtained depend solely on the individual contributor. There is a lack of shared philosophies and behaviors. Managers do not appreciate the significance of modern software engineering methods, and they do not provide an environment conducive to their application. Some of the traits displayed by such organizations follow.

Individual Behaviors

- Interactions among team members are characterized by territorialism and protection of knowledge. ("If I tell Susan the complete answer to her question, she'll be as smart as I am, and I don't want that.")

- "Coding cowboys" go their own ways, without alignment with group objectives and practices, and without repercussions. Troubled projects are saved through the heroic actions of talented individuals who operate any way they please, not through the effective teamwork of capable engineers who rely on tried-and-true techniques.

- There is no time for quality practices such as peer reviews, systematic testing, or documentation.

- Project leaders agree to ludicrous delivery time lines to look good to their managers or customers, and then they lose their credibility, their sanity, and perhaps their jobs when the project falls far behind schedule. Project management is a game, not a science.

Management Behaviors

- Poor management leadership, heavy workloads, unrealistic schedules, and little recognition lead to a high staff turnover rate.

- There are no systematic, management-driven improvement efforts in place. Project pressures keep everyone's nose firmly attached to the grindstone.

- Schedule is always put before quality.

- Brooks's Law, "Adding manpower to a late software project makes it later," is routinely violated [Brooks, 1995].

- Managers do not talk honestly with their staff. They seem to have hidden agendas, or personal goals that override the team's goals. Managers are not respected or trusted.

Organizational Characteristics

- One new method or tool after another is tried, seeking the magic solution that will generate a productivity breakthrough in the project. Frederick Brooks taught us that there is no silver bullet to lay software problems forever to rest [Brooks, 1987]. Believe it.

- There is a shelf full of standards and software development methodologies no one uses. Alternatively, development can only be performed according to the rigid and elaborate methodology that was created by a consultant ages ago.

- Developers are stuck in dead-end jobs, with no opportunities for growth. Local experts become indispensable because no one else could replace their knowledge of ancient and critical applications.

- High-pressure workloads and poor ergonomic environments lead to emotional stress and repetitive strain injuries, which reduce productivity and further increase the time pressures.

- Nothing is written down about how work is to be done in the organization, so individuals apply whatever processes they know. Completed projects do not go through postmortem analyses to discover why they succeeded or (more likely) failed.

I hope there aren't any real organizations that completely fit this description of software hell, but most groups exhibit some of these negative characteristics. Those that are currently causing pain for people in the group are ripe for immediate attention as part of the improvement effort. Use these checklists to assess the balance of healthy and unhealthy attributes in your organization.

Organizational Options

Larry Constantine describes four organizational paradigms that characterize very different cultures [Constantine, 1993]. Each type of organization will respond differently to attempts to change the way work is done. To launch a software process improvement or culture change effort, first understand which model your organization is most like. Then select the approach most likely to be successful for inducing change in your climate. These are the paradigms Constantine identifies (see Fig. 1.2):

> *Closed:* A traditional hierarchy of authority, with decisions usually imposed by those above you on the organization chart; such organizations are oriented toward stability and continuity.
>
> *Open:* Integrates stability with innovation, and individual with collective interests; adaptive collaboration, flexibility, and consensus-building are typical characteristics; change likely will succeed, provided that the team members participate in the decision-making, planning, and implementation.
>
> *Random:* Characterized by innovative individuals who go their own ways; change proceeds through creative autonomy; team members can be creative and energetic, but definitely are individuals.
>
> *Synchronous:* Features harmonious alignment of individuals with a shared vision of goals and methods, where rocking the boat is frowned on; the shared culture focuses on the status quo, with little conflict or chaos; groups operate efficiently through tacit agreement on roles and responsibilities.

It is not so much that any one of these organizational cultures is superior to the rest but that different change techniques are likely to succeed in the different environments. Also, the different cultures demand different leadership styles [Constantine, 1995].

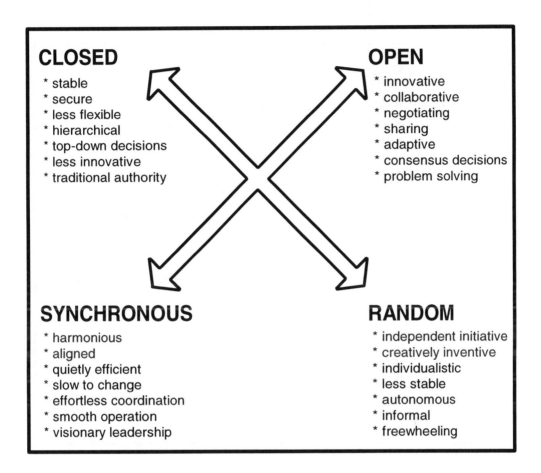

Figure 1.2: Characteristics of Constantine's four organizational paradigms.

Perhaps the best fusion of attributes selected from among these paradigms is found in the structured open team. Table 1.1 lists some of the special characteristics of a structured open team [Constantine, 1993]. The culture embodied in such a team is more likely to enable consistent software engineering excellence than is the culture in any of the four basic organizational types.

In a workshop Constantine presented on team composition and roles, he did not identify the presence of a leader as one of the distinguishing features of a team. While teams in some cultures can be successful without a leader, I believe an insightful, visionary, decisive, and sensitive leader can have an enormous positive impact on the effectiveness and group dynamics of most teams. Conversely, a team without such a leader might well turn into an unfocused group of individuals doing their own work as well as they can, with interpersonal problems going unresolved, resources applied inefficiently and to the wrong efforts, and results determined solely by individual capabilities and work ethics.

Table 1.1.
Characteristics of a Structured Open Team.

- A catalog of essential team roles

- Formal specification and institutionalization of functional roles, so everyone knows what someone playing one of these roles is expected to do

- Default assignment of roles to individuals to assure that essential functions are performed

- Rotation of roles to promote flexibility and skill acquisition

- A structured, externalized group memory for information management

- Clear, simple external accountability

- Technical consensus-building, not majority decision-making

- Promotion of personal ownership of work products

If you can find a group of talented individuals who interact effectively on a peer-to-peer basis in a self-managed team, that's terrific. Even on such a team, one person often emerges naturally as a de facto leader. Sometimes, multiple leaders emerge in various domains, with different individuals leading technical, organizational, administrative, and communication aspects of the work. A dynamic leader can be the dominant factor in getting a struggling group to jell and focus on a culture of taking the right actions at the right times for the right reasons.

Other models of culture in software organizations have also been proposed. In *The Olduvai Imperative,* Peter DeGrace and Leslie Hulet Stahl describe two opposing cultural views of software engineering, which they term "Roman" and "Greek" [DeGrace, 1993]. The Roman view reflects the characteristics of many larger, older development organizations. Greek thinking is more likely to be found in smaller, more dynamic software shops. Table 1.2 summarizes some of the attributes of these two cultural modes. Driving change in these two types of organizations will require very different approaches.

Table 1.2.
Aspects of "Roman" versus "Greek" Software Engineering Cultures.

The Roman Way	The Greek Way
• Structured methods	• Object-oriented methods
• More formality	• Less formality
• Excessively large programs	• Small scale programs
• Computer-aided software engineering tools	• Individual preferences in methods
• Standards that induce conformity	• Standards that enable uniformity
• Strictly managed software projects	• Undermanaged projects
• Left-brain thinking	• Right-brain thinking
• Volumes of low-quality documentation	• Minimum documentation
• Manages the projects	• Writes the programs

The Management Challenge

An effective software leader is more concerned with the work environment, attitudes, and behaviors of his developers than with meeting his own manager's expectations. A manager works for the people he supervises, not the reverse. His responsibility is to enable them to reach their peak potential as software engineers, while achieving the objectives of the customers, the project, the organization, and the company. If the team leader spends a lot of time working on committees and activities at the behest of senior management, little energy remains to address the day-to-day needs of the people in his group. Such neglect can lead to festering problems that never get solved, stagnation of the software processes used in the group, low morale, and high staff turnover.

The effective leader has a vision of how software engineering should be performed in his domain, and he has outlined a path to evolve from the current state to the realization of that vision. Since every work environment is different, the leader must assess how best to implement the steps leading to process improvement in his organization. Skill is required to pull all team members into the evolution process and to keep the right amount of gentle but steady pressure on everyone to grow and improve. All activities must strike a balance between doing and improving, since the project work has to get done. A good leader will strive for perfection, but will settle for excellence.

Building a quality-oriented software engineering culture is hard work. During construction, the culture is easily undermined by actions that are inconsistent with the words. Unless the manager exhibits consistent, congruent behavior, he will have zero credibility with the development staff. A group oriented toward good software engineering may regress back to the individual performance level unless the immediate supervisor reinforces the quality culture in everything he says and does.

In his autobiography, Air Force General Chuck Yeager related his experiences when he became the commander of a squadron of jet fighter pilots a few years after he broke the sound barrier as a test pilot [Yeager, 1985]. His comments on leadership can be applied to software engineering management and culture as well as to military command:

> To win their confidence, I had to perform up to expectations. Once they saw I was really good, they would follow my leadership—not just obey orders—because I had proved that I knew what I was talking about. . . . I had high performance standards and because the men respected me, they stretched to reach them. . . .
>
> All of us enjoyed being in a good squadron that was becoming even better.

It is not enough for a manager to be involved with efforts to improve the software engineering practices in his group: He must be committed to the changes. To understand the difference, consider a manned space flight. The people in Mission Control are involved in the flight, but the astronauts are committed. Managers and development staff share accountability for improving the effectiveness of the team. You will know you have been successful in your efforts to drive a cultural change if you see sustainable changes in the way work is done in your group. When you reach this stage, the team members have internalized the new behaviors. They are applied as a matter of course on future projects without the need for continual management reminders.

Table 1.3 lists fourteen software engineering principles that formed the foundation for constructive cultural changes in several software groups at Kodak. The rest of this book describes how each of these principles led us to select specific development practices to improve our software processes, work products, and team interactions. If you agree with our philosophy, make similar practices a part of your team's software engineering culture. If you do not agree with all of the cultural ideas presented here, decide what you do believe, and help your group evolve from a bunch of programmers to a team of software engineers. Create a clear and attainable vision, set a promising direction, and establish high standards, and most people will follow. This is one difference between being a manager and being a leader.

Table 1.3.
Software Engineering Cultural Principles.

1. Never let your boss or your customer talk you into doing a bad job.

2. People need to feel the work they do is appreciated.

3. Ongoing education is every team member's responsibility.

4. Customer involvement is the most critical factor in software quality.

5. Your greatest challenge is sharing the vision of the final product with the customer.

6. Continual improvement of your software development process is both possible and essential.

7. Written software development procedures can help build a shared culture of best practices.

8. Quality is the top priority; long-term productivity is a natural consequence of high quality.

9. Strive to have a peer, rather than a customer, find a defect.

10. A key to software quality is to iterate many times on all development steps except coding: Do this once.

11. Managing bug reports and change requests is essential to controlling quality and maintenance.

12. If you measure what you do, you can learn to do it better.

13. Do what makes sense; don't resort to dogma.

14. You can't change everything at once. Identify those changes that will yield the greatest benefits, and begin to implement them next Monday.

Summary

✔ Despite evidence that contemporary software engineering methods lead to improved quality and productivity, many developers continue to write software using undisciplined techniques that lead to low-quality products and unpredictable projects.

✔ The software manager or project leader faces the challenge of creating a culture in which team members consistently perform excellent software engineering in a healthy, supportive, and rewarding environment.

✔ Different types of organizational cultures demand different approaches to the change process.

✔ By working to align group objectives with a vision of superior products and processes, an effective leader/manager can drive improvements in all facets of an organization's work.

Culture Builders and Killers

Culture Builder: Have team members share their experiences in applying new techniques and methods at team meetings on a regular basis. It is even valuable to discuss the methods that didn't work. This approach to team meetings is much more stimulating than hearing routine progress reports on projects that are underway. Team meetings provide an opportunity to learn about new ways to solve problems and to leverage from what others have already done.

Culture Builder: If your group merges with another during a corporate reorganization, or if you hire several new developers at once, ask everyone in the new group to bring samples of specific work products to a team meeting to pass around. Examples are requirements specification documents, test plans, and system documentation. This open sharing can facilitate an attitude of seeking out best practices from wherever you find them, as well as helping to reach agreement on how certain engineering tasks should be performed in your environment.

Culture Builder: If your project team is getting swamped, take responsibility yourself for doing a part of the work. Even if the contribution is not substantial (and it probably shouldn't be; you have other responsibilities that should not be ignored), the symbolic value of the manager rolling up his sleeves and helping to carry the load can help motivate the rest of the team. It will also help you understand the problems they face and obstacles you can remove from their path.

Culture Killer: As the manager, make sure you have the most powerful workstation in the group, even if you use it only for e-mail. This shows that an individual's value to the organization is indicated by the number of MIPS on his desk.

Culture Killer: If your senior managers don't understand software, software engineering, or software process improvement, don't waste your time trying to educate them or persuade them to invest time and money in your improvement efforts. If they don't think you should be learning to work smarter, you might as well keep doing things the way you always have.

References and Further Reading

Boehm, Barry W. *Software Engineering Economics.* Englewood Cliffs, N.J.: Prentice-Hall, 1981.

> Chapter 33 deals with factors that affect software productivity and aspects of managing and motivating software developers. Personnel attributes and human factors provide by far the largest opportunity for improving productivity.

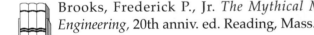

Brooks, Frederick P., Jr. *The Mythical Man-Month: Essays on Software Engineering,* 20th anniv. ed. Reading, Mass.: Addison-Wesley, 1995.

> Just as nine women cannot have a baby in one month, people and time do not exhibit a simple inverse relationship on software projects. In organizations where the managers have not read *The Mythical Man-Month,* you may find projects staffed with many fractional people. It is a fallacy to assign an engineer to work on four projects at 25 percent time each and expect him to be as productive as if all his time was devoted to a single project.

———. "No Silver Bullet: Essence and Accidents of Software Engineering," *Computer,* Vol. 20, No. 4 (April 1987), pp. 10–19. Reprinted in *Software State-of-the-Art: Selected Essays,* Tom DeMarco and Timothy Lister, eds. (New York: Dorset House Publishing, 1990), pp. 14-29.

> This essay debunks the myth that the next bit of magical software technology will finally be the one to solve development problems for the long run. Brooks proposes some steps by which an organization can develop the great designers who will determine the technical excellence of software products.

Constantine, Larry L. "Leading Your Team—Wherever It Goes," *Software Development*, Vol. 3, No. 1 (January 1995), pp. 26-34.

> Constantine discusses how to become a successful team leader in groups having different cultural paradigms: traditional hierarchy, independent initiative, collaborative negotiation, and alignment with a common vision.

———. "Work Organization: Paradigms for Project Management and Organization," *Communications of the ACM*, Vol. 36, No. 10 (October 1993), pp. 35-43.

> Constantine presents a four-pole model of organizational paradigms and explores how to apply this framework to the tasks of building teams and leading projects.

DeGrace, Peter, and Leslie Hulet Stahl. *The Olduvai Imperative: CASE and the State of Software Engineering Practice.* Englewood Cliffs, N.J.: Yourdon Press/Prentice-Hall, 1993.

> This intriguing book is really about two opposing cultural views of software engineering. DeGrace and Stahl discuss approaches for selecting and deploying methods, metrics, and tools in these two types of organizations. They provide a thought-provoking perspective on different schools of software engineering thought, behavior, and values.

 DeMarco, Tom, and Timothy Lister. *Peopleware: Productive Projects and Teams.* New York: Dorset House Publishing, 1987.

> *Peopleware* is a definitive resource on human issues in software development. In a highly readable style, it covers topics ranging from the factors that affect individual programmer productivity, to ways to build (and destroy) effective teams. Many ideas are presented for improving the work environment to enhance productivity and the quality of work-life. If your engineers are working odd hours to avoid interruptions, or if your project teams never seem to jell, read *Peopleware* immediately.

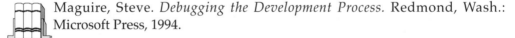 Maguire, Steve. *Debugging the Development Process.* Redmond, Wash.: Microsoft Press, 1994.

> Maguire candidly describes many of the errors he found project leaders making at Microsoft, and he gives concrete recommendations for how to avoid those problem situations. He presents much useful advice about how software engineers and project managers can work smarter, not harder, to achieve superior results.

McConnell, Steve. *Code Complete.* Redmond, Wash.: Microsoft Press, 1993.

> Chapter 31 addresses personal character issues that affect an individual's effectiveness as a software engineer. The traits, habits, and attitudes McConnell describes for individuals lay the foundation for an organization-wide software engineering culture.

Weinberg, Gerald M. *The Psychology of Computer Programming.* New York: Van Nostrand Reinhold, 1971.

> Weinberg addresses aspects of programming as human performance, a social activity, and an individual activity. While software has changed a great deal in the past quarter century, human nature has not. Weinberg provides insight into the ways programmers think and behave, both on their own and in concert with others.

————. *Quality Software Management, Volume 1: Systems Thinking.* New York: Dorset House Publishing, 1992.

> This book, first of a four-volume series, includes a discussion of six subcultural patterns of behavior found in software organizations. Weinberg provides guidance to help software managers understand their cultural pattern and work within it to steer their organization from variable software development behaviors toward congruent behaviors.

————. *Quality Software Management, Volume 3: Congruent Action.* New York: Dorset House Publishing, 1994.

> Weinberg emphasizes the need for managers to act congruently: They must not only understand the concepts of good software engineering, but also practice them. Weinberg's insights will help software managers think about their role, behaviors, and management style as they attempt to grow effective development teams.

Whitaker, Ken. *Managing Software Maniacs.* New York: John Wiley & Sons, 1994.

> Whitaker presents many practical tips about how to hire the right developers, lead them to success, and make the difficult decisions that result in delivering quality products on schedule. Many anecdotes from Whitaker's extensive experience in the commercial software field provide lessons on how to get development, marketing, management, and quality assurance to work together effectively.

Yeager, Chuck, and Leo Janos. *Yeager.* New York: Bantam Books, 1985.

Yeager's autobiography contains leadership perspectives that apply to software management as well as to military command.

 Yourdon, Edward. *Decline and Fall of the American Programmer.* Englewood Cliffs, N.J.: Yourdon Press/Prentice-Hall, 1992.

Yourdon grabs your attention by claiming that the high costs and low quality of much American software will lead to outsourcing of software development to programmers in other countries. After this provocative introduction, he presents a solid and highly readable overview of modern software engineering issues: people, processes, methodologies, CASE, software quality assurance, metrics, reusability, and reengineering. Yourdon also is the editor of *American Programmer,* a monthly magazine that addresses a wide variety of contemporary topics in software development. See the July/August 1990, June 1992, July 1993, December 1994, and January 1995 issues for many good articles dealing with software teams and their cultures.

Chapter 2

Standing On Principle

The only freedom that has any meaning is the freedom to proceed differently from the way your manager would have proceeded. This is true in a broader sense, too: The right to be right (in your manager's eyes or in your government's eyes) is irrelevant; it's only the right to be wrong that makes you free.

—Tom DeMarco and Timothy Lister, *Peopleware*

You may be asked to cut corners on the quality of the work you do or the way you do it. Sometimes, the person making the request is a manager who doesn't appreciate the value of the quality activities you practice, or someone who feels budget and schedule pressures you may not. Sometimes, it is a customer who wants you to address only her specific needs, even though you have identified an opportunity to generalize beyond her requirements to provide enhanced value to a broader user community within your own company. Customers and managers alike may press you to skip key engineering steps from time to time. It would be nice to think we are beyond the stage of "don't bother with those specs, start writing code," but this call of the software dinosaur still echoes throughout the land.

It's not easy to resist these pressures from the people who pay the bill or your salary. Sometimes you have no choice: Do what is asked of you, or head out the door. But people working in a quality-oriented software engineering culture will do their best to follow established and intelligent practices in times of crisis, as well as in normal times. Developers and managers must adopt personal standards that motivate them to stick to their software process guns in the heat of battle. You might need to temper this idealism with the reality of keeping your job, but start from the position of quality being paramount. Whenever a situation arises that calls for a value judgment, an ethical decision, or a choice between doing what is right and doing what you are asked to do, remember this: Never let your boss or your customer talk you into doing a bad job.

Integrity and Intelligence: With Customers

Perhaps it sounds like heresy, but the customer is not always right; however, the customer always has a point. Too often, software developers incorporate every feature requested by a customer into a requirements specification without regard to how much effort it will take to implement, or whether it is truly necessary to achieve the customer's objectives. While you must respect the attitudes and requests made by every customer, don't be blinded by the notion that you are hearing the "voice of the customer" and therefore must do whatever that voice says. Much of the value that a systems analyst adds to the application development process comes from looking for solutions that address the true user needs with creativity, efficiency, and thoughtfulness.

Some years ago, our software group at Kodak developed a PC-based system for controlling some lab equipment. The customers asked us to write a pop-up calculator program the users could invoke while they were running the program (this was before the advent of windowing systems that made such features commonplace). After a little thought, we concluded it would be cheaper simply to buy a basic calculator for each of the hundred-odd anticipated users and slap one on the side of each monitor with a piece of Velcro®. The customer need was for a calculator function—it didn't really have to be built into the software. That was just a cute, but unnecessarily expensive, solution the customer envisioned. There are two lessons here:

> **Look past the customer's request for a feature to find the underlying real need; and, look for simple and cheap solutions for the real need, not just the solution that the customer initially requested or one that looks neat.**

In a healthy software engineering culture, developers are empowered to take the actions they feel will best meet the company's objectives, in the context of project goals, customer needs, and resource realities. Sometimes, this means driving a paradigm shift in the way applications are built or delivered: new methods, new tools, new architectures, new platforms.

For example, one Kodak software group was asked to reengineer a large suite of scientific programs, written over a span of many years in Fortran on an IBM mainframe. We wished to migrate this into an object-oriented architecture in C++ running on a UNIX® platform. However, the current computing infrastructure would not allow the entire user base for this application suite to have direct access to the UNIX server right away. So, we devised an unconventional transitional architecture that helped move us toward the future, while keeping one foot firmly planted in the current reality.

This interim solution was an "inverted" client/server architecture, with the user interface component on the mainframe (to which all the users already had access) and the server component on a UNIX box. This unconventional solution effectively bridged the technology gap between the present and future states of our computing environment, which was in the early stages of migrating toward a more open systems architecture. The other solutions that were proposed were not consistent with the long-term strategic objectives of this organization. They would have resulted in software that few users could access immediately, or they would have further tied us to the older technology of the mainframe. The paradigm shift embodied in the approach we took addressed real user needs creatively.

Everyone is subject to tunnel vision. Customers think in terms of what functions they personally will use in the application, not those that should be included because of their potential value to other users. We ran into this situation on another project, which was requested by one area of the research laboratories at Kodak. Not surprisingly, the primary customer representative focused on the needs of the community she represented. However, the analyst spotted several places where the application could be made more generally useful without a lot of extra effort, thereby meeting the needs of other research departments.

This customer rep was reluctant to have us spend the extra time building in these generalizations. However, we felt they would enable Kodak to leverage the investment in this custom software over a broader internal user community. So, we went ahead and designed the system to incorporate these generalizations. In this case, we were willing to incur the unhappiness of the primary customer, because we were doing the right thing for the company. If her department had declined to pay for the extra work required for the more general solution, we would have funded it in some other appropriate way. The lesson here is

> **Look beyond the local interests of the primary customers to see whether you can easily generalize an application to meet a broader need.**

This rationale also applies to the identification of potentially reusable components in the course of application design. It will always take more time to design, implement, and verify a reusable component than to code a custom solution for one project. Think of designing for reuse as an investment you can cash in on multiple future projects, for the good of the company. Don't let resistance by your customer or your manager inhibit you from making smart strategic decisions.

Occasionally, you may encounter a customer who is a self-styled software engineer and who therefore wishes to provide a lot of technical input into how you design his application. This is usually a case of someone having just enough knowledge to be dangerous. The project leader must resist letting such customers become technically involved in design and implementation (unless, of course, the customer really *does* know what he's doing). Focus his energy on the requirements, or get him involved with testing and writing user aids, but do not let the customer drive the technical aspects of the project. The rule to remember is

> **Make sure you know where the customer's software expertise stops. Do not allow the customer to intimidate you into making poor design decisions.**

Developers must base their relationships with customers on mutual trust and respect. We expect our customers to be forthright with us about their requirements and constraints, and they expect us to be straight with them on cost and schedule. Conversely, when customers come to developers with changes in the established requirements baseline, we have to make sure they understand the impact of the changes they are requesting. New or modified requirements may not look so attractive once the customers know the cost, in terms of dollars or delivery time, of a late change. By the same token, if schedules slip as the project progresses, the customers have to be kept informed, even if they don't want to hear it.

I know of one developer who had originally promised to deliver a new application in October. He fell behind on the project, and as of September, it was clear that several months of work remained to be done. Unfortunately, the developer had not updated his delivery estimate with the customers: They still expected the system to be ready in October. We had to do some quick expectation management. As you might expect, the customers weren't happy about the "sudden" change in schedule. This developer didn't think about this principle:

> **Be honest with your customers. The project stakeholders are entitled to accurate information, whether or not it is good news.**

Do you say you will do something and then never get around to it? I feel this reflects a lack of personal integrity. Follow through on the commitments you have made. However, if something changes—you decided you won't do it, or you are unable to do it on time for whatever reason—talk about it! There are many reasons, some good and others not so good, why you might not be able to fulfill a commitment, but it is irresponsible not to notify those affected by your decision. So long as you are open about a problem, you can work out a solution. The message is this:

> **If you agree to a commitment, the other people involved expect you to do it. If anything changes, let them know as soon as you can, so you can work out an alternative.**

As a manager, I told my team members it was their right and their responsibility to tell me when their backlog pile became too high. Then it was *my* responsibility to help them deal with the pile. When I asked them to take on a new task, it was completely acceptable for them to reply, "Sure, I can do that, Karl. What would you like me to stop doing to free up the necessary time?" Until they told me the pile was too high, I had no way of knowing that this was the case. Naomi Karten suggests reasons and ways to "just say whoa" [Karten, 1994].

Integrity and Intelligence: With Managers

A colleague was once asked by a manager to estimate the delivery time for a planned large software application. He replied, "Two years." The manager said, "No, that's too long. How about six months?" My colleague's response was, "Okay." Wrong answer! What changed in the five seconds that elapsed between his first estimate of two years, and his second statement, agreeing to a schedule only one-quarter as long? Nothing, except that he thought the manager wanted to believe that six months was feasible. The project did not suddenly shrink by 75 percent, nor did the available staff increase four-fold or instantly become four times as productive. The project was not reestimated based on an improved algorithm. My colleague simply said what the manager wanted to hear, undermining his own credibility as a software estimator and project leader. To no one's surprise, the project extended beyond two years. Agreeing to unattainable commitments is unprofessional and unfair to all involved, including yourself.

How should this all-too-common situation have been handled? Here are a few approaches to try; there is no guarantee that any of them will work with unreasonable managers or customers, but try them first before caving in.

1. Explain your estimating method to the manager, and ask on what basis the manager's estimate is smaller. The manager may not really have an estimate, but he has a goal. You may not have an estimate, either, only a guess. It's harder to argue with an estimate based on some analytical, quantitative process than with a number pulled out of thin air. Historical metrics data can help build your case.

2. If you can't provide an accurate estimate because there are no written requirements, offer to provide a more precise estimate after some initial exploration of the project scope and general user requirements.

3. Point out that an estimate made very early in a project can be off by 80 percent or more. Present a range of estimates: best case, most likely, and worst case, with the approximate probability of meeting each one. Presenting a single estimate at the beginning of a sizable project sets an expectation that will persist in people's minds long after the original requirements and assumptions have drastically changed.

4. Negotiate for a larger team, fewer features, phased delivery, or reduced quality as ways to achieve an aggressively accelerated schedule. Make sure the stakeholders understand these trade-offs: They will not get something for nothing.

5. Redo your estimate with some different assumptions of project size, resources, or other factors, to see how close you can come to the manager's shorter goal. Make sure the assumptions are clearly communicated to everyone involved in the decision-making.

6. Make a counteroffer, showing the manager what fraction of the system's functionality realistically could be delivered in six months.

Concealing a project's scope from management is even more irresponsible than agreeing to a schedule you cannot possibly meet. One project leader was leading a long-term reengineering effort, but she never prepared a detailed project plan. She was afraid if her manager found out how extensive (and expensive) the project really was, the manager would squelch it. Both this project leader and her manager acted inappropriately. The project leader should have been forthright about defining the scope of the project and managing it properly, while the manager should have insisted on seeing a project plan and having some accountability. One purpose of project planning is to identify all the tasks that have to be performed to make the project a success. Pretending those tasks aren't there doesn't make them go away.

The Five Dimensions of a Software Project

There are five dimensions that must be managed on a software project: features, quality, cost, schedule, and staff (shown in Fig. 2.1). These dimensions are not all independent. For example, if you add staff, the schedule may be shortened (although not necessarily), and the cost may increase. A more common trade-off is to shorten the schedule or add features, and sacrifice quality. The trade-offs among these five dimensions are not simple or linear. For each project, we need to decide which dimensions are critical and how to balance the others so we can achieve the key project objectives.

Each of these five dimensions can take one of three roles on any given project: a *driver*, a *constraint*, or a *degree of freedom*. A driver is a key objective of the project. For a product that must ship on time to meet a marketing window of opportunity, schedule is a driver. Commercial desktop software, such as word processors and spreadsheets, are often created with features as the driver.

A constraint is a limiting factor that is not within the project leader's control. If a team of immutably fixed size is assigned to a project, staff becomes a constraint. Cost is a constraint on a project being done under a fixed-price contract, while quality will be a constraint for a project to develop software that runs a piece of medical equipment or an airplane's flight control system. Sometimes, you can regard cost as either a constraint or a driver, since it could be both a primary objective and a limiting factor. Similarly, a specified feature set may be the primary driver of the project, but you could view it as a constraint if the feature set is not negotiable.

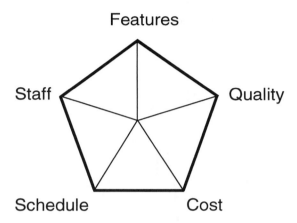

Figure 2.1: The five dimensions of a software project.

Any project dimension that is neither a driver nor a constraint becomes a degree of freedom. These are factors that the project leader can adjust and balance to some extent, to achieve the overall project objectives. For example, on some internal information system projects, the drivers are features and quality, and staff is a constraint, so the degrees of freedom become schedule and cost. The implication for this profile is that the features demanded by the customers will all be included, but the delivery time for the product may be later than desired.

An important aspect of this model is not which of the five dimensions turn out to be drivers or constraints on any given project, but that the relative priorities of the dimensions be negotiated in advance by the project team, the customers, and management. All five cannot be drivers, and all five cannot be constraints. This negotiation process helps to define the rules and bounds of the project. As in most games, we can play according to any set of rules, but all of the players must understand and agree to the rules that are in effect at any particular time.

A way to classify each dimension into one of the three categories is to think of the amount of flexibility the project leader has with respect to that dimension. A constraint gives the project leader virtually no flexibility, a driver has low flexibility, and a degree of freedom provides a wider latitude to balance that dimension against the other four. A graphical way to depict this is to use a Kiviat diagram, which allows us to plot several values (five, in this case) as an irregularly shaped polygon on a set of normalized axes. The position of each point on its axis indicates the relative degree of flexibility of that dimension for a particular project, on an arbitrary scale of zero (completely constrained) to ten (complete flexibility).

Figure 2.2 illustrates a flexibility Kiviat diagram for one of our group's recent applications. This project was constrained to a fixed staff size, so the value plotted on the staff axis is 0. The project was driven to meet a desired schedule, so the point on the schedule axis also has a low value. The project had varying amounts of flexibility around the features that would be incorporated into the initial release, the product quality, and the latitude for cost overruns. Therefore, the values for these degrees of freedom are higher on their axes.

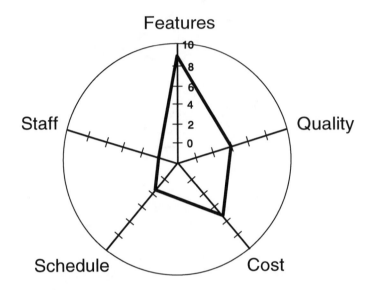

Figure 2.2: Flexibility diagram for an internal information system.

Figure 2.3 illustrates a flexibility diagram for a hypothetical project for which quality is a driver and the schedule shows the greatest latitude. The profile for a highly competitive commercial software product might look like Fig. 2.4, in which a specified feature set must be included (a constraint), the schedule is constrained to a specified ship date, and the quality is just whatever it turns out to be.

The shapes of the polygons in these examples provide a visual indication of the important aspects of each project. If you push the point on one of the axes inward to reduce the amount of latitude the project leader has in that dimension, you'll generally have to adjust the other dimensions to compensate: Nothing comes without a price. You can apply this sort of analysis to make management aware of the trade-offs and decisions they must make to meet a project's key objectives, and to negotiate realistically achievable commitments on each project. A form like that in Fig. 2.5 can be used to record the negotiated goals for driver dimensions, the limits for constraint dimensions, and the range of values associated with those dimensions that are degrees of freedom. The descriptions shown in Fig. 2.5 are for the project whose flexibility diagram was shown in Fig. 2.2.

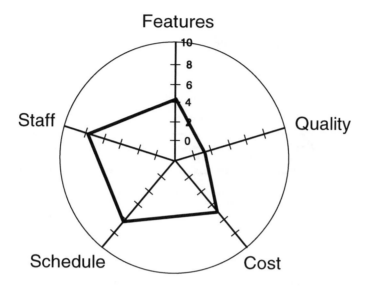

Figure 2.3: Flexibility diagram for a quality-driven application.

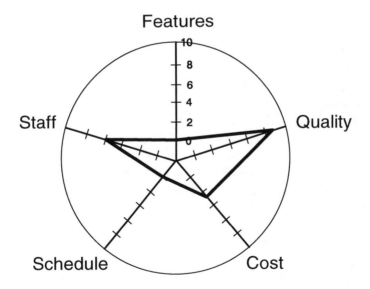

Figure 2.4: Flexibility diagram for a competitive commercial application.

Project Name: New Information System

Assessed By: _____

Date Assessed: _____

Dimension	Driver (State Objectives)	Constraint (State Limits)	Degree of Freedom (State Range)
Cost			up to 20% overrun from initial estimate is acceptable
Features			60-90% of priority 1 features must be in release 1.0
Quality			release 1.0 can contain up to 5 known major defects
Schedule	release 1.0 must be delivered within 4 months		
Staff		4.5 full-time staff available for duration of the project	

Figure 2.5: Sample form for documenting the negotiated dimensions for a project.

Too often, we focus only on one driver aspect (usually features or schedule), and we overlook the impact on the other dimensions. This is the sort of behavior that leads to those software engineering surprises nobody likes to hear about. Customers, managers, and the marketing department have to accept that they cannot have all the features they want, with no defects, delivered very quickly and at low cost by a downsized development staff.

Another way to apply the five-dimension model is to renegotiate when the world changes. If new requirements come along that simply *must* be included in the upcoming release, ask management what you should adjust to accommodate this request:

- Should other features be deferred?

- Can the schedule be allowed to slip? by how much?

- Can you add staff or pay for overtime to meet the new schedule?

- Or, as usual, does quality slip because sound processes and quality control practices are neglected in the press to ship something—anything—out the door?

The specific answer is less important than the discussion that is triggered when project leaders and developers push back against unexpected changes in any of these five dimensions. Customers and managers have to understand the impact of such changes on the other project dimensions so they can make the right decisions.

One characteristic of both a software engineering culture and a mature software development process is that project expectations and commitments are established through negotiation. To avoid unpleasant surprises late in a project's life cycle, the stakeholders all have to understand and agree on their objectives and priorities. Not everyone may be happy with the outcome of the negotiations, but people can commit to realistic schedules and deliverables only if all the parameters are discussed honestly. Unstated or unrealistic goals will rarely be achieved. A group with a culture in which people are afraid to say no or to discuss problem areas openly will always fall short of expectations. Tools like the flexibility diagram can facilitate these frank, and often difficult, negotiations.

Summary

- ✔ Never let your boss or your customer talk you into doing a bad job.

- ✔ The customer isn't always right, but the customer always has a point.

- ✔ Identify and creatively address the true customer needs, which may not be the same as doing whatever your customers ask you to do.

- ✔ Look for opportunities to generalize from a specific customer's request to a solution that offers broad potential for use in other applications or other customer domains.

- ✔ Do not let customers with a bit of software experience dictate how you should build their applications.

- ✔ Be forthright when discussing project status with your customers and managers, even if you are the bearer of bad news. The ostrich approach does not make the problem go away.

- ✔ If you agree to do something, either do it or explain to the people affected that you are unable (or unwilling) to do it, so they can make alternate arrangements.

- ✔ Do not commit to preposterous project schedules that are based on goals and dreams, rather than on a realistic estimating procedure.

✔ The software project stakeholders should establish the relative degrees of flexibility of five project dimensions—features, quality, cost, schedule, and staff—when the project is launched.

Culture Builders and Killers

Culture Builder: Strive to provide an environment in which you shelter your team members from political machinations, useless meetings, and unwarranted finger pointing. Your team members need to know that you will help fight their battles so they can work productively on the right projects. As a manager, take your share of the blame when things go awry, and take only your share of the credit when projects succeed. No one wants to work for a manager he neither trusts nor respects.

Culture Killer: Give your subordinates the responsibility for delivering a project, but do not give them the authority to take the actions and acquire the resources they need to be successful. Delegating any of your authority to project leaders will be perceived as a sign of weakness. Some may grumble that decisions are being made at too high a level on the organization chart, by people who are not close enough to the project to make good decisions, but you know you have enough information to make the right decisions.

References and Further Reading

Karten, Naomi. *Managing Expectations.* New York: Dorset House Publishing, 1994.

> Karten provides suggestions for working with "people who want more, better, faster, sooner, NOW!" Chapter 11 provides guidance on how to say "No" so it sounds like "Yes."

Maguire, Steve. *Debugging the Development Process.* Redmond, Wash.: Microsoft Press, 1994.

> In Chapter 3, Maguire describes the importance of using goals to drive your decisions, rather than the desire to please everyone who asks for something. He presents several anecdotes that illustrate the importance of saying "No" and the need to rely on one's personal integrity when asked to do something inappropriate. Maguire also discusses the importance of focusing on features that are of strategic importance to a product to keep the project on track.

McConnell, Steve. *Code Complete.* Redmond, Wash.: Microsoft Press, 1993.

> Chapter 31 discusses "personal character" issues that affect an individual's effectiveness as a software engineer, including communication and cooperation, creativity and discipline, and intellectual honesty.

Chapter 3

Recognizing Achievements Great and Small

Another major software player decided to "dangle" incentive money in front of its developers. . . . The dictated delivery date came and went and no product had been delivered. . . . Senior management withdrew the incentive and threatened jobs since developers were employed to deliver even without the need for extra compensation. Some of the software engineers (the good ones) left the company, morale was horrible, and by the time a product was delivered, the company's market share had eroded. What a terrible lesson to learn.

—Ken Whitaker, *Managing Software Maniacs*

When I first became the supervisor of the Kodak software group in which I had worked for several years, I initiated a simple (and slightly corny) recognition program. When someone reached a minor project milestone or made a small contribution such as helping another team member with a problem, I gave him a package of M&M® candies, with a message tag attached expressing congratulations or thanks, as appropriate. Bigger achievements generated bigger bags of M&Ms, or something more tangible. It wasn't much, but it was more than we were used to.

As I expected, the candy disappeared immediately, but I was pleasantly surprised to see that some people kept the message tags visible around their desks. To them, the important thing was not the bag of candy, but the words indicating that their manager noticed and valued the progress being made. It soon became apparent that group members preferred to have the presentations made publicly at our weekly team meetings, indicating their desire for peer recognition of even small achievements.

M&Ms worked with our group, but some other social recognition technique might work better for you. We also gave this sort of micro-recognition award to people outside the group who helped us in some way. It brought smiles to their faces and goodwill to our relationships. However you choose to do it, appropriate praise and commendation help to build the culture of teamwork and striving for excellence that we all want, and it can motivate your team members to do an even better job in the future, since they know you appreciate their efforts.

The form and extent of recognition and reward is a visible indication of an organization's culture. If managers believe the employees are lucky just to have jobs, they won't go out of their way to offer even small gestures of appreciation or congratulations. Conversely, in a market characterized by competitive hiring and high staff turnover, an effective recognition program can help retain talented developers. M&Ms won't make up for low salaries or unpleasant working conditions, but simple recognition is an important step in the right direction.

Software engineers are like other people (well, pretty much): We want to be appreciated, and we appreciate being wanted. Besides the internal satisfaction we obtain from interesting, challenging work and the tangible compensation in our paychecks, we want to feel that our efforts are noticed and valued by those around us. We all enjoy receiving compliments, especially when they come from various sources: peers, customers, team leader, senior managers, professional associates.

Praise for a job well done should be timely, direct, personal, and specific (see Fig. 3.1). If you are a manager, don't wait until performance appraisal or salary adjustment time rolls around to pass along some positive feedback. Tell the individual exactly what he or she did well and why you appreciate it. A mumbled "Keep up the good work" in the hallway is more likely to confuse than motivate the recipient. Your team members must know you are sincere when you offer compliments on their work. Though many people feel awkward when they receive a compliment, they appreciate that someone took the trouble to say how pleased he was with your work.

Figure 3.1: The simplest form of recognition.

Recognition can take many forms. Donna Deeprose presents more than one hundred ideas about how to select appropriate and meaningful recognition and rewards for your employees [Deeprose, 1994]. Ask the members of your team what kinds of recognition are important to *them*. Do they prefer a public pronouncement at the weekly group meeting, or are they more comfortable with private ceremonies? Should recognition come just from you, or is it meaningful to have higher-level managers participate in certain recognition activities? Tailor the reinforcement you offer to be significant to the recipients. The following paragraphs describe some of the things the groups in which I have worked have done to express appreciation and to build a positive culture. Some of these apply to individuals, while others are appropriate for teams of people.

Spend a few moments at weekly team meetings to give everyone a chance to pass along some positive reinforcement ("R+") to others. Did a coworker help you solve a problem this week? Did someone take some action out of the ordinary that helped the team? If yes, say so! The group may be uncomfortable when you first try this, but they should warm to the idea over time. If group members are so isolated from each other that no one ever has any R+ to pass along, you may have some serious issues of team dynamics to address.

A traveling trophy that moves from project to project can be used to recognize team achievements. In keeping with the M&M motif, we used a framed three-pound M&M bag (empty, sad to say) as a traveling trophy. Recipients displayed the prize in their office area until another project reached a milestone worthy of recognition. The trophy was ceremoniously passed from one team to the next in our group meeting. If you try something like this, be sure to keep the trophy traveling every few weeks, or its significance becomes lost.

Food and entertainment are also good ways to recognize someone's contributions or special achievement. Taking the team to a celebration luncheon when a milestone is reached can be fun for everyone involved. A gift certificate for dinner at a restaurant gives an individual recipient a chance to celebrate privately with friends or family. Whenever a member of my team earned a college or advanced degree, my wife and I took him and his significant other out to dinner. Maybe going to dinner with the boss is not everyone's idea of a great time, but it worked for us. On another occasion, I gave each team member a pair of movie passes as a symbol of how much I appreciated their time and teamwork when, during an intense period of selecting new members for our group, the entire team of ten pitched in on short notice to participate in the interviews. It was a small gesture but a sincere way of saying, "Thanks for the help, gang."

Recognize individuals outside your group for their contributions as well. It's amazing how much future cooperation you can secure with a simple gesture of appreciation. As the recipient of a few such gestures myself, it always makes me feel good to know that someone really appreciated something I did, however routine it may have seemed to me. We have thanked project customer representatives by taking them to lunch, giving them certificates to hang on the wall, and bestowing restaurant gift certificates upon those who shouldered the most responsibility.

One customer even reciprocated, throwing a lunch bash for the development group. This sort of customer-developer interaction helps build a culture of constructive teamwork.

Be sure to recognize people for attaining minor milestones, as well as when they complete a big project. Interim pats on the back help provide team members with the incentive to keep pushing ahead. Again, it says to the recipient, "Congratulations on making progress toward your goals."

As a manager, you must actively look for recognition opportunities, and seize the moment as soon as you spot one. The manager who realizes an achievement is worthy of formal recognition but waits to figure out what he wants to do about it, and waits to execute his plan, may provide recognition too far removed from the achievement itself to mean much to the recipient. "Oh, so you finally noticed what I did," is a typical unspoken reaction to a belated recognition effort. A manager who expects such opportunities automatically to pop up in front of him will miss many of them, and will not deliver consistent recognition messages. Also remember that managers who fail to reward exceptional contributions are sowing the seeds of discontent. The absence of well-deserved recognition is highly demotivating.

The Importance of Being Visible

The antithesis of being recognized for your achievements is feeling that your managers do not know who you are, what you do on the project, how you do it, or what your contributions are to the company as a whole. When was the last time your supervisor stopped by your office just to say hello and to ask how things are going? How about a visit from a manager farther up the corporate hierarchy?

Some people are uncomfortable with an unannounced manager visit, but others welcome the opportunity to share their concerns and show the boss what they are working on. "Management By Walking Around" is one way managers express interest in the individuals in their organization; it can and should be practiced by managers at all levels. Think about it: If you are a first-line supervisor and you never see your boss in the engineering staff's offices, chances are you'll conclude that he or she is hopelessly out of touch with the group.

People are more motivated to put in extra effort when they know the higher-ups value it. We have all worked for managers who represented the other extreme, having a limited awareness of the group's challenges and contributions. How excited can you get about trying to please such managers? As a supervisor, make sure you really know what the engineers in your department are doing. Who are the contributors, the innovators, the leaders? Who is just along for the ride? The team members will have no confidence that they can get fair performance appraisals if they rarely talk to their supervisor. Your employees need to have adequate opportunities to explain what they do and the problems they face.

When appropriate, a manager should also show interest in professional activities that are unrelated to specific projects. It is discouraging to put in extra time to prepare a presentation for a local software conference, then not to see your boss's face in the audience. Telling you he is pleased you are doing something extra is not nearly so meaningful as if he actually shows up for the event. Remember all those plays, dance presentations, and concerts you sat through because your children were on stage? Being a good manager demands some of the same actions as being a good parent. It means a lot to know your supervisor cares about what you are doing.

The Importance of Management Attitude

Here's a radical idea: Think of you, as a manager, working *for* the people who report to you, as opposed to the more traditional view of subordinates working for the supervisor. The people you supervise are the customers for your leadership and management services, including

- coaching and mentoring

- setting project goals and priorities

- resolving problems and conflicts

- providing resources

- evaluating performance and providing feedback

- career development

- leading process improvement efforts

- providing technical guidance when appropriate

Give your own people top priority over the demands of others for your time. Your priorities as a manager should be those shown in Fig. 3.2.

Unfortunately, too many managers are busy looking *up* the corporate organization chart, not down. The sequence in Fig. 3.2 is frequently inverted, with the key driver being what you think will make your own boss happy. In a healthy, congruent workplace, the boss should be thrilled if you are meeting the needs of your team and its customers. Not everyone is fortunate enough to work in such an enlightened environment; priorities are usually defined by the perception of who you think you have to please to keep your job.

One way a manager can tell if his priorities are straight is whether he ever receives any recognition from his team members. It meant more to me to get an R+ from one of the people I supervised than to get one from my own supervisor. If you are an individual contributor, remember to thank your managers for special contributions they make or extra help they provide to you. Managers are people, too, with the same desire to be appreciated that anyone else has.

Provide services to your team members.

Satisfy your department's customers.

Work on your own projects.

Please your own managers.

Figure 3.2: Priorities for the enlightened software manager.

Rewards for a Job Well Done

The skillful manager will use recognition and rewards to reinforce desired behaviors, rather than offering tangible incentives to individuals or teams to achieve specific goals. The main incentive for most software people to go to work each day is the opportunity to work on challenging projects with stimulating colleagues, in an environment that encourages quality work, in which software skills can be applied and extended.

Dangling extra cash as a carrot in front of a software engineer to try to get him to work faster-harder-longer can backfire [Whitaker, 1994]. If the ambitious goals are not met, and developers know the pot of gold at the end of the rainbow won't be forthcoming, how do you keep them motivated? Withdraw the incentives (thereby destroying morale), or renew the incentives (thereby showing that falling short of management's outrageous goals is just as meritorious as achieving them)? Either way, everyone loses. Instead of offering incentives, design a reward program that matches your organization's culture and means something to your team members. Motivate your team through frequent interim recognition activities, and reward them for a job well done when the job really is done. People should also be rewarded for taking intelligent risks, even if a great notion or great effort doesn't pay off for reasons outside the development team's control. Public rewards indicate to the rest of the group those behaviors you feel are desirable.

Rewards can be monetary or non-monetary. Slipping a few bonus bills in the pay envelope may seem like a sure way to please an employee, but often something else would be preferable. Talk to your people and understand what rewards they feel are significant. The corporate culture will have some influence in selecting feasible rewards. It may be easier to give someone a substantial, but non-cash, award, such as a trip to a conference or trade show. Some companies reward employees with frequent flyer miles, which can be purchased from airlines for a few cents per mile. Some developers might enjoy extra vacation time; others might want to buy a special software package with which to experiment, just because they heard it was interesting. If someone does an exceptional job on a project, he might appreciate a mini-sabbatical, a couple of weeks set aside to work on whatever he likes.

Another kind of reward is the opportunity to work on an exciting new project. In some groups, only the old hands have the skills and knowledge to keep the legacy systems alive. Less experienced people may be assigned to projects involving newer technology, which are more fun than maintaining ancient applications. This is a good way to drive your senior staff members out of the group, to search for opportunities where they can learn contemporary skills and work on the kinds of projects they read about in computer magazines. Creative and experienced engineers don't want to be mired in legacy code for the rest of their careers. Look for ways to reward your best workers by keeping them stimulated with new learning opportunities and project challenges.

Summary

✔ People need to feel the work they do is appreciated.

✔ Receiving positive reinforcement from peers, managers, and customers is highly motivating to most people. Failing to recognize someone's exceptional contributions and major achievements is demotivating. Why do extra work if your managers don't care?

✔ Recognition says, "I appreciate your effort," "Congratulations on your accomplishment," or simply, "I noticed what you did."

✔ Find out what kinds of recognition and rewards are meaningful to your people, and tailor your R+ program accordingly to foster a culture of desirable software engineering behaviors.

✔ Recognize minor accomplishments and milestones, to motivate individuals to keep working toward their major objectives.

✔ Managers can build better relationships with their team members simply by understanding the work they do and showing a sincere interest in it. Talk to your people informally, to find out what they are excited and unhappy about. Sometimes, this approach will let you deal with a concern before it becomes a crisis.

✔ A software manager should regard the people who report to him as his most important customers. The manager's top priority should be to address the needs of his team members.

✔ Reward your staff members, whatever their job, for a good performance, rather than offering big incentives to induce them to do great work in the future.

Culture Builders and Killers

Culture Builder: Distribute recognition awards equitably to your group members. Don't reserve recognition events only for project leaders, members of high-profile project teams, or your senior technical people. The scale and frequency of rewards does not have to be the same for everyone—after all, people are different—but it is demoralizing for an employee to see the same coworkers being recognized repeatedly without anyone noticing his own achievements.

Culture Builder: Make sure you are accessible to the people who report to you. Schedule one-on-one meetings with those who desire them, at whatever interval is mutually acceptable to you and each individual. A general open-door policy is important, too, but your team members may be reluctant to bother you if they know how busy you are. They deserve a slice of your undivided attention at regular intervals.

Culture Builder: If you make a verbal commitment to someone for a reward, be sure to follow through on it. Forgetting that you made this promise demonstrates a lack of sincerity. Be sure to reward the right people for the right reasons. If you aren't sure who made key contributions to a successful project, find out before you present any rewards or recognition. Few things are more infuriating than seeing a person receive praise (or more) for work that was actually done by someone else.

Culture Killer: In an era of political correctness carried to an extreme, you don't dare run the risk of anyone crying "Discrimination!" on any basis. Therefore, it is safest to offer exactly the same kinds of recognition to all of your team members, whether they excel in the performance of highly challenging work or they struggle to meet minimal expectations.

 Culture Killer: Here are some good reasons to cancel, cut short, or interrupt a regularly scheduled one-on-one meeting with one of your team members:

- Someone else has already stopped by your office to chat.

- You need to work on one of your own projects.

- Your telephone rings.

- You have been invited to join a new committee that meets at that same time.

- Your boss calls another meeting for that time.

- You have to travel to another site to meet with someone else.

- You forgot about it.

Whenever anything short of a true emergency interferes with a scheduled meeting with someone you supervise, you are sending a clear message: "Everything else I have to do is more important to me than you are."

 Culture Killer: Offer recognition, such as a luncheon with several important managers, to an individual who has done an ordinary job on an ordinary assignment, but offer nothing to other group members for taking significant initiative that extends outside the boundaries of their assignment. Word will get around that recognition depends on who you are, not what you do.

References and Further Reading

 Deeprose, Donna. *How to Recognize and Reward Employees.* New York: AMACOM, 1994.

> Deeprose presents ten guidelines that can give your recognition program more impact. She lists one hundred ways you might provide recognition and reward, in the form of structured reward programs, spontaneous rewards, and day-to-day feedback. You can recover the cost of the book the first time you provide an employee with recognition that motivates him to work a little bit harder or smarter on the company's behalf.

Whitaker, Ken. *Managing Software Maniacs.* New York: John Wiley & Sons, 1994.

In Chapter 3, "Attracting and Keeping Developers," Whitaker argues that managers should reward developers after the project is completed, rather than trying to motivate them by promising wonderful rewards in advance as an incentive. This book contains many horror stories of management actions that led to undesirable results.

Chapter 4

So Much to Learn, So Little Time

The average software developer, for example, doesn't own a single book on the subject of his or her work, and hasn't ever read one. That fact is horrifying for anyone concerned about the quality of work in the field; for folks like us who write books, it is positively tragic.

—Tom DeMarco and Timothy Lister, *Peopleware*

When my software group at Kodak interviewed candidates for some development positions, one question I asked every applicant was, "How do you keep up with the software literature?" The responses were discouraging. Some people didn't really understand the question. Few had read any software books recently. Even fewer were enrolled in academic programs pursuing additional education in some aspect of computer technology. Most of the magazines they read were free trade publications or weekly computing news updates, not technical periodicals. Almost none of the applicants belonged to a professional computing society.

My educational background is in organic chemistry. Imagine if someone who applied for a job as a chemist was asked to describe his experience in chemistry, and he replied, "I have a Gilbert chemistry set at home that I play with on the weekends, and it's a lot of fun." No one would consider hiring a scientist on the basis of such casual self-education, yet people who have written a 100-line BASIC program seem to feel qualified for software engineering jobs. Many self-taught programmers do not fully appreciate the huge difference between writing simple programs for their own use and designing substantial applications by systematically applying software engineering practices.

To be sure, many highly capable software developers come from non-computing educational backgrounds. Outstanding problem-solving abilities, creativity, and holistic thinking are more a function of how one's brain works than precisely what is in it. Many developers over the age of forty began their careers in some other discipline and learned software skills through a variety of nontraditional educational activities and work experience—I am one of these "retreads." Regardless of our education, all practitioners must work hard to keep up with the rate of growth of software technologies—new skills, methods, and tools. People in a healthy software engineering culture are committed to continuous learning:

- All team members strive to acquire and effectively apply new software development knowledge.

- Team members openly share their ideas and knowledge.

- Managers work to improve their own technical, management, and people skills.

- Management supports a variety of learning activities through funding and time released from project responsibilities.

- Management actively encourages and rewards those who work to improve their capabilities.

Managers should view improving the capabilities of their staff as part of the cost of quality. A diverse discipline like software development requires a significant investment for people to acquire the knowledge needed to successfully complete complex projects. Engineers with more tools in their tool boxes, and more ideas in their brains, will generate superior solutions to the challenges facing software organizations today. Remember that the quality of work and productivity of individual programmers spans at least a ten-fold range. Training can help you bridge the gap between the lower performers and the most capable members of your team.

A culture that does not encourage individual growth and the sharing of knowledge among team members is likely to stagnate and to suffer from high staff turnover. Steve Maguire recommends that managers align some personal growth goals for each team member with two-month project milestones [Maguire, 1994]. By encouraging them to learn and apply new skills, read technical books, and develop good engineering habits, all team members can continue to grow professionally in manageable increments. Organizations that strongly support individual career development and training generate considerable loyalty from staff members.

A company that takes software engineering seriously will encourage its staff to pursue continuing education and advanced degrees, to participate in professional computing societies, and to strive for relevant professional certification (see Fig. 4.1). Management plays a vital role by creating a culture in which those team members who better themselves by investing their own time and money are rewarded for their accomplishments. Management can provide tangible support for advanced education by providing some released time from work, by reimbursing tuition partially or in full, and by paying for textbooks. No software department should have any money left in its training budget at the end of the year. If it does, its managers are not taking training seriously enough yet. Yes, training costs money and time, but remember: "If you think education is expensive, try ignorance."

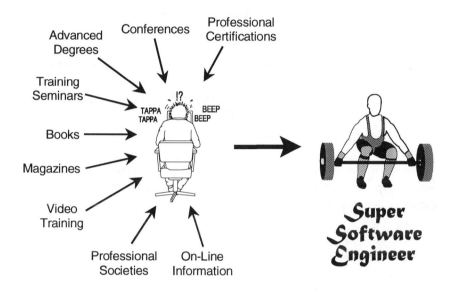

Figure 4.1: Growing better software engineers through continuing education.

What to Learn

There is much more to software engineering than knowing how to code programs. In addition to system construction and verification techniques, the professional software developer must have strong communication skills and the ability to plan and manage projects. We also must distinguish between the knowledge an individual has acquired and his ability to *apply* that knowledge effectively on a project. It is the set of practical capabilities possessed by each engineer that is important, not his training history.

Every software organization should maintain a skills and competencies database for its staff members. This can be used to identify individual skill gaps for which training or job experience is necessary, and to define career growth paths for each individual. Identify the mix of competencies and proficiency levels (novice, apprentice, practitioner, master) the organization requires for success, and then assess each individual's proficiency in those skill areas and schedule any necessary training. The database will also help you staff new projects effectively by pulling together people who have the necessary skills and proficiency levels.

One list identified some 130 skills pertinent to software development. There are the obvious technical software engineering skills, some of which appear in the left column in Table 4.1. Software organizations should also keep track of who knows about any specific packages and development tools used there. However, many nontechnical skills also are critical to software project success; selected examples are shown in the right column in Table 4.1. No developer needs depth in every one of these skill areas. Effective career development for software engineers should balance a broad range of capabilities with some areas of specialization. This field has become too large and too complex to expect every developer to be a fully proficient generalist.

Software managers are not exempt from the challenge of continuous learning and personal improvement. Many seminars and books are available on software *project* management, but the skills to effectively lead people and foster effective interactions among them also are critical to managerial success. All managers should evaluate their personal capabilities in the nontechnical skills listed in Table 4.1 and look for training opportunities to correct any deficiencies. It is disappointing to see software managers miss an opportunity to attend a presentation on effective leadership, process improvement, or other topics that are vital to becoming a dynamic leader of software people and projects.

Table 4.1.
Technical and Nontechnical Skills for Software Developers.

Technical Skills	Nontechnical Skills
general software engineering	application domain knowledge
analysis and design methods	knowledge of the organization
testing techniques	leadership
reviews and inspections	coaching and mentoring
gathering requirements	verbal and written communications
configuration management	presentation skills
project management	marketing
systems engineering	time management
estimating	team building
planning and scheduling	selling ideas
life cycle process selection	consulting
technology awareness	facilitation
networking and communications	conducting meetings
change management	conflict management

Where to Learn

Most software development knowledge does not come from the undergraduate college classroom. Computer science curricula often underemphasize the diversity of technical and communication skills that are required to build complex applications. Several universities offer master's degree programs in software engineering or software development and management, and some of these programs are flexible enough to accommodate those who are employed during the day and attending classes at night. Many members of Kodak's software groups have acquired master's degrees through such programs, and I have the greatest respect for people who make such an extensive commitment to furthering their own education. The rest of this chapter explores other valuable learning sources for the professional software development practitioner.

Professional Seminar Sources

Table A.1 in Appendix A identifies some of the companies that present seminars on many facets of software development. This is by no means a fully inclusive list of either such vendors or the courses presented by the vendors listed. These seminars typically cost around $400 per day, although some are even more expensive. Discounts often are available for government employees or for a group of employees from the same company attending the same session.

Seminars are presented in major cities throughout the United States. Some vendors will come to your own company site and present a class for a group of your employees, which can be cheaper than sending the same number of people to an off-site session. Having your entire team attend the same seminar can also reinforce your software engineering culture of common technical practices. Some of the seminars grant credits that can be applied toward professional certifications (and some certification programs grant credit toward college degrees).

Too often, managers view the mere act of sending someone to a training seminar as an accomplishment. This should be viewed as an investment, not an accomplishment. The accomplishment part comes when you have tangible evidence that the knowledge acquired at the class is being effectively applied on project work. This is the only way to tell if the investment you made in training is yielding the desired benefits. Too many training experiences fall short of the goals of effective technology transfer, the ability to integrate comprehension and judgment, and reduction to effective and routine practice.

Before one of your team members heads off to a training class, sit down together to discuss what the student should expect to get out of the learning experience. Upon the student's return, get together again to see what new techniques the student feels are immediately applicable to his or her work, or to the work of anyone else in the team. The answer may be "nothing right now," because of the nature of the class or the individual's current assignment, but you should ask. Look for opportunities to leverage the training investment over as many people as you can. One possibility is to have the student present an overview of the class to the rest of your group. Or, he or she might become the group's local subject expert in this area, serving as a mentor to others in the newly acquired skills.

To tell whether the training investment was sound or ill-advised, follow up several weeks or months later to see what the student is doing *differently and better* as a result of the training activity. The half-life of unused new knowledge is very short. If the student does not have a chance to apply what was learned quickly, the knowledge fades away, and with it fades your investment in the training activity. Whenever possible, look for just-in-time training opportunities. However, don't neglect courses that can build the student's general software development foundation. This speaks to the difference between *training* to acquire practical skills for a specific purpose, and *education* to acquire understanding of a topic and the judgment to determine how to apply it to a variety of problems. In either case, you should be able to identify some tangible benefit from the learning experience.

Some managers are reluctant to send their people to the softer people- or process-related courses, believing that only technical training is valid. I don't agree. The large communication component of a software engineer's daily work requires that hardcore technical skills be augmented by the engineer's ability to interact effectively with customers and teammates.

Make it a point to attend training seminars and conferences on software management, measurement, and process improvement yourself. Look for opportunities to apply the ideas and techniques as soon as you get back to work. This shows your team that you are serious about finding ways to improve the effectiveness of every team member, including yourself. I am always happy to see managers attend internal Kodak software conferences and classes I teach. Managers who do not take advantage of inexpensive learning opportunities may be sending a message that says, "I am too busy to learn how to do my job better."

Technical Conferences

Scores of conferences each year provide forums for learning about the latest technical thinking, seeing demonstrations of software tools, and hearing the practical experiences of users who tried to apply methods and tools. They also provide a good opportunity to network with professional colleagues to exchange ideas, problems, and business cards. Some conferences offer tutorial sessions on the days before or after the general sessions. Table A.2 in Appendix A describes several conferences oriented toward general software development or software quality issues. Many more are held each year on more specialized technical topics. The IEEE (Institute for Electrical and Electronics Engineers) alone sponsors about one hundred conferences each year. Schedules for upcoming specialized conferences can be found in the back pages of monthly magazines such as *IEEE Computer* and *Communications of the ACM*, or at the World Wide Web sites for these organizations (see Table 4.2).

Table 4.2.
Professional Computing Societies.

Organization	Stated Purpose
Association for Computing Machinery P.O. Box 12114 Church Street Station New York, NY 10257 phone: (212) 626-0500 e-mail: acmhelp@acm.org Web: URL http://www.acm.org	"To advance the sciences and arts of information processing; to promote the free interchange of information about the sciences and arts of information processing both among specialists and among the public; and to develop and maintain the integrity and competence of individuals engaged in the practice of information processing."
IEEE Computer Society 1730 Massachusetts Avenue NW Washington, DC 20036-1992 phone: (202) 371-0101 Web: URL http://www.computer.org for membership information: phone: (714) 821-8380 e-mail: membership@computer.org	"The IEEE Computer Society advances the theory and practice of computer science and engineering, promotes the exchange of technical information among 100,000 members worldwide, and provides a wide range of services to members and nonmembers."

Conference registration fees can reach hundreds of dollars per day, although discounts sometimes can be obtained for multiple attendees from the same company. Hint: Many conferences waive the registration fee for speakers, and some pay an honorarium, as well. Presenting a true-life software experience at a conference provides an opportunity to share development methods that worked for you with your peers.

When one of your engineers returns from a conference, spread the knowledge he or she acquired to as many coworkers as you can. Consider presenting the conference highlights at a team meeting, distributing throughout your company a trip report summarizing the conference, or posting a trip report on an electronic bulletin board. This sharing helps justify the expense of the conference to budget-conscious managers. I have taken home ideas and techniques from a conference that allowed my department to quickly recover the cost of sending me to it.

Publications

Recalling the quote from DeMarco and Lister at the beginning of this chapter, I am sometimes discouraged by how few software books I see in the typical developer's office. All professional engineers should have a set of textbooks and reference works on their desks, with a wider selection readily available from a nearby library or group collection. The many sources described in the References and Further Reading section of each chapter in this book can serve as initial acquisitions for your collection. Ed Yourdon suggests some fifty useful software engineering books in *Decline and Fall of the American Programmer* [Yourdon, 1992].

Group discussions of technical books can be an effective way to grow a cultural commitment to continual learning in your group [Cohen, 1991]. For example, every engineer in our group at Kodak has a copy of *Code Complete* by Steve McConnell, the most comprehensive collection of practical programming advice I have seen [McConnell, 1993]. Over a span of several months, we took turns summarizing a chapter for the rest of the team at our weekly group meetings. The team members who were most serious about acquiring useful knowledge were the ones taking notes during these informal presentations.

Don't read just technical books, however. There are hundreds of thought-provoking books which are not aimed at software developers, but which contain ideas that help you think about your work from different perspectives. One that contains philosophical insights about quality in general is Robert Pirsig's *Zen and the Art of Motorcycle Maintenance* (Bantam Books, 1974). *The 7 Habits of Highly Effective People*, by Stephen R. Covey (Fireside, 1989), contains valuable ideas that can improve the way nearly anyone works. Books on management in general, on leadership, and on people skills can help enhance your ability to positively influence the people with whom you work.

Unlike scientific and engineering disciplines that emphasize research literature, the computing world offers a wide spectrum of magazines. They range from many aimed at the home computing market and serious hobbyists, through those for practicing professionals, to still others directed toward academic researchers. In addition, many software and hardware vendors publish periodicals devoted to their products.

As a manager of a software group, subscribe to some pertinent periodicals, to encourage the team members to stay abreast of new developments in software engineering. Circulate them to whichever team members wish to see them. One downside of the circulation system is that some desks act as traps into which magazines sometimes disappear for months. If the circulation bogs down, individual subscriptions may be in order. No one has time to read all of the magazines, but every professional should follow a few on a regular basis.

Table A.3 in Appendix A lists some of the periodicals that frequently contain articles on software quality topics. Many other magazines are available on more specific computing topics, including both application-oriented and research-oriented magazines. Staying abreast of the huge volume of software literature is challenging. One tool that can help is the *Computer Literature Index*, a quarterly subject, author, and publisher index to computer and data processing periodical literature. Another option is to subscribe to *SoftWatch*, a quarterly publication that prints abstracts of key articles of interest to software development managers. Both *SoftWatch* and the *Computer Literature Index* are published by Applied Computer Research, Inc. (see Appendix B for contact information).

Videotape Instruction

Self-paced teaching through videotape instruction is another alternative for the motivated software engineer. An advantage of video courses is that several people can watch the same videotapes and amplify the learning experience through discussions and team exercises. As tapes can be costly, you may need to have a group of people view them to justify the expense. As an alternative, you may be able to borrow videos from a technical library to view at work or at home. Video instruction is an effective way to acquire just-in-time training in specific technical areas. One major source of video instruction is National Technological University, which offers accredited Master's Degrees in computer engineering, computer science, and software engineering (see Appendix B for contact information).

On-Line Information Sources

One benefit of the Internet is the plethora of discussion groups that has appeared on an enormous variety of topics. The Usenet computing newsgroups of general interest to software engineers include comp.software-eng, comp.software.testing, and comp.software.config-mgmt, in addition to scores of newsgroups on specific operating systems, vendor products, and so on. By exploring the archives of these newsgroups, reading the lists of Frequently Asked Questions (FAQs) that are posted periodically or archived, and posing questions to the collective wisdom of those who surf the 'Net, you can collect experiences from other practitioners and opinions of every sort. Well-known authors and consultants sometimes reply to inquiries that are posted to these newsgroups, entirely free of charge. Other interesting software discussion groups can be found on commercial network services such as CompuServe®.

Many World Wide Web sites also contain software engineering information. Because of the extreme rate of growth and change in the Internet, the exact locations of these sites will likely change over time. Web browsers can help you quickly locate software-related Internet sites, and hypertext links will let you navigate easily from one site to another.

Professional Societies and Certification

Professional societies, such as the Association for Computing Machinery (ACM) and the IEEE Computer Society, provide a collective way for practitioners to help shape public policy and opinions toward computing (Table 4.2). Members can participate at the national and local chapter levels in standards working groups, technical committees, and special interest groups (SIGs) on specific technical topics. ACM and the IEEE Computer Society also provide affordable group insurance and other benefits that might be attractive to self-employed computing professionals. Supporting these societies through membership dues is "the right thing to do" as a computing professional. Larger cities often have local associations devoted to software quality improvement or to software process improvement, such as the Software Process Improvement Network (SPIN).

Unlike many professional disciplines (law, medicine, other types of engineering), software engineers do not have to be certified as competent before hanging out the shingle reading "Have keyboard, will code." This may change one day, but for now, professional certification for software engineers is a personal choice. Table 4.3 describes several sources of certification for software professionals. Attaining any of these levels of certification requires substantial effort. Some companies organize study groups to enable a group of engineers pursuing certification to prepare together. Achieving certification requires that the candidate pass several hours of examinations on a broad range of material chosen from the relevant computing disciplines. Once certified, you have the right to place a set of letters after your name, which indicates to your peers (and to potential employers) that you have been recognized for reaching a professional level of competence in the field of software development. You must maintain the certification through ongoing educational activities and periodic recertification.

Table 4.3.
Professional Computing Certifications.

Certification and Organization	Description
Certified Computing Professional (CCP) Institute for Certification of Computing Professionals 2200 E. Devon Avenue, Suite 268 Des Plaines, IL 60018-4503 phone: (708) 299-4227	To achieve the CCP designation, the candidate must pass a core examination on several computing (and business) topics and a combination of specialty exams (selected from among several computing disciplines) and programming language exams. An Associate Computing Professional designation can be achieved by passing a smaller number of exams.
Certified Quality Analyst (CQA) Quality Assurance Institute Suite 350 7575 Dr. Phillips Blvd. Orlando, FL 32819-7273 phone: (407) 363-1111	The CQA has passed an examination designed to evaluate knowledge of both the principles and practices of software quality assurance. The CQA is also expected to be a change agent, someone who can change the culture and work habits of individuals to make quality happen. The CQA exam covers sixteen quality disciplines.
Certified Quality Engineer American Society for Quality Control (ASQC) 611 East Wisconsin Avenue P.O. Box 3005 Milwaukee, WI 53201-3005 phone: (414) 272-8575	ASQC offers several levels of certification to quality practitioners in a variety of fields, including Certified Quality Engineer, Certified Quality Auditor, Certified Reliability Engineer, and Certified Quality Technician. Each requires a specified level of education and/or work experience, in addition to passing an examination.

Summary

✔ Ongoing education is every team member's responsibility.

✔ In a software engineering culture, team members energetically pursue new sources of knowledge, and they freely share what they know with their teammates. Management actively supports continued education by funding book purchases, subscriptions to technical periodicals, training seminars, advanced education, and attendance at conferences.

✔ Software groups should assess the skills (technical and non-technical) and competencies of their staff members, as well as those that the organization requires to flourish.

✔ Sending someone to a training class is not an accomplishment—it is an investment. Students and their supervisors should plan how the information acquired at a training activity will be applied on the job and shared with others who could benefit. Follow up some time later to see if the training resulted in any tangible improvements in the student's work.

✔ All software engineers and managers should regularly read relevant technical magazines and books. Set a personal goal of reading at least four computing or management books per year.

✔ Videotape courses can supply just-in-time training, and they can lead to advanced degrees through National Technological University for those with enough perseverance.

✔ Engineers who are serious about their profession should join professional computing societies and consider pursuing professional certifications.

Culture Builders and Killers

Culture Builder: Join a computer book club, and give each member of your team a budget with which they can buy books they feel would be helpful to them. Make sure all of your engineers have on their desks, as their personal copies, a core set of practical books that are relevant to the work they do. In addition, buy books for reference use that you can add to your group library. Coordinate purchases to avoid unnecessary duplicates of general interest titles.

Culture Builder: Maintain an on-line file of references to interesting books and magazine articles that all team members can access. Anyone who reads an article that might be of interest to others in the group can add it to this reference file, with a short abstract. Keep the articles or journals in your group library for future access. Having such a resource file will make it easy to find publications that can help you solve a problem, without wasting hours reinventing a solution.

Culture Builder: Encourage your team to meet periodically to discuss software books, cogitate on recent articles from magazines, and view pertinent videotapes. Solicit volunteers to follow specific periodicals and summarize the highlights each month, so that the whole group gets exposed to a broad spectrum of new information. You might subsidize such a discussion group through a noon-hour pizza-and-software forum once a month. This can be a low-cost way to help compensate for cutbacks in the training budget.

Culture Killer: If you hear about a free software conference within your company or another low-cost learning opportunity, don't forward it to your staff, let alone encourage them to attend. If you let them all go to a conference for two days, all of your project schedules will slip by that amount. They will get more accomplished by sitting at their workstations and typing during those two days.

Culture Killer: When the budget ax looms, cut your allocations for training and travel first. Spending $400 per day for a training class is just too much. Don't incur travel expenses by sending anyone to a class in another city. Your people can read manuals on their lunch hours if they need to learn anything they don't already know.

Culture Killer: Send the same people to seminars and conferences all the time, and brush off the others when they request some training. Your top people should get their choice of training events as a perk for being so productive, while the run-of-the-mill programmers must earn the privilege of being trained.

References and Further Reading

Boddie, John. "Growing Better Managers by Doing Nothing," *American Programmer*, Vol. 8, No. 1 (January 1995), pp. 21-27.

> The time managers spend "doing nothing" actually is invested in staying current in technical knowledge, mentoring those they supervise, learning to manage better, developing customer contacts, and facilitating team improvements. Boddie points out that, too often, engineers "were promoted to management

positions with less task-specific preparation than McDonald's gives an employee moving from french fries to hamburgers."

Cohen, Rich, and Warren Keuffel. "Pull Together," *Computer Language*, Vol. 8, No. 8 (August 1991), pp. 36-44.

If you are interested in organizing a software study group for your team as part of their ongoing education, Cohen and Keuffel can help you get started.

DeMarco, Tom, and Timothy Lister, eds. *Software State-of-the-Art: Selected Papers.* New York: Dorset House Publishing, 1990.

Thirty-one significant articles from the software literature are collected, representing topics in the categories Management, Measurement, Methods, and News from Left Field. The papers are generally readable, not too formal or theoretical. They cover a wide range of contemporary thinking on software engineering.

 Maguire, Steve. *Debugging the Development Process.* Redmond, Wash.: Microsoft Press, 1994.

Chapter 6, "Constant, Unceasing Improvement," provides several recommendations about how a project leader can shape a culture that promotes the continual enhancement of each team member's software skills and knowledge.

 McConnell, Steve. *Code Complete.* Redmond, Wash.: Microsoft Press, 1993.

Code Complete should be considered a required acquisition for every software engineer's bookshelf. Chapter 33, "Where to Go for More Information," identifies a number of other books that are valuable sources of software construction wisdom.

 Pressman, Roger. *Software Engineering: A Practitioner's Approach,* 3rd ed. New York: McGraw-Hill, 1992.

Pressman's comprehensive textbook covers the breadth of the software engineering discipline in a substantive and readable fashion.

Raynor, Darrel A. "Team Training for Successful Projects: Using a Skills Matrix for Planning," *American Programmer*, Vol. 8, No. 1 (January 1995), pp. 11-14.

Raynor describes how an education skills matrix can help the software manager identify team members who need specific training to be effective on their upcoming projects.

Yourdon, Edward. *Decline and Fall of the American Programmer.* New York: Yourdon Press/Prentice-Hall, 1992.

Yourdon includes a sizable list of the important books in software development he feels should be accessible to every professional software engineer.

Part II

In Search of
Excellent Requirements

Customer requirements are the basis for all subsequent development work on a software project. Inaccurate and unstable requirements are the cause of many software product quality problems. They also reduce developer productivity because of the rework that has to be done to fix the problems created by poor requirements. Direct customer involvement in the project is a powerful remedy for the disease of inaccurate requirements. Software cultures that lack a systematic way for incorporating the voice of the customer into their requirements process face a higher risk of building the wrong product.

Software groups at Kodak and elsewhere have found the use of key customer representatives, or "project champions," to be an effective way to gather user needs. The project champion model was explicitly selected as the cultural foundation of a software group that supports the Kodak Research Laboratories when it was formed. A culture focused on building high-quality products will adopt effective strategies for capturing, representing, and interpreting customer requirements. Two cultural precepts are addressed in Part II:

✔ Customer involvement is the most critical factor in software quality.

✔ Your greatest challenge is sharing the vision of the final product with the customer.

Chapter 5

Optimizing Customer Involvement

There is a tendency in many projects purposely to exclude the user from the decision-making process. The usual reason is that the software developer feels that if the user does become involved, he will never make up his mind; his requirements will be constantly changing. There is a small degree of validity in this concern, but in practice the advantages of user involvement far outweigh this potential disadvantage.

—Glenford J. Myers, *Software Reliability*

"I'll go find out what they need, and the rest of you start coding." This cartoon caption is uncomfortably close to the way some software organizations still treat the requirements engineering process. Unfortunately, the stated specifications and the actual customer needs are not always the same thing. Converging these two components into a unified, shared vision of the final product is a linchpin of successful software development. Unless the true customer needs are thoroughly explored and documented, the probability of building a system that satisfies those needs is minuscule. In the words of Alan Davis, an authority on software requirements engineering, "Without requirements, design is either impossible or highly dangerous."

In *Quality Is Free* [Crosby, 1979], Philip Crosby wrote that

> We must define quality as "conformance to requirements" if we are to manage it. . . . Requirements must be clearly stated so that they cannot be misunderstood. Measurements are then taken continually to determine conformance to those requirements. The nonconformance detected is the absence of quality. Quality problems become nonconformance problems, and quality becomes definable.

"Conformance to requirements" is not a complete definition of what is meant by software quality, but it is one of the critical dimensions. Software quality is a complex function of conformance to requirements, user satisfaction, defect density, reliability, ease of use, and other less tangible factors. The bottom line is whether the customer views a product as having high value for the price paid.

In the movie *This Is Spinal Tap*, a comic "documentary" about a mythical English heavy metal band, a sculptress was commissioned to build a stage prop modeled after the eighteen-foot tall prehistoric structures found at Stonehenge in England. The "specification" literally was drawn on a napkin and resembled the sketch in Fig. 5.1.

Figure 5.1: "Specification" for a Stonehenge replica.

Some time later, the sculptress delivered a product that exactly conformed to this specification: It looked just like the drawing, and it was precisely one-and-a-half feet tall. The band manager was infuriated because the sculptress failed to grasp that he really wanted the piece to be life-size, not a scale model. Presumably she was supposed to divine this by telepathy, since the written specification clearly indicated a height of eighteen inches, not eighteen feet. The gap between actual customer requirements and the specifications provided to the sculptress led to a lack of conformance between the product and the customer need, not to mention major embarrassment to the band during the concert. Quality? The band didn't think so.

Software Requirements: The Foundation of Quality

Any successful enterprise requires that you both do the right thing, and do the thing right. We expect professional software developers to know how to do the thing—building a software product—right. Doing the right thing, though, requires a complete and unambiguous understanding of what your customer expects. In software, this is generally impossible. However, we have to do our best to define and understand customer requirements, or we are certain to miss the quality mark.

Collecting and analyzing the initial customer requirements is not enough; you also have to keep up with them as they mutate during the development cycle. Requirements management is one of the earliest improvement areas indicated by the Software Engineering Institute's Capability Maturity Model for Software (discussed in Chapter 9). Creeping user requirements (requirements that keep changing during development) pose one of the most common risks faced by software development organizations, affecting some 80 percent of management information systems projects and 70 percent of military software projects [Jones, 1994].

The "voice of the customer" is an essential prerequisite to creating a satisfactory product. How can we possibly expect to achieve the ultimate quality objective of "customer delight" without extensive customer involvement in the software development process? Arriving at a common vision of what the final product is supposed to be and do is very difficult. Without this shared vision, though, someone is bound to be surprised at what you eventually deliver. A major objective of software engineering is to minimize the surprise factor, the expectation gap between what the customers really need and what you think they need that tends to grow over time (see Fig. 5.2).

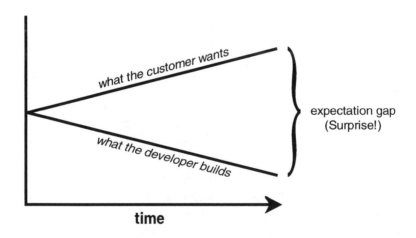

Figure 5.2: The software development expectation gap.

The problem of informal, incomplete, and poorly documented requirements plagues software groups of all types. One of our small software teams at Kodak focused on improved requirements engineering as the starting point for increasing our quality and productivity several years ago. We found that a culture that emphasizes high-quality requirements specifications does produce superior products, as judged by improved customer satisfaction and controlled post-specification requirements instability.

Our group's quest for excellent requirements specifications incorporates six techniques (Table 5.1). These techniques address the challenges of gathering, documenting, and validating user needs, as well as evaluating potential user interface designs. These six techniques fit into two general categories: (1) involving customers in the development project (this chapter), and (2) employing a variety of communication tools (described in Chapter 6). These methods are applicable to any software development life cycle.

Table 5.1.
Effective Techniques for Requirements Engineering.

Category	Techniques
Optimizing customer involvement in the application development effort.	• Use of a "project champion" model to build customer participation into the development team from the very beginning, and to ensure that the needs of diverse classes of users are properly understood.
Using effective communication tools to capture requirements and document them in easily understandable ways.	• Application of the "use case" method to analyze user needs. • Preparation of structured textual specification documents in a format based on the IEEE recommended practice for software requirements specifications. • Construction of "dialog maps," a variant of state-transition diagrams that effectively model user interfaces at a high level of abstraction. • Extensive use of prototypes to elucidate user needs and explore alternative designs for satisfying them. • Tracing individual requirements through design, implementation, and testing, to build a map of the system, the "requirements traceability matrix."

Actually, the life cycle you select for a particular project can itself serve as a tool for controlling risk. You may choose to develop a partial vision of the final product and implement it incrementally, rather than follow a classic waterfall strategy in which success hinges on acquiring high-quality requirements at the beginning of the project and assuming they remain stable for the duration. They rarely do.

The Need for Customer Involvement

Many years ago, I wrote Fortran programs for a scientist named Bill. As Bill was the sole anticipated user of these programs, we didn't have to worry about gathering requirements from different user communities or resolving conflicting needs. Bill and I were in adjacent offices with a common doorway, so questions that arose could be answered in an instant. I could show Bill what I was doing, and he could immediately confirm or correct my approach. When Bill moved about a hundred feet down the hall, I perceived an immediate drop in my productivity. Problems could not be resolved in real time any more. The frequency and quality of iteration between developer and customer declined, while the amount of rework I had to do increased. This was a powerful lesson on the importance of the customer/developer communication process, which was reinforced on subsequent projects.

The members of our Kodak research software groups are not experts in the specialized application domains we support. Consequently, it is not reasonable to expect us to make sound business or technical decisions on behalf of the customers. (I use the term "customers" to refer to the people who will actually use the software we write, not those managers who commission or pay for it.) Nor can we resolve conflicting requirements supplied by different users, or determine the relative priorities of a large group of requirements. We need to get actual customers involved in the project from the outset [Keil, 1995]. To begin, we must identify the different classes of customers that we anticipate will use an application. Then we need to think about how to get an actual member of each of those user classes involved with the development project.

When our Kodak software group became serious about customer involvement, our objective was to find a way to share the challenge of defining a new system between the developers and a few key customer representatives. We wished to avoid the common scenario of requirements changing every day as additional users hear about the application being designed and throw in their two cents worth. Several symptoms of an ailing project will alert you to the need for more direct customer involvement:

- You are continually chasing unsettled requirements.

- The number of TBD (to be determined) requirements never approaches zero.

- Consensus is not being reached on the desired feature set.

- Needs keep popping on and off your requirements list as you talk to new people.

- The development team is confused about how best to satisfy the most users.

Involving customers in development is relatively simple in a situation like ours, where our "customers" are fellow employees of the same company, often in our own building. The problem of customer involvement is more difficult when you are writing for the commercial marketplace; the involvement of marketing personnel adds another layer of uncertainty. In those situations, surrogate customers are necessary, but you still need confidence that the requirements that marketing generates are actually aimed at real customer needs. Marketing is responsible for accurately capturing the voice of the customer, while development has to translate marketing's interpretation into a system or software requirements specification. But for in-house development or even on-site contract work, there is no substitute for having actual users involved in every development project from day one.

The Project Champion Model

Since 1986, virtually all of our projects have included one or more key customer representatives, or project champions, as integral members of the development team. The project champion model is a cornerstone of our software development philosophy. I frankly do not feel comfortable approaching any nontrivial development effort without having a champion involved. In many of our projects, the role played by the champion has been a key determinant of success. We rely on the project champion model to incorporate the voice of the customer into our application development process.

The project champions serve as the primary interface between the customer community and the software developers. They are the focal point for collecting requirements from the potential users of a new application. We also expect the champions themselves to provide substantial input to the requirements for the proposed system. The champions also help to define the acceptance criteria that will be used to determine when a product is ready for delivery. The requirements analysis portion of development is now a shared responsibility of the software engineers and the project champions.

In a nutshell, the project champion is responsible for supplying the correct requirements from the perspective of the user communities. The software developer is responsible for documenting these needs and satisfying the resulting specifications. The champion must be empowered to make decisions on behalf of the entire customer community for the software system, or for that segment of the user domain each champion represents. Without the authority to make binding decisions, the champion is wasting his—and your—time.

We do not automatically fold into the requirements document requests for new features that we receive from other users. The project champions are the only "customers" we are working for in this model. Any expressed needs are filtered through the champions to see if they should be included in the requirements specification. By splitting the requirements gathering task among several user representatives, the analyst can focus on adding value in other ways:

- by clarifying and analyzing stated requirements

- by asking probing questions to dig down to the true user needs

- by synthesizing diverse perspectives into a unified view of the system

- by translating raw requirements into structured written specifications and analysis models like data flow diagrams

The notion of the project champion is a powerful cultural imperative in our groups. Every preliminary discussion about a new project considers who the project champions might be. Projects for which no champion can be identified are viewed, correctly, as high-risk, and they are undertaken with great reluctance. Early in a project, we spend considerable effort identifying appropriate champions, communicating with them and their managers, and agreeing on the role they will play on the project. The project champion model provides an example of how the cultural foundations of an organization can steer its decisions and behaviors.

When I am asked to consult on a troubled project, my first question usually is, "Who is the project champion?" If the answer is, "We don't have one," my first recommendation is to identify an appropriate candidate and see about getting him on board. Sometimes, it is clear that the current champion is not appropriate for some reason: He does not have a vested interest in the outcome of the project, he purports to speak for other user classes that he cannot accurately represent, or he is not able to devote the time needed to do a quality job. In these cases, I advise that a new champion be identified to replace or assist the current one.

A project champion is someone who will be an actual user of the system being constructed; he is not a manager, a funding sponsor, a marketing representative, or a member of the software group who feels he can speak for the users. If the champions won't be using the program in their own work, they aren't likely to have a commitment to devoting precious time to the project, nor an accurate perception of what the users really need.

Project champions hold a multifaceted job on the project. In addition to their primary role as key customers, their activities on our projects may include bits of systems analysis, internal marketing, customer support, and other roles. The ideal project champion

- is a respected member of the user community

- has a thorough understanding of the application domain

- has a vision of what the product should be and do

- eagerly anticipates delivery of the product

- has authority to represent the user community in defining the functionality of the system

- has management support for the often extensive time commitment he makes to the project

- has enough experience with computing systems to be effective and realistic

Project champions have to remember that we are not building the product just for their use. They represent a community of users having similar needs, and they are responsible for collecting input from their peers to help make the right decisions.

The champions should be able to recognize when a consensus on some issue conflicts with their personal preferences, and to compromise accordingly.

For large projects or those having diverse user communities, a team of two to four co-champions may be appropriate. Think about the different classes of users you expect to operate the system (you should do this anyway as part of the scoping of the project). Try to select a separate champion who can adequately represent the unique needs of each user class. Watch out for champion candidates who are highly territorial or who have a hidden agenda. They are likely to try to force their own narrow perspectives on the requirements analysis process.

A good way to overcome excessive parochialism is to have a small cross-section of the user community assisting each project champion. This resource team (which should include both frequent and occasional users-to-be of the system) contributes requirements, reviews specification documents, and evaluates prototypes to provide some additional user perspectives. Resource teams typically consist of one to five users.

Figure 5.3 illustrates the hierarchy of customer representation on a large project. The same analyst may work with more than one project champion. The champions that represent different user domains have to work together to reconcile conflicting requirements that were collected from the customers they represent. The analysts and project leader can facilitate workshops aimed at resolving these conflicts.

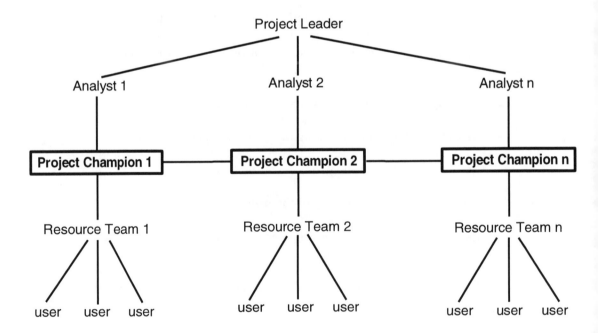

Figure 5.3: Project champion model for a large project.

For projects that do not have a specific customer clamoring for the program, such as those initiated by management directive, solicit project champions from among those potential users who seem the most enthused about the project. This does not work as well as when there are users who just can't wait to get their hands on the new software; they make natural choices for project champions.

Project Champion Expectations

The activities expected of project champions are described in the first section of our group's software development guidelines, making them a highly visible component of our written culture. The software project leaders are responsible for negotiating the exact roles and responsibilities with their project champions, using these written expectations as a starting point. Some of the specific activities we might ask champions to perform are described in the following paragraphs.

Planning: The champions might help define the business case for the system, interacting with management as appropriate. They work with developers to determine the scope and limitations of the system, and to define the boundaries between the system and the rest of the world. This boundary, sometimes represented as the single bubble drawn on a context diagram, separates those functions and components that lie within the system under development from those that do not (see Fig. 5.4). If team members do not agree on where this boundary lies, time gets wasted discussing needs that are actually outside the problem domain, while other necessary functions may be overlooked.

Gathering Requirements: Champions are expected to communicate with selected members of the customer community to provide additional input to the requirements for the new system. They also suggest other users to participate in prototype evaluations or beta testing, such as members of the resource teams shown in Fig. 5.3. Despite the involvement of other users through the resource team, the champion is still ultimately responsible for making decisions when a consensus is not reached by the group. Customers need to understand that the project champion plays this decision-making role, lest they believe (or expect) that the software team itself will take responsibility for making such decisions.

A critical role of the champions is to reconcile conflicting requirements so that a unified set of needs is presented to the developers. This may involve participation in group requirements gathering activities such as Joint Application Design (JAD) sessions, which are structured to bring together users and developers in a facilitated workshop to identify and document user requirements [Wood, 1989]. JAD sessions can minimize time delays and off-line communications by holding all major stakeholders captive in the same room until they make the necessary decisions.

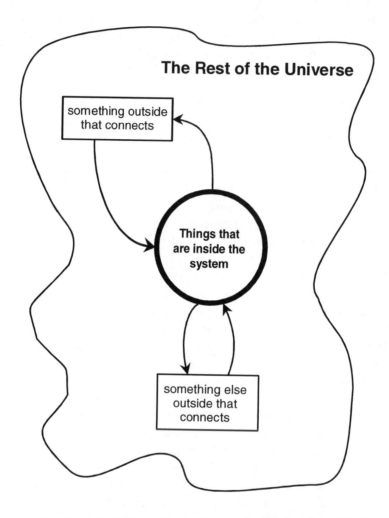

*Figure 5.4: The context diagram shows what is inside
the system and what is not.*

User representatives should be asked to distinguish between essential requirements and "chrome," and to establish implementation priorities accordingly. At
Kodak, we ask user representatives to classify individual requirements into three
classes of priority, as follows:

Priority 1:   Must be present in the initial release or the
product is not useful.

Priority 2:   Necessary but can be deferred to a subsequent
release.

Priority 3:   Would be nice to have if resources and time
permit.

It is safe to assume that items in the lowest (Priority 3) category will never be implemented. Sometimes, every feature seems to be essential, and you may have to push hard to get users to decide which ones really can be deferred. It is not reasonable to expect the developers to set rational priorities for implementing program functions if they are not intimately familiar with the application domain. We need the project champions to help us identify the correct subset of functions to implement first.

Champions may also define and assess security needs, performance requirements, and other software quality attributes, in addition to functional and user interface requirements. If these are not explicitly specified by user representatives, the development team will have to guess at what is important to the customer.

Validation: Our group requires project champions to participate in quality reviews of requirements specification documents, and we invite them to review high-level designs. They may also assist with writing acceptance test criteria and providing test data sets as appropriate. Sometimes, the champions and resource teams will walk through test cases to validate the requirements specification document. They also participate in prototype evaluations.

Documentation: Many of our champions have contributed extensively to the writing of user manuals and on-line help displays. They usually are responsible for writing those parts of the system documentation that pertain to the conceptual foundation of the application. Often, our project champions will draft the on-line help text, which the developers then structure into the format needed by the help display tool used by the application. The developers actually write the user manuals, but with considerable input from the champions.

For software to be installed on multiple computers, such as PCs, the project champions assist in defining the distribution process that will be used for the released software, such as mailing out disks, or downloading from a server on the network. They also define any security constraints that pertain to distribution or access to the application.

Advocacy: Champions may play a major advocacy role in "selling" the system to the customer communities and their managers. Customer and management reviews and demonstrations may be a part of this task. Project champions and their resource teams usually become early adopters of the new applications created, and a satisfied customer is the best advertisement. In fact, if the champion loses interest or moves to another work area before the project is completed, the likelihood of high user acceptance decreases. Project champions can help overcome the inertia that inhibits their peers from trying new and improved ways of doing their work.

Training: The champions sometimes play a major role in developing and delivering training in the use of the system to the user community, such as preparing a class or writing tutorial materials.

Change Management: We rely on project champions to help us evaluate requests from users for correcting defects and adding enhancements. All such requests are entered into the change control system, which automatically sends the request by e-mail to the maintainer and the project champion (see Chapter 15). The champion determines priorities for these items and presents change requests to the maintenance staff. Some larger projects use a more formal change control board to set enhancement and defect correction priorities. For smaller projects, the champion fills this role alone.

Not surprisingly, it is rare to find a project champion who has the right skills, the time, and the energy available to do all this work. In practice, the exact role of each champion is negotiated with the software project leader. It may look as if champions are expected to carry a disproportionate share of the analysis burden, but no one champion at Kodak has ever been asked to do everything on this list (nor should that be expected). Usually, though, we have found champions who perform enough of these tasks to make a great difference in the success of the project.

One of our best champions, Jackie, has worked with us on several projects over the years. Jackie is extremely knowledgeable about the application domain, and she is well respected in the user community. On one recent large project, Jackie was one of four project champions, each representing a different subset of the user community. Jackie made extensive contributions to this project, including

- providing application-specific algorithms and test data sets for them,

- working with other champions and the analyst to design user interface screens,

- communicating with other customers in the domain she represented to understand their needs,

- writing extensive text for the on-line help system and user manual,

- specifying the contents of certain data files and the functions required to manipulate them,

- prioritizing requirements to define an implementation sequence,

- participating in reviews of the software requirements specifications,

- planning a migration pathway from existing related applications to the new system, and

- providing training on the new application to his coworkers.

Not all project champions are equally qualified for, or dedicated to, the job. Sometimes, the analyst still has to pick up the slack, performing tasks that the best champions normally handle. The specific roles and responsibilities are negotiable, but the champion really must make the bottom-line decisions about what goes into the system and what does not. Project champions help control the risk of application development by increasing the probability that the right thing is being done.

I have been fortunate to collaborate with some outstanding project champions who work behind the scenes to collect and refine input from their peers and who step up to the challenge of making the many decisions that go into quality software construction. Such champions strive to define the best possible system for the largest number of potential users.

Our project champions learn enough about our structured software engineering process to appreciate why we use the approaches we do. They have been valuable advocates on our behalf in the conflicts that arise between engineers who want to build the product right and customers who wonder why it isn't done yet. Champions also have intervened with the managers sponsoring a project, supporting our commitment to spend time on requirements specification activities up front. A champion who insists on getting a quality system and supports the process we use to build one is a staunch ally indeed.

When the Project Champion Model Fails

Sometimes, the project champion approach has not delivered the desired results. These failings indicate the need to keep certain criteria in mind when selecting and working with a champion. Following are some examples of failure of the approach—with the results.

> **Problem:** The champion did not adequately communicate with his constituents in the user community; consensus was never reached on the direction the project should take, and the champion provided only his own, limited perspective of needs. **Solution:** The project was canceled in the requirements phase. **Observations:** The project champion approach has not worked well when the champion felt he had sole control over the system specifications. While we want people with opinions, they have to recognize that others will use the system, too. A project champion with too narrow a perspective may not see the need to incorporate certain functions, or to design programs for a range of user capabilities and frequencies of use.

> **Problem:** The project champion did not have a vision of the product, provided little input, and deferred many decisions to the analyst; whatever the analyst proposed was okay with the champion. **Solution:** The project champion was amicably replaced with one who had a stronger vision of the product, and progress accelerated nicely. **Observations:** When champions do not have both a clear

vision of and some opinions about what should be built, they cannot be helpful. If I choose to wander about aimlessly during the
analysis phase, I can do that on my own, without the intervention
of a project champion. We want champions who will start with a
mental image of the objective and work closely with us to shape
that vision into something we all agree is the best solution to the
problem.

Problem: The designated champion did not feel he had the
authority to make decisions and needed to consult frequently with
his resource team, leading to slow-motion decision-making and
reversals of decisions that had been made earlier. The champion
also failed to serve as an advocate for the system with his peers.
Solution: A good system was eventually delivered, which satisfied the champion's requirements and the needs of a broad user
community. However, because of a lack of advocacy and management support, it was not used nearly as much as it could have
been. **Observations:** Project champions must be empowered to
make binding decisions about the software system. If they have to
obtain approval from someone else—managers or other important
customers—they are probably not the right champions.

Whenever we had to work on a management-mandated (as opposed to customer-
driven) project and no champion was involved, we had a hard time assessing and
meeting customer needs. We have finally reached the state where we generally do
not undertake the project unless a project champion can be found to help us do it
right. Our culture is committed to building quality products, and if we know the
chance of this outcome is low, we would rather not waste our time and the company's money.

A major risk with the project champion model is that the champion's manager
will not appreciate the value of the contribution the champion is making to the
project, and therefore will not free up enough of his time to do a proper job. Only a
passionate and dedicated champion will put in lots of project time beyond his normal job responsibilities. The software team must share the reasoning behind its
commitment to customer involvement with the customer managers. Realistically
estimate the time commitment expected of each champion, to avoid blindsiding
any of the participants when the job grows way beyond an initial request to "participate in a workshop or two."

The project champion model is so effective that there is no excuse for not using
it when actual users of the system are available locally. If the project is important
enough to do, it's important enough to do well.

Summary

✔ Customer involvement is the most critical factor in software quality.

✔ A quality-oriented culture will maximize customer involvement in the requirements process to help all project members reach a common vision of what they are building.

✔ The use of project champions as key customer representatives is an effective approach for integrating users into the project development team.

✔ Document your expectations for project champions as part of your group's software development procedures—your written culture—and use them as a starting point for negotiating the champion's responsibilities on each project.

Culture Builders and Killers

Culture Builder: Project champions can be powerful allies, so treat them right. They are devoting their valuable time to help your software engineers, with the faith that you will build a quality product right for them and their peers. Make sure their managers are aware of the contribution the project champions are making to the cause. Remember the message of Chapter 3: Take the champions out to lunch to celebrate milestones, and give them more tangible gestures of appreciation when you can.

Culture Builder: If you are asked by management to build a system for internal use, and no project champions can be found from among the prospective user base, push back. Explain that you cannot guarantee a quality job if the voice of the customer is not heard when designing the program. You are reluctant to waste resources on a project you know is doomed to fail. If no users care enough about the product to help build it right, why should the software team devote any energy to it?

Culture Killer: Get the same champion assigned to several projects. Don't worry that his manager didn't reduce the rest of his workload accordingly, because talented people can always fit other responsibilities into their schedules. If the champion isn't attending the needs-gathering workshops, answering your questions, or making the decisions you present to him, ask the developers to fill in for the champion whenever necessary. They probably can do as good a job as the champion, after a little exposure to the application domain.

Culture Killer: One of your project leaders is having a hard time getting customer participation in the requirements gathering process and has come to you for help. The customers claim they have already told him everything he needs to know, so he should just start building the system. The project leader really doesn't have enough information to proceed, and tempers are getting short. Instruct the project leader to produce a requirements specification, even though he has never done this before, and don't offer to intercede with the unhappy customers. All software engineers know how to do requirements analysis and manage difficult customers, don't they?

References and Further Reading

Crosby, Philip B. *Quality Is Free.* New York: McGraw-Hill, 1979.

Crosby emphasizes the critical quality dimension of conformance to customer requirements. The concepts in this book provide the foundation for much of the contemporary thinking in the domain of software quality and process improvement.

Gause, Donald C., and Gerald M. Weinberg. *Exploring Requirements: Quality Before Design.* New York: Dorset House Publishing, 1989.

Gause and Weinberg concentrate on the human factors of getting a team to work together effectively to define the requirements for a development project. The goal is to develop a consistent understanding of requirements among all participants. They emphasize reducing ambiguity in requirements, asking the right questions of the right people, and running effective meetings.

Jones, Capers. *Assessment and Control of Software Risks.* Englewood Cliffs, N.J.: PTR Prentice-Hall, 1994.

Jones addresses some sixty software risks, including that of creeping user requirements (Chapter 9). Each risk factor is analyzed as to: severity; frequency of occurrence; root causes; methods of prevention and control; assistance available from software tools, consulting, education, publications, and standards; and known therapies.

Keil, Mark, and Erran Carmel. "Customer-Developer Links in Software Development," *Communications of the ACM,* Vol. 38, No. 5 (May 1995), pp. 33-44.

Fifteen techniques for establishing links between customers and developers of both package and custom software applications are discussed in this article. The most successful projects employed several of these links. This issue also contains several other articles that pertain to customer involvement in the requirements elicitation process.

Szmyt, Peter. "Get Over the Software-Centered Wall," *Software Development,* Vol. 2, No. 11 (November 1994), pp. 49-59.

For each of seven application development steps (functional analysis, design, implementation, and so on), Szmyt contrasts a software application-centered approach with its user-centered counterpart. This article also contains many references to publications on usability and user interface guidelines.

Thayer, Richard H., and Merlin Dorfman, eds. *System and Software Requirements Engineering.* Los Alamitos, Calif.: IEEE Computer Society Press, 1990.

This compendium of forty-four articles covers a wide range of topics in requirements engineering. A companion volume by Dorfman and Thayer titled *Standards, Guidelines, and Examples on System and Software Requirements Engineering* completes this comprehensive tutorial on the requirements engineering process.

Wood, Jane, and Denise Silver. *Joint Application Design.* New York: John Wiley & Sons, 1989.

Wood and Silver describe when and how to use Joint Application Design in the system development process. The steps of research, meeting preparation, the JAD session itself, and producing the final document are discussed.

Chapter 6

Tools for
Sharing the Vision

Any one "view" of requirements is insufficient to understand or describe the desired external behavior of a complex system.

—Alan M. Davis, *201 Principles of Software Development*

Software engineers are in the business of communicating to about the same degree that they are in the business of computing. Just look at the total number of meetings and volume of paperwork that is produced in conjunction with any sizable software project. Government projects are particularly notorious for generating massive quantities of documentation. Then there is the other extreme, in which an organization using informal development processes generates mostly code, with little supporting documentation. As with most things in life, the preferred state lies somewhere between these two poles.

The techniques described in this chapter focus on the critical communication interface between the creators of a new software system and those who will use it. If you build the product the customers initially tell you they want, you will always wind up building it again, once you (and they) finally understand their true needs. You need effective methods to elicit the real requirements from the users, document them in unambiguous and verifiable forms, and explore design alternatives. Our software groups at Kodak have used five tools to help the developers and their customers achieve a shared vision of the product they are creating:

- use case scenarios

- software requirements specifications

- dialog maps

- prototypes

- requirements traceability matrices

Use Cases

Often the customer will present as "needs" some combination of the problems she has in her work that she expects the system to solve, the solutions she has in mind for an expressed or implied problem, the desired attributes of whatever solution ultimately is provided, and the true fundamental needs, that is, the functions the system must let her perform. The problem becomes more complex if the systems analyst is dealing with a surrogate customer, such as a marketing representative, who purports to speak for the actual end users of the application. The challenge to the analyst is to distinguish among these four types of input and identify the *real* functional requirements that will satisfy the *real* user's *real* business needs.

Many techniques are used for eliciting user requirements, all of which attempt to include the voice of the customer in the product design process. A typical project might employ a combination of meetings with project champions and developers, facilitated workshops (for example, joint application design sessions) with analysts and users, individual customer interviews, and user surveys. The use case approach is an especially effective technique for deriving requirements, as discussed below.

The Use Case Method: Use (pronounced "youce," not "youze") cases were introduced as part of an object-oriented development methodology [Jacobson, 1992], but recently the concept has been extended into a general technique for requirements analysis and user interface design [Constantine, 1994]. Each use case describes a scenario in which a user interacts with the system being defined to achieve a specific goal or accomplish a particular task. Use cases are described in terms of the user's work terminology, not computerese. By focusing on essential use cases, stripped of implementation constraints or alternatives, the analyst can derive software requirements that will enable the user to achieve her objectives in each specific usage scenario. Figure 6.1 illustrates the overall process we found to be effective with the use case technique.

We recently applied the use case method to specify the requirements for a chemical tracking system. I worked as an analyst with a team of chemists (one project champion and a five-person resource team) to collect their needs for this application; other analysts worked with other project champions representing different user communities. Each community generated its own set of use cases, since each needed the system to perform different tasks. I began by asking the chemists to think of reasons why they would need to use this planned chemical tracking system. Each of these "reasons to use" became a use case, which we then explored in depth in a series of two-hour sessions that I facilitated.

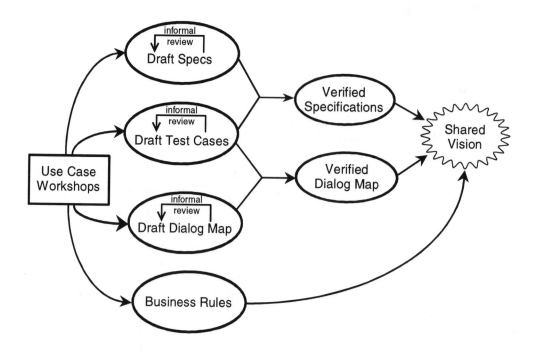

Figure 6.1: Process and deliverables from the use case method.

We used forms such as that shown in Fig. 6.2, drawn on a large flipchart. I prepared one flipchart for each use case prior to the group sessions. For each use case, we stated the goal that the user needed to accomplish—one reason someone would use this application. We also noted which of the various user classes we had identified for this application (chemist, technician, stockroom staff, purchasing department) would be interested in each use case. In addition, we estimated the anticipated frequency of execution for each use case. This gave us a preliminary indication of concurrent usage loads, the importance of ease of learning versus ease of use, and capacities of data storage or transaction throughput.

We spent the bulk of each workshop exploring the actions the user would expect to take with the computer for a specific use case, and the possible responses the system might then generate. As the chemists suggested user actions (or inputs) and system responses, I wrote them on sticky notes and placed them under the appropriate heading on the flipchart form. Often, a system response would trigger further dialog with the computer, necessitating additional user input, followed by yet another response. The movable sticky notes made it easy to revise our initial thoughts and to group together pieces of related information as we went along.

By walking through individual use cases in the workshops, we drilled down to the fundamental customer needs the system had to satisfy. We also explored many "what if" scenarios to reveal exception and decision situations that the system must handle. New use cases sometimes came to mind as we worked through those that the chemists had already suggested.

Some of the pieces of information elicited in the workshops were not really functional requirements. Instead, they were business rules about the system and the work processes it supported, stating such policies as: "Safety training records must be up to date before a user can order a hazardous chemical" and "A purchasing agent can modify a user's order only with written permission from the user." We documented these business rules separately from the true functional requirements, and then communicated them to the project champions of the other user groups, who had their own, sometimes conflicting, business rules. Any discrepancies were reconciled in a meeting between the analyst team and all the project champions.

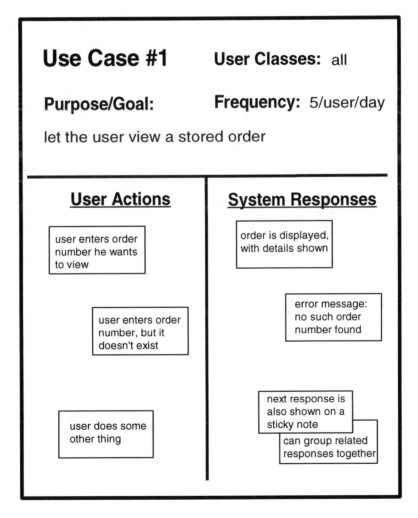

Figure 6.2: Use case flipchart created in a workshop with user representatives.

We found that the use case strategy of asking "What do you need to accomplish with this system?" kept us focused on visualizing how the application ought to perform some function. More open-ended discussions that begin with "What do you want this program to do?" can lead participants to suggest features that are not necessarily linked to specific user tasks. By the end of each workshop, we had a pretty good shared vision of how each usage scenario we explored should play out.

After each workshop, I took the flipcharts festooned with sticky notes to my office and began to extract functional requirements from each use case. After all the information was translated into structured textual requirements specifications, business rules, and structured analysis models, we were able to take another important step: deriving test cases.

Deriving Test Cases from Use Cases: I learned long ago that writing functional test cases is a great way to crystallize the fuzzy image in your mind about how a program should behave. Inventing test cases from our use cases proved to be easy, since we had already been thinking about how the user would interact with the program to accomplish various tasks [Ambler, 1995]. Each test case represented one specific scenario of interaction with the system, within the context of one of the essential use cases. The test case might result in a successful transaction, or it could generate an anticipated error response of some kind.

Using the requirements specification to provide details, we developed test cases without the chemists ever having sketched out screens or discussed the exact database contents. Our general concept of the sequence of events that characterized a use case provided enough detail to permit writing many test cases. If you can't readily think of test cases that demonstrate your understanding of a use case scenario, you haven't adequately clarified the vision.

Having test cases in hand this early in the development process provided several benefits:

- We could "test" parts of the specification long before it was complete. The chemist group walked through the test cases to find any changes that we needed to make in our specifications to make the tests execute properly.

- We could establish traceability between each test case and the requirements it addressed. Any requirements that were not covered meant writing more test cases; any test cases that relied on functions not present in the requirements document showed that some requirements were missing.

- We could use the suite of test cases to evaluate commercial products that might meet the needs of the project, enabling us to decide whether to build or to buy. We simply had to walk through the test cases with an evaluation copy of the commercial package to see which cases it handled and which it did not.

Developing test cases early in the project reinforced our fundamental software development cultural philosophy that quality activities must not be left to the end of the development cycle, but should permeate the entire project from the outset. This use case approach with immediate test case generation reinforced another valuable lesson. Every time I do any kind of systematic testing, the following three things happen:

1. I find errors in the work products (in this case, in the requirements specification document and the structured analysis models);

2. I find errors in the test cases (such as requirements that were not covered by the test cases); and

3. I correct both the work product and the test cases, and then rarely have additional problems with the product.

Use Case Technique Evaluated: The use case approach is an efficient and effective technique for collecting essential requirements from a group of customers, helping to focus on their real needs, not just what they initially say they need. It will help all those involved—analysts and customers—arrive at a common, shared vision of what the product they are specifying will be and do. This is key to constructing quality software.

There are two less obvious benefits to be derived from the use case method. First, the act of developing use cases helps analysts gain an understanding of the user's application domain. Second, it helps avoid superfluous requirements. When approached with the question, "What do you want the system to do?" customers are tempted to add features that just seem like good ideas and might be useful some day. From the use case angle, though, every requirement directly supports a specific task the user needs to accomplish with the help of the computer.

Software Requirements Specifications

No matter how software requirements are gathered, they must be documented in a way that permits them to be

- validated by inspection to make sure they are correct, complete, and consistent;

- used to correctly design the programs, databases, and user interfaces that will deliver the required functionality with the appropriate balance of quality attributes;

- traced into the design elements, and then into the code that implements the design; and

- used to derive test cases that can demonstrate whether the final software product in fact satisfies the requirements.

Software people are notoriously sloppy about documenting requirements. Even in groups that do write requirements specifications, each analyst is probably using a different style and format for the document, resulting in widely variable quality. Some developers feel their schedule does not allow time to go through a structured process to collect and record explicit requirements. Others believe they understand the problem well enough that it is not necessary to spend time writing down what the customer said he needs. Sometimes, requirements change so rapidly that it's hard to keep the written documentation current, so why bother to try?

These are all excuses, not reasons, for glossing over the requirements documentation step. They are recipes for failure, defined as delivering something that does not meet the needs of the customer (or not delivering anything at all). Nothing says the requirements document has to be a massive tome; it should be just large enough for clear communication, no larger, no smaller. Even if it fits on a single page, it provides the foundation for all the development work that follows. Indeed, if you are following a development life cycle in which small increments of functionality are designed and delivered frequently, the requirements specification for each increment will be short.

Without quality requirements, it is impossible to build a quality product. If the requirements are not documented, you have no way of knowing when you are done, and you cannot judge whether the work was done correctly. Excellent, documented requirements are a prerequisite for excellence in software engineering [Davis, 1993]. You should plan to spend 15 to 20 percent of the effort on a software project on gathering, analyzing, documenting, and reviewing the requirements.

Nearly all of our Kodak group's projects, even small ones for developing internally reusable software components, go through a formal, written requirements specification process. "Formal" need not mean "cumbersome, voluminous, incomprehensible, unchangeable, and interminable." Our objective is to prepare a consistent and unambiguous set of structured documents and models that clearly identify the features that must be contained in the delivered product.

The IEEE Software Requirements Specification: Our groups have standardized on using the IEEE Software Requirements Specification (SRS) template, as described in IEEE Std. 830 [IEEE, 1993]. The IEEE SRS provides a well-structured framework for recording not only the functional requirements of a system but also much of the ancillary information collected during analysis that is key to the success of the project (see Fig. 6.3). It provides the flexibility to organize functional requirements in a variety of ways, depending on what makes sense for your application: mode of usage, user class, object class, feature, stimulus, functional hierarchy, or hybrids of these. Figure 6.3 illustrates the organization of functional requirements by system feature, in section 3.2 of the SRS.

The hierarchical numbering scheme illustrated in Fig. 6.3 has some drawbacks. The numbers are not semantically meaningful, other than revealing hierarchical

Table of Contents

1   Introduction
   1.1   Purpose
   1.2   Scope
   1.3   Definitions, Acronyms, and Abbreviations
   1.4   References
   1.5   Overview

2   Overall Description
   2.1   Product Perspective
   2.2   Product Functions
   2.3   User Characteristics
   2.4   Constraints
   2.5   Assumptions and Dependencies

3   Specific Requirements
   3.1   External Interface Requirements
      3.1.1   User Interfaces
      3.1.2   Hardware Interfaces
      3.1.3   Software Interfaces
      3.1.4   Communications Interfaces
   3.2   System Features
      3.2.1   System Feature 1
         3.2.1.1   Introduction/Purpose of Feature
         3.2.1.2   Stimulus/Response Sequence
         3.2.1.3   Associated Functional Requirements
            3.2.1.3.1   Functional Requirement 1
               .
               .
            3.2.1.3.n   Functional Requirement n
      3.2.2   System Feature 2
         .
         .
         .
      3.2.n   System Feature n
   3.3   Performance Requirements
   3.4   Design Constraints
   3.5   Software System Attributes
   3.6   Other Requirements

Revision History

Figure 6.3: IEEE template for software requirements specifications.

relationships. When new requirements are inserted, the numbering can become complex unless you use a word processor that automatically handles renumbering. Some customers to whom I show the SRS find the four- to six-digit numbering scheme intimidating and clumsy.

To get around these limitations, Tom Gilb recommends a "tagging" scheme that uniquely identifies each specification with a mnemonically meaningful label [Gilb, 1988]. Tags such as AXIS, AXIS.TICKMARK, and AXIS.TICKMARK.SIDE show the hierarchical parentage of each requirement and are more meaningful than numbers like "3.1.3.5.2." Gilb's textual tags are easier to read and less prone to typographical errors than are numerical sequences, albeit much bulkier. Your word processor won't be able to generate textual tags automatically, either.

A textual software requirements specification, even one that is highly organized according to the IEEE SRS template, is not a panacea for the problem of representing user needs. Our groups at Kodak also use structured analysis techniques (such as data flow diagrams, entity-relationship diagrams, and state-transition diagrams) to augment textual documents. Each of these tools provides a different view of the problem we need to solve. The combination of a written SRS and visual modeling methods provides a complete and detailed picture of what has to be done to satisfy your customer's needs.

The essence of the SRS is the section on functional requirements or system features. Writing good functional requirements specifications takes practice. A specification can be written using narrative text, a more formal notation such as structured English, or a highly formal specification language such as Z. Regardless of which approach is used, a high-quality specification for a single requirement has the characteristics shown in Table 6.1 [Deutsch, 1988]. A specification that possesses these characteristics lays the foundation for a high-quality application. As you write and review specifications, look at them from each of these perspectives. For example, if you cannot readily envision how a requirement statement would be tested, perhaps you are looking at an attribute statement or a random piece of useful information, not a true functional requirement.

Quality Attributes: Section 3.5 of the IEEE SRS deals with software system attributes, or quality attributes. These attributes, taken together, define "quality" in software, beyond the simple implementation of functional specifications. Many specification processes fail to explicitly investigate the importance of various quality attributes, such as usability, maintainability, and modifiability. The users and developers may both have thoughts about which of the many "ilities" are important, but often they are not written down. If quality attributes are not captured as part of the vision of the new system, there is a good chance that the delivered product will not meet the implicit expectations of the customers.

Tables 6.2, 6.3, and 6.4 identify some of the quality attributes that can be important to a software project [Glass, 1992; DeGrace, 1993]. Some of these are visible to the users (software operation), while others are more significant to the developers (software revision and transition). Many of the quality factors cannot be optimized simultaneously; therefore, you must evaluate them for relative importance so appropriate design decisions can be made. For example, increasing the

importance of many attributes negatively affects program efficiency, while designing specifically for efficiency is detrimental to attributes such as portability, testability, and maintainability [Glass, 1992; Deutsch, 1988].

We attempt to incorporate quantitative and testable quality attributes in our
SRS documents. For example, a reusable component that we expected to be
enhanced frequently had a stated requirement for the maximum number of hours
needed to add a specific type of new feature. The presence of this requirement in
the SRS was a factor in designing the application to have high flexibility.

Table 6.1.
Characteristics of a High-Quality Requirements Statement.

Characteristic	Description
Complete	Nothing is missing; the requirement conforms to any applicable standards.
Consistent	It does not conflict with other requirements.
Correct	It accurately states a user need that must be satisfied.
Feasible	It can be implemented within existing constraints.
Modifiable	The structure and style of the requirement is such that changes can be made when necessary.
Necessary	It documents something the users need, not something the developers included because they thought the users would like it.
Prioritized	Requirements are ranked as to how essential it is to incorporate each one into a particular release of the product.
Testable	Tests can be devised to demonstrate whether the requirement is properly implemented.
Traceable	The requirement is uniquely identified so it can be traced into corresponding design, code, and testing components of the system.
Unambiguous	Each requirement has only one possible interpretation.

Table 6.2.
Some Quality Attributes for Software Operation.

Attribute	Definition
Accuracy	The extent to which results obtained from the program are free from error
Correctness	The extent to which the program solves the customer's problem, conforms to what was specified, and is free of defects
Efficiency	The extent to which minimal system resources are required by the program to perform its functions (memory consumption, speed)
Integrity	The extent to which access to the program or data can be controlled
Reliability	The extent to which the program can be expected to properly perform its intended functions without failing
Robustness	The degree to which the program continues to function correctly when presented with invalid inputs or unanticipated conditions
Usability	The effort required to learn, use, prepare input for, and interpret the output of the program

Table 6.3.
Some Quality Attributes for Software Revision.

Attribute	Definition
Adaptability	The extent to which the program can be used unchanged in environments other than the one for which it was originally created
Flexibility	The effort required to modify the program to provide some new function, or to adapt to a changed environment
Maintainability	The effort required to locate and correct an error in the program
Testability	The effort required to test the program to ensure that it performs its intended functions
Traceability	The ease of establishing connections between the program's requirements, design, code, and tests

Table 6.4.
Some Quality Attributes for Software Transition.

Attribute	Definition
Interoperability	The effort required to link the program to another software system
Portability	The effort required to modify the program to run in a new hardware or software environment
Reusability	The extent to which all or part of the program can be used in other applications
Understandability	The degree to which someone unfamiliar with the system can comprehend its architecture, as well as individual programs

Writing attributes to be testable is difficult, but if you cannot test the product against the attribute specification and measure it in some way, you will never know if the attribute goals were achieved. Specifications of quality attributes often cannot be tested until the product is nearly complete. Nonetheless, the act of documenting and studying such requirements can lead to design considerations that result in a better product, higher productivity, and fewer surprises. Keep these quality factors in mind throughout the entire project life cycle, and consider their implications for the decisions you make during design, coding, and testing.

What Can Go Wrong During Analysis: The requirements specification process is prone to two major pitfalls. At one extreme is the back-of-the-envelope specification that only crudely approximates the product you should be constructing to meet the user's needs. At the other extreme is "analysis paralysis," the attempt to perfect the functional requirements and user interface designs before implementing anything.

Analysis paralysis is most common when following a classic waterfall software development life cycle, in which the requirements specification is entirely completed first, then design is completed, then implementation. Other development models, such as iterative prototyping, incremental development, evolutionary delivery, or spiral development, can control analysis paralysis by getting some functionality into the user's hands quickly [Gilb, 1988]. Feedback from these initial deliveries is used to refine the specs for the next round. You can't hide behind one of these alternative life cycles as an excuse for not doing requirements engineering, though. Each development increment should go through a complete mini-cycle of analyze, design, build, and test.

Don't delude yourself into thinking you can freeze all of the requirements while you work on the system. Since requirements inevitably will continue to evolve as development is underway, you must define a process for managing changes in requirements and use it religiously. On a small project, you might be able to update the SRS with the new, modified, or canceled requirements every time you process a change request. The revision history at the end of the SRS should contain a complete history of the document changes, so the functions described in the SRS match the reality of the product when it is delivered. However, on larger projects, requirements changes must be incorporated in a disciplined way to minimize the impact on the development team.

For all but the most trivial projects, a formal change management process is required. Chapter 15 describes a combined change request, defect tracking, and user feedback tool that we have used to help us manage requirements changes. Track the number, frequency, and severity of changes, so you can decide if you need to develop methods to control this instability better on your next project. Always estimate the impact of a requirements change on the project's delivery schedule and cost, so you can obtain commitments to these changes from the development staff, the customer, your management, and any other affected parties.

Regardless of the development life cycle you follow, an essential step to assure quality is to conduct inspections, or peer reviews, of the SRS. It is well documented that the cost of correcting a defect increases dramatically the later it is found in the development cycle; therefore, requirements inspection is a high-leverage investment in quality (see Chapter 12 for more about software inspections). A well-organized textual document like the IEEE SRS is readily inspected by the development team, project champions, and other affected parties. Design models, such as data flow diagrams, can be understood by interested users, but most people will balk at reviewing a formal specification notation. In our inspections, we also include other software engineers who are not directly involved with the project, but who can critically evaluate the SRS from an unbiased perspective. Defects identified during the inspection are classified and recorded for appropriate action.

During the use case analysis method described above, we used the following review process: At the beginning of each week, we held a two-hour use case workshop with the team of customer representatives, followed within two days by delivery of the preliminary SRS to the customer team members. Next, the customers reviewed the SRS changes informally and on their own, in preparation for the next weekly workshop, at which we discussed problems they found during their review. The next iteration of the SRS incorporated any necessary corrections, as well as new requirements extracted from the latest use case discussion. The project champion also reviewed the test cases, which were also prepared in this incremental fashion.

By making multiple passes through the growing SRS in this way, we created a much higher-quality product than if we had waited until the complete SRS was done to begin the review process. Reviewing in smaller chunks was more manageable and less imposing to the reviewers than if we had just delivered a thick requirements document at the end for review. A formal inspection activity was used as a final quality filter after the use case exploration was finished and the preliminary SRS completed. Very few major errors were found, and the many minor errors were readily corrected. Then the project team was able to take a high-quality SRS on to the next step, which in this case was a buy-or-build decision.

Dialog Maps

In a program having a graphical user interface (GUI), the number of screens and their possible interactions and navigation pathways can be very large. Our SRS documents often include mockups of the major user interface screens, and individual screen images scattered throughout a document provide a detailed representation of the contents of each display. However, separate screen images do not show how the many displays in a large system connect to each other. Even a working user interface prototype can only show the immediate links from one screen to others, rather than revealing the complete network of possible windows connected to any particular display.

Different users will have different expectations of which window will appear when some action is taken at a particular screen. A user may expect to be able to jump from one screen to another, although the designer was unaware of this requirement. A technique is needed to provide an overall view of a complex user interface at a higher level of abstraction—the view from 20,000 feet.

The dialog map, a form of state-transition diagram or STD, is an efficient method for modeling an entire user interface and showing this high altitude view. In a user interface, only one screen or window (state) is active for user input at any given instant. A set of explicit navigation pathways and trigger conditions (transitions) has been defined for moving from one display to another. While an event-driven GUI may have a very large number of legal navigation connections, the number is still finite, and specific actions must be taken or conditions encountered for a particular window to become active.

Figure 6.4 shows a portion of the dialog map for one of our recent projects. Each display (rectangle) is identified only by name, with no detail at all shown about its fields or layout. The connections between one screen and another are shown as transition lines connecting the states; each transition is labeled with its trigger conditions. Dialog maps can be arranged hierarchically to further control the degree of detail revealed at any specific level. We have used dialog maps to model systems containing more than one hundred screens and pop-up windows.

The dialog map helps to communicate the vision of the user interface architecture among all the participants: project champions, other users, developers, software managers, and customer managers. Common or similar interface features can be identified and built as reusable components. Any duplicated or missing functionality can be detected and corrected well before implementation begins. You can draw a preliminary dialog map during the requirements gathering phase, providing an early and evolving view of how the user interface might be structured, without worrying about exactly how each screen looks.

You can test the correctness of a dialog map with the help of test cases derived during requirements analysis. This is a good way to search for states and transitions that are not covered by your test cases, or to find situations where your SRS does not match the view represented in your dialog map. On the chemical tracking system project described earlier in this chapter, we drew a dialog map of a possible user interface to help us visualize the many potential execution paths associated with one complex use case. As we walked through the conceptual test cases derived from the SRS, I traced the corresponding paths on the dialog map with a highlighter pen. This revealed allowable execution paths that we had missed in the test suite, as well as identifying test cases that could not be "executed" according to the current dialog map, indicating errors in the model.

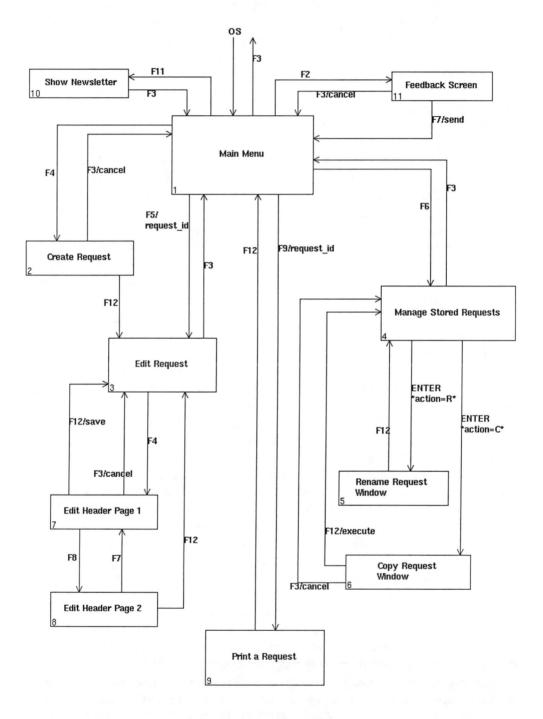

Figure 6.4: Sample dialog map.

Dialog maps can be drawn with computer-aided software engineering (CASE) tools, which assist with validation of the STD and facilitate frequent modifications as design progresses (Fig. 6.4 was drawn using Cadre's Team*work*® CASE tool). Or they can be drawn with any PC-based drawing program, or with a pencil and paper. After all, an STD is just a collection of labeled boxes and lines. The advantage of using a CASE tool over a generic drawing package is that CASE tools know the rules for STDs and can alert you when you make an error, such as having no transitions out of a particular state.

No matter which drawing method is used, there is great value in having the high-level view of the entire user interface that the dialog map provides. It is much less work to add a missing navigation pathway to a simple drawing than to connect two disparate functions in a completed system. Fixing such common faults early on helps avoid the blood-chilling customer response that begins with, "But I thought I would be able to . . ."

Prototypes

The user interface prototype is a powerful technique for refining customer needs and exploring design alternatives to satisfy those needs [Cornell, 1989]. Its purpose is to answer specific questions about both functionality and the look and feel of various interaction styles. (If you don't have any questions, don't bother with a prototype—just build the system.) Prototyping provides a general method for reducing application development risk by exploring alternative approaches early in the development life cycle.

Like an incremental development life cycle model, prototyping helps control the expectation gap by incorporating customer feedback at planned intervals during development (see Fig. 6.5). A culture that emphasizes customer participation in getting the requirements right will view prototyping as an essential tool. In the following paragraphs, we look at two types of prototype: horizontal and vertical.

A horizontal prototype consists of a superficial layer of a user interface, revealing the parts of the system that the user will see, but with little underlying functionality. Such a prototype is like a movie set, with realistic street scenes but only two-by-fours holding up the false fronts. Reasons to create a horizontal prototype include exploring dialog styles, determining if the required functionality has been planned for, assessing usability, and identifying the required navigation pathways among displays. While the dialog map provides the high-level view of the system's user interface, the horizontal prototype gets down to the level of detail necessary to make smart decisions about individual screens and their immediate navigation connections.

A vertical prototype consists of a complete slice of functionality for a limited portion of the whole system. Such prototypes are useful for validating design approaches and exploring alternative architectures or strategies for high-risk projects. For example, a vertical prototype of a client/server application might implement a small portion of the client user interface, all of the network communication component, and a few of the desired database functions on the server. Once the soundness of the technical approach is confirmed, the developers can implement the rest of the desired functionality.

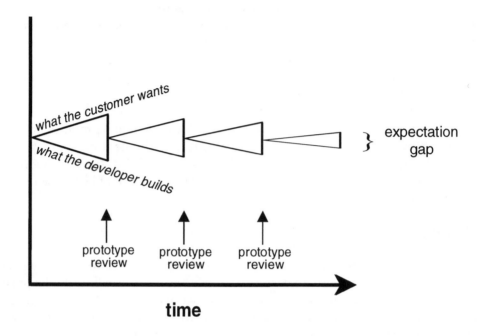

Figure 6.5: Prototyping reduces the software development expectation gap.

Because a prototype is not the final product, the effort required to build and evaluate a prototype that will provide useful answers to your questions should be kept to a minimum. If possible, use tools that allow the designer to construct the prototype quickly and modify it interactively, preferably as she sits with user representatives and hears their feedback. The effectiveness of prototyping is tied to the frequency and quality of iteration, as you sneak up on the best solution step by step.

Although some developers may be loath to write something that might well be thrown away, most will see the advantages of an approach that can provide creative alternatives for the users to evaluate. Providing choices through a prototyping experience enables developers to recognize the value of validating design approaches early in the life cycle, before committing to production code. Most developers will agree that the cost of fixing errors found through a prototype evaluation is much lower than the cost of fixing them in a delivered product. Providing choices is also a good public relations move, as it helps users to get involved in making contributions to the design of a system they ultimately will have to use in their jobs.

Note that electronic prototypes are not always necessary. Marc Rettig provides some excellent suggestions about how to build and use paper prototypes with minimum effort and maximum impact [Rettig, 1994]. Use simple prototypes to focus on the essence of what the interface should do, not on the details. For example, with a paper prototype, one person plays the role of the computer, while others attempt to use the paper model interface to accomplish tasks (perhaps derived from a use case analysis). The "computer" responds to user inputs by showing the appropriate response, based on the current design. The objective of the prototype evaluation is to find opportunities for improving the way the real interface, based on the paper model, would function.

It is tempting to perfect the prototype beyond the limited objective of answering your initial questions. This perfection usually adds little value, unless you intend to evolve the prototype into the deliverable product. An explicit decision should be made to either evolve or abandon the prototype once it has served its initial purpose [Davis, 1993]. A risk with prototyping is that the user will be enchanted with the false front of a horizontal prototype or the limited but real functionality of a vertical prototype, and therefore will conclude that the system is nearly complete. Clearly inform prototype evaluators that this is *not* the real system, but rather just a model of what the final application might look like. Prototypes rarely include production quality features for performance, error handling, or input validation.

Rather than simply letting users play with the prototype and offer comments, we use structured prototype evaluation scripts to generate answers to our requirements or design questions. The scripts should be short and focused, so the user is not daunted by the prospect of spending too much time working through them. In addition to many specific questions about the application, there are some general questions we have explored with prototype evaluation scripts, as follows:

- Does this program do what you expect it to do?

- Do you find any defects or omissions in the user interface?

- Do you like the interaction style?

- Which of several example interaction techniques do you prefer?

- Do any parts of the interface feel clumsy, awkward, or inefficient?

- Are there any missing navigation connections?

Watching users work with a prototype can be very informative. While few software organizations can afford to set up a full-blown usability testing lab, the things that users try to do with your sample program can tell you a lot. Where do their fingers move by instinct? When do they have that "I can't get there from here" look of frustration? When must they write down information on paper so they can re-enter it on another screen? As a result of watching users wrestle with a prototype, you can make improvements that might not have been apparent from written or verbal responses to prototype evaluation questions.

Requirements Traceability Matrices

The requirements traceability matrix (RTM) is another simple but effective quality tool. This tabular listing simply displays all of the functional requirements from the SRS, along with the design components that address each requirement, the source files and procedures within them that implement the requirement, and the test cases that verify the proper implementation of the requirement. The RTM provides several benefits. First, requirements will not be inadvertently overlooked during design or implementation. (If a requirement is explicitly canceled or postponed, that is shown in the matrix.) Second, developers and users can see at a glance what work has been completed, since empty boxes in the matrix represent items that are not yet complete. Third, if a test that has been mapped to a requirement fails, the source code entries in the RTM for that requirement tell you where to start looking for the problem in the code. And fourth, during maintenance, if a change is made in a specific requirement, the RTM identifies the other system components (designs, code, test cases) that may also have to be changed.

Figure 6.6 shows a portion of a RTM for a hypothetical project. For example, this matrix shows that requirement 5.1 is modeled by data flow process 2.3 and is implemented in function split_collapse of source file diagram.c. Test cases split.4 and split.5 are intended to verify that this requirement was properly implemented.

Req.	Design DFD	Source Files	Procedures	Test Cases
4.2.2	5.3.1.4 5.3.2.4	ge_lib.c dsp_lib.c	normal_section set_axes, get_y_scale	axis.1 axis.2, axis.3
4.2.3	5.3.7	ge_lib.c	required_key	axis.2
4.2.4	5.4	dsp_lib.c	calculate_step, adjust_graph	steps.1-steps.4
5.1	2.3	diagram.c	split_collapse	split.4, split.5
5.2	(canceled)			

Figure 6.6: Sample requirements traceability matrix.

Constructing the requirements traceability matrix on anything but a trivial system is a tedious manual task, but there are a few commercial tools available to help. Such tools must link the individual requirements in your specification document to design elements (perhaps stored in a CASE tool), to source files, and to test cases. Automated tool support is the only practical way to manage these linkages for a large system.

If you perform all of your system development tasks on a single platform, using various development tools, you might be able to find a traceability tool that can integrate your system components to construct the matrix. However, it is not uncommon to use different host computers for writing specifications (using a word processor on a personal computer), performing structured analysis and design (using a CASE tool on a UNIX workstation, for example), and writing code (on a mainframe). In such a hybrid development environment, you are stuck with creating the requirements traceability matrix manually.

Start the RTM as soon as the SRS is baselined. Populate it as development progresses, rather than waiting until the end of the project to fill in all the boxes. By entering information into the matrix as it becomes available, the matrix becomes a working tool that helps to prevent problems with the final product. Some developers feel that documents like the RTM are just wasted overhead activity. However, when would you rather learn that a requirement fell through the cracks—during the design phase, when the developer filled in the matrix and found the oversight, or when a customer calls? It seems like an easy choice.

From Requirements to Code

Excellent requirements specifications are a necessary but not sufficient condition for a successful software project. There are plenty of ways to drop the ball after the requirements analysis process. Watch out for these mistakes:

- Leave the requirements specification on the shelf and proceed with design and implementation without tracing all downstream deliverables back to a documented customer need.

- Freeze the requirements and allow no changes to be made during the rest of the development cycle, however long that may take ("what you said is what you get").

- Let new features creep in and old ones mutate or become obsolete, but don't update the requirements documentation to reflect the changes.

- Skip any kind of structured design activity, and dive right into the source code editor.

- Become a slave to the SRS, spending all your energy rewriting it as every little change comes up, rather than starting to build something useful, like a design, from it (a bad case of analysis paralysis).

These pathologies can be avoided by a combination of standard practices in your software engineering culture and common sense. All of these extremes increase the risk of project failure or, at the least, create inefficiency. The fact is that the requirements you've collected are *not* perfect, they *will* change, and you *should* document the changes in a revised SRS. But you cannot spend your entire career chasing the perfect SRS—it doesn't exist. Remember: Strive for perfection, but settle for excellence.

Skimping on design is the most common trap into which some of our Kodak software groups have fallen. There is a tendency to segue from requirements directly into code, with perhaps a brief layover at program architecture. This is particularly risky when considerable time has passed since the requirements and user interface components were originally specified. To maximize quality and minimize rework, revisit the specs prior to implementing them. No matter how carefully written and reviewed, they almost always contain errors of omission and commission. Just before jumping into code, dust off your prototype and probe the depths of the small subset of the specification you are preparing to implement.

A role-playing walkthrough of a portion of the specs with some users will help flesh out the details that no one can think of up front. Explore "what-if" scenarios, ponder the usability, and identify exception conditions that must be handled. Identify any reuse opportunities for this function, or any existing code you can borrow to do the job for you. Think about the context in which this function will operate, the different paths by which the user could arrive at the screen, and the various states the user's application might be in when this feature is encountered. A last-minute walkthrough to update the requirements and the way you intend to implement them can further reduce the expectation gap between initial concept and delivered reality.

In a culture that emphasizes excellence in software engineering, developers practice the discipline of requirements analysis and design, rather than writing code as soon as they have a general idea of what the customer has in mind. Think of these front-end stages of the software development life cycle as high-impact ways to reduce the risk of building a flawed system and to avoid expensive rework. Members of a software engineering culture recognize the value that customer involvement, structured communication processes, and well-written documentation add to the construction of a quality product.

Summary

✔ Your greatest challenge is sharing the vision of the final product with the customer.

✔ A quality-oriented organization will represent user requirements in a variety of ways that help communicate a shared vision of the product to all stakeholders.

✔ The use case approach is an efficient tool for exploring user scenarios and understanding the essential functionality the system must provide to the customers.

✔ The IEEE software requirements specification template provides a convenient framework for documenting user needs and associated information in textual form. It complements the views provided by structured system models.

✔ Dialog maps document the architecture of a user interface so project stakeholders can find errors and share a common understanding of the product design.

✔ Prototypes of both user interfaces and system architecture are valuable for refining the engineer's understanding of user needs and exploring alternative solutions.

✔ Each specification in the SRS should be linked to the design elements that address it, the code segments that implement it, and the test cases that verify it, using a requirements traceability matrix.

✔ Rather than coding programs directly from requirements specifications that may not be fully fleshed out or current, take a journey through design. Walk through the pertinent section of the requirements document to fill in the details and make any necessary updates before firing up the source code editor.

Culture Builders and Killers

Culture Builder: "We haven't got time to write a requirements specification; just build us a system." If you ever hear this from your customers, ask them how everyone will know that the work is done if there are no requirements. A pile of e-mail messages, scribbled ideas, and two-year-old meeting notes does not replace a structured SRS and system models. Show the customers examples of what you mean by a specification and explain the value of the document, but don't let your team proceed without creating an SRS and supporting models.

Culture Killer: Include every requirement requested by your customers in the specification document. It doesn't matter how often a proposed feature would be used, how much it will cost to implement, what impact it will have on other parts of the system, or whether it is technically feasible. The customer is always right; if he says he needs it, he must know what he is talking about. Priorities are not necessary—we can do it all (eventually).

References and Further Reading

Ambler, Scott. "Use Case Scenario Testing," *Software Development*, Vol. 3, No. 7 (July 1995), pp. 53-61.

> Ambler presents a clear and practical tutorial on how to combine the use case method with Class, Responsibility, Collaborator (CRC) modeling of object classes, and how to manually test user scenarios by role-playing.

Constantine, Larry L. "Design for Usability" and "UI to Fit the Uses: Essential Use Case Modeling," *Software Development '94 Proceedings*. San Francisco: Miller Freeman, 1994.

> In these workshop notes, Constantine describes the application of essential use cases to the design of interfaces that meet user needs and have a high degree of usability.

Cornell, John L., and Linda Shafer. *Structured Rapid Prototyping: An Evolutionary Approach to Software Development*. Englewood Cliffs, N.J.: Yourdon Press/Prentice-Hall, 1989.

> Cornell and Shafer describe various approaches to software prototyping, all of which are intended to reduce the risk associated with application development. They discuss the benefits of rapid prototyping, tools and techniques that can be used, and other practical aspects of building prototypes and evolving them into production systems.

Davis, Alan M. *Software Requirements: Objects, Functions, and States*. Englewood Cliffs, N.J.: PTR Prentice-Hall, 1993.

> In this comprehensive compendium of requirements analysis methods, Davis describes how to apply object-oriented, function-oriented, and state-oriented problem analysis techniques. He describes what should and should not be included in a good SRS and the importance of specifying both behavioral and nonbehavioral requirements.

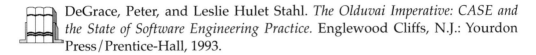

DeGrace, Peter, and Leslie Hulet Stahl. *The Olduvai Imperative: CASE and the State of Software Engineering Practice.* Englewood Cliffs, N.J.: Yourdon Press/Prentice-Hall, 1993.

> Chapter 3, entitled "Software Quality: An Odyssey Through the 'Ilities'," maps three kinds of customer requirements ("Get my programs up and running." "Keep 'em running and change 'em." "Move 'em to new platforms.") to eleven characteristics of good software—quality attributes—and to more than twenty software engineering practices.

Deutsch, Michael S., and Ronald R. Willis. *Software Quality Engineering: A Total Technical and Management Approach.* Englewood Cliffs, N.J.: Prentice-Hall, 1988.

> In this practical text, Deutsch and Willis discuss software quality factors and how to incorporate them into the software specifications.

Gilb, Tom. *Principles of Software Engineering Management.* Wokingham, England: Addison-Wesley, 1988.

> Gilb provides a fresh and readable look at many aspects of designing quality software systems. Several chapters address topics in requirements engineering, including distinguishing between problems and solutions, documenting functional requirements, and estimating and documenting attributes of the project. I got a lot of good ideas from this book.

Glass, Robert L. *Building Quality Software.* Englewood Cliffs, N.J.: Prentice-Hall, 1992.

> Glass describes seven key software product attributes (portability, reliability, efficiency, human engineering, testability, understandability, modifiability), and he explores the quality techniques that can be applied to achieve the desired balance of these attributes on a particular project.

IEEE Std. 830-1993, "IEEE Recommended Practice for Software Requirements Specifications." Los Alamitos, Calif.: IEEE Computer Society Press, 1993.

> This standard contains a detailed description of the different sections in the SRS, with examples of several different ways the user might choose to organize the functional requirements. It is easy to read and apply, and it contains a good discussion of the characteristics of a high-quality SRS.

Jacobson, I., M. Christerson, P. Jonsson, and G. Overgaard. *Object-Oriented Software Engineering: A Use Case Driven Approach.* Reading, Mass.: Addison-Wesley, 1992.

> A use case is a sequence of interactions, or dialog, between a user ("actor") and the system. Use cases and the requirements model, derived from the requirements specification, are the unifying threads that run through this object-oriented approach to systems development.

Rettig, Marc. "Prototyping for Tiny Fingers," *Communications of the ACM,* Vol. 37, No. 4 (April 1994), pp. 21-27.

> Rettig provides a wealth of practical ideas about how to build "lo-fi" prototypes using simple materials like paper, index cards, markers, sticky notes, and clear plastic sheets. He also describes how to conduct tests of your paper prototypes with users.

Part **III**

Improving Your Processes

An organization's culture is revealed through the processes it uses to build and maintain software. Members of a quality-driven culture recognize the need for continuous improvement in the ways they perform their work. They realize that increases in quality and productivity are achieved through systematic efforts to identify shortcomings and focus energy on high-yield improvement areas. Over time, the organization will accumulate a body of written procedures that represent the best available ways to perform the tasks that the group undertakes.

All members of the organization need to be involved in the assessment and improvement activities. This involvement promotes buy-in to the cultural commitment to continuous improvement. Top management sets the stage by making process improvement a priority and allocating the resources to make it happen. Project and group leaders reinforce the importance of established processes by expecting the team members to follow these processes even when the project is under a time crunch. All practitioners should continually seek better ways to do their work, while applying the group's currently established procedures as a matter of course.

Part III addresses two cultural premises:

✔ Continuous improvement of your software development process is both possible and essential.

✔ Written software development procedures can help build a shared culture of best practices.

Chapter 7

Process Improvement Fundamentals

The problems of software process change are often compli-cated by the fact that no one is responsible to make it hap-pen. If software process improvement isn't anybody's job, it is not surprising that it doesn't get done! If it is important enough to do, however, someone must be assigned the responsibility and given the necessary resources. Until this is done, software process development will remain a nice thing to do someday, but never today.

—Watts S. Humphrey, *Managing the Software Process*

C onsciously or unconsciously, we all follow some process for developing software, some sequence of steps that takes us from initial concept to exe-cutable code. This process is the set of procedures, methods, and tools we use to create a software product. In this sense, writing software is similar to any other construction activity.

For example, a manufacturing enterprise must define and control its processes to ensure that each widget made conforms to its specifications. Modern manufac-turing is done under conditions of statistical process control: The products created are randomly sampled, and some attributes are measured to see if they lie within acceptable tolerances of the specified values. A manufacturing process that is out of control will yield an unpredictable number of defective products that must be detected by inspection and either repaired or discarded. When the process is improved, the number of defective products will decrease, rework costs will decrease, productivity will increase, and profits should increase.

Do you have enough confidence in the quality of your code to test just one per-cent of it to estimate the number of errors in the whole program? How about ten percent? Most programmers would not trust this selective approach for quality assessment. And even if the coding step is perfect, it doesn't help us if we are writ-ing the wrong program because of defective requirements. Typical software requirements specifications contain so many errors that we cannot always tell if we are building the right product. We need processes that lead to quality products at every stage of development, not just coding. Software developers normally practice the quality techniques of inspecting or testing work products for errors. We also need to apply the quality techniques of improving and controlling the processes to prevent defects.

There are clear differences between a manufacturing enterprise cranking out many copies of the same item and software development, in which much of the effort is related to design and each program is only written once. Nonetheless, the concepts of process definition and improvement are fully applicable to software development. Members of an organization having a healthy software engineering culture believe in continuously improving the ways they design and construct software products. There is always something that can be done better on the next project.

The goal of process improvement is not to achieve perfection according to some guru's definition. It is to build software better, faster, and cheaper tomorrow than you did yesterday. "But," you say, "our group doesn't have any extra time to devote to improvement efforts. We are doing all we can to keep our heads above water as it is. If we fool around on process initiatives, we'll just have to work more overtime to keep up with the project deadlines."

You don't have time *not* to pursue process improvement opportunities. Process improvements are an investment in the long-term success and survival of your organization. Like any other investment, there is some risk, and the capital (time, money, and people) tied up in the investment is not available for other uses. A software group that makes this investment, devoting as little as five percent of its energies to activities aimed at increasing quality and productivity, will recoup its investment many times over.

Expect to pay a short-term price on project schedules while your group devotes some time to training and to developing better processes. But without this investment, you will only slowly push your software engineering capabilities to a higher plane of quality and productivity. Process improvement can help you escape the recurring cycle of slipped schedules and shipped bugs that plague so many software groups. Build some time for process improvement into your upcoming project schedules, rather than hoping the improvement work will somehow get squeezed into an already unrealistic project timetable. As you continue to apply the improved procedures on future projects, their completion costs and schedules should more closely match your estimates. This is partly because the estimates become more realistic, and partly because you will spend less time on unanticipated rework prior to delivery. From a competitive standpoint, you can't afford *not* to make this investment.

Principles of Process Improvement

Every software organization has opportunities for improvement. Unless you consistently produce defect-free software that satisfies user needs, always meet your time schedules, and never exceed your budget, things could be better. The scope of "software process" encompasses all the steps engineers go through when creating an application (see Fig. 7.1). If you compensate for shortcomings in individual technical skills, for technology limitations, and for management problems, yet your results still fall short of expectations, it is time to take a closer look at the processes your team is using.

An organization's culture is a fusion of its people, its processes, and its technology. Failure to address any one of these will diminish the potential impact of the changes you are trying to make. Processes that are applied sporadically, ineffectively, or inappropriately can cause more harm than good. Unused and underused technologies—shelfware—waste money, and people whose professional development is neglected are likely to seek more interesting employment opportunities elsewhere.

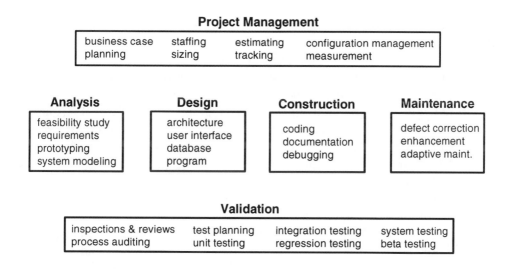

Figure 7.1: Activities involved in the effective practice of software engineering.

Because processes are performed by people, your team members will always be your greatest asset. Accordingly, your group's improvement efforts must include enhancing the capabilities, knowledge, and work environments of all team members. As we discussed in Part I, hiring and nurturing outstanding software engineers will give you a competitive edge no process definition can best.

To be an effective change agent, you must work within the existing organizational culture, while striving to modify the culture so as to yield long-term benefits. Cultural change can be encouraged by rewarding people for taking sensible risks, investing in the application of new processes and technologies, and breaking old paradigms that limit the performance potential of the organization. Examples of such paradigms include obsolete mandated methodologies that no longer meet the organization's needs, manual performance of testing and design tasks when automated tools are available, and informal project planning that is not based on historical data from past projects. If you entertain notions about making process changes, there are some principles to keep in mind:

- Process improvement should be evolutionary, continuous, and cyclical.

- Organizations and individuals both must change, but people change only when they have an incentive to do so.

- Process changes should be goal-oriented, data-driven, and non-dogmatic.

- Improvement activities must be treated as mini-projects.

Let's look at the first of these: *Process improvement should be evolutionary, continuous, and cyclical.* You can't go in to work on Monday and alter the entire way your group builds software, no matter how ineffective the process may be today, so try not to be overwhelmed by the number of changes you may be facing. Deal with them one at a time, in the sequence your team believes will add the most value to its work. The goal is to introduce change incrementally and sustain the altered behavior so that it becomes routine practice on all subsequent projects. (Chapters 19 and 20 contain some recommendations on the most important action items that software managers and engineers should tackle at the beginning of an improvement effort.)

Continuous process improvement, in which each individual strives to perform some aspect of his work better on the next project than on the last one, is another characteristic of a healthy software engineering culture. Completed (or canceled) projects should undergo postmortem examinations to diagnose what went right and wrong, so that tasks can be done better in the future. It is easy to slip into a complacent status quo when no one is beating on you, but at such times of relative tranquility you can make improvements to help head off future crises.

Teams and individuals both should set goals for improvement in specific technical areas. When an improved process has been learned, applied, and internalized, it becomes standard practice in the future. Then you can move on to the next improvement area. Once all of your major problem areas have been addressed, it's time to return to the first area you tackled for another round of process enhancement. The cycle of process and quality improvement is an endless, but profitable, journey.

Nontechnical improvements in areas such as communication are also important, since interpersonal communication is such a big part of the software engineer's job. Your team members need to be able to listen effectively, write clearly, give good presentations, resolve conflicts, facilitate meetings, and manage customer relations. Strong communication skills can make the difference between a proficient and respected information technology team and a group of programmers that customers prefer to avoid.

Next let's examine the second change principle cited above: ***Organizations and individuals both must change, but people change only when they have an incentive to do so.*** Processes encompass both organizational cultures and individual behaviors. While grass-roots improvement efforts by concerned professionals will enhance their personal results, it is better to modify the value system and philosophies of the whole organization to provide a coherent framework for the new work paradigm. People are more motivated to change when they see change happening around them and have been pulled into the improvement activities themselves. The ability of any one individual, in any position, to drive change across the organization depends on the size of the organization. The leader of a small project team can exert a lot of individual influence, but upper management must play an active supporting and enabling role in bigger departments or companies.

Commitment by members at all levels of the organization is a prerequisite for successful process change. While it's great if everyone agrees that a specific change is required, sometimes consensus is not reached. Consensus management in which no one's comfort level is permitted to be disturbed leads only to lowest common denominator results. Large corporations with historical cultural values cast in stone too often wind up seeking the "lowest common comfort level." The manager has to exercise leadership by communicating a vision, setting directions, and defining ambitious goals to make change happen. Such a leader has several responsibilities:

- Educate the staff so they understand why the changes are required for business success.

- Seek out and understand the real reasons for resistance.

- Use persuasion as a tool to build support for the change among a majority of the staff.

- Provide adequate support for the desired changes, including the time, training, and tools that are needed to successfully implement new practices.

- Adjust project schedules to free up time for team members to implement the changes, thereby demonstrating a serious commitment to the importance of the change.

- Educate upper management about the need for change and the support they can (and must) provide.

In the absence of management leadership at all levels, inertia will take over, and work will go on as it always has. Management should neither ignore the need to improve how software is being built nor force arbitrary process changes down the throats of the developers without their participation in the decision-making and implementation processes. Participative management is not the same as consensus management.

People are naturally resistant to change. To be an effective change agent or sponsor, you will have to learn how to induce and manage organizational change. The existing culture of attitudes and historical behaviors determines which change techniques are the most likely to be effective. It takes a combination of anticipated future pleasures, plus some pain suffered from shortcomings in the current situation, to encourage team members to go through an intimidating transition to new ways of working. Management techniques involving both positive and negative reinforcement may be required to encourage widespread changes in how people do their work.

There are numerous sources of pain that might originate from the status quo. External factors include customer complaints, product returns, and falling profits. Internal problems include low morale (for example, because many bugs are being reported), frustration (for example, because maintenance demands keep interrupting new development work), conflict (such as between engineering and testing groups), and the threat of outsourcing (to cheaper and faster—although not necessarily better—contract software houses). Sometimes, management generates pain artificially, by defining goals they hope will induce desirable changes in the organization. As a driver for change, this artificially generated pain is not nearly as compelling as the other, genuine sources of discomfort. The anticipated future pleasures from a proposed change could be that these unpleasantries go away, or that their arrival in your organization is forestalled.

When my software group at Kodak began an improvement initiative, we looked for sources of pain that we could address. Some of the issues that came up pertained to infrastructure, such as inadequate computer workstations and the need for better development tools. Others indicated frustration with the current process, including inadequate software quality assurance processes and a lack of documented expectations for the activities and deliverables associated with a project. Still others dealt with the desire for individuals to enhance their capabilities by attending conferences and gaining better access to technical publications. Some of these were small problems that could be addressed quickly, while larger issues helped us set a course of long-term improvement in the right directions.

The next principle to keep in mind in connection with process change is: *Process changes should be goal-oriented, data-driven, and nondogmatic.* Change for the sake of change will not attract many disciples. Instead, identify specific results you want to see, which will imply improvements that must be made in your processes to reach these goals. While top management may set overall corporate goals, first- and second-line managers are responsible for aligning project goals with the corporate objectives. They must also identify the paths that will take their staff into the future state. Don't wait to begin software process improvement until you have perfect quantitative data in hand to prove every point and justify every effort; you'll never leave the starting gate. (See Chapter 16 for examples of how to tie measurements to your improvement goals.)

You will need to establish a measurement program to quantify current problem areas and to assess the impact of process changes. If each of your goals is clearly stated and quantifiable, you should be able to tell when you are there. For example, a goal to "reduce the number of bad fixes going out to customers" is a worthy objective, and you can probably think of process changes to address this problem in your environment, but this goal does not state how much reduction is desired or when you wish to reach the goal. To assess whether such a goal has been attained, you will need to measure the current bad-fix frequency to establish a baseline, put into place the process changes you believe will help, and track the new bad-fix frequency to determine whether you have been successful. If you change several practices at once, it can be difficult to isolate the effect of any single process modification. But if you launch a process improvement by saying something like, "Our project tracking is *so* bad, . . . " and the team responds with a chorus of, "How bad is it?"—you had better have an answer based on actual data.

In addition to being goal-oriented and data-driven, process changes should not be made dogmatically. Unless you must meet specific externally imposed criteria, such as ISO 9001 registration, you can focus your energy on only those process improvement activities that will benefit your organization. This may mean selecting certain portions of established methodologies to address shortcomings in your current process. If your team agrees that some proposed change would be of little benefit, don't try it now. Decreeing that the whole organization must adopt an entirely new dogma (such as a commercially produced project management methodology, documented in a dozen thick binders) is a great way to stifle process improvement.

Avoiding taking a dogmatic approach to the improvement activity does not mean that developers are free to use whatever methods they choose. In a quality-oriented culture, best practices are accepted and applied by all team members as a matter of course. There is a stated expectation that agreed-upon processes will be used, and anyone wishing to make an exception should have a very good reason.

Nevertheless, some flexibility in tailoring standards and procedures to best meet the needs of individual projects can be necessary. If a team member can demonstrate that his approach is consistently superior to the one presently endorsed, it's time to rethink what you consider "best practice" for that particular activity.

In addition, one must recognize that no single solution fits all problems. You need to have multiple tools available for dealing with technical challenges that arise in the course of a project. The old adage "When the only tool you have is a hammer, all problems look like nails" definitely applies to software. Too often, programmers with limited programming language and method skills attempt to turn every problem into one they can tackle using the single tool they know well, however silly or inefficient that turns out to be.

The final principle guiding process improvement is: *Improvement activities must be treated as mini-projects.* An improvement effort is pretty much doomed to failure if management's involvement is limited to saying, "Make it so." Process improvement is an investment in the long-term health of the organization. It is not free, although the ultimate return on investment can be eight-fold or greater. Asking people to squeeze process improvement activities into their schedules without adjusting their other commitments simply is not realistic. Like any other project, improvement mini-projects should be planned and staffed for success. They should have stated schedules, clear deliverables, individual accountability, interim status reporting, and team rewards. In a software engineering culture, every member of the organization participates in these process improvement mini-projects. If the improvement activity is not accorded project-level status and given the necessary resources, you really shouldn't be surprised if the effort fails.

At Kodak, we have found that a structured sequence of Assess-Plan-Do-Verify provides an effective framework for improvement cycles (see Fig. 7.2). For each improvement mini-project, we write a project plan listing the expected deliverables from each of the four steps. The Assess step includes an analysis of the problem and its root causes, the current state of the practice, and the improvement goals. The deliverables are a short list of key result areas in which we want to improve and some measures we can apply to those result areas to determine the effectiveness of the improvement effort.

During the Plan step, we select several major improvement opportunities and develop action plans for attacking them. The Do phase centers around executing action plans that develop improved processes, with periodic progress reports to other stakeholders. Finally, the Verify step involves measuring the impact of the improvements and the effectiveness of the mini-project. If you have been successful, you move on to the next problem area and repeat the cycle. Don't overlook the very last step, to recognize the team for its efforts.

Getting Started with Process Improvement

To launch a process improvement effort, your group needs to identify a few high-impact problem areas about which something can realistically (if not always easily) be done. Group brainstorming sessions, described in Chapter 8, are a simple way to bring the sources of pain in an organization to the surface. When team members reach a consensus on the two or three most important areas to pursue, they can better align their energies toward appropriate organizational objectives. Once clear statements of both the problem and the goal of the improvement effort have been formulated, assemble a small team to identify the root causes of the problem and select a plan of attack.

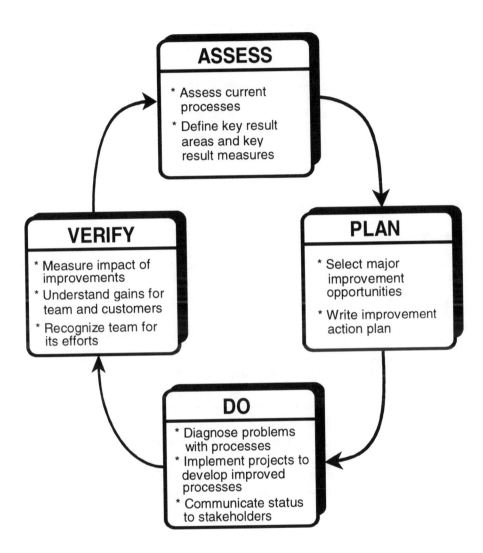

Figure 7.2: A process improvement task cycle.

Apply the improvement cycle in Fig. 7.2 to each mini-project that comes out of your action planning. Identify deliverables, assign responsibilities to individuals, establish schedules, and define criteria to verify that the mini-project is successfully concluded. The action plans do not have to be elaborate or formal, but they should focus on addressing specific problems. Figure 7.3 contains a simple action plan template that one Kodak group has used.

Problem:

[Concisely state the problem this mini-project is addressing.]

Goals:

[State a few precise, quantifiable benefits that will result from successful completion of the improvement mini-project.]

Root Causes:

[List the underlying causes of the problem.]

Possible Solutions:

[List several possible approaches that the mini-project team might pursue to correct the root causes of the problem.]

Action Item #1:

WHAT: [Describe one action to be taken or deliverable to be produced.]
WHO: [Indicate which mini-project team member is responsible.]
WHEN: [Indicate the completion date of the activity or deliverable.]
STATUS: [Track progress on all the action items periodically.]

Figure 7.3: Template for action planning.

Software process improvement can be a lot of work, but it can also be very rewarding as you help steer your team's culture toward better performance and a better place to work.

Summary

- ✔ Continuous improvement of your software development process is both possible and essential.

- ✔ Process improvement must be evolutionary, not revolutionary. Do not try a massive paradigm shift in the way your group does business all at once, but don't do nothing either.

- ✔ Understand what benefits you expect from a change you propose for the way your group operates, and define ways to assess the impact of the change.

✔ Treat the improvement activities as mini-projects, using a structured Assess-Plan-Do-Verify sequence with clear responsibilities, deliverables, and schedules.

✔ Incorporate process improvement activities into your way of life. Everyone should be contributing to at least one ongoing improvement mini-project at all times. Participation by all team members in the improvement activities builds a stronger sense of ownership of the process and the results.

Culture Builders and Killers

Culture Builder: Take every opportunity to educate upper management in the value of software engineering process improvement and quality practices. Identify your managers' hot buttons: If they like data, present some of your software metrics; if they are more touchy-feely, share the impact of your improvement activities on customer relations and job satisfaction. When managers see tangible benefits from better software engineering practices, they often become enthusiastic supporters—both of you and of your process improvement initiative.

Culture Builder: Set up a reuse accounting system for code and other software work products in order to encourage reuse as a productivity improvement mechanism. For example, lines of code (or modules, or object classes) contributed to the reusable library could be credited to a developer's "account." Give rewards to people who practice effective reuse by contributing to the reusable library or by using items already there. The details of this approach will have to be tailored to the kind of work you do and culture you have.

Culture Killer: When schedule pressures mount and everyone is working overtime, let the developers revert to the old way of doing things. The important thing is to get the code written, and the quickest way to do this is for each programmer to hack it together and test it himself. The QA group can just put in a little overtime to finish the testing when you get the pieces integrated together. Of course, when the pressure is not quite so bad, you certainly plan to get back into quality reviews and structured testing.

Culture Killer: When your managers launch an internal corporate project that includes an information system, you can safely bypass the front-end work that some people claim will prevent software project problems. If they've got to have a system, you'd better build them a system NOW! You can gloss over the requirements step since it will be easy to make changes after they've started using the system. Beta testing will catch any quality problems. Damn the defects; full speed ahead!

References and Further Reading

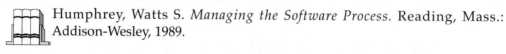 Humphrey, Watts S. *Managing the Software Process*. Reading, Mass.: Addison-Wesley, 1989.

In Chapter 2 of this classic treatise on systematic software process improvement, Humphrey describes the basic principles of process change.

Chapter 8

Process Improvement
Case Study

Much of the transition from one [SEI] level to the next is cultural. Consequently, one has to go from the stage of anarchy through a stage of informal consensus before reaching a stage of formal processes for system development.

—Edward Yourdon, *Decline and Fall of the American Programmer*

Years ago, our small group of five software engineers decided to embark on a course of process improvement. We had just moved into a new department and were starting off with a new team leader. The impetus for change was a sense that we had stagnated in our ability to systematically absorb and apply better practices, and that we had no strategic vision for the group's future and little technical leadership. It was time for a culture change—a paradigm shift from business as usual to a more aggressive search for improvements in our software capabilities and solutions to our nagging problems.

Our new department (primarily a non-computing service organization) had a strong push for improved quality, and we had good management support for our efforts. Our plan was to hold an initial informal brainstorming session to identify improvement opportunities. Then we intended to have every member of the group spend part of his work time addressing the most pressing issues that emerged. We realized this would be time diverted from current project work, but the appeal of a long-term investment in improving our quality and productivity was a strong driver for change.

A brainstorming session is the cheapest, quickest way to identify problem areas. Our goal was to think of as many improvement opportunities (a euphemism for "problems") as we could, then envision possible solutions and commence working on them in earnest. For about half an hour, everyone silently wrote problems and concerns on index cards and threw them in a pile on a table. As ideas dried up, we took each other's cards out of the pile and used them to stimulate

new thoughts. When the idea-generating period was over, we weeded out dupli-
cate ideas, leaving thirty-three unique issues. In a second pass through the cards,
each participant wrote possible solutions to the problem described on each card.
After some discussion to focus on the major items, we had identified several tangible improvement opportunities to tackle.

More recently, we used another group brainstorming method in a two-session
exercise to identify current barriers to our software productivity and quality. In
session one, all eighteen participants (our team had grown!) wrote their thoughts
about this topic on sticky notes, one idea per note. A facilitator collected and
grouped the ideas as they were generated, and at the end, we had about a dozen
major categories, which we then recorded on large flipchart sheets. In the second
session, the same participants wrote ideas for overcoming these barriers on sticky
notes and attached them to the appropriate flipcharts. Further refinement led to a
handful of action items that could be addressed as mini-projects in our effort to
break down barriers and help team members achieve their software quality and
productivity goals.

Both of these methods worked better than the more traditional brainstorming
approach of holding an open discussion with a facilitator recording ideas on a
flipchart. These techniques allowed the participants to generate ideas concurrently.
They also made it easier for team members who are uncomfortable speaking out in
front of a group to contribute their thoughts anonymously.

The objective of brainstorming is to generate ideas, building on what the other
participants say and applying the adage "Two heads are better than one." Here are
some basic guidelines to present to the group at the beginning of the brainstorming activity:

- No judgment or criticism of ideas suggested by others is permitted. (Saying things such as "We can't do that" or "I tried
  that—it doesn't work," or rolling eyes, smirking, giggling, and
  exchanging knowing glances will kill the spirit of brainstorming.)

- Go for volume of ideas.

- Wild and crazy ideas sometimes have the biggest impact.

- Look for inspiration in the ideas of others.

- Everyone participates. (If reticence keeps some from contributing publicly, try one of the silent or anonymous approaches
  described above.)

If you are not comfortable running a brainstorming session yourself, look for a facilitator from elsewhere within your company, or even a friend who is good at that sort of thing. I find that I am a less effective facilitator if I am too close to the problem being explored or have a personal stake in the outcome. It's hard not to let your own biases show.

It is of course impossible to simultaneously incorporate every available software engineering technique and tool into any one organization, even if all were valuable, which they are not. However, you can take baby steps to accomplish the task: Identify a small number of high-leverage changes that you can apply effectively to your group at low cost. Select just one or two key areas for improvement on each new project, based on appraisal of your weakest individual and team skills.

Our approach has been to learn a new technique while working on a project for which our ability to apply that technique is not a critical success factor. That way, when we do encounter a project for which the technique *is* critical, we will have had at least a little experience with it. As we master new capabilities and tools, they become a routine part of our activities on subsequent projects, so we can then focus on the next improvement opportunity. Continuous enhancement of your software skills gives your group a more powerful toolbox for future projects (see Fig. 8.1). Sustaining your previous achievements on subsequent projects is essential—process improvement is not a one-shot deal.

From our initial five-man brainstorming session, we chose several major objectives, put them in order of priority, and then chipped away at them. Among our improvement goals were the following:

1. Increase customer involvement in projects to facilitate our doing a better job of requirements specification.

2. Write group development guidelines to clearly define our preferred process and the deliverables expected at various stages during development.

3. Measure what we do by starting to collect certain software metrics.

4. Improve our knowledge of software engineering through training, conferences, books, and periodicals.

5. Improve the selection, acquisition, and application of software tools.

6. Define a formal software quality assurance process to apply to projects.

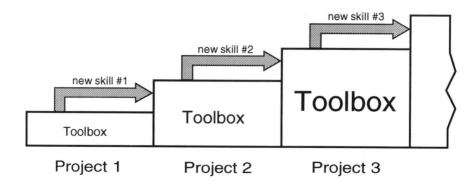

new skill #3

new skill #2

new skill #1

Toolbox

Toolbox

Toolbox

Project 1   Project 2   Project 3

Figure 8.1: Add new skills to your toolbox for future projects.

For each of these items, we agreed on objectives and assigned individuals from the team to work on them. We summarized the brainstorming results in a shared electronic file. As action items were addressed over time, we updated this file to reflect progress made. Everyone was involved in the improvement efforts, and progress was highly visible. Best of all, we accomplished our objectives, making process changes that, by and large, have been sustained for several years.

Here are some additional tips to help you get started: Do not try to do everything at once; the predictable results are failure and frustration, with a return to business as usual. Plan to devote around 5 percent of your team's time to process improvement activities, as a long-term investment in the professional health of the group. Select those portions of the many methods touted by the gurus that look promising for your particular environment, and discard methods that simply do not work for you. Avoid the temptation to swallow any dogma whole, but do not use this as an excuse to avoid trying anything new. Stay focused on the desired objective. Avoid being distracted by methods and tools that don't address your real problems, no matter how much fun they are to play with.

Software engineers want to build software. They tend to resist activities they perceive as draining precious time away from program-oriented work. They are also leery of anything they feel might stifle their creativity. The software manager may have to sell process improvement efforts to the staff as an investment in their ability to deliver on future projects, perhaps at the price of some schedule slippage in the current project. Our group's philosophy was that improved processes let us shift some of our creative energies from programming to the analysis and design parts of the project.

Organizational change is most effective if nearly every group member accepts (if not agrees with) the need for change and can see the importance of his own contributions to the change activities. Everyone on the software team should be asked to participate in improvement mini-projects as a job expectation that parallels their project responsibilities. Some organizations have succeeded by making software engineering process improvement a component of each practitioner's and manager's annual performance appraisal. A manager who is serious about driving process improvements to successful conclusions should be prepared to respond convincingly to the following objections:

- What makes you think we will benefit from that approach?

- I'm already using a state-of-the-art method; this change is a step backwards for me.

- I don't have time to work on those stupid process teams; I have real work to do.

- I know (or heard about, or read about) somebody who tried that already—it doesn't work.

- Our current process is fine; it's the fault of marketing (or the customer, or management) that we have problems.

- Our projects are harder (or different, or more complex); that method will never work here.

- Will I get the training I need to use these new approaches?

- I already do something just as effective as what you're proposing; just let me do it my own way.

- This won't do anything about my real problems.

Sometimes, managers are part of the problem, not part of the solution. Grass-roots efforts to improve software processes can only go so far. When developers see the need for changes and really want to work on them, it's highly frustrating if managers resist this bottom-up push. In this situation, try to educate the reluctant managers. They need to understand the nature and value of the improvements you believe are necessary, and you need to understand their concerns about your plan. Point out the price the organization is paying because of the current process problems, and propose a specific action plan for addressing the problems. Driving a process improvement initiative often requires the ability to sell ideas to managers at various levels.

Effective process improvement efforts require commitment at the individual, project, and organization levels, so the project leaders and department managers have to be on board. Bottom-up efforts will eventually run into a glass ceiling unless senior management provides an organization-wide focus to the improvement program. Our group was fortunate to have strong team leadership for driving improvements, broad participation among the practitioners, and endorsement from higher levels of management for the behavioral changes we attempted.

Making Change Happen

People react to pressures for change with a wide range of emotions, as shown in Fig. 8.2. We don't all experience the same emotions when confronted with the prospect of change, and we don't move through these phases in any orderly sequence. Anyone leading an effort to induce organizational change must be able to respond supportively and constructively to these responses. People have to feel they are part of the change effort, not victims of it. Communication, coaching, management leadership, and education can help an organization cope with change.

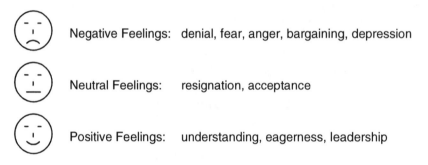

Figure 8.2: Emotional reactions to pressure for change.

As a large-scale change effort progresses, the number of people involved and the domains they represent should grow in a controlled way. Begin with a core group of visionaries and change agents who can set the directions and articulate the shape and value of the desired future state to other stakeholders. Then expand the effort by gradually incorporating others into the activities of the group. Pilot projects are a good way to road test a new approach. Design pilots as you would a software prototype, to answer questions you have about how to implement a proposed change effectively and the benefits you might obtain.

Any modification in the work we are asked to do or the way we are expected to do it pulls us out of our comfort zone. Fear of failure, fear of revealing ignorance, and fear of the unknown make us resist outside efforts at change. Effective change leaders must clearly communicate the reasons for change and the results the team can expect to see after the changes are made. Provide adequate training opportunities to prepare team members for the planned changes and to give them any new skills they will need. At Kodak, our brainstorming sessions set the stage for change because all team members had a hand in identifying problem areas. This made it easier for us to agree on the improvements we wanted to try.

Organizations operate in the context of various cultural paradigms, as discussed in Chapter 1. Understanding the areas affected by the changes helps you to select strategies that can effectively reduce the barriers. No single approach will work for all teams and all individuals. The present culture of the organization and the behaviors its leaders exhibit are key determinants in the effectiveness of any change strategy. Our team leader kept the change processes that were underway as a visible priority, maintaining a gentle positive pressure on the team members who were working on improvement mini-projects. Everyone on the team knew the leader was committed to the improvement activities—we weren't playing an idle game.

Well thought-out action plans have withered on the vine because the manager never mentioned them again after the initial brainstorming event. Since the manager gave no indication that he took the change efforts seriously, the group members were not motivated to work on them either. The time invested in revealing and discussing the problem areas was viewed as wasted, since the manager was not actively growing an improvement-oriented culture. The manager can't just say, "Everybody change now!" and expect something constructive to happen.

Sustaining Momentum

Working on process improvement efforts generally will have a lower priority to an engineer than working on an application project. It falls to you as the leader to keep the improvement efforts infused with energy. Provide status updates at group meetings and management reviews, and expect regular progress reports from the improvement mini-project teams. Leverage what each team accomplishes and learns by sharing their experiences with the rest of the organization. Success stories can help motivate those who have not yet jumped aboard the process improvement bandwagon. Skillful use of rewards and recognition can visibly reinforce your commitment to continuous improvement.

Our group sustained our process improvement energy by devoting at least one team meeting per month to a discussion of a selected process issue. We followed up with a written summary and a list of action items to address the deficiencies we identified. Below are some of the many questions we explored.

Who are our suppliers? What problems do we have with them? What can we measure to indicate trends of quality in the products or services they provide to us? From this discussion, we began to accumulate metrics on our interactions with key suppliers, which we summarized periodically and shared with them to see if improvements could be made.

How do our customers define "software quality"? To find the answer to this question, we held an open forum to which we invited our customers and their managers. This forum was valuable because it showed where our group's perceptions of what constituted quality did not match those of our customers. Understanding the differences can help you focus energy where it will yield the greatest customer benefit, not where it will provide the greatest developer satisfaction (in a perfect world, these would be the same).

How can we improve the testing procedures we use? What can we measure to help us know when a beta testing period can be completed and the product released? In less sophisticated development organizations, release criteria take the form of "the ship date is here; testing is therefore completed" or "the beta testers have pretty much stopped complaining, so I guess we're done." A data-driven approach uses trends in defect reporting rates and open problem reports to predict ship dates (see Chapter 15).

How can we improve our project estimation, planning, and management skills? To find the answer here, we discussed how to use our work effort metrics to prepare better estimates of development time. This analysis led to a correlation of our requirements specification size with implementation time, and from there to an estimating heuristic that was based on our historical project performance (described in Chapter 17). We also decided to get some additional training in software project management.

How should the performance of software engineers be assessed? Some people think annual corporate performance appraisals should be abolished, but such appraisals are still a reality at many companies. Since our group was not part of a software department, but rather belonged to a support organization that provided a variety of technical services to the Kodak Research Laboratories, we felt we should have some input into how our appraisals were derived.

What should go into a defect metrics database? We discussed the kinds of information about errors found during testing, reviews, and customer usage that we should capture and analyze so we might avoid similar errors in the future.

How can we use our people most effectively on our projects? In a small group, teams may consist of only one or two people, who must wear all the hats in the software development life cycle. We talked about the need for some team members to specialize in certain areas, and about how to staff projects for success by assembling teams of engineers with appropriate skill sets. This discussion also explored how to balance development work and maintenance responsibilities for the engineers in our group. Historically, each developer supported the applications he had written, a practice which can interrupt new product development and which can lead to problems in setting appropriate priorities. We did not find any magic answers, but at least we attacked the problem as a team, with the overarching objective of increasing both team productivity and individual job satisfaction.

What are the obstacles to improving our software productivity and quality? What are some solutions? The brainstorming process our group went through to generate improvement actions on this topic was described above. It is important to note that the ultimate success of an exercise like this depends on the diligence of the manager and the team members in implementing the action items and driving changes in the way work gets done. Action plans are useless unless they are followed up with action.

Another approach we used for sustaining process improvement momentum was to have the team agree on annual goals related to our products and processes. We shared our goals with our managers, took actions, and measured progress periodically to keep the goals visible. You will not achieve your goals by accident. The team leader must keep some positive pressure on the team members to drive them toward the goals to which all agreed. If you select a manageable set of four or five significant goals per year, you can systematically improve the way your group does its work. You will also build a stronger culture by sharing the satisfaction and rewards that come from achieving objectives as a team. Try to write your goals so you can objectively measure progress toward them. Here are some of the improvement goals we set for ourselves over the years:

- Have specific percentages of each kind of software work product reviewed by a group of peers (for example, 100 percent of requirements specifications, 60 percent of design models, 75 percent of source code, and so on).

- Increase the fraction of our work effort devoted to design and testing by 50 percent each over the cumulative levels from the preceding two years.

- Derive 20 percent of the code modules and database tables in next year's applications from those used in existing applications.

- Employ user interface prototypes to refine customer specifications and maximize usability prior to full system implementation.

- Design and document applications for high maintainability and usability, with a goal of reducing our maintenance burden to 15 percent of our total software work effort.

You may not achieve all of your goals each year. But, by focusing the group's improvement energies on just a few target areas at once, you can enhance your software engineering culture a little bit at a time.

Summary

- ✔ Begin your process improvement efforts with some form of assessment or brainstorming activity to identify the most pressing improvement opportunities.

- ✔ Following the assessment, devise a plan for implementing these new practices. Treat each improvement activity as a mini-project with explicit target dates, clear deliverables, and specific responsibilities accepted by different team members.

- ✔ Select target improvement areas for each project. Leapfrog from one project to the next, sustaining the improved practices acquired on earlier projects. Learn and practice new skills before they become critical factors for project success.

✔ Incorporate continuous improvement into your way of life. Participation by all team members in the improvement activities builds broad-based ownership of the process and the results.

✔ Because a culture will improve its performance faster if the sharing of ideas and methods is encouraged, aggressively look for better ways to do your work from the software literature, conferences, seminars, and the people down the hall.

Culture Builders and Killers

 Culture Builder: Match new members of your team or on-site contractors with experienced mentors to help them adopt your culture as quickly and comfortably as possible. Working with a supportive and effective coach will get a novice up to speed faster than simply giving him a copy of your procedures notebook. Selecting appropriate mentors is not just a matter of assigning a random senior person. Choose mentors who actively apply, and always seek to improve, the team's standard software engineering practices.

Culture Killer: Tell your group members what their collective improvement goals are for the next year, without wasting time getting their input. You have the big picture, and it is your job to think of these things.

Culture Killer: Work with your team members to agree on goals for the next year, then never mention them again. At the end of the year, check to see if they met the goals or not. These people are professionals. You can't be baby-sitting them by reminding them of their responsibilities every five minutes. Your engineers better not cut into the project schedule to work on these goals, though. This sort of activity is best done on their own time.

References and Further Reading

Binder, Robert. "Software Process Improvement: A Case Study," *Software Development*, Vol. 2, No. 1 (January 1994), pp. 59-70.

Binder describes a system development environment that was created to support a long-term process improvement effort in a company that markets a complex software product. Through models and text, the article describes the architecture of the process methodology, which incorporates elements of planning, plant, process, project, and product.

Chapter 9

Software Process Maturity

If you don't know where you're going, any road will do.

—Chinese Proverb

If you don't know where you are, a map won't help.

—Watts S. Humphrey, *Managing the Software Process*

The eleven to one ratio of organizational productivity that DeMarco and Lister reported in *Peopleware* suggests that the processes used by different organizations are not equally efficient for producing software. The diversity of software processes in use ranges from formless individualism, where everyone improvises and works as he pleases, to the discipline of standardized and measured procedures, in which the quality, cost, and schedule of projects are highly predictable. The Software Engineering Institute (SEI) defines software process maturity as "the extent to which a specific process is explicitly defined, managed, measured, controlled, and effective."

Figure 9.1 illustrates three of the scales that have been proposed to describe an organization's ability to efficiently produce quality software. These scales share the premise that an organization whose software engineering behaviors, attitudes, and practices place it at a higher level on the scale (that is, to the right) will, on average, enjoy higher quality and productivity than one operating at a lower level. Organizations functioning at the lower levels (on the left side of the scales) tend to produce poorer software at higher cost, with an increased risk of project failure, and with greater slippage of delivery schedules. To some extent, all of these scales are derived from Philip Crosby's earlier Quality Management Maturity Grid, which addresses management's attitude toward quality [Crosby, 1979]. Crosby described five stages of quality management maturity: Uncertainty, Awakening, Enlightenment, Wisdom, Certainty.

As shown in Fig. 9.1, Meilir Page-Jones describes a sequence of five ages through which an organization passes as it evolves toward more effective software engineering practices [Page-Jones, 1991]. Gerald Weinberg writes of cultural patterns of behavior in a software development group [Weinberg, 1992]. His scale of patterns essentially reflects "the degree of congruence between what is said and what is done in different parts of the organization." The cultural pattern reveals the attitudes and behaviors of software managers, and it influences the level of quality the organization can produce. Weinberg inserts a sixth, or zeroth-level, Oblivious pattern, in which practitioners are not even aware that they are doing software development. An example might be someone who writes a simple spreadsheet macro, or someone who creates a database on his PC.

Proponent	Term	Levels				
Page-Jones	Ages		Anarchy	Folklore	Methodology	Metrics	Engineering
Weinberg	Patterns	Oblivious	Variable	Routine	Steering	Anticipating	Congruent
Humphrey	Levels		Initial	Repeatable	Defined	Managed	Optimizing

Risk ⟸ ⟹ Quality
Productivity

Figure 9.1: Several evolutionary scales for software development.

Perhaps best known is the five-level scale of the SEI's Capability Maturity Model for Software (CMM). A federally funded software research and development center operated by Carnegie Mellon University in Pittsburgh, Pennsylvania, the SEI was established to provide leadership in software engineering and to assist in putting improved software technologies into practice. One initial goal of the SEI was to develop a mechanism to assist in selecting qualified software contractors for U.S. Department of Defense projects. This goal was the seed that led to the Capability Maturity Model [Humphrey, 1989; Paulk, 1993; CMU/SEI, 1995].

Very few organizations have been found that operate at the top two levels of Humphrey's scale or the top two patterns of Weinberg's scale. Nevertheless, there is reason to believe that Optimizing or Congruent organizations should be the most effective at producing software. Such organizations will have quality principles instilled at all levels of engineering and management, and they will continually measure and improve their software engineering processes.

The CMM is by no means a panacea for every software organization, and other process models have been effective in some companies. However, many companies, including Kodak, are now using the CMM as a framework for their process improvement efforts, and several have reported impressive improvements in their software development capabilities [Herbsleb, 1994; Dion, 1993].

The Capability Maturity Model

The CMM provides a framework for estimating the ability of an organization or project to produce software. The model provides a software organization with guidance during formal assessments to identify deficiencies in its processes, and it recommends key activities that should be mastered if the organization is to improve in its software development capability.

Figure 9.2 illustrates the five maturity levels in the CMM. The number shown by each level indicates the percentage of all the formal assessments whose results had been reported to the SEI that resulted in the corresponding maturity rating, as of April 1996. A large majority of the assessments indicated that the organization or project was operating at the Initial level, with very few at the top two levels. Only a small fraction of software-producing organizations worldwide have undergone formal assessments, so it's hard to know what the overall distribution of process maturity really looks like. The distribution in Fig. 9.2 is probably over-optimistic, if anything.

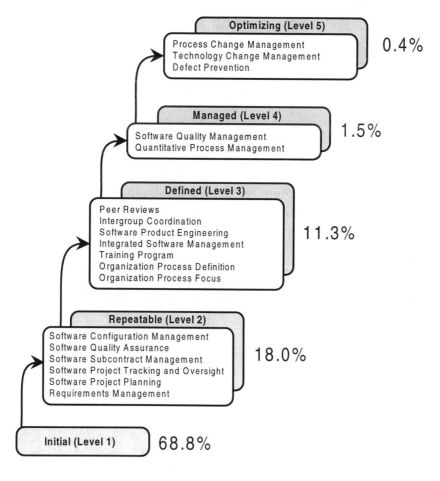

Figure 9.2: Software Engineering Institute's Capability Maturity Model for software.

Each maturity level except the first has a group of key process areas (KPAs) associated with it, listed in Fig. 9.2. The KPAs define several goals that must be satisfied across the organization to reach the associated maturity level. Several key technical and managerial practices that typically lead to achieving those goals are incorporated into each KPA. You don't have to apply all of the key practices to be assessed at a particular maturity level. However, you do have to demonstrate that you are satisfying all goals of all the KPAs at that level and all lower levels. Each KPA also addresses the organization's commitment to perform the activities associated with the KPA, the ability to perform the activities, measures related to the KPA, and ways to verify that the intent of the KPA is being satisfied.

Skipping levels in an attempt to zip up the maturity scale is not an option. The instilling of new management and engineering practices and a supporting culture takes time. The CMM is structured such that the KPAs at the lower levels provide a solid foundation for sustained performance as the organization climbs toward the higher levels. Ludicrous "stretch" goals announced by top managers who try to push an organization up the CMM ladder at an arbitrary rate, such as one level per year, simply are not realistic. "Continuous process improvement" means just that, not quantum leaps from one state to another without passing through the often painful learning process and behavior modifications that are associated with sustainable change.

Many factors will affect the rate at which an organization can implement real changes. Process evolution must take place through a series of planned stages and interim goals that are intended to infuse the improved practices into the group in an effective way. One responsibility of a process improvement leader is to see that senior managers whose support for process improvement is being sought are realistic about the investments required and the benefits they can hope to reap from them.

It typically takes two or three years to move from the Initial to the Repeatable level, and eighteen to twenty-four months to achieve each subsequent level, in the context of a systematic improvement effort. The length of time needed to climb a rung on the maturity ladder depends on where you start within the previous level, the resources that are devoted to process improvement activities, and the overall culture of the organization.

Now let's look at the characteristics and KPAs of each maturity level in the CMM. Complete details of the KPAs can be found in *The Capability Maturity Model: Guidelines for Improving the Software Process* [CMU/SEI, 1995].

Level 1: Initial

In a Level 1 organization, development activities are based on folklore and individual preferences, rather than on written standard practices. An oral tradition of techniques that work is passed from one generation of developers to the next. Any written standards that do exist probably are ignored. The ability to estimate project size and effort usually is poor. Success in a Level 1 organization is largely due to a few outstanding managers or individual programmers—heroes—who come through in the pinch with massive efforts that eventually get the job done, using whatever methods work. The Level 1 manager does not have good visibility into what is really taking place inside a project. Deadlines are more important than quality: When time pressures mount, discipline is discarded in favor of frenzied code-and-test. The organization operates reactively rather than proactively, fighting fires instead of finding ways to prevent them. Pejorative terms used in conjunction with Level 1 organizations include "chaotic," "undisciplined," "unpredictable," "ad hoc," and "anarchy."

Once when I was interviewing candidates for a software engineering position, I asked each one what factors he or she felt lead to success on software projects. One person told me that it boiled down to who was running the project. This is practically a definition of a Level 1 organization, reflecting a belief that the activities of a few outstanding individuals supersede organizational culture and defined procedures as the predominant success driver.

There are no key process areas for the Initial level. Work gets done however it gets done. Usually it does manage to get done, but with substantial overruns of cost and schedule, leaving little reason to believe that the next project will be any better.

Level 2: Repeatable

Project management and control are emphasized at the Repeatable level. A Level 2 organization has created documented processes for managing various aspects of a software project, and it has policies in place to see that the processes are followed. A new team member has some written guidance as to how to perform certain project activities. Metrics are collected to track project progress and to identify problems. This historical data can lead to improved estimating abilities. Target delivery times and costs may actually be higher than those estimated by a Level 1 organization, because they are more realistic. Therefore, there should be fewer overruns.

The key process areas and their associated goals that must be satisfied to move from the Initial to the Repeatable level are shown in Table 9.1. These KPAs are not selected arbitrarily. Often, they make the difference between successful and unsuccessful projects. On one Kodak project that was in serious trouble, we saw dramatic improvements when we began to implement practices in the requirements management and software project planning KPAs. In just a few weeks, this project went from a state of major trauma to being under control, with much less snarling among the participants.

Level 3: Defined

A Level 3 organization has standard, documented processes for developing and maintaining software in place across the organization. Tailoring guidelines are available to allow individual projects to modify the standard processes when necessary. As organizational effectiveness increases, targets for project costs and schedules shrink, as do the deviations between those targets and the actual delivery costs and schedules. A software engineering process group (SEPG) has been created to facilitate the organization's process activities. (You should really establish an SEPG even at Level 1, to guide your long-term process improvement program.) For an organization to be assessed at the Defined level, it must satisfy the goals of seven key process areas, described in Table 9.2.

Table 9.1.
Key Process Areas for the Repeatable Level.

Key Process Area	Description
Requirements Management	Requirements *management* is not the same as requirements *engineering*. This KPA addresses the need to establish a controlled software requirements baseline, to control changes in those requirements, and to keep software plans and activities consistent with the requirements as they change.
Software Project Planning	Project estimating and project planning are the areas most ripe for improvement in many software organizations. This KPA also stresses the need for affected groups and individuals to agree to their commitments related to the software project.
Software Project Tracking and Oversight	To meet project goals, the actual results of project activities must be tracked against the written project plan. When significant deviations occur, corrective actions must be taken.
Software Subcontract Management	This KPA provides guidance around contractual relationships between a software organization and other organizations to which project work has been subcontracted.
Software Quality Assurance	In the CMM, "software quality assurance" is an auditing and oversight function, not testing. People performing SQA objectively verify that applicable standards and procedures are being adhered to.
Software Configuration Management	A written software configuration management plan identifies selected work products as belonging to a controlled software baseline and specifies procedures to make sure that changes to these work products are controlled.

Level 4: Managed

Although measurement takes place at all maturity levels, measurement is the focus of the Managed level, particularly in the form of quantitative quality goals. Software development now approaches a state of statistical process control, since the process is being measured rigorously, and it is easier to tell if a project is performing out of the expected range. The quality of software products created should be both predictable and high. The two KPAs for the Managed level are described in Table 9.3.

Table 9.2.
Key Process Areas for the Defined Level.

Key Process Area	Description
Organization Process Focus	The software engineering process group is responsible for coordinating software process development and improvement activities across the organization.
Organization Process Definition	A Level 3 organization has developed a standard software process for the organization, and it collects and reviews information related to the use of the standard software process by individual projects.
Training Program	The presence of this KPA at the Defined level does not mean that training to build software technical and management skills can be neglected until the organization is firmly established at Level 2. However, it *requires* that training goals be defined and achieved for the organization to be assessed at Level 3.
Integrated Software Management	Projects in the Level 3 organization do not all have to follow the same process, but they must select and tailor their processes from a common parent set—the organization's standard software process.
Software Product Engineering	This large KPA covers most of the traditional software engineering life cycle phases, including requirements analysis, design, coding, testing, documentation, and maintenance.
Intergroup Coordination	All of the groups affected by a project must agree to the customer's requirements and to their commitments to each other. Intergroup issues among the engineering groups must be identified, tracked, and resolved.
Peer Reviews	Peer reviews are a powerful technique for identifying defects present in software work products. As with training, don't wait to start performing peer reviews until you reach Level 2. However, a defined peer review process must be in place to be assessed at Level 3.

Table 9.3.
Key Process Areas for the Managed Level.

Key Process Area	Description
Quantitative Process Management	A quantitative metrics plan that will allow the organization to understand its process capability and control its process performance is essential to achieving Level 4.
Software Quality Management	Measurable goals for software product quality are defined, and progress toward those goals is quantified and managed.

Level 5: Optimizing

At the Optimizing level, the emphasis is on defect prevention. Defects found are analyzed to learn how to prevent those same kinds of defects from being injected in the future. The entire organization is focused on continuous improvements in quality, productivity, and cycle time. A high priority is to reduce waste in the form of rework to correct defects. The organization has the ability to instill process changes based on a cost/benefit analysis leading to a decision to improve, rather than simply because other processes have failed. Because of higher productivity, the probability of meeting target delivery time lines and costs is much better than at lower maturity levels. The Optimizing level has three key process areas, described in Table 9.4.

Table 9.4.
Key Process Areas for the Optimizing Level.

Key Process Area	Description
Defect Prevention	Plans are in place to identify, analyze, prioritize, and systematically eliminate common causes of defects in software products.
Technology Change Management	Technology selection and transfer takes place in all software organizations. This KPA emphasizes the orderly incorporation of new technologies that are likely to increase the organization's capability for delivering quality software with ever-decreasing cycle times.
Process Change Management	Continuous process improvements are a way of life in a Level 5 organization, with participation across the organization in the improvement activities that are underway.

Only a very few SEI software process assessments have resulted in the Optimizing rating. One Level 5 assessment was done at the IBM Federal Systems Company Space Shuttle Onboard Software project (since acquired by Loral). This software has extremely high quality, due to rigorous defect detection (including seven discrete levels of testing), analysis, and prevention activities. For every defect found in the space shuttle software, regardless of significance, the following steps were performed: (1) determine the cause of the defect and correct it; (2) understand and correct the aspect of the process that led to the defect; (3) correct the quality control activities that permitted the defect to avoid earlier detection; and (4) search the product for similar defects that slipped through the defect detection nets [CMU/SEI, 1995].

This degree of rigor results in very expensive software, which is not unusual for programs having the potential for serious loss of life or major financial catastrophe. Few projects require this exceptionally high quality level, but if I were flying into space, I would prefer not to go with software written by the lowest bidder.

The goals of all the key process areas have a recurring theme of "activities are planned." This is the essence of the SEI's view of software process improvement: Improvement happens in a planned, controlled, and systematic fashion, rather than by exhorting team members to work harder and hoping that improvement goals are magically met. They won't be.

Dissenting Opinions

Not everyone agrees that the CMM is the best approach for pursuing improved ways an organization can build software. Some feel the CMM is a holdover from the days of mainframe development with hordes of programmers creating massive, expensive, complex systems that do not work well and are hard to maintain (these are not *requirements* of mainframe applications, but they are not uncommon characteristics). Part of the opposition to the CMM is based on misconceptions. Some people think the CMM does not allow you to implement practices from maturity levels higher than one above your current state, that it dictates a waterfall life cycle model, or that it requires that specific methods be used when applying the key practices. These three perceptions do not happen to be true.

In essence, the CMM framework is based on two premises: First, a systematic, institutionalized process defining how software is created in an organization is an important mechanism for achieving superior quality and productivity; and second, groups of certain key software practices lay the foundation for successfully implementing a subsequent set of practices that will lead to even better sustained results.

As with any other dogma, the CMM should not be swallowed whole. Indeed, some respected members of the software development community have raised serious objections to aspects of the CMM.

Author and consultant Gerald Weinberg objects to the term "maturity" as being too judgmental [Weinberg, 1992]. Mature implies a state of superiority over less mature. The differences between organizations are more in the nature of their behaviors and cultures, rather than how far each has progressed along some "quest for unjustified perfection." Weinberg favors evolving the patterns of management toward an effective steering level, rather than worrying about satisfying the particulars of a prescribed set of process definitions.

James Bach, a former software quality assurance manager at Apple Computer and Borland International, is a vocal critic of the CMM [Bach, 1994]. He contends that most companies in the packaged software industry would probably be assessed at Level 1, but this lack of formal maturity does not prevent some of those companies from prospering by producing what are often (but not always) regarded as quality products. Bach argues that more emphasis should be devoted to the nurture and interaction of the people who build software, rather than focusing so heavily on defining ideal processes as the only basis for consistent success [Bach, 1995]. The best software development process cannot fully bridge the considerable performance gap between the most and least capable developers. You must continually work to improve the capabilities of your team, by hiring the top people you can find, and by enhancing their skills, teamwork, and development environment.

Watts Humphrey has addressed the role of individuals in software processes through his Personal Software Process, or PSP [Humphrey, 1995]. Through the PSP, individual engineers learn to follow a defined process for software development and to manage and improve their own processes. The PSP covers a wide range of tasks and behaviors: defect recording, time recording, size measurement and esti-mating, task and schedule planning, code and design reviews, and use of design templates. The PSP promises to bring a new discipline and quality orientation to the work of those individual software engineers who choose to adopt it.

The SEI also has developed a five-level "People Capability Maturity Model" (P-CMM) [Curtis, December 1994]. The four higher levels identify practices that can help an organization attract, develop, motivate, and retain talented software engineers. The P-CMM helps software organizations characterize the maturity of their human resource practices, set priorities for improving their level of talent, integrate talent growth with process improvement, and establish a culture of soft-ware engineering excellence.

Capers Jones feels that the application of "artificial maturity levels" for catego-rizing software processes, methods, or life cycles is one of the major risks of soft-ware development today [Jones, 1994]. People invent artificial classification schemes in an attempt to simplify complex problem domains, often in the absence of adequate quantitative data. The costs that may be incurred by an organization pursuing CMM Levels 4 and 5 can be considerable; as yet, there is little evidence whether this is a sound business investment. Jones also believes that the SEI assessment process is flawed because it does not collect quantitative information on an organization's productivity rates or quality levels [Jones, 1995].

In my view, the risk is not so much that the arbitrary five-level CMM scale of ambiguous definitions like "Defined" and "Managed" has been promoted. The risk is that foolish decisions can (and undoubtedly will) be made solely on the basis of an assessment yielding some magic level number. Any dogmatic quest for perfection, on any scale, can lose sight of the primary software process improve-ment objectives:

1. To understand how an organization is performing software engineering today

2. To understand the shortcomings of the current approach and the price paid for those deficiencies

3. To pursue a systematic strategy for making sound investments in improved processes, within the context of a framework that holds the realistic promise of enabling the organization to achieve superior results.

The CMM does not dictate the specific practices that should be used in any key process area, such as what project management tools or peer review methods are to be adopted. It simply states that an organization's practices in each key process area should be defined, documented, and actually practiced by the engineering staff. The CMM outlines a sequence for laying the foundation of behaviors in a software group so that the adoption of key practices is more likely to succeed and yield the desired product improvements.

The CMM is a reasonable tool for guiding a serious software process improvement effort. However, it should be viewed as a framework, not a straightjacket or a checklist. Your goal should not be to attain a particular CMM level by a particular date, although sometimes this can be a useful way to bring focus to an organization-wide effort. The goal is to apply the CMM—and other process improvement approaches—to help you fix your organization's specific problems. Decide where you feel the arrow in Fig. 9.3 belongs for *your* department, and apply the guidance of the CMM accordingly.

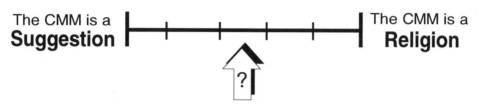

Figure 9.3: Where do you fit along the CMM philosophy spectrum?

The SEI has made some intelligent guesses about good places to start: project, requirements, subcontractor, and configuration management. But if you have different problems, address them directly. Just make sure, through an initial assessment activity, that you are working on improvements that will yield tangible benefits and whose value is apparent to enough stakeholders to obtain broad support. The formality of the CMM can help you grow a culture in which the improvements you make can be sustained over time, as individual projects, engineers, and managers come and go.

Process Assessments

Any process improvement initiative has to begin with an appraisal of your current software development practices. The goal of an assessment is to understand the root causes of your team's software problems so you can identify those changes that are likely to yield the greatest benefits. Undertaking an improvement effort without having the knowledge provided by an assessment can lead you to attack symptoms, rather than diseases. Several different process assessment approaches are available, ranging from quick and cheap brainstorming (as described in Chapter 8) or self-assessments, to formal and expensive assessments performed by external evaluators.

The SEI has defined several formal methods for conducting process assessments based on the CMM. Three major steps are followed during a typical CMM-based assessment. First, a group of representative practitioners and managers from the organization being assessed is assembled, along with a team of trained assessors, often including one or more members of the organization being assessed. Then, a questionnaire is completed and analyzed to develop a profile reflecting the implementation of key software practices throughout the organization. This profile provides a first indication of the maturity level at which the organization is operating. Finally, during an on-site visit, the assessment team interviews representative project leaders and practitioners and reviews documentation to better understand the software processes that are actually being followed by the organization.

The products from this on-site visit include lists of strengths and shortcomings ("findings") of the organization's software development process, in the context of the CMM's key process areas. A key process profile is constructed to show areas where the organization has and has not satisfied the goals of the KPAs. These deliverables from the assessment can be used by the organization's software engineering process group (be it half a person or a whole team) to guide their planning of an improvement effort.

A full SEI assessment can consume substantial staff time and money. The majority of organizations assessed to date turn out to be operating at the Initial level, but chasing levels is not what an assessment is all about. It is about identifying software practices that can be improved in an organization, by adopting more formal and sophisticated methods and by ensuring that current established procedures are actually applied on all projects. For a department committed to process improvement, an SEI assessment can establish a baseline of understanding about current practices. The assessment team points out areas in which process improvement investments are likely to yield the greatest returns.

To avoid the effort and cost of periodic full CMM-based assessments, several "mini-assessment" methods have been developed that let you take the process pulse of a software organization. Motorola (a leader in software process improvement) developed a technique for incremental, internal assessments [Daskalantonakis, 1994]. This self-evaluation tool can be used to track improvement over time, folding a sense of "progress assessment" in with the overall objective of "process assessment."

Kodak has developed a mini-assessment methodology that can be tailored to meet the specific needs of each project being assessed. Rather than defining a single technique, this methodology is modular, with various alternatives defined for each step in the assessment, which can be combined in many different ways. During a planning meeting between the assessors and representatives from the project team, the specific assessment approach is selected: which project team members will participate, who will fill out the process maturity questionnaire, whether a free-form process-oriented discussion will be held or not, and so on. The process maturity questionnaire addresses key process areas selected from Levels 2 and 3 of the CMM. Each question is phrased in terms of the frequency with which a specific activity within each KPA is performed by the project team: always, usually, sometimes, rarely, or never (don't know and not applicable are the other possible responses).

The results generated by a Kodak mini-assessment include identification of the three KPAs that will be the next focus of process improvement energy for that project team. Focusing action planning on these top three improvement priorities keeps the project team from being overwhelmed by trying to address too many changes at once. Since mini-assessments do not consume a lot of project staff time, it is practical to assess each project periodically, to track progress and to identify improved procedures developed by one project that can be shared with others.

Software Productivity Research, Inc. (SPR), has developed a methodology for assessing the factors that influence the outcome of software development projects [Jones, 1994; Jones, 1995]. The SPR assessment process covers about 400 factors, including about a hundred questions on strategic factors that affect all software projects within an enterprise, 200 questions on tactical factors that influence individual projects, and 50 questions relating to user satisfaction. The assessment also collects a large amount of baseline data on productivity, quality, schedules, costs, staffing levels, and other factors.

SPR uses a 5-point scale for each question, which is calibrated to reflect the distribution of answers across all projects that have been assessed. For example, a response of "3" for a particular factor means that the organization being assessed is in the middle 30 percent of all projects assessed. Fractional responses, such as 3.5, are also permitted. This higher resolution, relative scale contrasts with the more absolute yes/no scale used by the SEI's maturity questionnaire. As the general trend of improving software processes continues, the meaning of the ratings on SPR's relative scale will change over time. In this respect, an absolute scale such as the CMM is more appropriate, since the scale is constant with time, but the distribution of assessment results can evolve.

For do-it-yourselfers, Roger Pressman created a software engineering audit, which provides a set of questions to be answered by an assessment manager and representative practitioners from the department, along with guidelines for interpreting the responses [Pressman, 1988]. After completing the audit, you can follow Pressman's advice about how to select and implement methods, procedures, and tools that can improve the software engineering practice. Pressman provides a good starting point for small groups or companies that wish to launch a structured improvement initiative without investing in an expensive assessment.

Process Maturity and Culture

Software process is a fundamental component of an organization's culture. An organization committed to excellence in software engineering will consistently devote energy to improving the methods and procedures it applies to the construction of its products. A software engineering culture is characterized by

- clear organizational goals,

- management commitment to steering the team toward practices that will achieve those goals,

- an environment that enables the team members to develop their individual skills and to apply engineering procedures effectively, and

- measurements to track the effectiveness of the processes selected.

I recently met with a dozen employees of a software contract shop, not one of whom had ever heard of the CMM. Does this mean their culture doesn't care about software quality? Not at all. These people were very interested in learning how to improve the processes they use in their quest for business success through quality products. However, they would benefit from a better awareness of the established frameworks for improving software processes, which would give them additional tools to apply to their problems.

Process improvement begins with introspection, to understand the current processes being used and how they succeed and struggle. Regardless of the assessment approach you use, from simple team brainstorming to a full-scale SEI assessment, the objective is to gain honest insight into the ways your organization can change its attitudes, behaviors, tools, and methods to obtain improved results. A culture in which problem areas can be discussed frankly, without fear of retribution, has a big head start along the software process improvement pathway.

Summary

✔ The Software Engineering Institute defines a five-level scale of software process effectiveness, the Capability Maturity Model for Software. Most organizations that have been assessed are operating at Level 1. While few organizations will reach Level 5 any time soon, every software group has opportunities for improvement.

✔ The CMM identifies key process areas whose mastery across the organization is necessary to rise from one level to the next. However, the practices associated with these key process areas can be initiated at lower levels.

✔ Some strong objections have been raised to the CMM. It is clearly possible for some organizations to produce quality software while operating at relatively low levels of process maturity on the SEI's scale.

✔ Several formal and informal methods can be used for assessing the software processes of an organization. The goal of all these assessments is to identify high-yield areas for focusing improvement energy.

✔ A cycle of introspection, evaluation, and process improvement will almost certainly lead to a sustainable improvement in the software products you create and a decrease in the effort you expend to create them.

Culture Builders and Killers

Culture Builder: A high-level software manager can offer to provide direct assistance if the engineers in his organization feel the projects are not taking the right actions for creating quality products or if they need help changing the current approaches. When a manager asks if anything can be learned from a project's problems that will help us do a better job next time, he sends a message that he believes in continually improving on past performance. Lessons learned by one project team can be passed along to other teams in this way.

Culture Killer: Treat software engineering like a manufacturing line process. In the spirit of modern business process reengineering, reduce and combine steps to improve throughput, with no regard for the value added at each step. For example, skip low level design because that is so close to code anyway. Design the programs in your head and code them on the fly. Get rid of any process step that looks like it might slow down initial product delivery, even if you don't have any metrics data to show the real effect.

References and Further Reading

Bach, James. "Enough About Process: What We Need Are Heroes," *IEEE Software,* Vol. 12, No. 2 (March 1995), pp. 96-98.

> Bach contends that heroes (defined as "someone who takes initiative to solve ambiguous problems") are more central than process to successful software projects. He contrasts his "peopleware" model with the process orientation of the SEI CMM, and with the pathological heroism of the "cowboy" or "big magic" model of software success.

 ———. "The Immaturity of the CMM," *American Programmer,* Vol. 7, No. 9 (September 1994), pp. 13-18.

> Bach presents several criticisms of the CMM, and he proposes alternative process models that he has developed.

Carnegie Mellon University/Software Engineering Institute. *The Capability Maturity Model: Guidelines for Improving the Software Process.* Reading, Mass.: Addison-Wesley, 1995.

> This sequel to *Managing the Software Process* provides a technical overview and description of the CMM, Version 1.1. It covers the process maturity framework, as well as the key process areas and key software practices for each level of the CMM. Information for using the model in practice and a description of an actual Level 5 project also are included.

Crosby, Philip B. *Quality Is Free.* New York: McGraw-Hill, 1979.

> Crosby presents some of the concepts that underlie many contemporary views of software quality. While not all of the principles translate directly to the software world, this book contains many important ideas and tools for instilling quality attitudes and practices into any organization.

Curtis, Bill. "A Mature View of the CMM," *American Programmer,* Vol. 7, No. 9 (September 1994), pp. 19-28.

> Curtis addresses seven common misconceptions about the CMM, ranging from the notion that it "institutionalizes the mindless regimentation of processes," to the contention that the success of some PC software companies invalidates the CMM.

————, William E. Hefley, Sally Miller, Michael Konrad, and Sandra Bond. "Increasing Software Talent," *American Programmer,* Vol. 7, No. 12 (December 1994), pp. 13-20.

> The SEI's People Capability Maturity Model (P-CMM) is outlined in this article. The five maturity levels in the P-CMM are intended to lay successive foundations for an organization to continuously improve the talent of its software engineers, through a wide range of cultural and human factors practices.

Daskalantonakis, Michael K. "Achieving Higher SEI Levels," *IEEE Software,* Vol. 11, No. 4 (July 1994), pp. 17-24.

> In this clearly written article, Daskalantonakis describes the method developed at Motorola for performing incremental assessments of an organization's progress toward higher SEI maturity levels.

Dion, Raymond. "Process Improvement and the Corporate Balance Sheet," *IEEE Software,* Vol. 10, No. 4 (July 1993), pp. 28-35.

> Dion relates the benefits of software process improvement initiatives at Raytheon, including a 7.7-fold return on investment, doubling of productivity, changing of the corporate culture, and migration from CMM Level 1 to Level 3 over a span of some five years.

Herbsleb, James, David Zubrow, Jane Siegel, James Rozum, and Anita Carleton. "Software Process Improvement: State of the Payoff," *American Programmer,* Vol. 7, No. 9 (September 1994), pp. 2-12.

This article presents some of the benefits obtained by thirteen companies that had undergone SEI assessments and had vigorous software process improvement efforts underway, using the CMM as a process improvement framework. Significant improvements are reported in the categories of productivity gain, product cycle time reduction, and reductions in defects, both prior to and after product release.

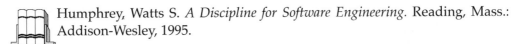 Humphrey, Watts S. *A Discipline for Software Engineering.* Reading, Mass.: Addison-Wesley, 1995.

Humphrey describes his "Personal Software Process" (PSP). The PSP, and other improvement efforts directed at individual software developers, complement the organization-wide focus of frameworks such as the CMM.

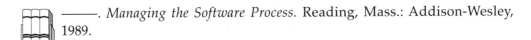 ———. *Managing the Software Process.* Reading, Mass.: Addison-Wesley, 1989.

Humphrey describes an early version of the SEI's process maturity framework. The key practices that are essential to attaining each maturity level are described in considerable technical depth.

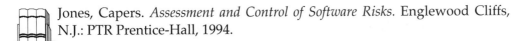 Jones, Capers. *Assessment and Control of Software Risks.* Englewood Cliffs, N.J.: PTR Prentice-Hall, 1994.

Jones devotes Chapter 5 to an explanation of why he feels that "artificial maturity levels" constitute a software risk. The SPR assessment process is described in Chapter 1.

———. "Gaps in SEI Programs," *Software Development,* Vol. 3, No. 3 (March 1995), pp. 41-48.

Jones presents his perception of deficiencies in several aspects of the SEI, the CMM, and the SEI's assessment methods. As a contrary example, he briefly describes the assessment method used by his company, Software Productivity Research.

Page-Jones, Meilir. "Managing in the Object-Oriented Environment," *Proceedings of the Fourth International Teamworkers Conference,* Cadre Technologies, Inc., 1991.

In this presentation, Page-Jones identified five ages through which a software engineering organization passes on its way from the anarchy of undisciplined programming, to the engineering of measurement-based continuous improvement, which leads to "productivity through quality."

Paulk, Mark C., Bill Curtis, Mary Beth Chrissis, and Charles V. Weber. "Capability Maturity Model, Version 1.1," *IEEE Software*, Vol. 10, No. 4 (July 1993), pp. 18-27.

This article describes the elements of the revised SEI CMM, including the behaviors expected at each maturity level and the key process areas associated with them.

Pressman, Roger S. *Making Software Engineering Happen.* Englewood Cliffs, N.J.: Prentice-Hall, 1988.

Pressman addresses the challenges of implementing a wide range of software engineering changes into an organization by starting with a do-it-yourself software engineering audit.

Weinberg, Gerald M. *Quality Software Management, Volume 1: Systems Thinking.* New York: Dorset House Publishing, 1992.

Chapters 2 and 3 in Volume 1 of Weinberg's series describe six software cultural patterns and his thoughts about what is needed to change patterns of behavior as the organization moves toward the more effective Pattern 3, Steering.

————. *Quality Software Management, Volume 2: First-Order Measurement.* New York: Dorset House Publishing, 1993.

Weinberg describes how to lay the foundation of a culture that supports measurement and quality. Appendix C contains a concise summary of the six cultural patterns.

SEI Technical Reports

The Software Engineering Institute publishes many technical reports on its activities. Many of these can be downloaded via the Internet using anonymous FTP (file transfer protocol, a tool for moving files from one computer system to another). Three groups of particularly interesting downloadable files are stored in different directories on the SEI's FTP server (Table 9.5).

Table 9.5.
FTP Site Directories for SEI Technical Reports.

Directory	Contents
pub/cmm	Contains reports CMU/SEI-93-TR-24 and -25 which describe the Capability Maturity Model for Software and the associated key practices in detail.
pub/documents	Contains a large number of additional SEI technical reports, grouped in subdirectories by year of publication.
pub/pm-cmm	Contains documents related to the People Capability Maturity Model.

From the Internet, follow this procedure for accessing the SEI's documents by FTP:

```
ftp ftp.sei.cmu.edu

login: anonymous

password: <your Internet userid>

cd pub/cmm (or pub/documents, or pub/pm-cmm)

get READ.ME

get <files>

quit
```

The READ.ME file in each directory contains information on the files available there, the various file formats supported (e.g., PostScript®, ASCII, RTF, and Microsoft® Word), downloading instructions, and World Wide Web sites that can be accessed for additional SEI-related information. Start in the pub/documents directory with files sei.documents.ascii (ASCII) and sei.documents.pdf (readable with the Adobe Acrobat® reader), which contain abstracts of the publications that are presently available for downloading. SEI reports can also be purchased from: Research Access Inc., 3400 Forbes Avenue, Suite 302, Pittsburgh, PA 15213; phone: (800) 685-6510.

Chapter 10

Software Development Procedures

. . . remember that standards establish a floor below which we dare not fall, not a goal to which we aspire. Because standards have to be a consensus, they tend to be weak.

—Boris Beizer

Peple have been building bridges for thousands of years. Each bridge built, whether it remained standing for centuries or collapsed with the cautious passage of the first pedestrian, contributed to the body of civil engineering knowledge. Such accumulated knowledge enables the builder of every new bridge to use the best of what is known about materials, designs, construction, and maintenance. Every legitimate engineering discipline has a body of standards that represent the accumulated best practices of that discipline over the ages.

Software developers generally feel free to use whatever approaches they like for the planning, design, construction, and maintenance of their products. This is due partly to the newness and complexity of writing computer software, but partly it is because software engineering is often taught only superficially in the computer science curriculum. Another contributing factor is the independent attitude of some programmers who resist anything they feel might constrain their creativity. This diversity of approaches is one cause for the wide variation in productivity and quality obtained by different software individuals and organizations. For software development to achieve the status of a true engineering discipline, an established body of standards must exist, based on empirical data rather than just the opinions of learned committees.

A group striving to practice quality software engineering will adopt and employ standard, accepted ways of performing common activities. A documented set of procedures for the tasks you perform provides a "group memory" in which to record the techniques you have found to be the most valuable. As these methods become routinely employed by all team members, they define a visible part of the group's software engineering culture.

It is not enough to point to the procedures notebook with pride—the members of the organization must actually apply the procedures in their daily work. If carefully selected and intelligently applied, software procedures and standards can facilitate your work by pointing to the best known ways to perform software development and maintenance activities in your organization. If poorly selected or injudiciously applied, standards become just a set of hoops you have to jump through to keep your boss off your back.

In many large shops, you are bound by previously defined (usually elaborate) standards and system methodologies, adopted and enforced up to the corporate level. Flaunting or bypassing these standards means that your system does not go into production. Whether yesterday's standards make good sense today may not even be open for debate. As technologies, processes, and application domains change over time, so too the software development procedures used by the organization must evolve.

The key to applying software engineering standards effectively is to use good judgment in deciding what degree of rigor is appropriate for each project. An organization risks wasting effort and losing good people when it insists on following all the steps in a purchased multi-volume methodology, even for small projects. Standard practices should define a software engineering framework that helps individuals contribute to the team, not a prison of sacred rituals that restricts their ability to find creative solutions to challenging problems.

Standards provide written expectations for the processes to be used and the deliverables to be produced by software developers. Team members may resist an effort to increase the structure of an engineering process if the manager's expectations are vague. "How can I give you what you want, when even you don't know what you want?" is the legitimate lament of those being asked to change without adequate guidance. Existing standards sources can point to areas that should be considered for standardization, in addition to providing templates of standard documents a group may choose to adopt. In this chapter we will look at some of the sources of software development standards that do exist, and see how one software group at Kodak went about creating and applying its own set of development guidelines.

Standards, Procedures, and Guidelines, Oh My!

Standards, procedures, and guidelines form the foundation of effective software engineering practices in an organization (Fig. 10.1). A standard is the strongest written statement of how work must be performed according to a specific set of rules: "a set of protocols that should be followed unless a formal deviation is approved" [Jones, 1994]. Standards typically are established by a professional society such as the Institute for Electrical and Electronics Engineers (IEEE), an official standards body like the International Organization for Standardization (ISO), or the U.S. government, including the Department of Defense (DoD) and the Food and Drug Administration (FDA). A standard may specify the contents of required documents, the activities that must be performed to fulfill the intent of the standard, and the individuals or groups responsible for these activities.

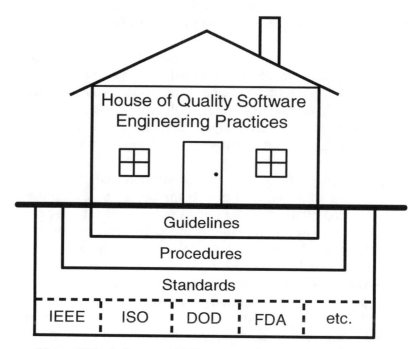

Figure 10.1: Software guidelines, procedures, and standards.

Procedures constitute a step-by-step formula for how a specified task is to be performed—a process definition. Unless there are external demands for compliance with specific standards, as is often true for software created under government contracts, most software organizations follow development procedures. The SEI's Capability Maturity Model refers to activities being performed "according to a documented procedure." To satisfy the goals of a key process area in the CMM, you must follow the pertinent procedures when performing such activities. Organizations often have policies in place mandating that specific documented procedures be followed when performing certain types of work.

Guidelines are suggested approaches that help the practitioner who wishes to apply established techniques, rather than choosing whatever she likes or inventing her own. Acceptance of the guideline is optional and can be decided by the project manager or individual practitioner. Guidelines are the simplest way for a group to start formalizing and documenting the way it builds software. Software development guidelines often recommend that existing external standards should be followed for certain activities.

Some IEEE standards documents are actually recommended practices (like procedures), while a few are called "guides." The guides suggest practical ways to apply certain of the standards. For example, IEEE Std. 1042 is the "Guide to Software Configuration Management." It provides implementation guidance for IEEE Std. 828, "Standard for Software Configuration Management Plans."

Software certification and process assessment activities may require that you prove that you have established written processes for development tasks, and that they are actually used. For example, an audit for ISO 9001 registration looks for both documented processes and evidence that they have been applied consistently. If you already have a collection of software development procedures, could you prove to an auditor which of your developers and projects routinely apply them?

In the CMM framework, the need to have an organization-wide standard software process appears at the Defined level (Level 3). However, individual projects can tailor the standard process to meet their particular needs. In other words, every project performed by the organization has to follow some defined process, but they do not all have to use exactly the same process. The Level 3 key process area (KPA) called Organization Process Definition addresses the need for an organization-wide process, while the Integrated Software Management KPA pertains to the tailoring of a standard process to meet a project's needs [CMU/SEI, 1995].

Local Development Guidelines

By documenting your development procedures, you move away from informal traditions toward improved ways of transmitting accumulated software wisdom from one generation of engineers to the next. No single set of prepackaged procedures is appropriate for every software department. Therefore, each organization must come up with a set that is tailored to meet its own needs. The exact details of your procedures are less important than the fact that they have been thought through, written down, accepted by the group, and applied to project work.

The procedures you adopt should address your group's specific problem areas, not necessarily the entire software development life cycle. Begin by defining procedures that will reduce the variability of how certain critical tasks are performed in your group. If you tried any of the process assessment techniques described in Chapter 9, you should already have a list of improvement opportunities identified. Begin by documenting how you perform the tasks in each of these areas today, so you can look for shortcomings to rectify. There is little point in writing procedures that do not directly address those aspects of software work that cause your group the most trouble.

Carefully plan how any new recommended practices that are defined in your procedures document will be phased into the culture of the group. This should be done as part of your process improvement planning. Rather than implementing many new procedures at once, begin with those that promise the most benefits. Good initial candidates are software configuration management, change control, writing requirements specifications, and project planning. Piloting new procedures on specific projects will give you valuable experience and demonstrate how much value they add. Lessons learned by the pilot projects can be used to refine the procedures, and then they can be extended to other projects in the department.

The impact on the culture is smaller if the written procedures simply document existing established (albeit informal) practices. Expect more pushback from the staff if your group tries to adopt procedures in an area in which developers are used to having complete freedom of style and method. A successful pilot project can serve as a selling point. Unspoken peer pressure also can help propagate the use of new procedures, as the early adopters obtain better results than those who resist what they perceive to be infringements on their right to unbridled freedom of action.

Don't rely on a collection of standards as a mechanism for implementing new practices; a fat rule book is intimidating to anyone. If your procedures are nothing but shelfware, they are worthless. They must be usable and practical for your developers, reflecting realistic expectations, not a fantasy of how you would like work to be done in a perfect world. It is easy to write a procedure stating that 137 metrics will be collected on each project. But if the reality is that nothing is ever measured in your culture, that part of your procedures adds no value to the organization.

Don't fall into the "not invented here" trap when it comes to acquiring software development procedures. If you work in a good-sized company, there are probably several sets of departmental procedures around that you can borrow. Have your team members study them, looking for those areas in which the procedures would and would not meet your local needs. Don't worry about style and format. If your team decides they can live with the guidelines as they are or with minor tailoring, this will help propagate common development processes and philosophies throughout your company.

With the wealth of published standards, you should be able to select some that will help address your team's most pressing problems. Our group has adopted IEEE standards for several aspects of development, including writing software requirements specifications (see Chapter 6), preparing test documentation, and quality assurance planning. We tailored the contents of these standards to meet our needs, rather than blindly applying every component of the standard.

If you do decide to create your own set of software development guidelines from scratch, get the whole team involved. The team should agree on the areas for which guidelines are needed. Ask different individuals to investigate existing standards that might be relevant and to draft the necessary sections for your own guidelines. Have everyone in the group critique each draft guideline. This will build a shared sense of ownership because everyone feels he or she had a chance to contribute to the guidelines.

Given the natural resistance many programmers have to following standards, it is important to remove any barriers that make applying the standard inconvenient. To facilitate the use of a standard document format throughout your group, get some examples to pass around and discuss, either from outside your area or from the team member who tries it first. Create templates of the documents and store them on your network for easy access by anyone who needs them. Give the standard a fair shake before you conclude whether or not it will do you any good. Perhaps you can adapt it slightly to meet your needs, rather than just throwing it out. Customizing standards to meet local requirements can increase the team's willingness to follow them.

Our Software Development Guidelines

In Chapter 8, we saw how one of Kodak's software groups conducted an informal brainstorming session as an initial process assessment method. The whole team agreed that the lack of defined expectations for how an application should be built was a handicap to our reaching peak performance. Consequently, one of our earliest improvement activities was to write a concise set of software development guidelines. This activity provides a good example of how to grow a software engineering culture through team consensus on improvement opportunities. Each team member drafted one or two guidelines, and all team members approved every one before it went into the notebook. To help us get started, some team members studied the pertinent IEEE standards to glean ideas. We selected those parts of the standards that looked most helpful and incorporated them into our guidelines.

These are guidelines, not laws: If there is a good reason for doing something other than what the guidelines indicate, fine. But it should be a *very good* reason, not just a whim or personal preference. Our team readily agreed on the topics for which we should begin writing guidelines. If you aren't sure where to begin, try these approaches:

1. Hold a group brainstorming session to identify areas where you think the team would benefit by applying common best practices. Which group member is using the best local technique in each of those areas already?

2. List all the software activities you perform during the life cycle of a typical project. Which activities result in the most rework? Which do the developers struggle with the most? Which have the most uncertainty about how best to accomplish the task? These are the areas most in need of some documented procedures.

3. If all else fails, look at the Level 2 key process areas in the CMM (Table 9.1), and create procedures to address those common sources of software development problems.

Our guidelines total fewer than fifty pages, but they address many of the important aspects of our work. We did not get into details of coding style, specific analysis and design methodologies to be used, or certain other areas that are also good candidates for standardization. Avoid getting bogged down with too much detail in the early stages of exploring software guidelines. Try a few things, change what doesn't work for you after a six- to twelve-month trial period, and retain the guidelines that do add value. The sections of our development guidelines document are described below. We created some during our first round of process documentation, while others were added during subsequent annual guideline reviews.

Project Champion Responsibilities: This section describes the expectations we have for our project champions and their managers, as discussed in Chapter 5.

Software Development Life Cycle: Two pages describe the creation of a project plan and the life cycle phases through which our projects typically pass. IEEE standards that are to be followed for certain of these phases are indicated.

Documentation Guidelines: This is the largest section, with six pages defining the expectations, plus an example of internal module header documentation. We included subsections on both internal program documentation (for example, source file header comments) and the external system documentation that belongs in a project maintenance notebook.

Since it is much more fun to write code than to write documentation, we created some utilities that produce standard header comment templates for programs written in various languages (see a sample portion of the template in Fig. 10.2). The output file produced by these utilities contains information extracted from the compiler and source listings, such as variable name lists, internal and external procedure lists, and a procedure call tree. The rest of the template contains boilerplate prompts to remind the programmer to supply other information. Programmers insert the bits of documentation that really ought to be present for a particular program, and omit the rest based on an explicit decision to do so, not because they neglected to think about what is important.

The external system documentation guidelines describe the following sections to be prepared for each application:

- purpose and description
- software operating instructions
- computer resource requirements
- security and access considerations
- hardware components
- system specifications, design, and architecture
- list of system programs
- build instructions
- copies of user interface displays

- list of help files

- routine maintenance procedures

Not all of these topics are relevant to every application created. The project leader is expected to see that the appropriate sections are written and placed in the project maintenance notebook. We use this section of our software development guidelines as a checklist when we perform documentation reviews at the conclusion of an application project.

```
/*********************************************************
Program Name:
Purpose:
Written by:
Date Written:
Modifications:
Arguments Passed:
Return Codes:
Libraries Needed:
Internal Procedures:
External Procedures:
Array Variables:
Scalar Variables:
Files Read:
Files Written:
Procedure Call Tree:

*********************************************************/
```

Figure 10.2: Sample source file header documentation template.

Software Quality Assurance Guidelines: Our small software group does not have a separate QA department available. Therefore, this section of our procedures defines the expectations of individual project members in performing SQA functions (see Chapter 11 for more on this topic). A description of how software inspections are conducted in our group is included, along with sample forms for documenting the inspection results. This section also itemizes the metrics that are to be collected on each project.

Feedback and Change Request Process: The purpose and use of our change request process and tool is described in this section of the guidelines. See Chapter 15 for a discussion of our change request process.

Test Plan Guidelines: This section is a condensation of effective and expected testing practices into just four pages. The first two pages address the components and outline of a test plan, how to specify test designs and test cases, and incident reporting. The last two pages contain guidelines for writing unit and system tests. This short guideline is hardly a comprehensive manual on software testing practices. It is simply a reminder of the minimum levels of testing activity expected of each of our team members.

User Interface Guidelines: When life was simpler and most of our development was on a mainframe, we wrote a short guideline for user interface screen design, including recommendations for screen layout and standards for function key definitions. Our philosophy was that our users should be able to identify a new application as one of our group's products because of the way it looks and feels, but they should not be able to tell which group member designed the user interface. Now we develop for many platforms and many kinds of interfaces, so this old guideline is of less value. Graphical user interface (GUI) standards are extremely important these days. Every organization that develops GUIs should follow established conventions for optimum usability and consistency on specific platforms. Few things irk users more than interfaces that do not conform to the standards, explicit or implicit, they have come to expect in a particular GUI environment. When your fingers are used to reaching for certain keys to perform common functions, anything unexpected that happens is a time-wasting nuisance, at best.

Configuration Management Guidelines: This section introduces the practice of software configuration management, or SCM. SCM involves procedures and tools that control access to the components of your software system and allow you to re-create a specified version of a file or application from a database of historical changes that have been made to a set of base files. People most commonly think of source code control when discussing SCM, but any kind of document (including your software development procedures) can and should be placed under configuration management.

User Manual Guidelines: The final section of our guidelines describes our preferred style and layout for user manuals. Some general guidelines are accompanied by style standards for specific manual sections, and by a sample document that illustrates how to apply the styles to those different sections. We derived these guidelines by studying existing commercial and locally written manuals, and by conducting surveys to see what layout and style options our customers preferred. User manuals should be designed for the convenience of your customers, not the preferences of your developers.

Glossary: We appended a short glossary defining some of the terms in our guidelines document. For comprehensive glossaries of software engineering terms, refer to IEEE Std. 610.12, "Glossary of Software Engineering Terminology," or the 600-item glossary of software assessment and management terms found in *Assessment and Control of Software Risks* [Jones, 1994].

That's it! Just over forty pages of text and examples represent our collected best practices and the distillation of industry wisdom to guide our team members in selecting methods to perform their jobs. These guidelines work for us, but they will not cover the needs of every software group. You may want to add guidelines around other areas, such as project management, estimating, graphical user interfaces, design methods, and tools. As time goes on and life becomes more complicated, our guidelines will evolve and grow, but we do not expect them ever to become really large. They don't need to be big to be valuable—just focused, rational, and practical.

One of our continuous process improvement efforts involved reviewing our guidelines a year after we wrote them, to discard any components that had not proved useful and add others that we needed. We have periodically revisited the procedures since that initial review, each time tuning them to the new state of our team composition and project mix. Another good time to review the procedures is during a postmortem analysis of a completed project. This discussion about which procedures worked and which did not can lead to more timely improvements than simply reviewing the entire guidelines document on a calendar basis.

With time, we found that some of the practices we included in the original guidelines were not appropriate for our current culture. For example, we found that we really were not collecting all the project metrics that our guidelines indicated we should; the group members had simply not yet accepted that this data was important. Whenever we discovered one of these discrepancies, we decided either to start applying the practice (thereby changing the culture itself), or to stop pretending we were going to do it and delete it from the guidelines for now. Perhaps the time will come when these more stringent expectations can be added back to the guidelines document. As teams change, so must their supporting foundation of standards and practices.

It is important for written procedures to reflect the reality of how you intend to build software, not a hypothetical state you hope to magically reach someday. An outside auditor should be able to snoop around in your project documentation and determine whether the practices you claim to be using actually are being applied by the development staff. If they are not, you should find out why, and then decide which part of the picture is out of focus: Are your current procedures impractical or not valuable, or are the team members simply not performing work in the way you have all agreed that they should? In either case, something needs to change.

IEEE Standards

Table 10.1 lists the software engineering standards, recommended practices, and guides that are currently available from the IEEE. The document numbers listed are typically followed by the year each standard was most recently revised (for example, 830-1993). Most of these standards are also accepted by the American National Standards Institute (ANSI). All of these documents are included in the *IEEE Software Engineering Standards Collection,* which is published every year or two.

Many of the IEEE standards are practical, clearly written, and broadly applicable to organizations working in different application domains. Some that groups at Kodak have found to be particularly valuable are those for software quality assurance plans (Std. 730), configuration management plans (Std. 828), test documentation (Std. 829), and requirements specifications (Std. 830). Some of the other standards are less well-written, which makes it difficult to see how the contents can best be applied to your own organization. Nor do IEEE standards reflect the software state-of-the-art. The rapid rate of change in the software industry, coupled with the slow pace of any consensus-oriented activity involving a large committee of geographically separated participants, makes it impossible for such standards to incorporate the latest thinking in software development.

As written, the IEEE standards contain little guidance for scaling the contents to projects of different sizes. Blindly applying all of the elements of a standard to a small project can result in excessive quantities of documentation that add little value. On the other hand, mammoth projects can collapse under their own weight without a supporting framework of standards and common processes. As with all software engineering methods and tools, use the parts that are appropriate for your projects. Unless you are working under a mandate to conform to specific standards, you should strive to implement the spirit of a standard, not necessarily every detail included in the often lengthy text.

Other Standards Sources

Two of the most important sources for software standards are the International Organization for Standardization (ISO) and the U.S. government, but there are many others. Leonard Tripp led a team that compiled a comprehensive listing of hundreds of available standards that pertain to software engineering [Tripp, 1993].

ISO publishes international standards and guidelines pertaining to quality management, assurance, and auditing. ISO 9001 is a broad, industry-independent standard for quality assurance in all aspects of products and services. A supporting guideline is ISO 9000-3, "Quality Management and Quality Assurance Standards—Part 3: Guidelines for the Application of ISO 9001 to the Development, Supply and Maintenance of Software." This guideline particularly addresses contracts with suppliers who produce software. It does not specify the actual practices or methods that are to be used for any phase of software development work. Rather, it emphasizes the need for a documented quality system, which assures the use of sound software engineering practices [Ince, 1994]. ISO 9000-3 provides detailed guidance around such topics as

- the responsibility of both supplier and purchaser management for the quality system;

- documentation, planning, and audits that must be in place in the quality system;

- the contents of a development plan and a quality plan;

- aspects of design, implementation, and testing activities that should be considered; and

- supporting activities for quality, such as configuration management, document control, measurement, and purchasing software.

Table 10.1.
IEEE Software Development Standards.

IEEE Document Number	Title
610.12	Glossary of Software Engineering Terminology
730	Standard for Software Quality Assurance Plans
828	Standard for Software Configuration Management Plans
829	Standard for Software Test Documentation
830	Recommended Practice for Software Requirements Specifications
982.1	Standard Dictionary of Measures to Produce Reliable Software
982.2	Guide for the Use of Standard Dictionary of Measures to Produce Reliable Software
990	Recommended Practice for Ada as a Program Design Language
1002	Standard Taxonomy for Software Engineering Standards
1008	Standard for Software Unit Testing
1012	Standard for Software Verification and Validation
1016	Recommended Practice for Software Design Descriptions
1016.1	Guide to Software Design Descriptions
1028	Standard for Software Reviews and Audits
1042	Guide to Software Configuration Management
1044	Standard Classification for Software Anomalies
1045	Standard for Software Productivity Metrics
1058.1	Standard for Software Project Management Plans
1059	Guide for Software Verification and Validation Plans
1061	Standard for a Software Quality Metrics Methodology
1062	Recommended Practice for Software Acquisition
1063	Standard for Software User Documentation
1074	Standard for Developing Software Life Cycle Processes
1209	Recommended Practice for the Evaluation and Selection of CASE Tools
1219	Standard for Software Maintenance
1228	Standard for Software Safety Plans
1298	Standard for Software Quality Management Systems, Part 1: Requirements

As more companies are required to achieve ISO 9001 registration to compete in the global marketplace, application of the ISO 9000-3 guideline for the software components of products will become more widespread. To achieve certification, you must demonstrate to an external auditor that documented procedures are in place to satisfy the quality management system objectives stated in the guideline; that you are, in fact, following those procedures in the creation of your software products; and that your quality management activities are effective.

The U.S. Department of Defense publishes numerous standards that must be followed by programmers developing software under military procurement contracts [Roetzheim, 1991]. While these standards do enable consistency from one project to the next, they can lead to vast amounts of documentation being generated on a software project. Capers Jones states that, "Large military projects routinely create up to 100 discrete document types and more than six pages of paper per Function Point (equivalent to some 400 English words per Ada statement)" [Jones, 1994]. I guess this is not surprising for a government standard that is intended to be used for a wide variety of projects. But if you are programming for that market and the boss says you have to follow the standard, then you have to follow the standard.

Summary

✔ Written software development procedures can help build a shared culture of best practices.

✔ To build a sense of joint ownership of your guidelines, get the team members involved in selecting, writing, and critiquing them.

✔ The guidelines you select cannot simply reflect the lowest common comfort level of the developers in your organization. They should help each team member produce the highest quality products using common tools, methods, and documents.

✔ For procedures to be useful, they must be short and realistically applicable to each project. Look for the value added to your process and products by each procedure you write.

✔ Become familiar with the software engineering standards published by the IEEE and any other standards bodies that are relevant to your company's line of business.

✔ Borrow as many procedures as you can from other sources. Don't invent anything you can buy or adapt from others. Seek out best practices wherever you find them and incorporate them into your procedures.

✔ Plan to review and update your guidelines periodically as part of your continuous improvement activities.

✔ When you become serious about having the procedures followed, set up a quality assurance function to facilitate their application in practice, audit the extent to which they are applied on each of your projects, and assess whether the procedures are delivering the intended benefits or not.

Culture Builders and Killers

Culture Builder: One of your team members approaches you with a question as to what technique would be most appropriate for dealing with some problem. You know this topic is covered in your group's software development guidelines. The two of you can look up the pertinent section in the guidelines and discuss it. This encourages team members to look to the guidelines first when seeking advice, while sending the message that you believe the guidelines should be taken seriously.

Culture Builder: When new engineers join the group, give them copies of your software development procedures. Explain your expectations and the philosophy around the procedures. Coach the new people in how to apply the right procedures at the right time to keep them from being overwhelmed. Mentoring or partnering with an experienced team member who you know follows the procedures is a good way to help the newcomers fit into your culture.

Culture Builder: When a project documentation review is held, use the guidelines document as a checklist, to make sure the correct items have been included in the documentation notebook. Actively using parts of the group software development guidelines during any team activity will reinforce the notion that they are there to be used, not simply to sit on the shelf.

Culture Killer: Give everyone in your group a copy of the *IEEE Software Engineering Standards Collection*, and ask them to start applying all the practices contained therein immediately. The book is only about a thousand pages long; it shouldn't be too hard for your staff to change their development practices to conform to those standards. While you're at it, buy a copy of that eighteen-volume project management methodology and make sure your project leaders follow it, too. Tolerate no deviations from the standards. After all, that's why they're called "standards."

Culture Killer: Enforce whatever software development procedures your organization has adopted on certain projects, but not on others. Some programmers are so good they don't need to follow the procedures. Any project that falls behind schedule should be free to disregard the established development procedures and get things done any way they can.

References and Further Reading

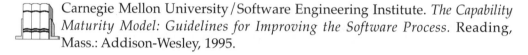

Carnegie Mellon University/Software Engineering Institute. *The Capability Maturity Model: Guidelines for Improving the Software Process.* Reading, Mass.: Addison-Wesley, 1995.

> Several of the key process areas for the Defined level pertain to the creation, maintenance, and application of an organization's standard software process.

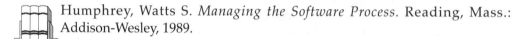

Humphrey, Watts S. *Managing the Software Process.* Reading, Mass.: Addison-Wesley, 1989.

> Chapter 9 discusses software development standards, including examples of some major standards and how to establish standards in an organization. Humphrey states that the goals for a software quality assurance department include ensuring full compliance with established standards and procedures for the product and the process, and bringing to management's attention any inadequacies in the standards so that they can be corrected.

IEEE Software Engineering Standards Collection, 1994 ed. Los Alamitos, Calif.: IEEE Computer Society Press, 1994 (IEEE product number SH94213).

> All of the IEEE software engineering standards from Table 10.1 are found in this collection. To purchase IEEE software engineering standards, contact: IEEE Customer Service, 445 Hoes Lane, P.O. Box 1331, Piscataway, NJ 08855-1331.

Ince, Darrel. *ISO 9001 and Software Quality Assurance.* New York: McGraw-Hill, 1994.

> This slender volume examines each facet of the ISO 9001 system as it pertains to software development. It also includes a checklist of questions you can use to assess your existing quality process in comparison to an ISO 9001 expectation.

Jones, Capers. *Assessment and Control of Software Risks.* Englewood Cliffs, N.J.: PTR Prentice-Hall, 1994.

>   Chapter 31 addresses the risk factor of "Inadequate Software Policies and Standards." Each of the other 59 software risks he discusses includes a section on standards that might help alleviate the risk. Sadly, many of these sections indicate that no pertinent standards are available at present to address that specific risk.

Layman, Beth. "ISO 9000 Standards and Existing Quality Models: How They Relate," *American Programmer,* Vol. 7, No. 2 (February 1994), pp. 9-15.

>   In addition to this article on the relationship between the ISO 9000 standards, the SEI Capability Maturity Model, and other software process models, this issue of *American Programmer* contains several other articles on ISO 9000 as it pertains to the software industry.

Roetzheim, William. *Developing Software to Government Standards.* Englewood Cliffs, N.J.: Prentice-Hall, 1991.

>   This book describes major government standards for software development and advises how to follow them. Guidance is included on how to prepare nearly twenty of the document types required by these standards, and how to conduct seven different types of mandated reviews and audits.

Tripp, Leonard, ed. *Survey of Existing and In-Progress Software Engineering Standards* (1993) and *Master Plan for Software Engineering Standards* (1993).

>   The Survey lists more than 300 existing standards that apply to software development, issued by more than 60 organizations from many countries. The Master Plan contains sections on the user expectations, process objectives, and general requirements and constraints for software engineering standards. These unpublished documents can be obtained for a fee from IEEE Computer Society Headquarters, 1730 Massachusetts Avenue NW, Washington, D.C. 20036.

Part IV

The Bug Stops Here

An organization having a software engineering culture takes quality very seriously. Its commitment to quality is reflected in the understanding and effective application of established software quality practices throughout the organization. There is an attitude that quality is the responsibility of each individual, not just the province of the testing department. All practitioners are trained in defect removal techniques, including inspections and various forms of testing. Defect detection and removal activities are explicitly planned for each project, with written software quality assurance plans that identify who is responsible for performing various quality functions. Records are kept of the defects found, so the effectiveness of the defect detection methods being used can be measured and improved.

We will look at several aspects of software quality assurance and control practices in Part IV. Rather than condense the vast body of knowledge on software quality into a few pages, I will focus on techniques that members of some groups at Kodak have found to be effective in improving the quality of their software. I will present some data that suggests these quality practices have brought our corrective maintenance (bug fixing) work under control, although there is still opportunity for further improvement. Individual engineers should begin to apply these techniques as part of their contribution to the group's software engineering culture.

Two cultural premises are explored in Part IV:

✔ Quality is the top priority; long-term productivity is a natural consequence of high quality.

✔ Strive to have a peer, rather than a customer, find a defect.

Chapter 11

The Quality Culture

There is absolutely no reason for having errors or defects in any product or service.

—Philip B. Crosby, *Quality Is Free*

Bug. Defect. Error. Fault. Incident. Anomaly. Problem. Spoilage. Imperfection. Leaders in the software industry disagree on just what something found to be wrong with a computer program ought to be called. Some object that "fault" suggests that it is somebody's fault that the program has something wrong with it (often it is). But "bug" makes it sound as if these things just come out of nowhere, all by themselves (usually they don't).

An "incident" sounds like something from a Robert Ludlum novel; "anomaly" is a broad-reaching euphemism for anything out of the ordinary; "spoilage" makes it sound like the code on the disk goes bad as it sits on your shelf. No one wants to be "defect"ive, and no one wants to make "errors." But, being "imperfect" humans, we all do.

Then, there are those who say that "bug" is best, because programs are written by people and people are simply going to make mistakes. Bugs *are* a normal, albeit undesirable, consequence of software development: They are unavoidable. Our challenge as software engineers is to learn as much as we can about how to find them, squash them, and keep them from coming back.

By any name, programs and their associated documentation usually have things wrong with them. Rather than get into semantic subtleties to distinguish them, I will use the terms bug, defect, error, and fault interchangeably to refer to such software problems. One important term to keep distinct, however, is "failure," which refers to a malfunction in a software system (abnormal termination or incorrect behavior) because of an underlying fault. A single fault can be the cause of many failures, while a failure that occurs because of one fault might mask the presence of other faults in the program.

Customers do not want anything to be wrong with the software products they use. The user's perception of software quality depends heavily on defects in the application, be they usability problems, misunderstandings that originated during requirements analysis, or inconsistencies between the program and its user manual. Customers are not concerned so much about actual source code errors, but rather the frequency of software failures caused by these errors. Simply having bug-free code is no guarantee that your users will perceive your product as having quality or value, but it is an important term in the quality equation.

The intent of frank discussion about software quality problems is not to fix blame and create a generation of guilt-ridden programmers. It is to help engineers deploy effective technologies, practices, and attitudes that lead to injecting fewer defects into a program in the first place and to more efficiently finding those bugs that are present as early as possible.

In an organizational culture committed to excellence in software engineering, considerable effort is devoted to both defect prevention and early detection. An organization less committed to quality will focus more on finding errors through more expensive late-stage testing, which leads to releasing (and sometimes withdrawing) buggy programs. In a software engineering culture, developers want to find their errors themselves or with the help of their peers, rather than shipping the errors to their customers. You know the customers will not be in a good mood when they eventually encounter the bugs that your quality filters missed.

The quality commitment must be present at every level of the organization. In a healthy engineering culture, finding errors in unreleased products is viewed as a good thing (up to a point, anyway; if too many errors are found, process improvements are in order). Engineers who are serious about achieving consistently superior quality keep records of the defects they find in their own work products. They analyze defect records to understand

- where the defects originated,

- why they were not caught earlier,

- what they can do to avoid making similar errors in the future,

- how to catch such defects more efficiently in the future, and

- where to look for similar defects that might already be present in the product.

Software quality depends on the individual attitudes of software engineers and managers, the processes used to prevent errors during development, and the practices employed to detect those bugs that do wind up in the work products. In *A Discipline for Software Engineering*, Watts Humphrey describes a Personal Software

Process that a developer can adopt to improve in all three of these areas [Humphrey, 1995]. Through the PSP, developers learn to follow a defined and disciplined process for designing, coding, and validating individual programs. The skills acquired through the PSP can be scaled up to improve the developer's effectiveness in creating high-quality software applications.

The Cost of Quality

One benefit of creating nearly defect-free software is that you don't have to waste time on rework during the long maintenance phase. The cost of quality is the price you pay for doing things wrong, not the cost of doing them right. Put another way, the cost of quality is the sum of all costs that would disappear if everything was done right the first time. As shown in Table 11.1, the cost of quality is defined by the total effort and money spent on defect prevention, quality appraisal, and costs associated with product failure [Crosby, 1979]. Failures can be internal to the organization prior to product delivery, or they can be experienced by the customer. On top of these direct expenses are future business opportunities lost because of a reputation for producing low-quality products.

Table 11.1.
Some Components of the Cost of Quality for Software.

Category	Examples
Defect Prevention	• Effort devoted to understanding the root causes of defects • Process improvement activities • Quality assurance efforts • Quality training and tools
Quality Appraisal	• Inspection to find defects • Testing to find defects • Measuring the quality of the product
Product Failure	• Reproducing and diagnosing the failure • Rework (fixing the defect, rebuilding the product, reinspecting it, retesting it, reinstalling it) • Engineering and requirements changes • Warranty repair or replacement • A support function to help customers with products that are defective or difficult to use • Program redesign • Programs, documents, or entire applications that are abandoned, or scrapped and rebuilt

It might not seem as if defect prevention activities are part of the "cost of doing things wrong." But consider: If you had perfect processes that never produced defects and were always followed, you would not have to analyze the causes of your defects, nor improve your processes, nor audit to see that they were being applied. More realistically, a quality-oriented culture will focus on defining processes that prevent defects from being created in the first place, rather than squandering its resources fixing problems reported by customers.

Do you know the cost of quality in *your* organization? To accurately calculate the cost of quality requires that you look in a lot of places for unobvious labor and expenses. You probably won't like the answer you get. "Quality is free" means the investment you make in improving the quality of your development process (defect prevention, quality appraisal) is more than recouped by reducing the costs due to defects (product failure) over the lifetime of the product.

Too many quality efforts are sacrificed on the altar of productivity, as managers and programmers alike claim they could produce more if only they didn't have to do all of the quality-related tasks. However, the time invested in building a quality product in the first place is repaid over the lifetime of the product through lower maintenance costs. A less tangible benefit is the goodwill of the customer. Most customers are willing to wait a bit longer to get a better product that will help them do their work correctly, without wasting their time through program failures and poor usability. And they might not even have to wait: Finding defects early in the development process can save a lot of time during late-stage testing and debugging.

The ultimate goal of a software quality program is to eliminate the time and expense wasted on internal rework and post-release maintenance to correct defects (see Fig. 11.1). Internal rework can consume 30 to 40 percent of the effort on a software project. The time saved by not performing rework translates into a direct productivity increase, because that time can now be spent creating new software products. While you do have to invest money and time in applying the appropriate quality assurance and control methods, you will still experience a net gain if you can produce software that does not have to be fixed so frequently. Capers Jones states that every dollar spent on defect prevention will reduce future defect repair costs by three to ten dollars [Jones, 1994]. *It is always cheaper to do the job right the first time.*

Assuring Software Quality

The term "software quality assurance" (SQA) is used in several different ways. In some companies, QA refers to the testing department. Many small software groups do not have an independent QA department at their service, so to them, SQA refers to all actions that are performed to find, eliminate, and prevent errors in software work products. People who perform these broad-definition SQA activities are sometimes known as software quality engineers. In larger organizations, the QA department may be an independent unit that assesses the quality of the procedures used and products created by the organization.

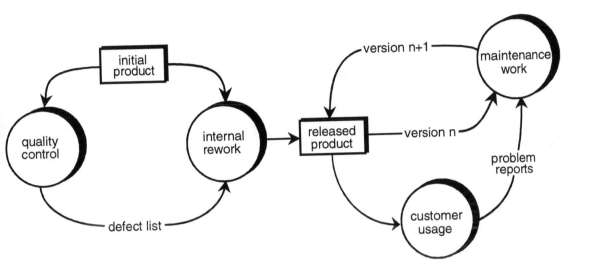

Figure 11.1: Internal rework and post-release maintenance.

The Software Engineering Institute's Capability Maturity Model states that, "The purpose of Software Quality Assurance is to provide management with appropriate visibility into the process being used by the software project and of the products being built" [CMU/SEI, 1995]. The "IEEE Standard Glossary of Software Engineering Terminology" (IEEE Std. 610.12) defines *quality assurance* as: (1) a planned and systematic pattern of all actions necessary to provide adequate confidence that an item or product conforms to established technical requirements; and (2) a set of activities designed to evaluate the process by which products are developed or manufactured.

Let's use the following definitions for tasks associated with creating quality software products. *Quality control* (QC) is defined as activities intended to find defects that exist in a software work product, including all forms of testing and inspection. *Quality assurance* (QA) is defined as: (1) activities intended to verify that established software development procedures and quality practices have been properly and effectively applied on a project; (2) activities that measure the quality of a software work product and assess its suitability for release; and (3) activities intended to define improved processes that will minimize the injection of defects into future software work products.

The focus of quality control functions is on error detection, while quality assurance functions emphasize error prevention and quality measurement. The commonly held view of "QA = testing" oversimplifies the multiple and distinct purposes of the QC and QA functions in an organization.

How Dense Are Your Defects?

Both QC and QA activities are intended to create software containing the fewest possible bugs when delivered to the customer. How small is "fewest"? A typical commercial software application has a defect potential—the number of defects injected during all development stages—of about five defects injected per function point (a measure of software size, discussed later in this chapter) [Jones, 1994]. This corresponds to some forty to sixty defects per thousand lines of procedural language source code (KLOC), depending on the language. Other sources suggest that typical defect potentials range up to a hundred defects per KLOC [Humphrey, 1995].

Based on the effectiveness of typical quality control practices in catching these *injected* defects, the application might contain in the range of five to twenty *delivered* defects per KLOC. A high-quality application might contain less than one delivered defect per KLOC. Some software created using the most stringent development and defect management practices is essentially free of errors. For example, the Space Shuttle onboard software achieved a defect potential as low as five injected defects per KLOC, all of which were removed prior to delivery through rigorous quality control techniques.

An increasingly common measure of quality in any product or service is to express defects in units of parts per million (ppm). That is, the defect rate is the number of defects per million opportunities to create a defect. In software, what constitutes an opportunity to create a defect? The answer is not obvious, because software is different from a manufactured product in which millions of copies of the same item, such as a roll of film, are created. In one sense, each source statement is a defect opportunity. In another sense, every keystroke qualifies. How about errors in requirements specifications, system designs, and user manuals? Is every character or word or sentence a defect opportunity? There is no simple, universal definition of "opportunity to create a defect" for software.

Several companies are using "lines of assembly-equivalent source instructions" as a measure of software size. An opportunity to create a defect in software is then defined as one assembly-equivalent source instruction. This approach attempts to normalize different high-level languages to the number of assembly language statements that would be necessary to deliver the same functionality. Capers Jones reported the average number of assembly language instructions that correspond to a single source statement in each of several languages, as shown in Table 11.2 [Jones, 1991]. For example, a 1,000-statement program of average complexity written in C would require approximately 2,500 statements of assembly language to deliver the same functionality. (We'll look at the rightmost column in Table 11.2 a bit later.)

Table 11.2.
Source Statements, Assembler Instructions, and
Function Points (Adapted from [Jones, 1991]).

Language	Assembler Instructions per Source Statement	Avg. Source Statements per Function Point
Basic assembly default	1.0	320
C	2.5	128
FORTRAN 77	3.0	105
ANSI COBOL 85	3.5	91
Pascal	3.5	91
PL/I	4.0	80
Ada	4.5	71
QuickBASIC	5.0	64
Statistical language default	10.0	32
Object-oriented default	11.0	29
Fourth generation default	16.0	20
Query language default	25.0	13
Fifth generation default (graphic icons)	75.0	4

Motorola, one of the American companies that has led quality improvement imperatives for several years, has set the objective of "six sigma" quality as a goal to approach a zero-defect condition. Sigma refers to one standard deviation in a normal distribution of variability of some process or product. The full statistical description of sigma quality levels is somewhat involved, and there are some questions as to exactly how to relate it to software. For our purposes, we can simply discuss defect densities in terms of sigma levels and parts per million of defects. Table 11.3 shows the parts per million of defects that are found as a function of sigma. Note that the six-sigma level corresponds to 3.4 ppm of defects. This means that if your software organization is operating at the six-sigma quality level, and you have defined an "opportunity to create a defect" as one assembly-equivalent source instruction, your programs will contain only three or four defects per million assembly-equivalent source instructions.

On this scale, a more typical delivered defect rate of ten errors per KLOC of COBOL 85 corresponds to $10 \div 3.5 \approx 2.9$ errors per thousand assembly-equivalent lines of code (LOC), or 2,900 ppm (applying the factor of 3.5 for COBOL 85 from Table 11.2). This falls short of the extremely ambitious six-sigma target of 3.4 ppm by a factor of 850. To make matters worse, larger systems are more error-prone than smaller ones, making it that much more challenging to create nearly defect-free software on a big scale.

Table 11.3.
Defect Levels Associated with
Different Sigma Values.

Sigma	PPM of Defects
1	697,670
2	191,690
3	66,810
4	6,210
5	233
6	3.4

As another example, an application that contains 100,000 lines of source code written in C is entitled to only one defect if it is to reach the six-sigma quality level:

$$\frac{1 \text{ defect}}{100,000 \text{ LOC in C}} \times \frac{1 \text{LOC in C}}{2.5 \text{ LOC assembler}} = 4 \text{ ppm} \approx \text{six sigma}$$

An interesting consequence of the assembly-equivalent normalization is that a single fault in a higher level programming language has less impact on the defect density expressed in assembly-equivalent statements than does one fault in a lower-level language. For example, one error in 1,000 LOC of relatively low-level C corresponds to a defect density of 400 ppm in assembly-equivalent terms, whereas a single error in 1,000 LOC of a high-level query language (25 assembler statements per LOC from Table 11.2) is only 40 ppm. The normalization to assembly-equivalent statements compensates for the greater functionality that can be delivered in the same number of statements in the higher-level language, but one defect is still just one defect.

Recently, I was involved in a software group discussion about defect densities and Kodak's six-sigma goal for product quality. Everyone seemed to understand that the six-sigma quality level was an extremely ambitious long-term goal. When I asked the group what defect level we were at now, the room fell silent. This loaded question pointed out the need for careful measurements to establish a baseline of defect densities in current products, so that progress toward six sigma (or any other goal) can be tracked.

Lines of Code versus Application Functionality

Whether lines of code is a useful measure of anything at all is a source of religious argument in the software community. Two problems with line-of-code measures are a lack of standardized definitions and counting methods, and the inability to meaningfully compare statements written in different programming languages. Some standard source code counting rules can be found in Appendix A of *Applied Software Measurement* [Jones, 1991], and in IEEE Std. 1045, "IEEE Standard for Software Productivity Metrics."

There is an increasing movement toward the use of functional metrics, which attempt to quantify the functionality delivered to a user by an application, rather than simply counting the source statements. In the best-known functional metric counting scheme, the number of function points contained in an application is derived from the number of input types, output types, file types, inquiry types, and external interfaces in the application [Dreger, 1989]. Functional metrics often can be estimated early in a development project from the requirements specifications and screen layouts.

Functional metrics themselves have some shortcomings. Counting function points accurately and consistently requires training and practice. While function points work well for many types of management information systems software, they are not as easily applied to real-time systems, embedded software, libraries, or software components that do not contain a user interface. From the relatively straightforward scheme proposed by Allan Albrecht of IBM in 1979, the methods for counting function points have evolved to a 250-page *Function Point Counting Practices Manual,* published by the International Function Point Users Group (see Appendix B for contact information).

Functional metrics are appealing from the perspective that the quantity of useful functionality contained in an application is an indication of the value provided to the customer. They also eliminate the problems that can arise from comparing line of code measures from programs written in different languages. What the user perceives is functionality, and he does not care what programming language was used. Unfortunately, the complexity of the function point counting rules and the difficulty of automating the counting process inhibit the widespread use of function points. Capers Jones, one of the most fervent advocates of functional metrics, has proposed a somewhat simpler function point counting scheme [Jones, 1991].

One of our small software groups at Kodak attempted to learn to count function points on three separate occasions and with some training, but we found it difficult to get consistent point totals on the kinds of applications developed by the group. We spent a lot of time discussing the assumptions and conventions we were using, in an attempt to converge toward the same counts on some small applications. Careful mastery of the counting rules and agreement on local conventions for specialized cases (such as adapting the rules for reports to apply to graphical plots) are necessary. One Kodak organization that has achieved very good results from function point counts has a few specialists who do the counting on many applications.

The majority of the existing software quality literature expresses data in terms of lines of code, usually loosely defined as something like "number of noncomment source statements." If you are going to count lines of code, you must use consistent, precise definitions. An effective approach is to employ source code analysis tools, using the count of logical source statements provided by the tool as your lines-of-code value. This will avoid inconsistencies in the way different developers count their code, and it also reduces the impact of coding style on the LOC counts obtained.

Jones has published factors that can be used to relate the number of noncomment source statements to the number of function points for programs written in many languages, as illustrated in the rightmost column in Table 11.2 [Jones, 1991]. According to this table, a program written in assembly language requires about 320 source statements to deliver one function point. Higher-level languages require fewer source statements to encode one function point. The fewer the number of statements needed to deliver a function point, the higher the language level.

Radical differences in programming style can influence the relationships between lines of code and function points. For example, a series of five function calls might be coded as five separate statements, or as a single complex statement having five nested function calls. The impacts of style and variable counting methods can be reduced by using coding standards, source code reformatting tools, and automated tools to perform the line-of-code counts in standard ways.

Jones describes a process called "backfiring" that can be used to estimate the number of function points in an existing application, by applying the factors in Table 11.2 and adjustment factors for problem, data, and code complexity to the source statement count [Jones, 1991]. Backfiring provides a way to normalize programs written in different languages to permit comparisons, provided the programs are relatively large (several thousand source statements). Because of this relationship between LOC and function points, it is generally appropriate to discuss defect densities for programs of comparable complexity written in the same language in terms of LOC counts.

Many software errors originate well before the coding stage, and code quality is not the only determinant of application quality. Therefore, defect metrics based solely on lines of source code can only approximately measure anything pertaining to software quality. Nonetheless, source code is a major deliverable from a software development process. As such, counting the defects contained in a source program is as valid as counting defects in any other deliverable document, provided that you normalize LOC counts for differences in programming language (for example, by using assembly-equivalent lines of code) and coding style.

How Good Is Good Enough?

The programs I have written over the years, however good they may be, have never come anywhere near the six-sigma standard. Can they? Should they? Must they? Many customers are not willing to pay for six-sigma quality, and not all software has to achieve that extraordinary quality level. Sometimes software just has to be "good enough," not perfect. The acceptable quality level for a given application should be based on the risk associated with a failure of the application.

The risk attributable to any possible fault depends on both the impact and the probability of a failure caused by that fault. For individual productivity software, such as a word processor, a severe failure might result in the loss of a few hours' worth of typing. For business software, substantial financial losses can be the consequence of a particularly egregious bug. And one failure in some medical or aircraft flight control software might result in people dying and gigantic lawsuits. The highest-risk systems need to use every available method to prevent and eradicate defects before delivery.

Rather than setting an arbitrary defect objective like six sigma, you should determine the error level that is acceptable to your customers. If asked, customers will usually say that no defects should be permitted. Realistically, though, customers can help you identify the higher-risk portions of the system. In our research software groups at Kodak, we sometimes allocate quality control resources based on a simple risk analysis.

For a real-time laboratory process control application, we assessed the risk in terms of how much time or precious chemicals could be lost if a failure took place in certain software components. We also looked at the risk associated with getting the wrong experimental result because, say, the temperature control module did not operate correctly. Even a rudimentary risk analysis will let you allocate limited testing and inspection time to the most critical modules, so you can strive for an appropriate quality level for each program.

Analyzing software quality in terms of defects per assembly-equivalent source code size addresses only the internal view of quality, that visible to the developers. It does not take into account the vitally important external quality factors visible to the customer, such as meeting user needs, usability, and delivering "customer delight." Nor are other internal attributes like maintainability and portability addressed by the simple defect density count. Your quality improvement efforts should focus on the dimensions of software quality that are most critical in your own environment. This may vary from one project to the next, which is why it is so important to negotiate the appropriate balance of quality attributes with the customers during the requirements phase, as was discussed in Chapter 6.

To approach anything like six-sigma quality, the defect-detection processes you use must have a very high success rate or yield. You can't know how efficient your testing and inspection processes are unless you measure how many bugs are found by these quality control activities, and how many are found after the product is released to customers. These pieces of data can be combined to calculate the efficiency of your quality practices, as shown in Fig. 11.2. The analysis in Fig. 11.2 assumes that no additional faults are introduced by bad fixes when performing rework following inspection and testing, although they almost always are. It also assumes that all remaining defects in the delivered product are eventually discovered by users, although some may never by found by anyone. Before you estimate the total number of defects that were shipped in the product, track the data for customer bug reports until the rate of new bug discovery approaches zero.

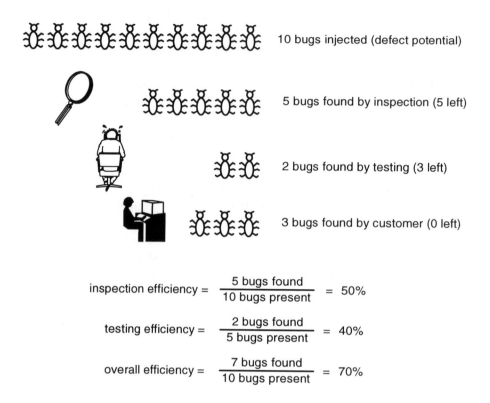

Figure 11.2: Example of how to calculate defect detection efficiencies.

An empirical way to estimate the yield of any single defect removal practice is to seed a known number of artificial but representative errors into a software work product, so you can see what fraction of the seeded errors are found by your quality control filters. Suppose you seeded ten typical errors into a source code module before it underwent unit testing. The unit testing process found four of the seeded bugs and six actual bugs. If you assume the likelihood of finding the real bugs is the same as that of finding the seeded ones (40 percent), you can estimate that your program still contains about nine real bugs:

$$6 \text{ real bugs found } \times \frac{10 \text{ total seeded bugs}}{4 \text{ seeded bugs found}} = 15 \text{ total real bugs}$$

$$15 \text{ total real bugs} - 6 \text{ real bugs found} = 9 \text{ real bugs remaining}$$

The error seeding technique is still somewhat experimental, so it should be used with caution. If you decide to try this experiment, don't forget to remove any undetected seeded bugs before you ship the product!

So, how can you achieve six-sigma quality in software? There are only two knobs to turn: (1) Increase the effectiveness of the various defect detection methods you use, and (2) reduce the defect potential by injecting fewer in the first place. Table 11.4 illustrates the impact of adjusting both of these factors.

Table 11.4.
Reaching Six-Sigma Quality in a C Program.

Defect Potential, Defects/KLOC	Assembly-Equivalent PPM	Inspection Efficiency, %	Testing Efficiency, %	Cumulative Efficiency, %	Final Defect PPM
50	20,000	80	80	96.00	800
50	20,000	99	98	99.98	4
10	4,000	80	80	96.00	160
10	4,000	97	97	99.91	3.6

Assume a representative defect potential of fifty errors per KLOC of C source code, or 20,000 ppm in assembly-equivalent terms (recalling the factor of 2.5 assembler instructions per C source statement from Table 11.2). Using representative numbers for highly effective inspection and multistage testing practices as quality control filters, line one of Table 11.4 shows that we can get a cumulative defect removal effectiveness of 96 percent, resulting in 800 ppm of defects in the final product. This level represents high-quality software by today's standards. To approach six-sigma quality at this same defect potential of fifty per thousand lines of code, we would need to raise our inspection efficiency to 99 percent and our testing yield to 98 percent, getting us down to 4 ppm (other combinations will work, also). That is quite a quality control leap from the current yield levels for these techniques.

What if we could reduce the number of errors made during development by a factor of five, so we start with a defect potential of only 4,000 ppm? The current inspection and testing efficiencies of 80 percent each reduce the residual defects in the final product to only 160 ppm; six sigma could be attained if both inspection and testing reached yields of 97 percent. This is a little more feasible, but it still requires extremely effective methods for finding errors. These calculations assume that no additional errors are introduced through bad fixes, a totally invalid assumption in today's software world. Clearly, reaching six-sigma quality in software is not a trivial task.

The message is that we need to work on improving both defect prevention and defect detection if we want to substantially improve the quality of our software, whether measured in terms of defects per million assembly-equivalent source statements or by more direct measures of customer satisfaction. It isn't enough to throw the code over the wall to the testing department and have the testers clean it up. Every software engineer is responsible for controlling the defects injected into his or her work products.

An Assault on Defects

One way to think about software quality is to consider that each step in the software development process is the customer of the previous step. This notion is adapted from the manufacturing concept of Next Operation as Customer. For example, products created during requirements analysis become raw materials for design. In that pairing, the analysis step is the supplier, and the design process is the customer. This reasoning is true for any software development life cycle—waterfall, spiral, incremental development, and others—since all involve the tasks of analysis, design, implementation, and testing.

The model in Fig. 11.3 depicts some customer/supplier relationships of the software development process. The key concept is that the product quality that can be attained in any transformational process is limited by the quality of the raw materials supplied to it. No matter how talented the designer, he cannot do a quality job if the requirements specification provided to him contains errors. Similarly, the quality of the code written cannot exceed the quality of the design, although it can certainly fall short if new errors are introduced during coding. Feedback loops between pairs of supplier and customer processes help catch some of the errors, but many slip through unnoticed. This customer/supplier view shows that we must adopt practices that will assure the quality of the deliverables produced at each step in the development cycle, not just at the end of the project.

Our Kodak software groups have several selfish reasons for emphasizing quality in our products. First, our customers are fellow employees, right down the hall from us. Quality software that meets user needs is good for the company and good for our personal relationships with these people. Second, we have to support our products for the rest of their (and, it seems, our) lives. Since most of us would rather do new development work than maintenance, it is in our own best interest to build applications correctly the first time. Reducing maintenance burdens through improved initial quality and robust, maintainable designs should appeal to every development group that also supports its applications. Even if your intent is to grow a new application by successive iterations or increments, quality in the early increments will facilitate changes on subsequent cycles.

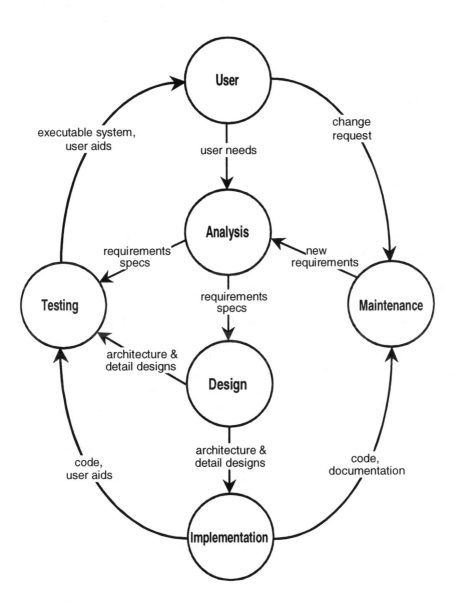

Figure 11.3: A customer/supplier process model for software.

Software defects can be introduced at any stage of the life cycle, so quality filters to remove them must be effectively applied at every stage. Jones identified several major root causes for low software quality in delivered products, including these [Jones, 1994]:

- inadequate use of reviews and inspections to find defects

- insufficient or careless testing

- lack of quality measurements

- lack of understanding by management that quality is on the critical path to user satisfaction, time to market, and market share

- excessive schedule pressure, leading to unwise shortcuts in quality control techniques

- unstable and ambiguous user requirements

To attack these causes and others that affected our Kodak software teams, we implemented a set of practices that have significantly improved the quality of our delivered software systems. One quality metric we use is the fraction of our total work effort that is devoted to correcting defects in delivered systems. This is an indirect measure, in that we are not specifically counting bugs. However, it is highly practical, since it directly indicates how much time we are spending on post-release rework. (You should also quantify internal rework, another important part of the cost of quality). The reduction in maintenance effort has freed up more time for new development activities. It also provides the psychological benefit of not being interrupted so frequently by those pesky bug reports from our customers.

The five major initiatives that have had the greatest impact on the quality of our software are

1. extensive customer involvement in preparing excellent requirements specifications (discussed in Chapter 5)

2. explicitly assigning SQA responsibilities to project team members

3. conducting inspections and reviews of all types of software work products (see Chapter 12)

4. application of structured unit and system testing methods (see Chapter 13)

5. use of a combined change management, defect tracking, and user feedback system (see Chapter 15)

I cannot claim that every member on all of our teams applies all of these practices on every project. However, we have always obtained better results when we followed these approaches than when we did not.

Explicit SQA Responsibilities

Software quality does not happen by accident. Specific activities must be carried out during development, and specific individuals must be responsible for these activities. In many small teams, identifying, assigning, and fulfilling these responsibilities is not done in a conscious way, resulting in quality gaps.

Software engineers are in the business of *making* things, ultimately building a piece of application software that performs certain functions. In contrast, quality control experts are in the business of *breaking* things. Their objective is to find as many errors as possible in a piece of code or a design document. The attitudes and behaviors of makers are different from those of breakers, so there is a good chance that an individual will not excel in both kinds of activities.

This dichotomy is particularly significant when it comes to testing your own work products. The maker part of your brain wants desperately for the product to be error-free, while the breaker part fiendishly wants to uncover the bugs it knows are lurking in there. Rather than collapse under the strain of this subconscious battle, programmers often skimp on testing, confidently assuming that their brilliant programming skills have come through once again. For this reason, it is better to have someone else test your code. Glenford Myers said it well:

> ... It is extremely difficult, after a programmer has been constructive while designing and coding a program, to suddenly, overnight, change his or her perspective and attempt to form a completely destructive frame of mind toward the program. . . . Hence most programmers cannot effectively test their own programs because they cannot bring themselves to form the necessary mental attitude: the attitude of wanting to expose errors [Myers, 1979].

Large companies set up separate testing departments for just this reason. In some cases, independent verification and validation groups are used to provide objective testing by highly skilled specialists. But small software groups have fewer degrees of freedom and have to be more creative in addressing their quality control demands. In the Kodak Research Laboratories, we wanted to provide some of this outside perspective to our quality activities, within the constraints of a small team, and so we identified and carried out a plan for SQA responsibility, which evolved through three stages.

In Stage 1, all developers were responsible for the quality of their own products. This default approach is limited by individual attitudes, knowledge, skills, and priorities. None of us had received any formal training in software quality practices, and the outcome was informal development methods, variable quality, and unpredictable results.

Our dissatisfaction with this state led to Stage 2, in which we assigned an SQA coordinator to each project. This was simply another group member charged with certain quality activities on that project, in addition to his own development responsibilities on another project. The SQA coordinator was expected to write system test plans from the functional requirements and to conduct reviews of work products. Another group member, or someone from a different software group, also was assigned to each project to provide a fresh perspective during reviews. The SQA coordinator was not expected to spend more than five to ten percent of his time on the project.

This second-stage approach resulted in improved quality only when the SQA coordinator actually did his part. Unfortunately, it was too easy for SQA coordinators to let the pressures of their own development work override their commitment to the quality of someone else's project. The team leader sometimes had trouble convincing engineer A that it was okay to spend time working on quality tasks for engineer B's project, because engineer C would be helping with those same quality issues on A's project. Another weakness of this strategy was that it still relied on each team member to be proficient enough in testing, inspection, and other quality practices to be an effective SQA coordinator. While we did get some training and experience in these areas, there was still a wide range of capability among the team members.

In Stage 3, in order to circumvent these limitations of the SQA coordinator approach, we designated one group member to take SQA responsibility for multiple projects. This approach functioned more like having an independent QA department, but on a very small scale, and proved to be a superior solution as the group grew in size from five members to ten and beyond. The result was more consistent practices across projects, as one member of the group acquired strong SQA skills and experience that could be used to coach the others in testing, inspection, and quality planning.

You'll have to judge at what point your team is ready to have someone specialize in software quality engineering, and what ratio of development engineers to quality engineers is appropriate to meet the quality demands of your customers. A group size of eight to ten provides a critical mass that can support some specialization of software skills. The number of developers a software quality engineer can support depends on the way quality activities are apportioned among them.

Our Kodak group has begun writing software quality assurance and test plans according to IEEE standards for each project in the group. IEEE Std. 730 provides guidance on software quality assurance plans (SQAP), while IEEE Std. 829 guides our writing of software test documentation. These plans help us first to identify and document the quality tasks that should be carried out on each project, and then to allocate responsibilities to individuals and set schedules. By itemizing the quality activities scheduled for each project, we assure that they are less likely to fall between the cracks and be overlooked by busy engineers. A group that does not routinely create written SQA or test plans does not yet have a software engineering culture. In such an environment, it is no wonder that testing takes longer than the developers anticipated, and that there are still many bugs left in the code.

Table 11.5 shows how we apportion several quality tasks. Individual developers are responsible for unit testing, creating the requirements traceability matrix, and informing the quality engineer when work products are ready for review. The quality engineer writes the project SQA and test plans, as well as conducting both formal and informal reviews of work products. For those projects on which he has testing responsibilities, the quality engineer also leads the system testing effort, which may involve writing test cases based on the requirements, building or acquiring automated test driver tools, and conducting formal system testing. In addition, he is responsible for keeping metrics of defects found and recommending process improvements based on defect trends.

Table 11.5.
Allocating Software Quality Responsibilities.

Player	Roles
Developer	• Perform unit testing • Complete the requirements traceability matrix • Tell quality engineer when a product is ready for inspection
Quality Engineer	• Write project SQA plan • Write project test plans • Conduct inspections and reviews • Perform system testing activities • Record metrics on defects found • Recommend process improvements

You may choose to allocate responsibilities in some different way. However you split them up, make sure the expectations are explicit, so that people know the aspects of software quality for which they are accountable. The assignment of responsibilities and a schedule for executing them becomes part of the project's SQAP. The project manager is responsible for tracking progress on these QA activities, to ensure they are being performed as planned.

While none of our quality task allocation schemes was perfect, they all helped improve our ability to detect errors in software work products. By identifying specific individuals as responsible for performing certain quality practices, the expectation of a personal commitment to software quality becomes more ingrained in the group's culture.

Why Do We Think Quality Practices Pay Off?

Early in 1990, one of our Kodak software groups launched a work effort metrics program (discussed further in Chapter 17). Since then, we have recorded all of the time devoted by team members on every software project we have worked on. Work effort is classified into one of six development and four maintenance phases. Our group's accumulated post-release defect correction effort over a span of five years is shown in Fig. 11.4. The raw percentage of our group's total software project effort that was devoted to fixing bugs found in operation is shown for each calendar quarter. The running average of data from the previous four quarters, which damps out oscillations in the quarterly data and reveals the long-term trend, is also shown.

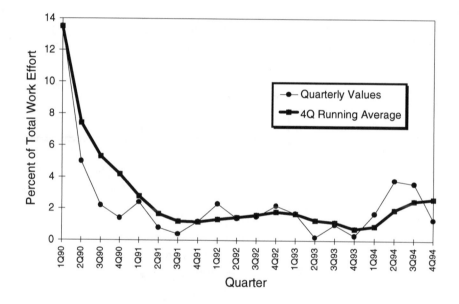

Figure 11.4: Trends in defect-correction work effort over five years.

Our data reveals a steady decline in the fraction of work effort required for post-release defect correction once we began the quality improvement program. From an initial level of 13.5 percent of our total work time, defect correction effort has declined to a steady state in which only about 2 percent of our time is spent fixing errors in released software. Short-term rises in the defect correction effort usually coincided with the initial release of new products, indicating that we still must improve our defect detection practices prior to delivery.

The metrics data helps us pinpoint the applications on which we spend most of our maintenance time, so that we can focus improvement activities for the greatest leverage. The whole team discusses our metrics data on a quarterly basis, so as to identify trends and determine where to better allocate the time spent in various work areas. If certain projects are requiring unexpected quantities of bug-fixing time, we try to understand why and see what we can do about it.

The data in Fig. 11.4 suggests that the quality of our products has improved as a result of our software quality practices. Better quality translates to higher productivity, too. Every hour we do not spend fixing an existing program is an hour we can spend writing something new.

Summary

- ✔ Quality is the top priority; long-term productivity is a natural consequence of high quality at all stages of the software development life cycle.

- ✔ A software engineering culture fosters a commitment to finding defects as early as possible, and a desire to learn from the pattern of defects found to reduce their future occurrence.

- ✔ To maximize quality, apply improved processes that reduce the number of defects injected during development, and use methods that find bugs as efficiently and early as possible.

- ✔ Think of each step in the software development process as the customer of the preceding step. The quality that is potentially achievable at any stage of the development life cycle is limited by the quality of the inputs supplied to that step.

- ✔ The quality assurance and quality control tasks that are to be carried out on a software project should be explicitly planned and allocated to individuals on the project team.

- ✔ Defect densities in source code provide only part of the software quality picture. Do not overlook the importance of quality characteristics that are not related to defects per line of code, including customer acceptance, usability, portability, maintainability, and so on.

Culture Builders and Killers

Culture Builder: If other software groups in your company ask your team to adopt their software for eternal maintenance, do not accept it unless it meets your group's written standards for testing and documentation. Resist the pressure to be treated as a dumping ground for user-written or other orphan software. Share your quality practices with other programmers to help them attain your level of quality software development.

Culture Builder: Do not start a quality improvement initiative by aiming for a stratospheric quality goal like six sigma at some long-distant future date. Instead, strive to achieve a defect density that is one-half your current level in a shorter time period, such as twelve months. This is more realistically achievable and indicates that your objective is a measurable and sustained improvement in quality. Setting a quantitative goal indicates the need for data collection and for analyzing the effectiveness of your current quality control practices.

Culture Builder: If a particular module is causing lots of problems during integration, rebuild it. While it is difficult to admit that a program needs to be rewritten, this is a sound investment. There is no reason to believe that extensive patching will make it more reliable after it has been delivered to the customer. Don't force your developers to struggle with a poor piece of code that keeps breaking as every new component is integrated. That would send a message that your quality credo is, "We'll get it right—eventually."

Culture Killer: Give your engineers and secretaries individual office cubicles and their own workstations, but double up the testers. Save costs by having them use shared workstations located in a common area. The testers should be able to adjust their schedules to obtain adequate access to the public workstations. Besides, if you can keep them away from the keyboard, they won't be able to hold up the project by continually reporting what they think are bugs and what you think are either features or user errors. Testers should always be subordinate to developers in the organization's cultural pecking order.

Culture Killer: Exhort your team to apply good quality practices but not to let quality activities interfere with their productivity or schedules. Quality is all well and good, but the main thing is shipping something—anything—on the scheduled date.

Culture Killer: Give your project managers authority to override the QA department's recommendation to delay release because they think the product is still unstable. Those QA guys won't get off your back unless they think every single bug has been eliminated. Half of their tests are things no real user would ever try to do anyway.

References and Further Reading

Carnegie Mellon University/Software Engineering Institute. *The Capability Maturity Model: Guidelines for Improving the Software Process.* Reading, Mass.: Addison-Wesley, 1995.

The SEI's definition of software quality assurance as an auditing and oversight function is quite different from the definition of SQA used in most software organizations.

Crosby, Philip B. *Quality Is Free.* New York: McGraw-Hill, 1979.

Crosby's analysis of the cost of quality is highly relevant to software development. He provides suggestions about how to measure the cost of quality, and
how to insert a quality improvement program into an organizational culture.
Crosby contends that investing in quality practices to avoid doing things
wrong, doing them over, or working on the wrong problem will have a direct
positive impact on any business's bottom line.

 Deutsch, Michael S., and Ronald R. Willis. *Software Quality Engineering.*
Englewood Cliffs, N.J.: Prentice-Hall, 1988.

This is a practical text that focuses on how to engineer in quality, and how to
use verification and validation techniques to review out defects and test out
errors. It provides an excellent presentation of the major issues around engineering quality into software, with a high density of information and many
good ideas explained clearly.

Dreger, J. Brian. *Function Point Analysis.* Englewood Cliffs, N.J.: Prentice-
Hall, 1989.

Dreger describes the method for counting the function points in an application. A lengthy exercise presents a requirements definition report from a
planned system as the subject of a function point count.

 Glass, Robert L. *Building Quality Software.* Englewood Cliffs, N.J.: Prentice-
Hall, 1992.

Glass provides a good overview of technical and management factors and
practices in software quality throughout the development life cycle. This book
is easy to read, and it contains many valuable entry points into the software
quality literature.

Humphrey, Watts S. *A Discipline for Software Engineering.* Reading, Mass.:
Addison-Wesley, 1995.

Humphrey describes the Personal Software Process, which brings a new level
of systematic and analytical behavior to the writing of individual programs.

———. *Managing the Software Process.* Reading, Mass.: Addison-Wesley,
1989.

While Humphrey's focus is primarily on process maturity, this book includes
several insightful chapters on software quality assurance. Chapter 8 presents
an overview of SQA, Chapter 10 and Appendix C cover inspections, and
Chapter 11 addresses testing. Chapter 16 discusses managing and quantifying
software quality, a key process area of Level 4 (Managed) of the SEI Capability
Maturity Model.

Jones, Capers. *Applied Software Measurement.* New York: McGraw-Hill, 1991.

> Jones includes a large chapter on measuring software quality and user satisfaction, as well as an extensive section on U.S. averages for software quality and productivity, based on partial historical data derived from about 4,000 software projects developed between 1950 and 1990.

———. *Assessment and Control of Software Risks.* Englewood Cliffs, N.J.: Yourdon Press/Prentice-Hall, 1994.

> Chapters 35 and 51 deal with the software risk factors of inadequate tools and methods for quality assurance and low quality in delivered products.

McConnell, Steve. *Code Complete.* Redmond, Wash.: Microsoft Press, 1993.

> McConnell includes several highly practical and readable chapters (23 through 26) on software quality practices that are useful for individual programmers.

Myers, Glenford J. *The Art of Software Testing.* New York: John Wiley & Sons, 1979.

> This classic treatise also explores some human aspects of software testing.

Perry, William E. *Quality Assurance for Information Systems: Methods, Tools, and Techniques.* Wellesley, Mass.: QED Information Sciences, 1991.

> Perry's treatise contains over 800 pages of information on structuring the QA function: allocating QA time; performing reviews; verification, validation, and testing; improving maintenance; metrics and quality attributes; and so on. This is a useful resource if you want to set up a QA function, but it's not a general technical testing or inspection book.

Weinberg, Gerald M. *Quality Software Management, Volume 1: Systems Thinking.* New York: Dorset House Publishing, 1992.

> Section IV, "Fault Patterns," addresses many aspects of thinking about software errors, the relationships between faults and failures, and issues around fault resolution practices in a software organization.

Yourdon, Edward, ed. *American Programmer.* Arlington, Mass.: Cutter Information Corp., published monthly.

> Periodically, an entire issue is devoted to topics of software quality assurance or testing. For QA topics, see the November 1990, February 1992, June 1993, and October 1995 issues. For testing, see the April 1991 and April 1994 issues.

Chapter 12

Improving Quality by Software Inspection

The bitterness of poor quality remains long after the sweetness of meeting the schedule has been forgotten.

—Anonymous

I began programming computers in college using punched cards on an IBM 360. With just a couple of compilation cycles per day, there was plenty of time to study the listings and look for those elusive bugs. Now, we write programs at the keyboard and compile them as frequently as we like. We rarely print out complete listings for entire applications, let alone get people together to examine listings line-by-line on a bug hunt. Ironically, this very process, officially termed software inspection (or, more generally, peer review), is one of the most effective methods available for identifying errors in a program. So much for progress.

Every time I actually sit down and read through an entire program listing, I find ways it can be improved: redundant logic, incorrect Boolean tests, comments that don't match the code, and many other errors that make me glad I took the time to look. Software inspection is a proven technique for reducing the number of defects in a program before it goes out the door. If you work in an organization of two or more people, some kind of peer review activity should be a part of your standard software development process. If you work alone, at least read the code.

A variety of related manual bug-detection activities go by such names as inspection, formal inspection, Fagan inspection, walkthrough, peer review, and formal technical review. In the most general sense, these are all ways in which someone other than the creator of a software work product examines the product with the specific intent of finding errors in it. These are in-process reviews, as opposed to manufacturing style inspections, which examine completed items for

189

defects. Don't confuse inspections with management reviews held at the end of a development phase, which are not defect detection activities.

Inspections and Culture

Instilling inspections into an organization's culture can be a challenge. You need to overcome the protectionistic tendencies of some people to shield their work from review by others. You may have to defuse the fear that inspection data might be used against the producer in some way. New participants in code reviews sometimes do not see the benefits. Often, this is because they test their code thoroughly before submitting it for review, which will reduce the value of the review (many of the original errors will already have been removed). To help get your team members on board, provide training in inspections so the activity is as effective as possible.

Submitting one's work for peer review is a step on the path to egoless programming, a concept based on the premise that we tend to be blind to errors in our own work because we perceive our value as people to be linked to the quality of our work [Weinberg, 1971]. If we can weaken that link, we become more willing to seek the opinions of others regarding how the products we create can be improved. It's impossible to be completely egoless, since we are proud of the good work we do, and therefore we feel badly if flaws in it are pointed out by others. However, if you really would prefer to have a peer, rather than a customer, find a defect, you have to be receptive to constructive criticism from your associates, through a healthy peer review process.

It is possible to undermine a group's culture by abusing the review process. A colleague once worked at a company where code reviews were used in an attempt by a misguided manager to prove that a particular individual was responsible for a project's problems. When the project fell behind schedule, this manager announced that "regular code reviews would be held," with himself as one of the reviewers. The review of my colleague's program was essentially an inquisition; although no actual bugs were found, the manager claimed that this program was responsible for the project's problems. Later on, the review policy was changed so that only programmers who were announced to be "incompetent" had to have their code reviewed. Reviews were performed not as a quality-oriented development activity but as a punitive demonstration of a programmer's inability to get a program running. Clearly, this behavior is the antithesis of a software engineering culture.

Benefits of Inspections

Figure 12.1 illustrates the trend in the cost of correcting a bug as a function of the stage in the life cycle in which it is found [Boehm, 1981]. While exact numbers from different sources vary, this profile is typical. One implication of this data from Boehm is that we should not be inspecting only source code, but also any software artifact that people can read: requirements specifications, design models, test plans, system documentation, project plans, and user aids are all candidates. Inspection is one of the few testing techniques available for software work products other than code.

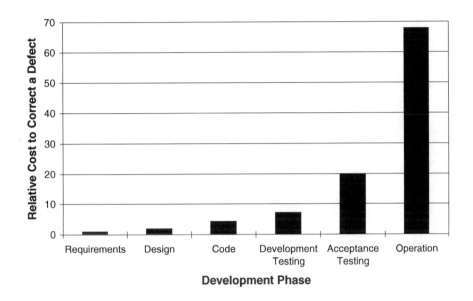

Figure 12.1: Increase in the cost of fixing bugs throughout the life cycle [Boehm, 1981].

The greatest leverage from the time spent on software inspections comes from examining requirements and design documents, early in the life cycle. If you rely solely on testing to find defects, those that slip into your product design early will stay in there a long time, spawning related errors and growing into an invasive tumor so entwined with the healthy parts of the system that radical surgery may be needed late in the development cycle. Inspections shorten product delivery time by reducing the time spent in the integration and system test/debug phases, since a cleaner product is passed into those late stage quality filters [Weller, 1993].

Incorporating inspections into your software engineering process is not free. Defect detection through inspections is part of the cost of quality, and a rigorous inspection process can consume 5 to 15 percent of the total project budget. However, many companies have learned that the results yielded by a good inspection process far outweigh the costs of performing them; see Table 12.1 for some examples. You can estimate dollar savings by multiplying the number of bugs found by inspection before the product is shipped times the approximate cost of fixing a bug that is found by one of your customers. While it is difficult to compute a precise anticipated return on investment for implementing inspections in a particular organization, the software literature contains many examples that justify this investment. The excuse "I don't have time to do inspections" simply does not hold water.

An organization functioning at a high process maturity level can use the data collected from inspections to improve its process further [Gilb, 1993]. Data from inspection summary reports can be used to identify the most common or most costly kinds of bugs, determine their root causes, and change how work is performed so as to prevent those types of errors. Inspection and test defect data can be used to plan test activities, estimate the number of bugs to be found at various test stages, and track and analyze project progress [Weller, 1994].

Team reviews provide a unique opportunity to see how other software engineers do things. Knowledge is effortlessly exchanged about programming language features, coding and commenting style, design notations, the application domain, and all the other aspects of the software development process. Inspections reinforce the cultural values of common practices and shared efforts to improve the quality of any product created by the team.

Table 12.1.
Benefits from Software Inspections.

Company	Cost Impact	Productivity Impact	Quality Impact	Reference
Aetna Insurance Company		25% increase in coding productivity	inspections found 82% of programming errors	[Humphrey, 1989]
AT&T Bell Laboratories	cost of finding errors reduced 10X by inspections	14% increase in productivity	10X improvement in quality	[Humphrey, 1989]
Bell Northern Research	avoided 33 hours of maintenance effort per defect found	inspections 2-4X faster than testing for finding defects	found 80% of all defects by inspection	[Ebenau, 1994]
Bull HN Information Systems		late stage testing period shortened because defects removed earlier by inspection	inspections found 70-75% of all defects	[Weller, 1993; Weller, 1994]
Hewlett-Packard	save $21.5 million per year; 10X return on investment	reduced time to market by 1.8 months		[Grady, 1994]
IBM		inspecting test documentation reduced unit testing time by 85%	inspection found 93% of all major defects detected over life cycle of one product	[Fagan, 1986]
Jet Propulsion Laboratory	$7.5 million savings from 300 inspections			[Ebenau, 1994]
Standard Bank	maintenance cost for inspected projects was 28X lower than for uninspected projects			[Gilb, 1993]

Inspections and testing tend to reveal different kinds of errors. Table 12.2 shows some common types of programming problems and techniques that are effective for detecting them. The combination of formal inspections and systematic, multistage testing provides a powerful tool for creating defect-free programs.

Jones reported on the impact of four quality methods, singly and in combination, on defect removal efficiencies [Jones, 1991]. The four methods are: formal design inspections; formal code inspections; formal testing by trained specialists; and use of a formal, professionally staffed, quality assurance group. If none of these methods is used, the defect-removal efficiency ranges from 30 to 50 percent, with a median of 40 percent. Not very comforting: We are shipping six out of every ten bugs that were injected into the product. If all of these quality techniques are employed, the defect-removal efficiency ranges from 95 to 99 percent. Design and code inspections were the most effective quality factors in this study. So, if you can't immediately apply *all* quality methods in your organization, start with those that can have the greatest impact: inspections of requirements and designs.

Table 12.2.
Errors Found by Code Inspection or Testing.

Error Type	Inspection	Testing
Badly structured code	x	
Boundary value errors	x	x
Excessive code complexity	x	
Failure to meet requirements		x
Module interface errors	x	
Performance problems	x	x
Unreachable code	x	
Unrequired functionality present	x	
Usability problems		x

Inspections are more efficient than testing because when you find an error by looking at the code, you know exactly where the problem lies. Testing, on the other hand, reveals the presence of errors indirectly, through a program failure or an unexpected result. Now that you know something is wrong, you still have to hunt through the code to find the underlying fault (or faults). A lot of debugging time is spent pinpointing the exact cause of a program failure. Inspections let you look right at the sickness, not at its symptoms. You can also find multiple defects during an inspection, whereas otherwise they might be revealed one at a time through a lengthy test-fix-compile-test sequence.

If you don't have time to inspect every work product, select items to be inspected on the basis of risk. First, examine the items that can cause the most damage if undiscovered bugs remain. You should inspect 100 percent of your requirements specifications, because an error there causes many problems down the road. Consider inspecting 75 percent of designs, 50 percent of code (but 100 percent of the code in reusable components or high-risk sections of an application), and 50 to 75 percent of test documentation.

Inspections, Walkthroughs, and Reviews

Michael Fagan developed the formal software inspection process at IBM in the mid-1970s, hence the term "Fagan inspection" [Fagan, 1976]. This process is the most formal of the various peer review activities, and is arguably the most effective at locating errors. To qualify as a true formal software inspection, the activity follows a specified process and the participants play well-defined roles with inspectors receiving formal training in how to perform effective inspections [Ebenau, 1994]. The typical formal inspection process is described below.

An inspection team consists of three to seven members and includes several specific roles in addition to the inspector. The *moderator* schedules and controls inspection meetings, reports inspection results, and follows up on rework issues. Moderators should be trained in how to conduct inspections, as well as in the fine art of keeping participants with strong technical skills but low social skills from killing each other.

The *reader* describes the sections of the work product to the team as they proceed through the inspection meeting. The reader may paraphrase the product's functions and features, such as describing what a section of code is supposed to do, but the reader does not usually read the product verbatim. (It's hard *not* to read a requirements specification verbatim.) For example, during a code inspection, the reader describes the task performed by a block of several source statements, much as in-line block comments describe the function of the following statements.

The *recorder* classifies and records the defects and issues raised during the inspection meeting. (Note that the moderator might perform this role for a small inspection team.) This written record provides a list of action items for the author to use when performing rework. Summaries of defect types found also can be stored in an inspection metrics database, which is used to reveal trends in the number and types of defects being detected.

The *author* either created or maintains the work product being inspected. The author can answer questions about the product during the inspection and also looks for defects. The author cannot serve as moderator, reader, or recorder in a formal inspection.

Each *inspector* attempts to find errors in the product. All participants are acting as inspectors, in addition to any other responsibilities they have. Good people to consider as inspectors include: the person who created the predecessor specification for the work product being inspected (for example, the designer for a code inspection); people responsible for implementing, testing, supporting, or maintaining the product; a quality assurance representative to act as standards enforcer; or someone who is not involved in the project at all but who has the skill set and defect-detection abilities to inspect a work product of this type constructively.

Our research software groups at Kodak also require that our project champions (see Chapter 5) participate in inspections of requirements documents. Gaining customer, or even surrogate customer, participation in such inspections may not be possible in organizations that develop commercial applications or embedded systems software.

Did you notice that the word "manager" did not appear in the list of participants? The conventional wisdom is that managers do not belong at inspection meetings, as their presence may inhibit the process of finding defects. Also, the presence of managers may change the tenor of the meeting from a defect-detection inspection into a management review presentation. However, in many small software groups, the first-line supervisor is also a developer. Such a person probably creates products that ought to be inspected and is technically qualified to contribute to inspections of products written by others. If the culture permits (ours did), it is appropriate for these types of managers to participate in reviews. In fact, if the manager's work products are reviewed to the same standard as those created by anyone else, this can reinforce the cultural foundation for the inspection process and the personal commitment to quality by all members of the group.

The inspection process involves more than just a single meeting. To satisfy the criteria for a formal inspection, several distinct activities must be performed, as depicted in Fig. 12.2.

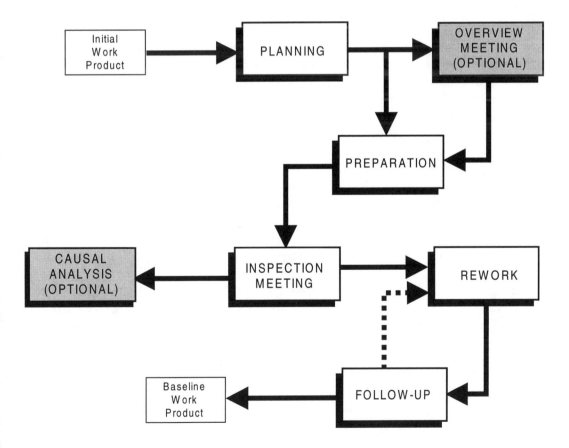

Figure 12.2: Stages in a formal software inspection process (adapted from [Ebenau, 1994]).

Planning. The moderator selects the inspection team, obtains the materials to be inspected from the author, and distributes them and any other relevant documents to the inspection team at least three days prior to the inspection meeting. Relevant documents include the specification for the product being inspected, pertinent standards and guidelines, an inspection checklist for the specific type of work product, and test cases for the work product. The responsibility for requesting an inspection may rest with the author, but the project management plan should indicate at what points inspections are to be held. Establish some entry criteria for assessing readiness of a product for inspection. For code, you might require that it compiles cleanly, all text has been spell-checked, and the source listings provided to inspectors include line numbers.

Overview Meeting. This meeting gives the author an opportunity to describe the important features of the product to the inspection team. It can be omitted if this information is already known by the other participants.

Preparation. Each participant individually examines the work products prior to the actual inspection meeting, noting any possible defects found or issues to be raised. Perhaps 75 percent of the errors found during inspections are identified during the preparation step [Humphrey, 1989]. The product being inspected should be verified against any predecessor (specification) documents to assess completeness and correctness. If you are using any standards that pertain to this class of work product, at least one inspector should look for deviations from the standard during preparation. Checklists of defects commonly found in this type of work product should be used during preparation to hunt for anticipated types of errors. Checklists for inspecting nearly a dozen types of software work products can be found in *Software Inspection Process* [Ebenau, 1994], but these should be tailored to meet your own needs.

Inspection Meeting. During this session, the moderator and reader lead the team through the work product. If the moderator determines at the beginning of the meeting that the participants are insufficiently prepared, the meeting should be rescheduled. During the discussion, all inspectors report potential defects and raise other issues from their individual preparation, which are documented on a form by the recorder. Do not try to solve problems during the meeting—just find them.

The synergy of the inspection meeting leads to the discovery of new defects, as one person's observation triggers related thoughts in the minds of the other participants. During preparation, an inspector might gloss over something that doesn't seem quite right but is not an obvious error either. The meeting provides an opportunity to drill down deeper into such issues, sometimes uncovering serious problems that no one fully recognized on his or her own.

The meeting should last no more than two hours. At its conclusion, the group agrees on one of several assessments of the product: accepted as is (I have never seen this happen); accepted with minor revision; major revision needed and a second inspection required; rebuild the product; or inspection not completed (schedule a follow-up meeting to complete the process).

Causal Analysis. An important long-term benefit of an inspection program is the insight it can provide into the kinds of defects being found and process changes you can make to prevent them. The causal analysis step, which seeks to understand the root cause of each defect found, provides that understanding. Causal analysis is one characteristic of a highly mature, quality-driven organization. You might conduct a causal analysis discussion right after the inspection meeting or as a separate event, although the inspection can be considered to be complete without this step.

Rework. The author is responsible for resolving all issues raised during the inspection. This does not necessarily mean making every change that was suggested, but the author must make an explicit decision about how to deal with each issue or defect recorded. Rework should not be attempted during the inspection meeting, although it is very easy to slip into problem-solving mode.

Follow-up. To verify that the necessary rework has been performed properly, the moderator is responsible for following up with the author. If many errors were found, or if a significant fraction (say, 10 percent) of the work product were modified, an additional inspection may be required. This is the final gate through which the product must pass for the inspection to be completed. Your group should define explicit exit criteria for completing each inspection, for example, requiring that all major defects are corrected and issues resolved, with uncorrected defects documented in a defect tracking system. Remember, the full inspection consists of the entire seven-stage process, not just the inspection meeting.

To some, the formal inspection process may seem to have excessive structure and too many steps. Are there simpler ways to conduct a hunt for bugs in a software product? The answer is, "Yes," but experience has shown formal inspections to be the most effective way for a group of people to find defects in a software work product. Between the one extreme of a formal Fagan inspection and the other extreme of no review process at all lies a whole spectrum of methods. In fact, most organizations probably practice one of the less rigid technical review processes, such as group reviews, walkthroughs, or peer deskchecks.

Walkthrough generally refers to a group activity in which the producer of the artifacts being discussed guides the review meeting. In code walkthroughs, the review team may simulate execution of the program line by line. Walkthroughs are less rigorous than either formal inspections or peer reviews in which the author plays a more passive role. They can easily turn into a presentation by the author, which misses the point of having others less familiar with the product attempt to understand it and find errors in it. Preparation is not normally required, and formal records need not be kept. Walkthroughs are usually less successful at detecting bugs than are more formal review methods, although they work well for reviews of maintenance projects, in which a number of changes are sprinkled throughout a large source listing.

Two review approaches that our Kodak software groups have found to be useful are *group reviews* and individual *peer deskchecks*. Our group reviews are not quite as rigorous as Fagan inspections, but they involve many of the same activi-

ties and participant roles, such as individual preparation and the use of a moderator and recorder. We generally bypass the overview meeting, causal analysis, and
follow-up steps (the author is responsible for follow-up).

This is sort of an "inspection-lite" method: It yields most of the benefits, without all the formality. Our experience has been that the formal inspection, in which
a reader paraphrases the product aloud, does reveal more errors than the "any
problems on the next page?" approach of our less formal group reviews. However,
these moderately formal group reviews have become well-established in our culture, and they add a lot of value.

Individual peer deskchecks are the least expensive review technique, because
only one person besides the author examines the material. This approach can be
effective if you have coworkers who are extremely good at finding defects on their
own. Peer deskchecks also provide a great learning opportunity for the person
doing the reviewing. A buddy system provides an effective technique for passing
the organization's culture to the next generation, as well as a terrific chance to
learn about program design and implementation by looking over an experienced
developer's shoulder. On the minus side, a peer deskcheck lacks the synergy of a
group review; the errors found will be those that the brain of the single reviewer is
best at spotting.

The moral? Strive for formal inspections, because you will find the most errors
this way, but do not abandon an attempt to instill reviews into your team if formal
inspections don't fly. Relax the rules a little and try some less stringent peer review
processes. They are still worth the effort.

Guiding Principles for Reviews and Inspections

Someone who submits a product for peer review should not be made to feel like
the victim of an intellectual assault. A healthy review mindset pits the entire
review team against the defects lurking in the product, not the reviewers against
the author. If you lay the right foundation for implementing an inspection or
review process in your group, team members will seek input from their peers as a
matter of course, to everyone's benefit. Every inspection or review process should
follow these basic guiding principles:

- Check egos at the door.

- Critique the products, not the producers.

- Do not try to fix problems during the inspection.

- Limit inspection meetings to a maximum of two hours.

- Avoid style issues unless they affect performance or understandability.

- Review early and often, formally and informally.

Let's look at these principles in detail.

Check egos at the door. It is not appealing to expose your carefully crafted products to a bloodthirsty mob of critical coworkers, and it's easy to become defensive about every prospective bug that is brought up in the meeting. A climate of mutual respect helps minimize this polarization. The group culture must actively encourage and reinforce the attitude of having peers, rather than customers, find the defects. Inspections can then be viewed as a nonthreatening way to achieve quality, rather than as an ego-destroying experience. The inspectors should also look for positive things to say about the product. An inspection is really a supportive activity, as the whole review team shares some responsibility for the quality of the product, even if only a single team member created it.

Critique the products, not the producers. The purpose of the inspection is not to point out how smart the inspector is compared to the author, but rather to make a software work product as error-free as possible. The moderator should promptly deal with any behavior that violates this principle. A polite reminder of inspection etiquette should be enough, but if inappropriate comments persist (which can happen if there are some social dynamics going on behind the scenes, such as competition, mutual antipathy, lack of respect, or catfighting) the moderator should terminate the meeting. Sit down with the transgressor and, if necessary, the manager, to straighten things out. If developers can expect to be personally criticized during a software inspection, they won't be willing to participate.

Do not try to fix problems during the inspection. It is easy to fall into the trap of interesting and interminable technical discussions about the best way to solve a particular problem. The moderator should squelch these tangents pretty quickly. The author is responsible for fixing defects after the inspection meeting, so just concentrate on identifying them during the meeting. The recorder can make note of issues that the team agrees should be pursued off-line. My general rule of thumb is that if a problem can be resolved with no more than 30 to 60 seconds of discussion, go ahead and resolve it. Otherwise, defer resolution until after the meeting. If the group concludes that a side discussion is sufficiently valuable, go ahead with it, but make sure that the material under review does get completely covered, perhaps in a subsequent meeting.

Limit inspection meetings to a maximum of two hours. Our attention spans are not conducive to meetings that run longer than two hours, and an inspection's effectiveness decays quickly after this duration. If the material was not completely covered in two hours, schedule a second inspection meeting to complete the task.

Figure 12.3 shows an example of the number of defects found per thousand lines of source code as a function of the rate of inspection. The shape of the curve described by this data is typical for inspections: Fewer defects are found when the material is inspected more rapidly, with the optimum balance around 150 to 200 lines of commented source code covered per hour. This guideline limits the quantity of material that can be covered in a single inspection to 300 to 400 lines of source code, or six to eight pages of design or text documents. The effective inspection rate depends on how complex and critical the work product is. Rapid inspection is appropriate for straightforward code in a domain well understood by the inspectors, but slow down when examining an unfamiliar, highly risky, or highly complex program or design document. Choosing the appropriate quantity of material to cover in a single two-hour inspection is part of the planning discussion between the moderator and the author [Ebenau, 1994].

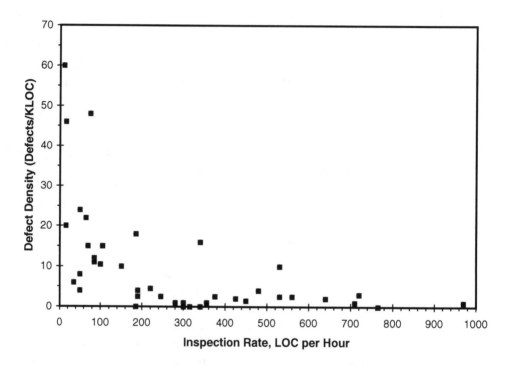

*Figure 12.3: Defects found versus inspection rate (data courtesy
of Kirk Bankes [Bankes, 1994]).*

Avoid style issues unless they affect performance or understandability. Everyone writes, designs, and codes a little differently. When a group begins to hold reviews, people raise style issues that are not about defects so much as about preferences. Style issues that affect clarity, readability, or maintainability (such as nesting function calls five levels deep), can certainly be raised. However, discussing whether code indentation should occur in two- or three-character increments should not come up as an inspection issue. The use of coding standards or source code reformatting tools can eliminate many distracting style issues from the inspections. An inspection record form containing mostly style issues hints that actual errors may have been missed. Don't spend time in the inspection discussing trivial typographical or grammatical errors, but pass these minor defects along to the author on a separate list or a marked-up copy of the document being reviewed.

Inspectors should be checking for completeness, correctness, clarity, and traceability to predecessor documents (code back to design, designs back to requirements). Focus on uncovering errors in logic, function, or implementation, not just on physical appearance. Avoid the temptation to impose your own coding style on other programmers while still sharing your best practices with the other inspection participants when appropriate. If coding standards are supposed to be followed, your quality assurance representative can verify whether a work product is in compliance with the standard.

Review early and often, formally and informally. Most of us are reluctant to share incomplete products with our peers for review. This is a mistake. If a product has a systematic shortcoming, you want to learn this when a small amount of code has been written, not in a completed 5,000 line program. So long as reviewers know what state the product is in, most people can examine it from an appropriate perspective.

You may want to establish your own conventions for how best to review various types of products. For example, during a code inspection, is it better to go through the source listing page by page or to trace down the hierarchical call tree as you encounter calls to functions within the program being inspected? You may have to experiment to settle on the best approach for your team, or simply agree to use multiple approaches.

Keeping Records

Record keeping is a major distinction between informal and formal review activities. There are three aspects to this task: recording defects during the inspection meeting; collecting data from multiple inspections; and analyzing the defect trends to assess inspection effectiveness and identify ways to improve your software development process to prevent common types of defects.

Figure 12.4 shows the technical review summary report form that our groups use; our issues recording form is shown in Fig. 12.5. These are typical of the forms depicted in many books that address software inspections [Freedman, 1990; Humphrey, 1989]. As inspectors raise issues and defects during the review meeting, the recorder enters them all on the issues list from Fig. 12.5. We distinguish "issues" (questions, points of style, or places where clarification is in order) from "defects," which are subdivided into five categories: missing, wrong, extra, performance, and usability. Each error or issue found is described in enough detail so that the author can refer to this list during the rework step and understand the point that was raised. We also note the development phase in which the underlying error was introduced (requirements, design, implementation, testing). This indicates the sources of process flaws we should try to correct.

In addition to defect class and origin, we rank errors according to a severity scale. Our scale (which we also use for errors found by testing) includes these four categories:

- cosmetic (screen text is misspelled)

- minor (nuisance or a work-around exists)

- severe (some functionality is not available)

- fatal (program will probably crash)

A simpler method is to classify defects either as major (some product failure is expected) or as minor (the product may not be perfect, but it will work). This simpler scheme is preferable if the recorder finds it hard to keep up with the discussion because he has to think a lot about defect classifications.

Inspection Identification: **Product Identification:**

Project: KARAT   Product: Code for the manifold housing
Inspection Number: CODE-3   coupler linkage and datalogging
Date: 11/4/95   system
Time: 10:00 AM   Developer: Fallacious Wiscenowskowicz
Location: Room 352   Customers: Gem exploration team

Inspection Team

                                               SIGNATURE

1. Author: F. Wiscenowskowicz___   _____

2. Moderator: Emerald Ize_____   _____

3. Reader: Sir Findsalot_____   _____

4. Recorder: Diamond Gym_____   _____

5. Inspector: Ruby Lipps_____   _____

6. Inspector: _____   _____

Product Disposition

ACCEPTED (*no further review*)   NOT ACCEPTED (*new review required*)
___   as is   ___   major revision necessary
___   with minor revision   ___   rebuild
                                        ___   inspection not completed

Pages Scheduled to be Inspected: _____   **Preparation Time:** _____ hours
Pages Actually Inspected: _____   **Inspection Time:**   _____ hours
Lines of Code: _____   **Rework Time:**   _____ hours

Figure 12.4: Inspection summary report.

The defect list from a single inspection should be distilled down to a summary report with a count of the defects in each category you are using for classification. This summary can be entered into an inspection database, if you are maintaining one. You should also prepare an inspection report for management. The management report contains information about the material that was inspected and the disposition of the product (accepted with minor revision, and so on). However, it should not include details about or counts of the actual defects found. This data is private to the author and the inspection team. The moderator is responsible for preparing these post-inspection reports. In a quality-oriented culture, the managers will want to see these inspection reports to better understand how the project is coming along and to know that the planned quality control activities are being performed.

Project: _____	**Type:**	Requirements, Design, Implementation, Testing
Inspection Number: _____	**Class:**	Missing, Wrong, Extra, Usability, Performance,
Inspection Date: _____		Style, Clarity, Question
Recorder: _____	**Severity:**	Cosmetic, Minor, Severe, Fatal (or Major, minor)

Type   Class   Severity   Description

1. ____ ____ ____   _____
                       _____
2. ____ ____ ____   _____
                       _____

Figure 12.5: Inspection issues list.

If your organization has an ongoing inspection process, you can combine data from multiple inspections to gain insight into the quality of both the inspection process and the products being inspected. Your ultimate objective is a collection of inspection data from which you can draw quantitative conclusions about defect trends and inspection effectiveness. A serious metrics program will combine defect data from inspections with that from testing and customer problem reports. This allows you to assess your defect-removal efficiencies, as was discussed in Chapter 11, as well as tracking your progress toward higher-quality products—the payback from process improvement efforts.

We use a simple spreadsheet, as shown in Fig. 12.6, to pool data from inspections of particular types of work products (in this case, source code). In this spreadsheet, all issues raised in an inspection are tallied, but only items other than style or clarity issues are termed "defects." The data shown in Fig. 12.6 represents our recent experiences with both peer deskchecks and group reviews. Only a few rows of data are shown, but the Totals line accurately summarizes the results obtained from twenty-three reviews.

This spreadsheet allows us to compute various review process parameters. Our data for 20,000 lines of code shows an average of eighteen defects found per thousand lines of code, an average inspection rate of nearly 200 LOC/hour, and an average of 3.5 defects found per staff hour of preparation and review time. All of the reviews summarized in Fig. 12.6 involved programs written in similar procedural programming languages, so comparisons based on the number of noncomment source statements are reasonable. As we saw in Table 11.2, different languages can embed a wide range of functionality in the same number of source statements. Therefore, we cannot legitimately compare raw defect densities in languages having substantially different numbers of assembly-equivalent statements per source statement.

Date	Project	Review ID	Author	Reviewers	Programs	Prep+Review Hours	Extra	Wrong	Missing
7/26/95	A	CODE-3	TRW	[initials]	[file names]	20	6	9	2
11/15/95	A	CODE-1	IBM			13.0	21	40	19
12/23/95	C	CODE-2	MS			8.5	14	14	4
1/3/96	B	CODE-5b	AC			11.0	22	18	22
...	...	...	...	...	...	...	...	...	...
Totals for 23 reviews:						103			

Usability	Performance	Style/Clarity Issues	Total Issues	Total Defects	LOC	Defects/ KLOC	LOC/ Hour	Defects/ Hour
0	0	25	42	17	1700	10	85	1
1	5	12	98	86	3585	24	276	7
0	0	25	57	32	6059	5	713	4
6	4	15	87	72	1676	43	152	7
...	...	...	...	...	...	...	...	...
Totals for 23 reviews:		544	363	20017	18.1	194	3.5

Figure 12.6: Record of code reviews carried out (bottom section is an extension of the top section to the right).

Inspection results will vary from one organization to the next for many reasons. If you begin recording and analyzing your inspection data, you'll be able to determine which review techniques work best for you, and you can begin to assess the quality of your work products. Our data suggests that we still have plenty of opportunities to improve our programming work, but the authors of the twenty-three programs summarized in Fig. 12.6 were happy to have 363 defects found by their coworkers, rather than lingering into the final products.

Making Inspections Work in Your Culture

An organization's culture of shared beliefs and behaviors has a big impact on whether any software review process can be implemented successfully. Inspections will be most effective when the team members share certain values and attitudes:

- a desire to make every work product generated by any team member as defect-free as possible before it passes to the next development stage or to the customer

- a level of mutual respect, which ensures that problems found are with the product and not with the author, and which makes each participant receptive to suggestions for improvement

- a sense of unease when the author is the only person who has viewed a completed product

- confidence that spending time on quality activities up front will save time for the whole organization in the long run

To steer a culture toward these values, a manager should remember two key principles. First, demonstrate respect for team members in all situations. Mutual respect is a foundation for any kind of peer review process. And second, never punish a team member for the results of an inspection. The first time the outcome of a peer inspection is held against the author is the last time that person will submit his work for review.

You can't change your culture overnight, but there are some additional steps you can take to increase the chance of successfully initiating inspections in any organization. First, provide inspection training for all team members who will participate in inspections. Moderators may require additional training, as they have to deal with sensitive issues of human interactions. Software managers should at least receive overview training on inspections. Second, build inspections into the project schedule. Be sure to factor in time for preparation, as well as for the inevitable rework that follows a successful inspection. If the inspection is treated as a milestone, rather than a task, in your project plan, the time needed for rework may be overlooked.

To judge the need for inspections, measure the time spent on internal rework of products you thought were completed. To assess the impact of inspections, compare the number of post-release defects found in older products with the number found in newer ones. Did you get fewer bug reports from customers after you started an inspection program? Share bug report trends with the team to help steer them toward a shared belief in the benefits of quality practices.

Finally, identify a local advocate who preaches the merits of inspection from experience, coaches others as they get started, and strives to improve your group's inspection processes. Make sure all team members understand that the time they devote to inspecting another person's product is for the benefit of the whole organization; others will assist their own project efforts in the same way. This quid pro quo balances the resistance team members may express against diverting time from their own work to review someone else's products.

As with any other technology, organizations are not always successful in their attempts to begin software inspections. Assess your group's readiness for inspections by considering these common reasons for failure:

- Developers are concerned that inspection results may be used against them at performance appraisal time.

- Authors are unable to separate their egos from their work products, claim their products do not need reviewing, or become defensive during the inspection meeting.

- Participants do not prepare adequately prior to the inspection meeting.

- Participants skip important steps because of a lack of training, or they dogmatically follow the letter of some inspection rule book rather than seeking the spirit of the activity.

- Authors do not take the results of the inspection seriously and resist making the suggested changes.

- Inspection meetings lose their focus, wander into interesting discussions about technical solutions, and fail to cover the scheduled material.

- Reviews with the desired participants cannot be scheduled in an appropriate time frame for the project schedule because people are too busy or inspections are not a priority for them.

- Inspection teams are too large or have the wrong players. (Participants are invited because of their position in the project team, not because of their ability to contribute to an effective inspection.)

- The project schedule does not include time for inspections, so they are cut when schedule pressures mount.

Any group of software developers can improve quality through some form of peer review process. If you don't feel the time is right for doing formal inspections, begin with individual peer deskchecks through a buddy system. Continue to learn about inspections, and evolve your review activities toward the more formal approaches: record keeping, defined roles, pre-meeting preparation, and so on. You, too, can experience the sense of relief that comes from having one of your professional peers find a major error that likely would have crept into the product had you not held an inspection.

Summary

- ✔ Strive to have a peer, rather than a customer, find a defect.

- ✔ A software engineering culture fosters a commitment to finding defects as early as possible, and learning from the pattern of defects found to reduce the future occurrence of similar errors.

- ✔ Peer reviews and inspections are effective techniques for finding errors in any software work product. The greatest leverage comes from inspecting requirements specifications and designs, since the cost of fixing a defect increases dramatically the later it is discovered.

- ✔ Formal inspections require that participants assume specific roles: moderator, author, reader, recorder, and inspector. A formal inspection involves several discrete steps: planning, overview meeting, preparation, inspection meeting, causal analysis, rework, and follow-up.

- ✔ It is not essential to follow a strictly formal inspection process to obtain benefits. Less formal forms of peer reviews are valuable, too.

- ✔ Keep records of your inspection results to assess the effectiveness of your inspections in finding defects and to understand the kinds of errors that are most frequently made.

Culture Builders and Killers

 Culture Builder: If you are a first-line manager who still writes code or creates other software work products, put your own products through the same inspection and testing gates as those created by anyone else in your group. This will demonstrate your commitment to producing high-quality products. In a healthy software engineering culture, all inspectors attempt to find defects, no matter who created the product being inspected. Your receptiveness to the issues raised by inspection sets an example for the others and helps to institutionalize quality practices in your group.

 Culture Builder: Seed one or two realistic errors into a product that is being inspected. Whoever finds the bugs first gets some token prize, such as movie tickets. This might encourage inspectors to look harder and to point out anything they think might be an error. If you have too many inspections where the seeded errors remain undiscovered, investigate the inspection methods being used and see if they need to be improved. Tell the inspectors that the errors have been seeded, and be sure to reveal the errors if they were not found during the inspection.

Culture Builder: The organization's standard peer review policy should apply to all members of your team, not just to those who think it's a good idea. Some programmers believe they are so talented that their products do not require reviewing. Reviews are not punishment for mediocre engineers; they are a valuable quality improvement method from which anyone can benefit.

Culture Killer: Collect the defect reports from inspections and use them as input into the performance appraisal for the individual developers. This will send the message that you trust inspections to point out your most and least competent programmers.

References and Further Reading

Bankes, Kirk. "Ford Systems Inspection Experiences," *Proceedings of the 1994 International IT Quality Conference.* Orlando, Fla.: Quality Assurance Institute, 1994, pp. 3-83 to 3-114.

Bankes described the effective implementation of inspections in Ford's Customer Service Systems division.

Boehm, Barry W. *Software Engineering Economics.* Englewood Cliffs, N.J.: Prentice-Hall, 1981.

Boehm explores the factors that most strongly influence software costs and uses them to determine the estimated costs of a future software project. This book shows how to apply economic analysis techniques to software engineering decision situations.

Ebenau, Robert G., and Susan H. Strauss. *Software Inspection Process.* New York: McGraw-Hill, 1994.

This comprehensive text covers every aspect of formal inspections of software work products. The core of the book is Chapter 8, "Software Inspection Procedures Manual." Extensive sections are included on implementing and managing inspections in an organization, inspection data analysis, and education and support for inspections.

Fagan, Michael E. "Advances in Software Inspections," *IEEE Transactions on Software Engineering,* Vol. 12, No. 7 (July 1986), pp. 744-51.

> Fagan presents additional studies and experiences of software inspections in this paper.

———. "Design and Code Inspections to Reduce Errors in Program Development," *IBM Systems Journal,* Vol. 15, No. 3 (March 1976), pp. 182-211.

> In his seminal paper, Fagan concludes that design and code inspections can both improve program quality and increase productivity. He stresses that the conduct of the trained moderator and the attitude demonstrated by management are key determining factors in how well the inspection process is accepted by programmers.

Freedman, Daniel P., and Gerald M. Weinberg. *Handbook of Walkthroughs, Inspections, and Technical Reviews,* 3rd ed. New York: Dorset House Publishing, 1990.

> Employing a question and answer dialog format, this book covers the technical, managerial, and personal aspects of software review activities.

Gilb, Tom, and Dorothy Graham. *Software Inspection.* Reading, Mass.: Addison-Wesley, 1993.

> These authors emphasize collecting and analyzing a wide variety of inspection metrics as a tool for quantifying products and processes. I doubt whether any organization is (or should be) measuring all of the more than fifty inspection metrics suggested here. I prefer Ebenau and Strauss's *Software Inspection Process* as a general handbook for inspections.

Grady, Robert B., and Tom Van Slack. "Key Lessons in Achieving Widespread Inspection Use," *IEEE Software,* Vol. 11, No. 4 (July 1994), pp. 46-57.

> Grady and Van Slack describe the experience and benefits of implementing software inspections at Hewlett-Packard during a span of ten years. Metrics for tracking the penetration of inspection into a large organization are presented, along with data showing a return on investment greater than ten to one from the inspection process.

Humphrey, Watts S. *Managing the Software Process.* Reading, Mass.: Addison-Wesley, 1989.

> Chapter 10 and Appendix C deal with software inspections.

Jones, Capers. *Applied Software Measurement.* New York: McGraw-Hill, 1991.

> Jones reports on the effectiveness of several software defect removal and quality factors.

McConnell, Steve. *Code Complete.* Redmond, Wash.: Microsoft Press, 1993.

> McConnell covers reviews and inspections in a chapter that surveys software quality techniques.

Weinberg, Gerald M. *The Psychology of Computer Programming.* New York: Van Nostrand Reinhold, 1971.

> Weinberg originated the notion of "egoless programming" here. He also describes aspects of human behavior and psychology in the context of programming groups, teams, and projects.

Weller, Edward F. "Lessons from Three Years of Inspection Data," *IEEE Software,* Vol. 10, No. 5 (September 1993), pp. 38-45, and "Using Metrics to Manage Software Projects," *IEEE Software,* Vol. 11, No. 5 (September 1994), pp. 27-33.

> These articles describe Weller's years of experience with inspections at Bull HN Information Systems. He addresses the methods used to collect, analyze, and apply the inspection data to project planning and tracking. These articles provide a good case study in the large-scale application of inspections.

Chapter 13

Structured Testing

More than the act of testing, the act of designing tests is one of the best bug preventers known. The thinking that must be done to create a useful test can discover and eliminate bugs before they are coded—indeed, test-design thinking can discover and eliminate bugs at every stage in the creation of software, from conception to specification, to design, coding, and the rest.

—Boris Beizer, *Software Testing Techniques*

Recently, a colleague asked me to assist him with devising thorough unit tests for one of his programs. He said he had spent about two weeks writing the program and three weeks testing it. I asked him if he had written down any of the tests. "No," was the predictable reply. I pointed out to my colleague that we had to start all over with the testing process—all the mental effort he had put into devising tests, however excellent or poor they were, went down the drain. By documenting your tests so you can re-execute them in the future, you will see an immediate increase in your software testing effectiveness and efficiency.

According to the IEEE, testing is "an activity in which a system or component is executed under specified conditions, the results are observed or recorded, and an evaluation is made of some aspect of the system or component" [IEEE, 1990]. Testing is the one quality control technique that is practiced by nearly every software organization. However, it is frequently performed in an ad hoc, unstructured way, consuming far more time than anyone likes and leaving far too many defects in the code for the customer to find. In a software engineering culture, testing is not a frenzied activity performed just before the product ships, but rather a planned and disciplined activity that begins early in the project's life and continues in a controlled fashion until the project is completed.

Not long ago, I conducted a survey of several dozen software developers in the Kodak research and development community, to understand the current state of the practice of quality control activities. The facts that emerged from this survey were worrisome. Only 20 percent of all respondents had had any formal training in software testing. Fully half the respondents indicated that all of their testing is performed manually. Nearly half of the responses with regard to how unit, integration, and system testing are performed reported they were "pretty thorough, but I don't record any of the tests" (see Table 13.1). Just 24 percent of the respondents said they record unit tests for regression testing. Only 11 percent said they create written system tests that trace back to specific requirements, and the same 11 percent indicated that they designed tests to cover 100 percent of the software requirements.

Table 13.1.
Survey of Testing Practices Among
Kodak R&D Software Engineers.

Test Practice	Unit Testing	Integration Testing	System Testing
Systematic and structured; tests are recorded for future use	24%	11%	26%
Pretty thorough, but tests are not recorded	43%	49%	40%
Ad hoc: not systematic or documented	14%	17%	26%
Don't perform this as a discrete activity	5%	11%	3%
Don't really know what this kind of testing is	14%	11%	6%

The survey responses may not be representative of Eastman Kodak Company as a whole or of the U.S. software industry at large. However, they do indicate that this one community of software engineers ought to significantly improve its testing practices. People are not born knowing how to test software, nor do they get a lot of instruction in structured testing techniques in most college computer science courses. In fact, many of us taught ourselves all we know about testing; sometimes that isn't enough.

Testing and the Quality Culture

The first code testing gate is *unit testing*, an activity that involves the testing of individual programs or procedures within programs. It is typically performed by the person who wrote the program. In an organization that has not yet adopted the concepts of a quality-driven software engineering culture, much of the unit testing is performed on the fly. Tests are neither systematic, repeatable, documented, thorough, based on risk, nor based on a testing strategy (such as structural path analysis or data flow analysis). Testing is intimately entwined with implementation, rather than being treated as a discrete function. The quality of a module after such casual unit testing really is not known.

The next step is *integration testing*, which is intended to verify the interfaces among parts of a system, such as multiple modules or entire subsystems. The interfaces among software components provide many opportunities for errors that are difficult to track down and correct. Integration testing should be based on the architectural design of the program, and it should be conducted in association with a documented plan for building the final executable from its components. Unfortunately, both architectural design and explicit build plans are often lacking or incomplete in organizations that are not yet serious about software engineering.

System testing is intended to verify the final program in its entirety, after all software and hardware components have been integrated. It also validates that the completed system actually meets the customer requirements. System testing is usually performed in an actual or simulated production environment. Too often, though, system testing is unstructured and inefficient, with many program features being executed redundantly and others not executed at all. Many exception conditions are not triggered, and the level of requirements coverage by the test suite is not known. It's no wonder the products delivered after such testing still contain bugs.

One goal of a software engineering culture is to combine effective testing with other quality control and assurance methods, as part of a systematic effort to eradicate and prevent errors. Testing needs to be planned as an explicit set of activities early in the project life cycle, not tacked on as part of the end game. The test plans, procedures, and infrastructure should be developed in parallel with the requirements, design, and code development. Test activities should be documented, tracked, and analyzed. Anyone who is expected to test software should be trained properly, and automated tools should be procured to accelerate the more tedious aspects of the testing process.

Quality cannot be tested or inspected into a product—it must be designed in. The goal of all software testing activities is to identify defects in the program. Testing can never prove the absence of errors; it can only reveal their presence. Testing is prone to human errors, and it can never be totally comprehensive. Decades ago, Glenford Myers stated several insightful axioms about software testing, some of which are presented in Table 13.2, and all of which are still valid [Myers, 1976].

Writing down your tests forces you to translate your fuzzy vision of how you think the program should operate into explicitly defined scenarios of program behavior under specified conditions. This act leads you to spot oversights, inconsistencies, and ambiguities in the requirements, designs, or code, long before you ever actually run the tests. As with inspections, the highest payback from testing comes from finding errors prior to the coding step with the help of your test design.

Table 13.2.
Myers' Software Testing Axioms.

- A good test case is a test case that has a high probability of detecting an undiscovered error, not a test case that shows that the program works correctly.

- Write test cases for invalid as well as valid input conditions.

- A necessary part of every test case is a description of the expected output or results.

- Avoid nonreproducible or on-the-fly testing.

- As the number of detected errors in a piece of software increases, the probability of the existence of more undetected errors also increases.

- Assign your most creative programmers to testing.

- Ensure that testability is a key objective in your software design.

To improve your testing process, begin writing test plans with clear expectations and staff responsibilities. The IEEE states that the test plan is "a document describing the scope, approach, resources, and schedule of intended test activities. It identifies test items, the features to be tested, the testing tasks, who will do each task, and any risks requiring contingency planning" [IEEE, 1990]. Our software group now frequently follows IEEE Std. 829, "Standard for Software Test Documentation," adapted as appropriate for the scope and intended use of our systems. We pay particular attention to the comprehensive testing of components that are intended to be reusable. A culture in which reuse is extensively practiced demands great confidence in the quality of the reusable components, confidence that can be built partly by thorough, documented test plans and automated test drivers. It's wonderful to be able to run a suite of 300 tests that fully exercises a reusable function library in just a few seconds.

A personal commitment to producing superior programs must include excellence in software testing practices. In view of the customer/supplier software process model from Fig. 11.3, every programmer is responsible for removing as many defects as possible from the modules he writes prior to passing them to the next process, be it integration testing or the ultimate user.

Most forms of testing have a bug detection efficiency of less than 30 percent, so multiple stages must be combined in order to achieve high test effectiveness [Jones, 1994]. Dynamic testing, in which the program is actually executed, is only one of the defect removal filters available to you. Combine testing with inspections, walkthroughs, checklists, and other quality tools to build an effective defect removal strategy. During a testing activity, the tester (or the programmer wearing his testing hat) should have the attitude, "This program has flaws in it, and I'm going to find them." Do not be lulled into a false sense of security because a single defect detection activity failed to reveal any new bugs.

A Unit Testing Strategy

The absolute minimum acceptable level of testing for a program written in a procedural language is that every instruction in it has been executed at least once. This is called *100 percent statement coverage* (sometimes shortened to just "statement coverage," wherein the 100 percent is implied unless some other percentage is explicitly noted). If a statement has not been executed, you should assume you do not know whether it is correct. Further, the tests you employ should be designed to reveal every bug that might occur in each executed statement. Boris Beizer expressed his thoughts on this guideline more strongly: "Testing less than [100 percent statement coverage] for new software is unconscionable and should be criminalized" [Beizer, 1990]. What fraction of the code in *your* last application was executed by your test suite?

A more appropriate minimum level of unit test coverage is to ensure that every decision statement (branch) in the program has been executed at least once in each direction. This is called *branch coverage*. Decision statements include if/then/else constructs, switch/case constructs, and loop termination conditions. Except in rare situations (such as unstructured modules with multiple entry points), branch coverage automatically provides statement coverage.

Better still, devise test cases that will execute each logical expression (a Boolean clause, or predicate) in a complex decision statement at least once in each direction, which provides *condition coverage*. You can select the test cases that provide condition coverage so that they also achieve branch and statement coverage. This should be the starting point for your unit testing. As you extend your testing rigor beyond this starting point, add tests that systematically probe the impact of different data values on the behavior of the program, and tests that trace the flow of data through various execution paths [Gianturco, 1994].

Effective testing requires a combination of *white box* and *black box* testing methods. White box tests are based on an examination of the internal design and structure of a program, such as path coverage tests, while black box tests are designed without regard to the internal structure of a program, based on the external functional requirements of the program. Don't think you can neglect structured white box unit testing just because you have a pretty good set of black box system test cases.

An important test coverage criterion is the fraction of the functional require-ments executed by your test cases. At the system testing level, test cases derived from the functional requirements document can test the external behaviors of the program; you should aim for 100 percent coverage of these requirements. Even at the unit level, every module or procedure has some specification that defines the output the procedure is supposed to generate and how it should respond to input conditions. A good unit test plan will cover all of these specified behaviors, as well as covering the source statements themselves. You may be able to execute every theoretically possible path through perfectly clean code without finding a bug, but if the module does not satisfy its specification, the program is defective.

You can buy coverage monitor tools that will measure the extent of code cover-age achieved by executing a test suite and show which sections of the code were not executed. Coverage monitors work by inserting code into ("instrumenting") either your source code or the object code in a preprocessing step. At execution time, the inserted code writes information to a log file that indicates which seg-ments of the code are executed as you run your test cases. Table A.4 in Appendix A lists some sources of information on coverage monitors and other testing tools. Updated compendiums of testing tools are posted periodically to the Usenet news-group comp.software.testing, as are comments from practitioners who have used various tools.

According to Beizer, good programmers testing without benefit of a coverage tool are only achieving about 80 percent code coverage, while average program-mers are getting 50 to 60 percent, and poor programmers are hitting less than 30 percent [Johnson, 1994]. Test strategies that emphasize only the functional behav-iors of the software may cover the requirements adequately, but this is no guaran-tee that the internal structure of the program has been thoroughly exercised.

Dozens of test coverage measures can be applied in addition to these code cov-erage testing criteria [Kaner, 1995]. Code coverage testing strategies are less appro-priate than some other coverage measures for programs that are not written in procedural languages. Applications developed using code generator tools also require different test strategies, since you may have little control over, or visibility into, the generated code. Comprehensive black box testing approaches are required to verify the proper functioning of these types of applications.

A relatively simple technique can be used to help you reach the goal of 100 percent condition coverage by selecting appropriate unit test cases. Following is a description of a systematic unit testing approach I have found to be effective and efficient for testing structured programs written using procedural languages such as C (unstructured code riddled with GOTOs are extremely difficult to test thor-oughly by any method, including this one). While this approach does not include all the rigor possible in unit testing, it provides a solid test foundation.

1. Run the program through a source code metrics analyzer tool to identify those procedures having relatively high complexi-ties, based on the McCabe cyclomatic complexity metric (described later in this chapter).

2. For the more complex procedures, draw a "control flowgraph" (first cousin to a flowchart) and identify those tests necessary to achieve branch or condition coverage [Beizer, 1990; Mosley, 1993]. Some of the commercially available testing tools can draw the flowgraphs, and some will tell you which tests are required to achieve condition coverage. Make sure you can predict the outcome of each test, or you won't know if it passed or not. Automatic test generators won't help you much with outcome prediction.

3. Augment this initial list of tests with

   ■   boundary value tests to probe such troublesome spots as the ends of loops and Boolean inequalities for common defects, like off-by-one errors and greater-than when you really meant greater-than-or-equal-to;

   ■   data flow tests to cover code segments based on where a data value is set and where it is used;

   ■   error guessing to handle parts of the program you intuitively (or insightfully) feel are more likely to contain certain kinds of errors; and

   ■   other tests derived from your understanding of how the module should work based on its requirements. This is a black box testing strategy, so I think of the combination of structural and functional testing described here as a "gray box" approach to software testing.

4. Document the test conditions and their expected results in comments at the top of the source code module. This avoids the problem of having a separate unit testing document to maintain and keep in sync with the source code. You may choose to record your unit tests in some other fashion, but regardless of the method you select, *write them down*.

5. If feasible, incorporate the tests into an automated test driver to facilitate future regression testing. (Regression testing is a form of testing intended to determine whether changes in the software have caused any unintended side effects that damaged other functions. It is typically performed by re-executing a selected subset of the test cases after a change is made.) Kevin Weeks described an effective approach for incorporating test code directly into C source files, where it can be invoked when

needed through conditional compilation directives [Weeks, 1992]. Strategies recommended for testing object-oriented programs often suggest that you incorporate special testing methods into each class, which again can be excluded from the production software through conditional compilation.

6. Print out a complete listing of the source code and your tests, and perform a deskcheck prior to executing the program. You will be amazed at how many bugs you can find yourself, simply by reading the code—and test cases—all the way through.

7. Execute the tests, followed by: (a) correcting errors found in the code, (b) correcting errors in your test suite, and (c) rerunning the corrected test suite to verify your code corrections.

While you can easily derive test cases to provide the desired code coverage level, actually forcing execution down all of those paths is not always feasible. It can be difficult to generate all anticipated error conditions, simulate bad return codes from library function calls, force or simulate database and hardware failures, and so on. Some testing tools allow you to return failure from system calls, in order to test your program's handling of conditions such as memory allocation failures. If you design your test cases to achieve 100 percent condition coverage and keep records of the execution results, you will know exactly which of these difficult-to-reach tests have not been hit by your testing activities.

Cyclomatic Complexity and Testing

Ideally, your test suite would cover every possible execution path through a program: this is termed *100 percent path coverage*. In practice, this is rarely possible, due to the combinatorial explosion of possible execution sequences of branches and loops. How, then, can we design the fewest possible test cases that will achieve our more realistic goals of statement, branch, and condition coverage?

Tom McCabe devised the concept of "cyclomatic complexity" as a measure of how many unique basis paths exist in a structured program written in a procedural language [McCabe, 1982]. A basis path is one sequence of decision branches that goes from the entry point in the program to the exit point, thereby executing a subset of the code segments contained in the program. Traversing all the basis paths will execute every statement in the program with the fewest number of distinct tests, providing a useful foundation for structured unit testing. The technique of selecting control paths and test data based on cyclomatic complexity is called the "baseline method."

There are two variants of cyclomatic complexity—basic and extended. The extended version treats the multiple decisions in a compound logical expression independently, while the basic method treats every logical expression the same way. To calculate the basic cyclomatic complexity, simply count the number of decision statements in the program and add 1. When calculating extended cyclomatic complexity, count each Boolean expression in a compound predicate statement (that is, an expression containing logical AND or OR operators) separately. The resulting total is the *minimum* number of tests required to force execution of all statements, yielding statement coverage. By selecting these tests to make sure each decision is exercised in both true and false directions, you will also achieve the more desirable branch coverage. (Unstructured programs filled with GOTO statements complicate the analysis.)

To identify the fewest test cases that will provide statement coverage, you need to devise certain execution paths through the code based on specific combinations of true and false values for all of the logical decisions. For the first test case, identify a pattern of true and false values for all of the decisions in the module that results in a representative execution path through the program. Then, generate additional test cases by switching each of the decisions to the opposite response one at a time, while holding the others at their original values. The number of test cases generated in this fashion equals the number of binary decision statements plus one: the cyclomatic complexity number for that module. The resulting list of test cases will generally provide branch coverage in addition to statement coverage. This minimal set of test cases is by no means a complete test suite for any module, but it provides a starting point for structured unit testing.

The baseline method for unit testing is most applicable to programs written in procedural languages [Mosley, 1993]. It is less useful for testing database-oriented programs, where a data-driven approach is needed, and object classes, which tend to have many relatively simple procedural methods for each class, with potentially complex interactions among the objects.

The cyclomatic complexity of a module provides one way to judge whether its complexity has become excessive, based on the number of control flow decisions in the program. The conventional wisdom is that modules having cyclomatic complexity greater than ten, or extended cyclomatic complexity greater than fifteen, should be examined for possible simplification or partitioning into subroutines. If you have committed yourself to the minimum testing standard of executing every statement in the program, the cyclomatic complexity tells you the fewest possible tests that are required to achieve this goal. I once saw a programmer report a cyclomatic complexity of 930 for a single procedure in a large program! That programmer did not appreciate the implications of such a high complexity on the quality of his program, or on the test suite required to achieve even statement coverage.

Various sources in the software literature point to increased maintenance problems with larger and more complex programs. Cyclomatic complexity has been correlated with the number of errors in a program, the time to find the errors, the effort to test it, and the effort to maintain it. Do not emphasize reducing cyclomatic complexity for its own sake to meet some numeric target. Instead, use it as a guide to identify overly complex modules, so you can make sure they can be adequately verified for correctness. Nor is cyclomatic complexity the only measure that should be used for assessing module testability and maintainability; it is just one such indicator.

Software tools are available to calculate cyclomatic complexity and other metrics on source code. The tools sources listed in Table A.4 can point you toward some commercial or freeware candidates for various platforms. I use PC-Metric, from SET Laboratories, Inc. (see Appendix B for contact information). Versions of PC-Metric are available for several procedural languages, and a related product called UX-Metric is available for UNIX platforms. PC-Metric generates reports that include basic and extended cyclomatic complexity, software science or Halstead metrics (another set of metrics that indicate the size and complexity of a program), number of physical and logical source statements, number of blanks and comment lines, and other source code metrics.

Test Management and Automation

Once you have identified a set of tests that will achieve your aims, you must write a suite of test cases containing specific input data that will force the execution of all the test paths you selected from the white box test design. Sometimes multiple tests can be combined into a single test case, leading to a more efficient testing process, provided the results of one test will not mask the results of another in the same test case.

Whenever possible, use automated test drivers for your programs, particularly for reusable components or code libraries that do not include a user interface component. Sophisticated capture-and-playback tools can even be used to automate the testing of programs having a complex graphical user interface. Organizations that perform only manual testing of their software products will spend far more time than necessary on testing, and the tests they execute likely will not be reproducible. Test automation guarantees that the test suite you execute today is identical to the one you executed yesterday.

With an automated test driver, you can store the test case descriptions and expected results in an external data file, which is easily updated. Test datasets or modifiable templates can be stored in other files, and scripts can be written to build the actual input dataset you need for any particular test. The data flow model in Fig. 13.1 illustrates this approach to test automation. One down side is that automated test aids need to be maintained as the program being tested changes. Remember, too, that tester programs are themselves prone to defects.

Our group recently developed an application called the Graphics Engine. The Graphics Engine program reads a "plot specification file" written by an application that needs to generate terminal or hardcopy graphics. We wrote nearly 700 individual tests for the Graphics Engine, mapped to the functional requirements, which were combined into about 450 unique test cases. Each test containing invalid input data that should cause the program to terminate had its own test case, but tests that generated specific independent plot features could be combined, with up to several dozen tests in a single test case. This led to some funny looking plots, but we were able to assess the success or failure of each test in these combination test cases by examining the plot that was generated.

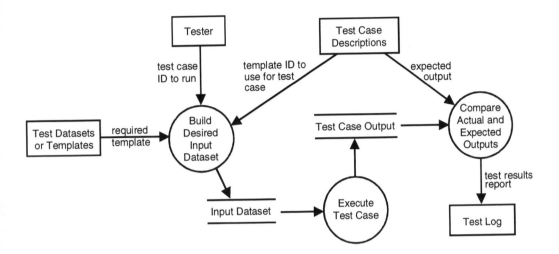

Figure 13.1: Data flow model for operation of an automated test driver.

We wrote an automated test driver program for the Graphics Engine, which made it easy to execute any subset of these 450 test cases. The test driver worked from a library of template plot specification files, with some editing directives that were applied to generate the specific input file that was needed for any particular test case. The Graphics Engine test driver produced a report that indicated whether each test case executed in a single run passed or not (Fig. 13.2). A test case was considered to have passed if the actual return code matched the expected value, and, for non-zero return codes, if the actual error log message matched the expected message.

The test driver program could not actually look at the plots and tell if the plot features were all generated correctly—we still had to do this manually, to see if the test case really passed. Automatically comparing the actual results with those expected is a better way to more fully automate the testing process, but that was not very practical with graphical output in the environment in which we were working.

For those test cases that produced the expected return code and (for failures) error log message, a simple "Test passed" message was written to the report file. Test cases that were not passed resulted in a more verbose output in the report file, identifying all we could learn about the nature of the error. Remember that the point of testing is to find errors, not to confirm success, so a test that I say "passed" could also be thought of as having failed in its mission to find an error.

Building an elaborate automated test mechanism like this takes a lot of time. As usual, the decision to make this investment should be based on risk. The Graphics Engine was a highly leveraged reusable component, relied on by several large applications, and we knew it would be enhanced frequently in an evolutionary development mode. It was essential for us to know whether the existing functionality had been injured in the process of adding a new feature. Having this comprehensive automated test suite, with about twenty composite test cases for routine regression testing after we made changes in the software, gave us a lot of confidence in the quality of the application whenever it was rebuilt on either of its two delivery platforms. The investment of effort in test automation was repaid by the speed, correctness, and convenience of running repeated tests during development and maintenance.

```
              Results of Graphics Engine Test

Test ARROWCOL.1 has passed
Test ARROWHEAD.1 has passed
Test ARROWHEAD.2 has passed
Test AXISTYPE.1 has passed
Test AXISTYPE.2 has passed
-----------------------------------------------------------------
Test DEVICE.9:   FAILED

Expected return code was: 5
Actual    return code was: 6
Expected error text  was: neither terminal nor plotter specified
Actual    error text  was: terminal key has no value
=================================================================

TEST RESULTS SUMMARY:

Number of tests executed =    6
Number of tests passed   =    5
Number of tests failed   =    1

Execution time = 17 seconds
```

Figure 13.2: Sample test report from the Graphics Engine.

Structured Testing Guidelines

Along with formal inspection, systematic unit testing is an important technique for individual programmers to use before passing their code on for integration with other software or hardware components. On smaller projects in which the same programmer is responsible for module design, coding, and integration, it is easy to gloss over the unit testing step, which can result in excessive program failures during integration and system testing. Since bugs are much harder to hunt down and eradicate in a fully integrated system, any technique that finds them earlier in the development life cycle should be diligently applied. The value of structured testing became apparent when I realized that every time I applied the techniques described in this chapter, I found errors in my code and in my tests, but few problem reports were received after the program was delivered. Keep these guidelines in mind as you plan and execute the testing of the next program you write.

1. Write down the tests you think of, so you can

    ■   execute exactly the same tests again in the future;

    ■   fully define the inputs, actions, and expected outputs;

    ■   avoid having to waste time reinventing them in the future;

    ■   grow a comprehensive suite of test cases;

    ■   add them to the test driver when you write it (even better, capture them in the driver program as you think of them).

2. Take a risk-based approach to concentrate your testing time on highly complex modules and on those that will do the most damage if they fail during operation. Strive to minimize complexity as you design and code your programs. Use a static code analyzer tool to calculate complexity metrics on your source files to identify error-prone modules.

3. Design unit tests systematically, not haphazardly, based on the structure of the code (white box tests). Use testing tools to help you design unit tests to obtain condition coverage efficiently. Test the boundary conditions of loop indices, data values, and counters. Augment path-based testing with data flow-based testing strategies. Include invalid data values, to try to make the program fail in as many ways as possible.

4. Create tests to generate all the unique outputs that are specified for the program, and create tests to stimulate all of the return codes and error handling conditions you can force. Create additional tests that you think will expose likely sources of errors, based on your knowledge of the program and the ways it will be used.

5. Remember that testing itself is error-prone. Inspect your test plans, test cases, and test drivers. Test your automated test drivers to confirm that they are executing the correct test cases.

> Examine the results of the tests carefully to make sure you are
> seeing what really happened, not just what you expect or want
> to happen.

Every software developer has a responsibility to apply quality filters to his or her
work products. Don't expect the next person downstream in the development
process to catch your errors. If you can develop a group culture that emphasizes
the use of systematic and repeatable testing, your team members should be able to
avoid late nights spent in a frantic cycle of code, test, fix, and test again, as the ship
date inexorably draws nearer and the bug count doesn't seem to be decreasing.

Summary

- ✔ A software engineering culture promotes a synergistic relationship between testers and developers, in which members of
  both groups apply structured testing methods to detect errors
  as efficiently as possible.

- ✔ The first line of testing defense against software errors is unit
  testing, which should be systematic, structured, repeatable,
  documented, and automated when possible. The minimum
  level of unit testing you should strive for is 100 percent condition coverage.

- ✔ Cyclomatic complexity analysis of programs can point out
  excessively complex modules that should be thoroughly
  inspected and tested, or restructured.

- ✔ Effective testing involves a gray box approach, combining
  structure-based white box strategies with function-based black
  box strategies. Your testing goals should include generating all
  distinct types of expected outputs, including all anticipated
  exception conditions.

Culture Builders and Killers

Culture Builder: When you have individual meetings with your developers, ask to see a current unit test plan. You may not care how many
errors were found, but you do want the developers to conduct structured
testing, record their tests for future regression testing, and keep records of the
errors found so they can learn from them and assess their overall defect removal
efficiency.

Culture Builder: Encourage your group to set standards for unit testing that include 100 percent statement and condition coverage as minimum criteria, and provide tools for your team to facilitate and measure test coverage. When discussing the quality and test status of a project, ask to see the tracking chart that shows what percent coverage the test suite has yielded so far. This will reinforce the concept of measuring coverage as one unit testing criterion.

Culture Builder: Track the test coverage on a project and share the results with the project team members (after all, it's their data, even if someone else is actually making the measurements). Make the test results visible. Get people to actively look at the defect removal effectiveness. Track the number of bugs found as a function of test coverage, to see if you can convince yourselves that a coverage-based strategy for testing is indeed discovering more bugs than did the older ad hoc approaches.

Culture Killer: If your group makes minor changes in a library that is used by other software products, you can safely bypass integration regression testing with those other components and make the new library directly available to the final customers. You have confidence in your team; they would not say the revised library was reliable unless they were certain. Formal verification of software revisions is a waste of time if the programmers know what they are doing.

Culture Killer: If you're getting pressure from the boss to show progress, your developers can save some time by foregoing inspections and formal unit testing. The programmers can test the code on the fly as they write it. If there are any problems at integration, the testers in QA will take care of them. Isn't QA's job supposed to be to make up for any quality problems that slip through the engineers' hands?

References and Further Reading

Beizer, Boris. *Software Testing Techniques,* 2nd ed. New York: Van Nostrand Reinhold, 1990.

> Written by one of the leaders in the software testing arena, this volume presents a thorough treatment of the topic. It includes chapters on flowgraphs and path testing, transaction flow and data flow testing, domain testing, metrics and complexity, logic-based testing, and graphical testing methods. This book is among the most comprehensive in its field.

Gianturco, Mark D. "Testing Techniques for Quality Software," *Software Development*, Vol. 2, No. 8 (August 1994), pp. 45-61.

> This article is an excellent place to begin reading about testing techniques. It provides a concise, understandable, yet substantive overview of several important methods. Gianturco describes the relative effectiveness of different testing techniques.

IEEE Std. 610.12-1990, "IEEE Standard Glossary of Software Engineering Terminology." Los Alamitos, Calif.: IEEE Computer Society Press, 1990.

> This standard contains an extensive glossary of terms related to software engineering.

Johnson, Mark. "Dr. Boris Beizer on Software Testing: An Interview. Part 1," *The Software QA Quarterly*, Vol. 1, No. 2 (Spring 1994), pp. 7-13; "Part 2" (Summer 1994), pp. 41-45.

> This is a frank and interesting interview with an outspoken member of the software testing profession.

Jones, Capers. *Assessment and Control of Software Risks.* Englewood Cliffs, N.J.: Yourdon Press/Prentice-Hall, 1994.

> In Chapter 51, Jones addresses the risk area of low software quality.

Kaner, Cem. "Software Negligence and Testing Coverage," *The Software QA Quarterly*, Vol. 2, No. 2 (1995), pp. 18-26.

> 101 test coverage measures are described here.

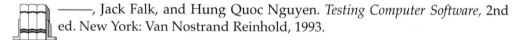

————, Jack Falk, and Hung Quoc Nguyen. *Testing Computer Software*, 2nd ed. New York: Van Nostrand Reinhold, 1993.

> This contemporary treatise on virtually all issues of testing software components includes chapters on types of tests and software errors, reporting and analyzing bugs, testing hardware devices, and internationalization testing. Testing of user manuals, test planning and documentation, and testing tools also are covered.

McCabe, Thomas J. *Structured Testing: A Software Testing Methodology Using the Cyclomatic Complexity Metric.* National Bureau of Standards Special Publication 500-99, 1982.

> McCabe gives a clear introduction to cyclomatic complexity and his approach to structured testing using control flowgraphs.

Mosley, Daniel J. *The Handbook of MIS Application Software Testing.* Englewood Cliffs, N.J.: Yourdon Press/Prentice-Hall, 1993.

This book contains many examples of diverse techniques for structural and functional test design. Using an effective tutorial approach, Mosley walks through the application of several different white box test case design strategies to the same sample COBOL program.

 Myers, Glenford J. *The Art of Software Testing.* New York: John Wiley & Sons, 1979.

Myers wrote one of the classics in this field. It is a bit dated, but it provides a concise presentation on test case design techniques, testing, and debugging approaches. The newer testing books described in this section are much more extensive resources.

———. *Software Reliability.* New York: John Wiley & Sons, 1976.

Myers discusses fourteen timeless axioms that pertain to software testing.

Weeks, Kevin D. "Glass-Box Testing," *The C Users Journal,* Vol. 10, No. 10 (October 1992), pp. 47-54.

Weeks has written a clear and practical guide to glass-box (a.k.a. white box) testing, with examples of how to incorporate test code in programs written in C.

Part V

Methods, Measures, and Tools

Culture is reflected in the methods and tools used by an organization. A quality-oriented software engineering culture acquires contemporary tools for designing, building, and measuring software. The tools are regularly and rationally employed by the members of the team. Consensus has been reached (often painfully) as to when and how the tools and methods should most appropriately be used, and the team members recognize the value the tools add to their work.

People who work in a healthy software culture are willing to measure their products and processes. The metrics program should be designed by a team of practitioners, not simply imposed by management fiat. The measurement objectives must be clearly stated, and management must scrupulously avoid using the data collected to evaluate individuals. Accurate measurement of software yields insights that can be used to identify improvement opportunities and assess the impact of new processes.

Four cultural premises are addressed in Part V:

- ✔ A key to software quality is to iterate many times on all development steps except coding: Do this once.

- ✔ Managing bug reports and change requests is essential to controlling quality and maintenance.

- ✔ If you measure what you do, you can learn to do it better.

- ✔ Do what makes sense; don't resort to dogma.

Chapter **14**

The CASE for Iteration

Measure one thousand times; cut once.

—ancient Chinese proverb

Design one thousand times; code once.

—modern software engineering proverb

Plan to throw one away; you will, anyhow.

—Frederick P. Brooks, Jr., *The Mythical Man Month*

The first solution a software engineer devises for a problem is rarely the best solution. During the process of designing a solution, we gain a much better understanding of the problem, making our first approach inferior to the one we would take if only we had a chance to start over. This is the rationale behind "planning to throw one away." It is also the premise of prototyping, in which we create a partial or exploratory solution to a problem and tweak it until (1) we thoroughly understand the problem, and (2) we have a pretty good idea of what the best solution will be. Evolutionary delivery, incremental development, and spiral life cycles are other ways to deal with the reality of needing more than one attempt to create an excellent solution.

A resident of a software engineering culture recognizes the value of iteration. He knows his first approach is not optimized, so he has some peers review his initial ideas to find errors and improvement opportunities. Then he can improve the design until he is confident that it provides a quality route to the objective. Reaching a high level of quality *demands* iteration, removing errors and building confidence in the correctness of your solution at each pass.

In an organization that has not yet achieved a software engineering culture, a developer typically begins writing a program as soon as he has a cursory understanding of the user requirements. Little effort is devoted to drawing pictures that represent various views of those requirements, or to designing and redesigning an effective architecture to implement them. As the developer acquires a clearer understanding of the user needs and identifies weaknesses in the initial design, much of the code may have to be rewritten, with the architectural design becoming less stable and more error-prone with each rebuild. Iterative refinement of both requirements and designs can reduce the time spent on more expensive code rework.

The value of iteration was vividly revealed to me when I was gathering requirements for the chemical tracking system described in Chapter 6. Each week, I held a needs-gathering session with the customer representatives, and then wrote a new portion of the software requirements specification (SRS). The customers reviewed the revised SRS informally prior to our next meeting (the number of errors they found during each review was pretty amazing), enabling weekly corrections. We also iteratively reviewed the evolving suite of test cases, with the same results. After several pairs of eyes had made multiple passes through the products, we felt confident that the final SRS represented an accurate statement of the chemists' needs for this system.

Most software engineers cannot really discard version 1.0 of their applications, so we need some other way to build iteration into the development process. The later in the life cycle that a change is made in a system, the more it costs to make the change. Therefore, we want to make the big changes as early as possible. This leads to the philosophy of multiple iterations at the analysis and design stages, so that the initial code you write is as nearly correct as possible. While it is often more fun to change the code than to change drawings, it is also more expensive.

The "design many times, code once" philosophy does pose a risk. The designer might become mired in analysis paralysis, the fruitless quest for perfection in the requirements or designs. Do not interpret this philosophy as "design infinitely, code never." The time comes when you actually have to build something, based on the current status of your design. The purpose of iteration is to sneak up on the best solution one step at a time, not necessarily to reach ultimate design utopia. The requirements and designs do not have to be perfect, just good enough to reduce the risk of rework that you incur by proceeding with the next development step. Remember: Strive for perfection, but settle for excellence.

The idea of iterating during the analysis and design activities is the basis for software system modeling. Through modeling, we draw pictures that represent different views of the system, and we iterate on the pictures, rather than on code. It takes a minute or two to add a line to a drawing, or to alter a definition in the data dictionary. Implementing the same change on a completed application might require days of software surgery, perhaps leaving the patient in worse shape than when you picked up the scalpel. The models allow you to visualize system components at various levels of abstraction. You can study the interconnections of the components, and make sure the development team members have a common understanding of the composition and behavior of each piece of the puzzle.

Software engineers use modeling as one technique for controlling some of the risks that threaten the success of a software project. Such risks include building a system that does not meet customer needs, and constructing an architecture that is not sufficiently robust to enable modification over time. Engineers who wish to maximize quality and minimize rework spend quite a bit of time drawing models before diving into a source code editor. The most practical way to draw models is to use automated tools that facilitate drawing and revising the models, called computer-aided software engineering (CASE) tools. Even if you do not have automated tools available to help tune your models, you can still draw a picture of your system by hand before you attempt to implement it. One design iteration is better than none.

Types of CASE Tools

Progress in software development research seems to move upstream, from the later stages of the development cycle toward the earlier ones. For example, structured programming techniques were developed before structured design methods, which preceded structured analysis. The same sequence held for object-oriented development methods, with object-oriented languages being invented before techniques for object-oriented design and analysis came along. Similarly, the earliest software development tools supported the coding process: assemblers (the lowest level code generators), compilers, and linkers, for example. More recently, tools were developed to support structured and object-oriented design and analysis activities. The spectrum of CASE tools now extends to reverse engineering and maintenance support on the downstream side, and to project planning and estimation on the upstream side.

In the broadest sense, any software application that is used by programmers to do their jobs but is not ordinarily used by the general public can be classified as a CASE tool [DeGrace, 1993]. "Upper-CASE" and "lower-CASE" are terms commonly used to classify the tools that help automate software production (see Fig. 14.1). Upper-CASE tools assist with the early life cycle activities of project planning, systems analysis, and design. They typically run on graphics-based personal computers or workstations. Lower-CASE tools include those that generate code from design models or user interface designs, as well as other tools that facilitate the construction, testing, maintenance, and reconstruction processes. In this chapter, we'll focus primarily on the use of upper-CASE tools, because the quality of an application depends so heavily on the early life cycle activities.

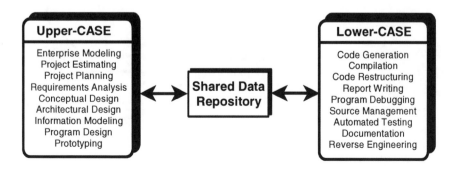

Figure 14.1: Some upper-CASE and lower-CASE tool categories.

CASE tools can be integrated (I-CASE) into a software engineering environment that addresses the full spectrum (or a selected subset) of life cycle activities. With I-CASE, a variety of tools can access project information that is stored in a shared data repository [Sharon, 1995]. An I-CASE environment will let the developer go full circle, generating code from a design model as well as reverse engineering existing source code back into a model.

CASE tools that support analysis and design activities are based on one or more of the many published methodologies for systems development. Most of the tools provide support for the classical structured analysis and design methodologies. They include models such as data flow diagrams (DFD), entity-relationship diagrams (ERD), structure charts, and state-transition diagrams (STD) [Robertson, 1994]. The definitions stored in a data dictionary provide the logical glue that joins these complementary views of a software system. An increasing number of tools include support for various object-oriented analysis (OOA) and object-oriented design (OOD) methodologies. For an overview of OOA methods, some CASE tools that support them, and many pointers to the OOA literature, see "Object-Oriented Analysis with CASE," by Christopher G. Jones, in [Bergin, 1993].

By support, I mean the CASE tool designers incorporated capabilities to let the user draw the kinds of diagrams that the methodology defines, as well as building in the rules that are applied to validate the correctness of these diagrams. For example, a validation report on the DFD fragment shown in Fig. 14.2 would state that process 2 has no data flows coming out of it, an error in any DFD methodology. Some tools force you to correct anything they interpret as an error. Others will report syntax errors only if you explicitly ask for model validation, allowing you to proceed even with the method violations present. With experience, you learn which kinds of validation error messages to take seriously and which ones are more of a nuisance.

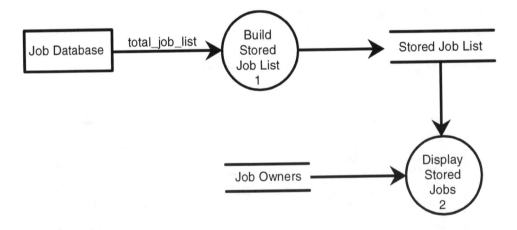

Figure 14.2: Sample data flow diagram that will generate a validation error.

Table A.5 in Appendix A identifies some sources of information on CASE tool vendors and their products. Vendors and their products frequently come, go, merge, and change in this business, so I will not attempt to compile a summary of specific CASE tools here. Any list would be hopelessly out of date by the time you read it. Current information about CASE tools can be found at various locations on the World Wide Web and in certain Usenet newsgroups, particularly comp.software-eng.

Hypes of CASE Tools

Once there was a lumberjack who, having heard how much a new tool called a "chain saw" would increase his productivity, bought one and went to work with it. The first day, he cut about half the wood he usually chopped by hand. The next day, he skipped lunch and rest breaks, and wound up with two-thirds of his normal output. The third day, he worked from dawn until dark with the chain saw, and still just barely matched his productivity with the ax. Exhausted and disgusted, he took the chain saw back to the hardware store and demanded a refund—clearly it was not delivering on the claimed productivity increase. The hardware store owner said, "Let's see if it's working right," and fired up the engine. "What's that noise?" asked the lumberjack.

I think of this joke every time I read a claim about how much a CASE tool will increase my software development productivity. When I attended my first CASE conference in 1987, some of the speakers were claiming that ten- to twenty-fold productivity increases were possible through the miracles of CASE. To be sure, some companies really did obtain five-fold improvements, but this was from lower-CASE tools that generated code for a narrow range of application types, often by starting with frameworks or templates for these specific application classes. More typical, and more realistic, are reports of productivity increases of ten to thirty percent for new development projects. Even these modest gains require that you learn how to use the tool correctly, a step that our lumberjack skipped.

Productivity gains alone are not the best justification for investing in CASE technology, tools, and training. More recently, the contributions that CASE can make to software quality have been recognized as the most significant impact of these tools [Dixon, 1992]. As we saw in earlier chapters, improved initial quality reduces the effort that has to be devoted to future maintenance. CASE tools can enhance quality by

- improving communication through the use of standard notations for depicting system components;

- improving comprehension and manageability through the use of abstraction, which allows the project stakeholders to view portions of the system at varying degrees of detail;

- making it easy for a designer to change the system models when these changes are inexpensive to make;

- catching certain errors and inconsistencies in the design models more easily than people can;

- reducing rework on subsequent development stages by improving the quality of the specifications supplied to those steps;

- explicitly revealing and documenting the interfaces among system components; and

- providing comprehensive documentation of a system, from several perspectives.

The conventional wisdom (with which I agree) is that you can expect only small benefits from upper-CASE tools unless the people using them are skilled in applying the underlying methodologies. Attempting to get developers to employ tools based on unfamiliar notations and design rules will fail. Your staff should be comfortable with the methods so they can: select the appropriate modeling techniques for each problem; use the power of the CASE tool to draw, redraw, and validate their models efficiently; and know when to violate the rules built into the tool and still achieve their objectives of accurate communication.

Lessons from Our CASE History

My first exposure to structured software development methods came in 1986, when I took a five-day class on structured analysis and design using the Yourdon methodology. I had never before thought in terms of building models of software systems, and the approach made good sense to me. As soon as I got back to the office, I began to apply these new methods to my current project, drawing DFDs, writing module mini-specifications, and creating a data dictionary. The value of the methods was immediately obvious to me: They allowed me to design and think through the system components using models before I started banging out code. However, I learned three lessons along the way. First, I learned that

Changing a model is faster than changing a program.

The second time I had to redraw a diagram to make improvements, the value of having a drawing tool to help me edit my initial models also became obvious, leading to the second lesson:

You cannot get the models right on the first try.

In fact, it always takes me several tries to get a model that feels right. I draw one, print it out, scribble changes on it, then redraw it to make it readable so I can revise it once more. This cycle quickly led to the third lesson:

If you have to completely redraw your models by hand every time you make a change, you probably won't bother drawing models at all.

As a result of my initial attempts, I began to search for a tool that would help me and other members of my team draw these useful pictures. A CASE conference I attended promised fabulous benefits, so our team agreed we should give some upper-CASE tools a try. As another Kodak department had already selected a PC-based upper-CASE tool, we asked for a demonstration. The product, which I refer to as PaleoTool, looked reasonable and the demonstrator extolled its virtues. We bought a copy for each of our five group members.

We successfully used PaleoTool to develop one small system, but we found its character-mode user interface to be clumsy and inefficient. For example, I spent considerable time redrawing the flows that automatically were relocated to silly places every time I moved a bubble in a DFD. This observation led to lesson four:

CASE tools must be sufficiently usable to encourage you to iterate, rather than forcing you to do a lot of tedious cleanup every time you change a diagram.

If changing the model is more trouble than it's worth, people won't take the time to change it and you will lose the benefits of iteration. You'll stick with your first model, even if you know it has shortcomings, because you just won't want to go through the hassle of making modifications. (This experience reminds me of the days before word processors became prevalent, when we prepared one or perhaps two drafts prior to the final version of a document. A word processor vastly improves writing quality, because it makes editing so easy. In the same fashion, a CASE tool must facilitate rather than complicate the revision of software system models.)

After we reached our frustration tolerance with PaleoTool, I called our demonstration contact, explained our problems, and asked why her department thought it was such a great tool. Her response explained a lot: They had used it to document a completed system, not to design a new one. That department did not face the usability problems we experienced, because *they were not iterating*! It is easy to draw a picture of a stable system if you don't have to change the picture in the future. In addition, the tool's knowledge of software design methods is useless to you, if you aren't exploiting its built-in diagram validation functions. Hence, lesson five:

A CASE tool is more than a drawing program. Use the tool for iterative design, not just after-the-fact documentation. Let the tool's intelligence detect errors that are difficult for people to see, by validating the diagrams according to the tool's methodology rules.

PaleoTool contained a plethora of different symbols that could be used for drawing software models or generic diagrams. Drawing certain infrequently used symbols actually required the user to press five keys simultaneously. I felt like I was playing a piano, not a computer keyboard. At that time, some of the experts writing about CASE gushed over tools that allowed users to define whatever symbols they liked. These writers claimed that you should be able to define triangles (or anything else) to represent the processes on a DFD, rather than the more conventional circles (DeMarco-Yourdon) or rounded rectangles (Gane-Sarson). "Why should I be constrained by the methods that are hard-wired into the tools?" they asked.

I don't agree with the premise of complete tailorability of tools and notations. CASE tools facilitate communication among the project participants precisely because of their ability to enforce a limited set of standard notations. Supporting multiple conventions is important, since no single design methodology satisfies all needs. But creating a software Tower of Babel to accommodate designers who wish to be artistically creative with their individual symbologies will inhibit communication, not facilitate it. (Of course, individual developers can still benefit from their use of the tool, no matter what unique notations they decide to use.) My viewpoint led us to lesson six:

Choose one of the standard modeling notations, and use it until you determine that it no longer meets the needs of your team or your project.

Having the team use standardized modeling notations facilitated sharing our high-level analysis and design documents with our key customers. Some customers interact with more than one of our development teams, and we would not have been as successful in getting customers to accept our design models as a communication mechanism if each developer had been using his own diagramming conventions.

After we returned four of the copies of PaleoTool we had purchased (keeping a single copy to support the one system we had built with it), we worked with another simple PC-based product for a couple of years. This one had substantially improved usability and performance over PaleoTool, but it was limited in the variety of models it supported. We used it successfully on five small projects, however, and all in all found it to be a good investment. These first-generation upper-CASE tools have since been replaced by much more capable and less expensive PC- and Macintosh®-based products.

At that first Yourdon training class in 1986, I was overwhelmed by the variety of structured analysis models that were introduced: current physical, current essential, new essential, new implementation, processor, task, and other models. I wondered whether it really is necessary to draw so many different kinds of models. I concluded, "Not usually." Subsets of the various model types meet most needs, with the exact members of the subset depending on the project.

For example, I worked on one project in which the new implementation model was quite different from the new essential model. Building both models led us to a more efficient design than if we had stopped with the essential model and began programming. On another project, modeling the current physical system really was necessary before we could begin to design the future essential model. The conclusion I drew from these early experiences is summarized in lesson seven:

Don't feel that you have to swallow any methodology whole. Just use the parts that add value to your project.

During this period of growing into CASE, we spent considerable time during group meetings struggling to learn how to make both the methodologies and the modeling tools work well for us. One issue we confronted was how best to model the different types of applications our group constructed: information systems, real-time process control programs, and scientific software. We could not figure out how to collect all the significant elements of each application class—process-oriented components, data storage relationships, and control flow processing—onto a single diagram. Eventually, we reached the conclusion of lesson eight:

No single model can show all the important aspects of the system; often you need to create multiple views.

Several different kinds of models can be used to represent different views or projections of the system. The *context diagram* identifies the external entities to which the elements of the system must interface and the data that flows between the system and each external entity. *Data flow diagrams* identify the processes in the system that transform inputs into outputs and the data used by each such process. The *control flow diagram* adds control processes and flows to the DFD to show how one event stimulates another. Events that result in changes in the system's state can be represented in a *state-transition diagram.* (In Chapter 6 we saw how to apply the STD in a dialog map for modeling a user interface.) The *entity-relationship diagram* depicts the architecture of the data collections in a system. These views are not all independent. For example, entities on the ERD often map to data stores in the DFD.

Object-oriented modeling notations often do a better job of fusing data, process, and control elements into a single diagram than do traditional structured diagramming techniques. Object diagrams identify object classes and their hierarchical and compositional relationships. They also show how collections of objects interact by exchanging messages and performing actions upon receiving requests from other objects.

No single modeling technique is perfect for every application. The challenge to the designer is to select the appropriate modeling views that will facilitate communication and minimize rework by creating a clear, shared vision of the application prior to casting it in code.

Despite our understanding of what models best fit a particular situation, we had some heated group meetings in which we haggled over exactly what rules the team should follow for different design models. We struggled with questions such as the following:

- If your system interfaces to an external database, should you show that database as an external entity (terminator) on the context diagram, or as a data store?

- Is it ever okay to draw more than one bubble on a context diagram?

- Should you use a data store to represent *any* data that is passed from one process to another (such as an argument list), or just for data that has some persistence over time (a file, a database, or global variable storage)?

- Is it appropriate to show externals on lower-level DFDs, or only on the context diagram?

These may seem like trivial issues, but resolving them seemed to be on the critical path to successfully implementing CASE and structured methods in our group, thereby moving us toward an improved software engineering culture. We finally converged on some conventions we could all live with, or else we agreed to disagree when doing so did not impair our use of the models as communication tools. Then, we went about our business of using the methods and tools to get useful work done. There were two lessons here. Lesson nine was

Align the team on the spirit of the method and the tool, not necessarily the letter of "the rules."

Remember that two main objectives of system modeling are to facilitate the iteration that leads to design quality and to facilitate communication. Anything that supports these goals is acceptable; anything that inhibits them is not acceptable. We need not be dogmatic about how either the method or the tool is applied, provided the two objectives are met.

A related lesson was

Expect to pass through a sequence of forming, storming, norming, and performing when your group begins to use CASE or other software development tools and methods.

The stages of forming, storming, norming (or standardizing), and performing describe the interpersonal dynamics of a new team. They also define a typical sequence for groups incorporating new methods or tools into their development process. During forming, the team selects a CASE tool it wishes to adopt. During storming, team members argue incessantly about how to use the tool, discussing whether it is a good investment or a waste of money, whether they intend to use it at all, and how to interpret the rules embodied in the tool or its underlying methods. If you stop at the storming stage, the culture does not evolve to the future state the team anticipated when they launched the CASE initiative. The team leader should recognize when storming is taking place and control it so that no blood is shed nor personal relationships destroyed, but allow the discussions to take place.

Push through the storming, relying on the mutual respect and professionalism of your team members and their willingness to compromise. Sometimes, these elements are lacking, which indicates a need for the manager to provide leadership, technical insights, individual coaching on interpersonal skills, and possibly even an executive decision (the last resort). When you get past storming, the team should enter a norming stage, in which the members reach agreement on how to apply the methods and tools, in line with the overarching objectives of effective communication and achieving software quality through iterative design.

The ultimate stage is performing, in which project team members are able to achieve better results by using the new tool than they did without it. When you see team members performing, you should be proud of them—and yourself—for staying focused on quality software engineering objectives, and for carrying the technology change through to routine practice in an improved culture.

While our group has not made a practice of quantifying developer productivity, we still can sense whether some change in our development process is having a positive effect. Once we reached the stage at which neither lack of knowledge of the methods nor lack of experience with the tool was an inhibitor, we asked ourselves whether we were reaping the great productivity gains promised by CASE vendors and writers. The answer was, "No." In fact, using upper-CASE tools caused us to spend more time on up-front analysis and design than we otherwise would have spent. While the resulting design quality certainly reduced the extent of code rework that had to be done, we perceived little direct impact on the delivery schedule. Therein lies lesson eleven:

> **Benefits from CASE come mainly in the quality of the delivered product. The biggest productivity gain comes over the long term, as defect-repair efforts are reduced because of improved initial quality, and enhancements are facilitated by design models, documentation, and more robust system architecture.**

To be fair, we never conducted a controlled experiment in which two comparable teams built the same product, one with the help of CASE technology and one without, measuring the productivity difference between the two teams. No one outside a university or software research organization is likely to attempt such an experiment. Our development process was not so precise that we could accurately predict how long it would really take us to complete a specific project. Developers always underestimate the amount of rework they will end up doing, anyway. So while I cannot quantify my claim, I still believe the quality improvement outweighs the delivery schedule impact of upper-CASE tools, at least in this one group's experience.

We verified the contention of accelerated enhancements thanks to CASE when we had to add a major extension to the one system we had built using PaleoTool. We hired an internal Kodak contractor to work on this project, who began by studying the architecture and functions of the current system as described in the design models. We then took the specifications for the desired enhancements and modified the current design models to incorporate a new subsystem, connected to the existing functionality. Implementation of the new subsystem went smoothly, with little post-delivery debugging required. The models thus served their purpose as a communication tool: The contractor said she found them to be extremely helpful in gaining an understanding of the current system.

No matter how great a job software engineers do during analysis and design, the programs we write never exactly match their designs. The design models therefore become inconsistent with the software that is ultimately delivered. On our projects, we had to decide what to do with the CASE models when system construction has been completed, and we came up with four options.

1. Update the models to match the reality of the system as it was built, and keep them current as modifications are made in the future. This approach demands the most effort. It has the advantage that the design documentation is always accurate, making it more valuable during maintenance work. If you are using a lower-CASE code generator tool that writes programs based on design models, you *must* maintain the models.

2. Keep the models as a historical record of the system as it was originally designed. This option is fine, provided that future readers of the models understand that they reflect only a generally correct view of the current system, not one that is accurate in every detail.

3. Discard the models once they have served their purpose, which was to assist with construction of a quality system. This choice avoids any possible confusion due to conflicts between the real system and the design diagrams. There is a military aphorism that states, "When the map and the terrain do not agree, always believe the terrain." Source code is the ultimate "terrain" of software reality. Inconsistencies between code and documentation cause confusion, wasted time, and possible errors.

4. Reverse-engineer the design models from the finished source code, which is feasible only if you have appropriate CASE tools available. This approach gives you the as-built design documentation directly from the final code. You can repeat this process any time code changes are made in order to generate a new and accurate set of models.

Any one of these alternatives is acceptable, so long as everyone affected understands which path was taken and the implications for the future of the system. Lesson twelve can therefore be stated as

Explicitly resolve the issue of as-designed versus as-built documentation for each project.

Integrated CASE, in which a collection of tools interact effectively to let you work on all stages of the software development life cycle in a unified fashion, sounds like a great idea. Unfortunately, our group worked in a heterogeneous computing environment, in which we performed pieces of the development work on an assortment of platforms (Fig. 14.3).

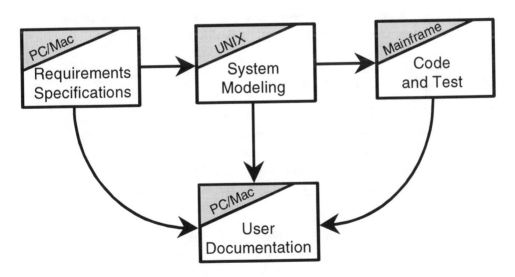

Figure 14.3: Different platforms used for development steps.

The CASE tools we had available provided no help with writing structured textual requirements specifications, so we did that on either a PC or on a Macintosh. We performed analysis and design using CASE tools on a PC or a UNIX workstation. The major delivery platforms were an IBM® mainframe and PCs running MS-DOS® or QNX™ (a real-time multitasking operating system). While we did our best to make the pieces fit together, we were faced with the cold reality of lesson thirteen:

> **You cannot reap the full benefits of CASE in a highly heterogeneous development environment. Keeping system development components synchronized manually across multiple platforms is tedious and time-consuming.**

There is a common belief that CASE tools are only useful on giant projects involving armies of developers. I don't agree. After using several CASE tools on a variety of projects over a span of seven years, I concluded that structured systems modeling with automated assistance provides value to all but the tiniest applications. One-person projects should pass through some explicit and systematic design activity, just as monster projects should.

I am disheartened when I see programs being rewritten to fix problems that could have been avoided by doing a better job of modeling the requirements and designing the architecture prior to writing code. Even for programs having only a few hundred lines of code, I sketch out a data flow model or structure chart on paper. Sometimes, one sketch is enough to keep me on track; if not, into the CASE tool it goes. The final lesson from our group's CASE experience is

> **Nearly all projects can benefit from the discipline of iterative structured design that upper-CASE tools facilitate.**

Fitting CASE into Your Culture

Incorporating CASE into a software development organization is not as simple as buying the latest tool and plopping a copy of the user manual on each engineer's desk. The shelfware rate for CASE tools can approach 80 or 90 percent. As with any technology migration, the organization has to prepare for change through planning, training, and communicating. As James Wilson pointed out [Wilson, 1993]:

> When you introduce new methods, techniques, and CASE tools, you're introducing a new technology which will change the way you construct software. You're changing the way people perform their jobs. You're changing the skills needed to perform those jobs. Companies that have been successful with CASE tools have realized that you must take the focus off the tools and focus on the underlying methods and techniques. Your ultimate objective is to change the way your information systems department does business.

An organization that attempts to incorporate CASE technology into its culture typ-ically passes through the stages of disenchantment, resignation, commitment, implementation, and finally maturity [Hughes, 1990]. At CASE maturity, project participants are able to select from a palette of tools and methods that can help them meet their objectives. The techniques for successfully inducing the changes required for an organization to adopt CASE depend on the cultural characteristics of the organization [DeGrace, 1993]. For example, a tool choice imposed by man-agement decree will not be well received in a culture that emphasizes collaborative teamwork and consensus decision-making. In addition, introducing CASE causes a conflict between the part of your brain that wants to start cutting code right away and the part that admits the importance of understanding the problem before building a solution. The group's orientation toward a quality-focused soft-ware engineering culture helps define the relative sizes of these two cerebral com-ponents.

Given the many potential pitfalls, it is no wonder that so many CASE projects fail, leading to disenchantment on the part of all those involved and a return to development as it was done before. You can minimize the risk of CASE failure by managing the organizational changes skillfully and by focusing on the needs of your specific projects, not the hype you read in the most recent stack of vendor lit-erature. The best chance of successful tool adoption comes if the capabilities of the tools and their underlying methods will attack some source of pain in your organi-zation. In *CASE on Trial*, a paper by John Parkinson entitled "Making CASE Work" identifies eight critical success factors that are required for the successful introduc-tion of CASE into an organization [Spurr, 1990]:

Pick the right approach. Decide why you want to start using CASE tools, and understand the problems you expect them to solve, before you take the plunge. Merge the tools into the department, gradually evolving your culture to exploit the tools, rather than trying to radically change the culture to fit the tool vendor's software development paradigm.

Obtain management commitment. You will need to educate your man-agers in the value of investing in CASE, so they understand that this is not just a toy to amuse the software people. Management must be persuaded that the non-trivial cost of CASE is a sound investment.

Build on a methodology. Unless you already have an established develop-ment methodology in widespread use, you will not be able to adopt CASE success-fully. Do not rely on the tools to teach your engineers the fundamental methods, any more than you can learn arithmetic by using a calculator. In the groups with which I have worked, the individuals who used CASE tools most effectively were those who had a solid understanding of the methods that the tools support. New ways of thinking lay the foundation for new ways of working.

Acquire training. As with the lumberjack and the chain saw, someone needs to show your staff how to derive the maximum benefit from the new tools. Without training in how to use the tools effectively, you cannot fully leverage your investment. If the trainees do not have the opportunity to use what they have learned soon after they return from the training class, much of their newly acquired knowledge will fade away. Training delivered by the tool vendor can inflate the hype of the miracle cures awaiting users of the tool, which then fail to materialize when the students try to apply the tool to their own projects.

Involve users. Exposing application users to CASE tools and the diagrams they produce can help engage them more in the development process. Many of our project champions learned to read DFDs, STDs, and data dictionaries with just a little explanation about the notations that are used. A single diagram may seem overwhelmingly complicated to the novice, but the beauty of structured modeling techniques is that you can focus your attention on the immediate environment of one diagram element (such as a single DFD bubble or object class description) at a time. It doesn't matter what appears elsewhere on the page.

Select appropriate tools. Make an explicit decision to select either a tool with a simple user interface, so that developers can become productive with it quickly, or a more powerful tool suite that supports most of the development life cycle. The strategy our software group took was to start with a simple and inexpensive tool, replacing it with a more capable product when our needs exceeded its limitations.

The two-stage approach does require making a second investment in CASE products and associated training. An alternative is to acquire a high-function tool initially but only use a subset of its features at first. A third strategy is to use a collection of tools that work well with each other, rather than trying to find a single one that will meet all of your team's needs over the long run. Whichever approach you select, make sure your developers have desktop access to the tools, rather than having to go to some inconvenient location to access the single workstation you bought for the CASE tool.

Get help. Particularly during your first projects using CASE tools, be willing to bring in expert consultants to get your team over the learning curve as quickly as possible. But be cautious: I have had consultants offer to work with me on a project so they can learn along with me!

Manage expectations. As with so many of the techniques I have addressed, a CASE tool is not a silver bullet for your software troubles. Nor is it a substitute for good analytical skills. The tool can let you generate poor designs faster than you ever could before, as well as enabling the skilled designer to do a much better job. CASE tools may know the rules for validating models according to someone's methodology, but they know nothing about how to generate good solutions for your customers' needs. Make sure the stakeholders in the CASE experiment have a realistic understanding of what value they can expect the tool to add to their process and products. Your first CASE-based project likely will take longer than it would have without the tool, because of the learning curve. Share your failures, as well as success stories, within the team, so that all can learn from another's experiences.

Other Benefits from CASE

The use of upper-CASE tools can encourage your developers to focus consciously on explicit design activities. This design process produces tangible artifacts—models—that can be reviewed to assess design quality, prior to casting them into hand-written code or generating code from a lower-CASE tool. A conscious design process is far superior to the jump from requirements directly into code that characterizes many software projects. Great programs can't compensate for a poor system architecture.

A model can help reveal the interfaces among system components, as well as the interfaces between your system and external entities to which it connects. These interfaces usually cause headaches at system integration time, but by explicitly defining the interface elements—such as data flows, object messages, and relational database tables that are logically connected—the development team can agree on structures and behaviors so the pieces fit together more smoothly.

The instructor for my Yourdon structured analysis and design class taught us that "bubbles don't talk to bubbles" in a DFD. He advocated placing a data store between any pair of process bubbles that are connected by data flows. While this clutters the diagram, it explicitly identifies the interfaces around each process. In the DFD fragment shown in Fig. 14.4, the dashed line around the process labeled Retrieve Reference Requests cuts through the middle of each attached data store. This conceptual line is not really part of the DFD, but it isolates that process and its data interfaces as an independent object, which can then be assigned to any appropriate developer for detailed design and implementation. Provided that everyone respects the data dictionary definition of the connecting stores (and assuming they are correct), programs written by different developers should integrate properly.

CASE tools and their underlying methods facilitate collaboration through the use of standard notations and definitions. On one system that I specified and helped implement many years ago, the three-person development team did not use a data dictionary, or any other structured methods. While assembling some documentation after completing the system, I was dismayed to discover that such a simple data item as a user's name was not defined consistently. We used five different variable names in two programming languages, with inconsistent definitions for the length of the name. The same programmer (er, um, me) had even used different variable names for this data item in two subroutines. Had we created—and respected—a common data dictionary, this sort of error would not have taken place.

Building design models can make reuse opportunities visible. If multiple processes in a DFD require the same functionality, or if similar classes appear in multiple parts of an object model, a REUSE sign should begin flashing in the designer's brain. Identifying reusable components at the design stage is much more effective than hoping they pop out of the code. This way, you can explicitly design the components to satisfy multiple needs. Often, the requirements can be adjusted slightly to facilitate reusing an existing component.

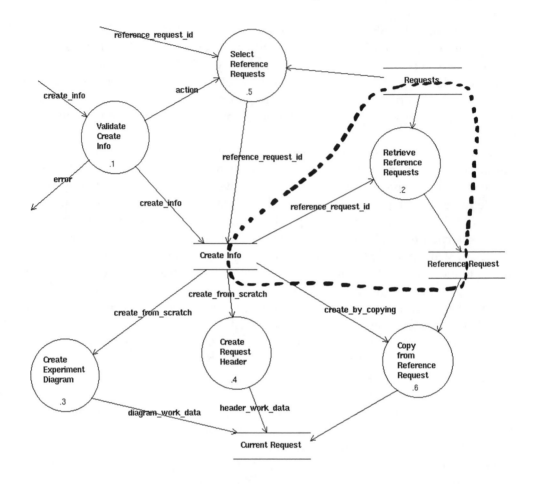

*Figure 14.4: The data stores connected to a DFD process
define its external interfaces.*

Culture Change for CASE

Part of the cultural resistance to CASE arises because some developers fear that automating aspects of software engineering will inhibit their creativity. On the contrary, CASE tools can handle some of the drudgery of routine tasks, allowing developers to focus their creativity on high-impact activities. The software engineer's project contributions will start to shift from creating correct source code to accurately representing user requirements and designing high-quality solutions that satisfy them. Exceptionally creative application designers are scarcer, and more valuable, than clever programmers. The skill sets used by analysts and designers are different from those required for writing programs.

Expect some of your team members to require training in the new skill areas, including design methodologies, customer interactions, meeting facilitation, technical writing, and other people and communication skills. Anticipate that others will be uncomfortable with the changing expectations; they will need some mentoring, persuasion, and examples of success stories before they climb on board. Still others just won't be able to make the cultural shift.

The discipline required to build and improve models will also be a big culture change for those who disdain structured approaches and can't wait to "say it in code." Those team members who do migrate successfully into modeling and CASE application can expect considerable improvement in the quality of their work products, through rapid iteration of system analysis and design models. They should also enjoy increased productivity through reduced rework and more effective reuse of the fruits of previous labors.

Summary

- ✔ A key to software quality is to iterate many times on all development steps except coding: Do this once.

- ✔ To iterate efficiently on analysis and design activities, you need a structured notation to represent the information and a tool that lets you make changes quickly and easily.

- ✔ When using a structured development methodology, you need to create multiple views of the system being designed. CASE tools help to integrate these views and keep them consistent, using a data dictionary as the common vocabulary.

- ✔ Make sure your staff understands how to effectively apply the methods you select before you invest in CASE tools that support the methods.

- ✔ CASE tools can improve the quality of your delivered software, because of the improvements made through iterating on designs. This higher quality will reduce subsequent internal rework stemming from design errors, as well as lowering your maintenance and support burdens for the life of the product.

- ✔ A cultural transformation takes place as an organization moves from less structured, manual methods to the discipline of structured methods and automated tool usage. The roles your engineers will play during systems development will change. Facilitate this change by acquiring management commitment, providing training, selecting the right tools for your organization, and managing the expectations people have of the new technology.

Culture Builders and Killers

 Culture Builder: Before you embark on a CASE tool selection journey, work with your development staff to evaluate their current work environment. Explore questions like these:

- What methods do they use for system and program design now, and how well do they work?

- Do they need training in structured or object-oriented development methodologies to be able to use them more effectively?

- What kinds of tools do they think would provide the most improvement leverage?

- How stringently do they want the tool to enforce the methodology rules?

This analysis will help you select the initial software tools that are likely to benefit your organization. Try to find people who have already used the tools in which you are interested, on projects similar to yours. What value did these other users obtain from the tools? What difficulties did they encounter? What can they tell you that will save you the pain of solving unanticipated problems yourselves?

Culture Builder: Once you have selected a set of CASE tools, apply them on a project in which their use is not critical to success. As with any new technology adoption, be prepared to take a productivity hit during the implementation and learning stages. Avoid the temptation (and, perhaps, the pressure from upper management) to shorten the project schedule because you have this wonderful new tool available. Technology infusion rarely works quick miracles.

Culture Builder: Sponsor a user group in your company to allow practitioners who are using the same methods and tools to share their experiences. If different groups are using different tools, try to get some hands-on exposure to a new tool before you purchase your own copy. True-life experiences are a valuable supplement to vendor literature and canned demonstrations. Kodak had a Structured Methods Users Group (SMUG) for several years, which was helpful and fun. User groups like this also help build a corporate culture of sharing best practices and exchanging ideas that work.

Culture Builder: Even though CASE tools can be expensive, buy enough copies to provide ready access for every member of your development staff who needs to use them. Don't try to economize by installing single copies on a walk-up workstation. Your team won't be motivated to use the new tool if they have to work evenings and weekends to get access to it. A manager in a software engineering culture invests in the tools her staff needs to perform their tasks efficiently.

Culture Killer: When you purchase CASE tools for your team, you can save some money by not sending anybody to training classes for the tool or for the new development methods that you want them to use. Save even more money by not signing up for the vendor maintenance and support costs. Your people are clever; they should be able to work through any problems they encounter with the tool. They can read the manual to answer their questions.

Culture Killer: Select the CASE tool you want your team to use by studying some vendor literature, then tell your engineers to use it, without getting their input into the selection process. Alternatively, commission a comparative evaluation of CASE tools, then select something other than the one the evaluators recommended. If they are not able to apply the tool effectively, it's their own fault. Many other companies are getting great results with this very tool—it said so right in the vendor brochure.

References and Further Reading

Bergin, Thomas J. *Computer-Aided Software Engineering: Issues and Trends for the 1990s and Beyond.* Harrisburg, Penn.: Idea Group Publishing, 1993.

> This large volume contains twenty-two papers by different authors, in the categories of integrated CASE, managing the transition to CASE, methodology issues in existing tools and methods, case studies of tool usage, and the future of CASE. I highly recommend it.

DeGrace, Peter, and Leslie Hulet Stahl. *The Olduvai Imperative: CASE and the State of Software Engineering Practice.* Englewood Cliffs, N.J.: Yourdon Press/Prentice-Hall, 1993.

> DeGrace and Stahl describe the implications of CASE for organizations having two distinct types of culture, which they call "Roman" and "Greek". The authors are disdainful of the top-down, management-driven Roman approach to deploying CASE. They suggest an alternative, Greek approach, which focuses on those who will use the tools—the engineering staff.

Dixon, Robert L. *Winning with CASE: Managing Modern Software Development.* New York: McGraw-Hill, 1992.

> Since the most common reason why CASE tool insertion fails is resistance to change by the developers, Dixon discusses aspects of change management in an organization. A useful appendix contains a comprehensive outline of criteria for classifying and evaluating CASE tools.

Hughes, Cary T., and Jon D. Clark. "The Stages of CASE Usage," *Datamation* (February 1, 1990), pp. 41-44.

This article describes a five-stage sequence through which organizations evolve as they attempt to incorporate CASE technology into practical use.

Page-Jones, Meilir. "The CASE Manifesto," *Computer Language,* Vol. 10, No. 6 (June 1993), pp. 39-52.

Page-Jones looks at what is wrong with CASE tools today. One big problem he cites is poor usability: Making a simple change in a CASE model can require an inordinate number of editing steps. The ideal tool would conduct a dialog with the user, with the computer walking through a series of questions designed to elicit precisely the required information from the tool user. Page-Jones presents twelve attributes that CASE tools ought to have.

Robertson, James, and Suzanne Robertson. *Complete Systems Analysis: The Workbook, the Textbook, the Answers.* New York: Dorset House Publishing, 1994.

This contemporary guide to system modeling describes the structured methodologies that form the foundation for many upper-CASE tools. The principles of structured analysis are freshly presented and extended in this two-volume set, which applies the methods to an actual project. A unique "trail guide" approach suggests appropriate sequences of book sections that novice, intermediate, and experienced analysts might choose to follow.

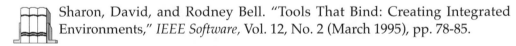

Sharon, David, and Rodney Bell. "Tools That Bind: Creating Integrated Environments," *IEEE Software,* Vol. 12, No. 2 (March 1995), pp. 78-85.

This article describes the kinds of tools that would fit into an integrated software development environment. Sharon and Bell itemize nearly thirty tools that have demonstrated the ability to be integrated into a cohesive tool suite by conforming to established industry standards.

Spurr, Kathy, and Paul Lazell, eds. *CASE on Trial.* Chichester, England: John Wiley & Sons, 1990.

Fifteen papers on CASE methods, evaluating and selecting CASE tools, and organizational considerations for CASE are included in this collection. I especially liked "Making CASE Work," by John Parkinson. Parkinson provides a realistic perspective on the benefits of CASE, how to insert CASE technology into an organization, and critical success factors for implementing CASE.

Wilson, James D. "Methodology Mania: Which One Fits Best?" *Journal of the Quality Assurance Institute,* Vol. 7, No. 2 (April 1993), pp. 18-22.

> Wilson provides a seven-step process for selecting a systems development methodology for your organization. He identifies the strengths and weaknesses of twelve commercially available methodologies with respect to ten dimensions of the software development life cycle.

Yourdon, Edward. *Decline and Fall of the American Programmer.* Englewood Cliffs, N.J.: Yourdon Press/Prentice-Hall, 1992.

> Chapter 6 provides a concise history of the evolution of CASE tools and their capabilities, along with recommendations for bringing CASE tools into an organization.

Chapter 15

Control Change Before
It Controls You

You can't control what you can't measure.

—Tom DeMarco, *Controlling Software Projects*

One quality management practice that several software groups at Kodak have found helpful is a system that assists with software change management, defect tracking, and user feedback. Unrestrained changes in software are a common cause of quality degradation. Managing change requests is necessary throughout the development life cycle, since requirements changes can have a severe impact on work that has already been completed. Recording and tracking the status of defects identified in a system is important for quality assessment, process improvement, and managing the perennial maintenance backlog.

In a reactive software development culture, changes are poorly managed. Customers have no formal process for requesting enhancements in a product or reporting bugs they encountered. No one knows exactly how many change requests are pending in the backlog. No rational prioritization process is used to make sure the important things get done first. The status of any particular problem at any given time is not always clear. Two people might work on the same reported problem at the same time, resulting in the need to reconcile any conflicting changes. Change requests sometimes become lost before they can be addressed.

In such a culture, records are not kept to understand how much time is spent on different kinds of maintenance work on each project. The rates at which new defects are reported and corrected during testing are not known. This makes it more difficult to anticipate when the product will reach an acceptable (that is, shippable) level of quality, and what that level of quality might be. Without accurate records, there is no certain way to identify those system components that generate the most problem reports or requests for user support. No historical records exist to indicate when, why, and by whom decisions to modify the product were made.

In contrast, managers and practitioners in a healthy software engineering culture want to manage product changes effectively. They want to know who is responsible for resolving each problem report, and how quickly problems are being solved. A reported error should not linger in the to-do queue forever because no one gets around to dealing with it. Nobody wants to waste time fixing the same bug more than once because of miscommunication.

An accurate count of the bugs found during testing and after a program is released is necessary, so the team can determine the efficiency of their inspection and testing practices. Members of a culture focused on continuous improvement want a history of program failures, so they can understand the faults that led to the failures and reduce those kinds of faults in the future. A problem reporting and tracking system, and a defined process that integrates it into the development and maintenance work, can help you achieve these objectives.

Benefits of a Problem Tracking System

We have already seen that minimizing the effort spent on all types of rework is one pathway to improved software development productivity. Activities that can be considered as rework or maintenance include: correcting defects found after a product is released; correcting errors that slipped through the previous development stage's quality control filters; adding unanticipated new functionality to completed products; making modifications to adapt to changes in the execution environment that are imposed by external forces; providing assistance to customers, such as supplying workarounds for known bugs, shipping code patches, and explaining obscure user documentation; and restructuring programs in order to avoid future maintenance problems.

The purpose of a problem reporting and tracking system is to bring order out of the chaos of uncontrolled change. By accumulating well-characterized data rather than just vague perceptions, team members acquire greater insight into their products and processes. Project leaders and department managers can feel that their work is under control, instead of being victims of the chaos. A problem tracking system provides visibility into the status of both prereleased and released products, so priorities for work can be set intelligently. You can track the effort devoted to fixing specific faults, and you can assess how well your support staff responds to customer problems.

The system also serves as a historical repository of previously reported problems, to which a support person can refer in search of a known solution to a fresh trouble report. This historical record can show whether an unusual problem has occurred before, to help reveal patterns. It is easy (and tempting) to dismiss a bizarre and nonreproducible error report as being spurious, attributing it, for example, to a hardware problem, user error, or cosmic rays. However, we sometimes find old, but still open, problem reports in our database that match a new one, proving that there really is a software error lurking in there somewhere.

Collecting comprehensive data on the defects reported also lets you analyze the root causes of those defects. One Kodak project performed just such a fault analysis on the defects identified during testing. The bugs responsible for all failures were classified as to type, and trends in the prevalence and cost impact of each bug class were examined. This analysis revealed that most of the defects could be attributed to errors in either the user requirements or the user interface. This understanding led to improvements in the way user requirements were gathered and documented and to better user interface prototyping. Without the insights provided by the defect data, any improvement efforts this project attempted might not have focused on the most important sources of errors.

A Software Change Management Case Study

Early in 1990, my group devised a simple system that combined three functions: change request and management, defect recording and tracking, and user feedback. This system, called SWCHANGE, has contributed a lot to the quality of our software products and processes. At the time we decided we needed a problem tracking system (PTS), nothing was commercially available for our dominant development platform, so we wrote one. While you can always build your own PTS (Lotus Notes™ is a popular choice for a tool on which to base such a system), I suggest you look into one of the many commercial options now available. A good source of information on such tools is the Usenet newsgroup comp.software.config-mgmt, in which a descriptive list of many problem management tools is posted periodically.

SWCHANGE has helped us in many respects. It serves as a central repository for change requests and bug reports for our many applications, so they do not get lost. We can track the status of pending change requests and measure our response times for resolving requests of different types. If those response times are not what we want them to be, we can set goals to improve them and track our progress toward the goals. This is an example of using process data to point out improvement opportunities and to measure progress.

Through SWCHANGE, we monitor the number of problem reports for each application, look for trends, and determine if we should take action to head future problems off at the pass. For example, a lot of user assistance requests for one application might indicate a need to improve its user interface, provide better on-line help, write a user manual, or provide some user training. We can turn the raw data in the PTS into information that helps us make smart decisions.

We can generate reports of the pending change requests for each application. The project leader, project champions, or change control board can use these reports to set priorities for work to be done. Often, the support person for the application is not in a position to set reasonable priorities for adding new features or correcting noncritical bugs. Life is much easier for the support staff if they can take a stack of SWCHANGE reports to the project champions and ask them to prioritize the change requests.

Figure 15.1 illustrates the SWCHANGE architecture, which is typical of many commercial bug tracking systems. SWCHANGE entries are stored in a file-based hypertext tool we wrote. Commercial systems may use flat files, proprietary database formats, or an interface to a commercial relational database management system like Oracle® or Sybase®.

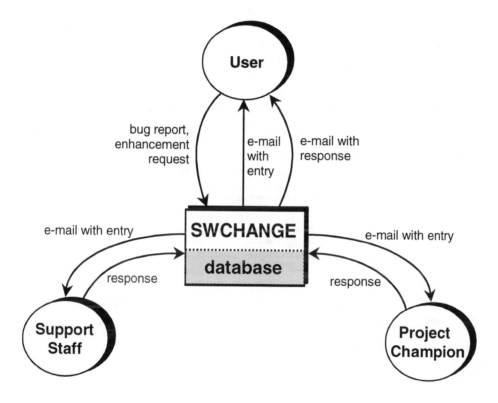

Figure 15.1: Architecture of the SWCHANGE problem tracking system.

When a customer submits an entry to SWCHANGE, it is stored in the database. E-mail messages are generated automatically to route the new entry to the designated support staff member and the project champion for that application. These might be the same person, such as for our internal reusable components. The submitting customer also receives a copy of the note, so he knows the entry was logged properly and who was notified. This approach insulates the customer from having to know whom to call to get help with each of the over one hundred applications that currently use SWCHANGE.

SWCHANGE runs on an IBM mainframe, and many of our mainframe applications employ it as the user feedback/problem reporting screen. SWCHANGE can be hooked into an application as a reusable component with only one line of code, or the users can access it as a stand-alone utility. The error reporting function of a non-mainframe application can feed messages directly into SWCHANGE through an e-mail interface. By the same token, the mail messages that are generated when an entry is submitted into SWCHANGE can be sent to a user on any computer that can be reached from this mainframe.

An SWCHANGE user can report a perceived bug, suggest an enhancement, or request assistance with a problem, using the screen in Fig. 15.2. Information identifying the user is added to the entry automatically. The support person and project champion can then decide how each entry will be handled. Either of them can enter a response to an entry, which is added to the database and e-mailed to the customer who submitted the entry in the first place.

```
            Submit an SWCHANGE Entry for SOME_APP              SWC020

Customer Name: MARVIN GLEASON      Userid: marvin    Phone: 78880 Dept: 756
Request Class:  _ Bug Report    _ Enhancement Request    _ User Assistance
Descriptive Title: _____
Description of problem or desired enhancement:
_____
_____
_____
_____
_____
_____

For bug reports only:
Version of software being run: _____ Is the error reproducible? _ (Y/N)
Kind of terminal or computer used: _____
When was the last time this
function worked correctly, if ever? _____
-------------------------------------------------------------------------
PF1-Help      PF3-Cancel      PF10-Reset Screen      PF12-Submit this Report
```

Figure 15.2: SWCHANGE entry submission screen.

Every SWCHANGE entry is assessed as to the effort that will be required to make the necessary changes in the software. The assessment is automatically set to *To Be Determined* when the entry is first created. The following are the other assessments that an entry can have.

> *Minor.* The change can be made, tested, and documented in two days or less; no special user testing is required.

> *Major.* The change can be made, tested, and documented in two weeks or less; definitive user testing will be required to validate the change.

Severe. The change involves restructuring a significant fraction of the program, or it may have a large impact on the way the user interacts with the program. It may take longer than two weeks.

Impossible. The change cannot be made because of hardware or software limitations or conflicts, performance constraints, lack of access to required data, or other technical reasons.

User Error. The reported problem is due to improper use or understanding of the program by the customer; no software change is indicated. It may be appropriate to modify user aids (on-line help, user guide, on-line newsletter) to prevent such misunderstandings in the future.

Unknown. The developer cannot adequately assess the scope of the change request at this time.

In addition to its assessment, each entry always has a status specified. When the customer's initial entry is accepted into the change database, the status is set to *Submitted.* The other possible statuses that an entry can have are: *Assessed* (the developer has reported his initial assessment); *Pending* (the project champion has requested that the change be made, and the developer has scheduled the change or is actively working on it); *Completed* (the change has been completed and the new software has been released); *Canceled* (the change request has been canceled); and *Deferred* (action on the change request is deferred to a future time).

The status and assessment for an entry can be changed only by individuals who are authorized to respond to entries for that application in the database, usually the support person and project champions. Every project that employs SWCHANGE uses the same assessment and status codes. This facilitates collecting consistent metrics data across several projects.

Since a problem tracking system is a communication tool, all parties involved—developers, testers, support staff, customers, and managers—must share the same vision of how the tool will be used. The way the system is employed by these stakeholders is a reflection of their software engineering culture. At one extreme, the PTS may be viewed as an embarrassing way to air the group's dirty laundry for all to see. A more enlightened culture will recognize the PTS as an enabling tool that provides honest insight into the quality of its software products, processes, and services.

As an example of how the data can be used for process improvement, suppose your PTS allows the engineer who corrects a defect to log both the location of the error in the source code and the time he spent correcting it. You can use this data to identify those program modules that are hogging your maintenance resources. You can then decide whether a troublesome module should be rewritten or some other corrective action should be undertaken.

The data can also point out projects in which too many bugs leaked through the quality control filters, so the filters can be improved on the next project. If you calculate predicted maintainabilities from source code metrics (described in Chapter 17), the information in your PTS will let you determine how well the predictions correlate with reality. This will help you use source code metrics analysis as a better predictive tool on your next project.

If you have a defined process for managing changes in place, the PTS can help enhance your software engineering culture. Some of the principles that went into the design and use of SWCHANGE are described in the following paragraphs. Your rules may be different; the important point is to have all the stakeholders share an understanding of how the PTS will be used.

If a change request has not been submitted through SWCHANGE, it does not exist. This requirement has reduced the chaos that results when change requests come in by e-mail, telephone, scribbled notes, and quick conversations in the hallway. Perhaps half of the requests we receive verbally never materialize after we ask the customers to submit them through SWCHANGE (we conclude that such requests must not have been very important). This principle is not intended to inhibit customers from submitting change requests or reporting problems, but to let us provide a superior level of service through a defined process and tool. In short, SWCHANGE helps us focus on those changes that add the most value for the customers.

Anyone can submit an entry to SWCHANGE, and anyone can view the contents of the SWCHANGE database. We don't want potential bug reports or enhancement requests to be screened by the project champions or developers, who sometimes have their own agendas. We want to hear what the customers are thinking directly, not through a filter.

Sometimes, a developer submits an entry into SWCHANGE on behalf of a customer who has approached him. This is okay. It doesn't matter how the requests get into the system, so long as they are documented in the PTS so they can be prioritized against other pending change requests.

Once submitted, the entry cannot be modified or deleted from the database. We do not want anyone changing what a customer reported or removing it from the historical record. Even if the customer's original report is erroneous, it reflects his raw perceptions and opinions, which are important to capture.

All change request entries will be acknowledged as quickly as possible. If users do not perceive the PTS to be an effective mechanism for getting action, they will not use it. The support person should contact the submitting customer within twenty-four hours, even if no resolution is available yet, just to acknowledge receipt of the problem report. The average time it takes to close out entries in the three categories of bug report, enhancement request, and user assistance indicates whether we are being adequately responsive to customer needs. If not, we may need to adjust our work priorities. Management is responsible for monitoring the responses to customer requests in the PTS to see if they are being addressed within the desired time frame.

The overall objective is to assess the quality of our team's products and services, not to assess any individual team member's performance. As with other metrics data, the change management tool is intended to monitor and improve the group's processes, not to punish individuals.

Any problem tracking system should provide a variety of sorting and reporting options. The reports generated by SWCHANGE can summarize the entries for a single application, or they can combine data from multiple applications. One of the most useful reports indicates the number of entries in each of the classification, status, and assessment categories, along with the average time to reach a status of "Completed" for each of the three types of entries. Another report format lists all the entries from a single application, sorted by any displayed column. Sorting by status helps the user see at a glance which entries have not yet been closed out (completed or canceled).

A problem tracking system built on top of a relational database management system will provide the widest range of query options, since anyone skilled in the query language (SQL, for example) can write her own queries or reports. A PTS based on a proprietary database may provide a more limited range of canned reporting options, so before selecting a commercial tool, make sure it can produce the types of reports your team members want to see.

The Software Change Control Board

An effective change control process requires more than just a standard way to collect and organize requests for software changes. Someone still has to make decisions regarding which of the requested changes shall be made and in what order. A software change control board (SCCB) provides just such a formal mechanism for deciding how to handle change requests. The board typically includes representatives from software management, development, quality assurance, and either marketing or actual customers. The group meets periodically to review and prioritize change requests, and to determine which new features or bug fixes are to be incorporated into each software release. Without an SCCB, the software build-and-release process tends to be chaotic.

The board one of our project teams assembled includes six customer representatives, seven representatives from the business areas supported by the team's application, one business manager, and all four members of the development team. In addition, customers who submit the change requests that are discussed at each monthly meeting are invited to attend the pertinent meeting (generally, about half of them show up). This results in a large committee, but the size has not restricted its ability to get the job done. During the meeting, fifteen to twenty entries from the SWCHANGE database are discussed and prioritized. Typically, ten are new submissions, while the rest are older submissions that were deferred for future handling. The prioritized list of changes that emerges from this meeting constitutes the project team's maintenance task list for the next month.

This process has worked well for this project team for three years, although customers are not always delighted with the priorities assigned to their pet change requests. One weakness in the process is that if a key representative misses a meeting, no decisions can be made on change requests falling in that person's domain. For an SCCB to be effective, the participants must be empowered to make binding decisions on the requests being considered each month.

How Change Control Can Simplify Your Life

An incident that took place in our group illustrates the value of managing software changes with the aid of a defined process and a supporting tool. One of our engineers, Mark, was working with a project champion, Bill, on a scientific application, which produces hard-copy plotted output. Janice, a strong-willed and influential scientist, was one of the key users of this application. She wanted all of the plots to be grouped together and sent to the plotter at the end of a user session, rather than sending them one at a time, as specified by Bill and implemented by Mark. Janice approached Mark directly and strongly requested that he make this change.

Mark was torn. On one side, Janice was growling at him; on the other, the project champion preferred the program the way it was. Mark suggested giving the user a choice of output options, but Janice insisted that the change she described be put in place. Mark was caught in a position where he could not win, and he was upset about it.

Mark's response to Janice's demand should have been to politely ask her to submit her request through SWCHANGE. Then, it could be properly evaluated by the project champion and programmer and prioritized against other pending change requests for that application. This way, Mark would be out of the decision-making loop. The project champion is responsible for deciding which of the requested changes to implement. Therefore, Bill could negotiate with Janice to decide which solution would provide the greatest value to all users of this application, not just to Janice. It doesn't really matter how Bill and Janice reach their decision: rational analysis, drawing cards, or pistols at dawn. But once they do decide, Bill can tell Mark what, if any, changes to make in the system, schedule them appropriately, and update the SWCHANGE entry to show that Janice's request is either canceled or pending.

By using the change management tool and process as they are intended, the developer avoids being caught in the internecine battles among various customers. Fighting these battles is one of the roles of the project champion, as described in Chapter 5. If project champions are not part of your development process, someone else must make decisions about enhancements—possibly someone from the marketing staff, project management, or customer management, for example. Developers are usually the *last* people who should make software change decisions, unless all the stakeholders have great confidence in the developers' ability to properly represent the best interests of the customers. However, developers can assess the potential ripple effect of a seemingly simple change on other parts of the system. The priority of an enhancement may depend on the cost of making the change, and only the developers can estimate this with any accuracy.

Learning from Bug Detection Trends

Unless you have an exceptionally efficient software inspection process, formal testing will reveal many program defects. Use your PTS to record defects that are found during system, alpha, and beta testing, as well as after the application goes into production. This approach provides a mechanism by which to collect defect information in a standard way and to display the status of all identified bugs. SWCHANGE has helped us improve our management of the testing cycle by facilitating communication between programmers and testers. Trends in the rate at which new defects are reported help us decide when a product is ready to be released.

The study of failures experienced and faults discovered as a function of time is part of the discipline of software reliability. Musa et al. define *software reliability* as "the probability of failure-free operation of a computer program for a specified time in a specified environment" [Musa, 1987]. Accurate recording of faults and failures and their rates of detection during testing are essential to the quantitative estimation of software quality based on reliability models.

James Walsh analyzed trends in defects submitted to a tracking system by users and testers of a 230,000-line, 700-class CASE tool written in C++ [Walsh, 1993]. By looking at defect discovery rates as functions of both calendar time and CPU time consumed, Walsh was able to estimate the number of undiscovered bugs remaining in the product at any given time, within some reasonable bounds. Figure 15.3 shows one of Walsh's defect discovery plots, which illustrates how you can use the contents of your PTS to help manage your projects.

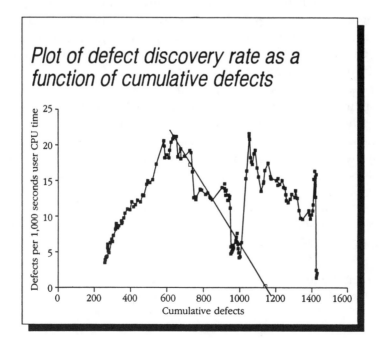

Figure 15.3: Example of reliability modeling from defect discovery rates [Walsh, 1993].

Based on Musa's reliability models, Walsh plotted the defect discovery rate versus the total number of defects discovered over time. He fit a regression line to the falling slope of this defect rate data in the range of 600 to 1,000 cumulative defects. From this line, Walsh estimated that the current iteration of the product contained a total of 1,154 defects (intersection of the regression line with the X axis). Subtracting the number of bugs that had already been found at the time he made the plot (1,011) predicted that some 143 defects remained in that version of the product. Since reliability modeling is a statistical process, it is safe to assume that the true number of remaining errors is not exactly 143. However, if continued testing only reveals, say, twenty additional defects in a situation like this, the projected figure of 143 should cause you to take a closer look before you declare victory.

Armed with this sort of fault detection information, you can make a risk-based decision to ship the product or to continue testing. Testing should not stop until your defect discovery rate indicates that you have reached your target quality level.

Sharing defect metrics trends with the team lets everyone see how they are progressing toward their goal of producing a quality product by the scheduled ship date. An automated bug tracking system is essential if you want to pursue this level of defect management sophistication. A quality-oriented software engineering culture should permit the scheduled delivery date to be adjusted based on this kind of quantitative analysis of product quality. If your culture does not, you're likely to be frustrated when management overrules your warnings about remaining bugs and sends a crummy product out the door. Some companies that have taken this approach have faced the unpleasant consequences of poor market response, unfavorable reviews, and a reputation for low quality they must struggle to overcome. Pulling a defect-laden product off the market after it has been shipped will more than negate the pleasure of shipping on schedule.

Analyzing the types and origins of defects found in your products allows you to identify the weak aspects of your development process. Armed with such knowledge, you can focus your improvement activities for the greatest bottom-line impact. Figure 15.4 shows the way Hewlett-Packard® categorizes the sources of software defects [Grady, 1993]. Information recorded for each defect includes the development activity in which it originated, a classification of defect type, and the reason this item is considered to be an error (mode). Patterns in the distribution of the sources and types of defects were used to identify those portions of the software process that required improvement.

Several other bug classification schemes exist [Beizer, 1990; IEEE, 1993]. Perhaps the most elaborate is Boris Beizer's "taxonomy of bugs," a hierarchical scheme for classifying software faults with a high degree of resolution. The complete taxonomy includes nearly 120 distinct categories of bugs, although it can be used more simply to group bugs into as few as nine classes (Table 15.1). An organization that is just getting started with serious bug tracking should stick with these basic nine categories, tailoring as needed. Having defect classification data available will help you make smarter decisions about how to reduce your most common and irksome bugs in the future.

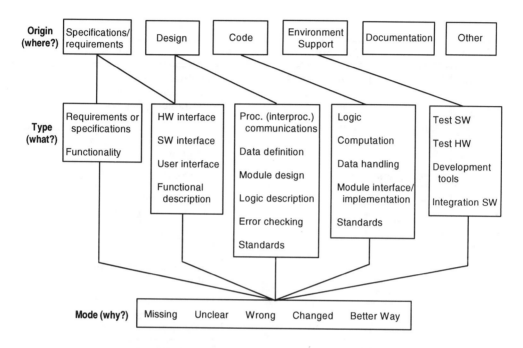

Figure 15.4: Categorization of sources of software defects at Hewlett-Packard [Grady, 1993].

Proactive Failure Reporting

A problem tracking system requires that users, be they customers or testers, must manually generate an entry to the database, supplying a description of the problem encountered or the change desired. Customers will not always bother to report the failures they encounter, and the information they do provide may be incomplete or inaccurate. In some environments, though, it is possible to more proactively communicate the details of a program failure directly to the appropriate support staff member.

Many of our group's older applications run on an IBM mainframe; most of them include programs written in REXX, a language useful both for scripting and for developing user interfaces. Some years ago, we wrote a utility called ERRFLAGR that is called whenever a syntax error occurs during execution of a REXX program (an "exec"). ERRFLAGR generates an e-mail message that is sent directly to the support person for the application that failed (Figure 15.5). The user sees a

Table 15.1.
Top Level of Beizer's Taxonomy of Bugs
[Beizer, 1990].

Code	Description	Subcategories
1	Functional requirements and features	Requirements incorrect, logic errors, completeness, verifiability, documentation; requirement changes
2	Functionality as implemented	Correctness, completeness, input domains, user messages and diagnostics, exception handling
3	Structural bugs	Control flow and sequencing, processing
4	Data	Data definition, structure, or declaration; data access and handling
5	Implementation	Coding and typographical errors, standards violation, documentation
6	Integration	Internal interfaces, external interfaces and timing
7	System and software architecture	Operating system bugs, software architecture, recovery after failure, performance, incorrect exception handling
8	Test definition or execution bugs	Test design, test execution, test documentation, test case completeness
9	Other bugs, unspecified	(none)

polite screen message saying that we are terribly sorry, but an error has taken place, and this support person has been notified. When possible, the application attempts to recover gracefully from the failure. An automatic failure reporting tool like ERRFLAGR provides a number of benefits.

■ Any failure for which you can set a trap in the program gets reported, not just those that the user chooses to report. The failure report can be routed directly into your PTS, without the user having to take any manual action.

■ The failure report can include more accurate and more complete information than you will get from the user. The user can only report the externally visible symptoms of the failure, whereas the reporting tool may be able to pinpoint the underlying fault in the code.

```
An error has been found in an application
which has been identified as one maintained
by you!  Hopefully the following information
will be of some assistance.

        Application name:   SOME_APP
        Exec in question:   LINKPLOT EXEC
       REXX error number:   34
      REXX error message:   Logical value not 0 or 1
    Found on line number:   21
               Line text:   if (mode) then do
                Found by:   MARVIN GLEASON
                  Userid:   marvin
                   Phone:   78880
                    Date:   28 Jan 1996
                    Time:   12:23:07
```

Figure 15.5: Sample e-mail message from a trapped REXX error.

- Since the application's support person receives the failure report immediately, he might be able to contact the user by telephone while the user is still running the application. Users are really impressed when they get such a quick response to a software problem. It is also easier for a user to recall the actions that preceded the failure, instead of trying to reconstruct them days later, when the support person finally calls in response to a manually entered problem report.

While not every language provides services that make it this easy to generate failure reports, seek proactive ways to have your programs trap and report any failures they encounter. Your program may write an error log file, which is embedded in an e-mail message and is then sent to a support person or into your PTS. Any environment that includes a program-accessible e-mail interface should support such an approach.

Making Change Management Work in Your Culture

Instilling a formal change management process into an organization that is used to handling changes informally requires a significant cultural adjustment. The team should be involved in defining the change processes to be used, evaluating and selecting tools, and monitoring the effectiveness of the process. Most software engineers have horror stories to tell of badly managed application changes; draw on these experiences when searching for solutions to the group's change control problems.

Begin by recording user problem reports in a standard, electronic way. A spreadsheet will work as a low-cost start, but in the long run you will be better off with a more robust commercial problem management tool. Keep the process and its supporting tool simple to encourage use. Define standard terminology around the status and classification of defect reports, so the support staff members use the system in a consistent fashion. Integrate your problem tracking tool into your e-mail system to facilitate communication of a problem report to all the stakeholders.

Another cultural change is to begin keeping records of the defects found during development. From them, you can determine which quality control techniques (inspections or various types of testing) are most effective for you, what kinds of errors are most common, and when a product being tested reaches the level of quality you desire for release. Make sure the team understands that the purpose is not to point to individual developers as causing problems. Instead, you need to deal openly with quality issues as a pathway to customer satisfaction. Separate the data for alpha test, beta test, and various production releases. This will help you get a handle on the number of defects that leak through your quality control procedures.

Require your customers to use your system for reporting problems and requesting enhancements. This sort of cultural change has an impact beyond the software group. It will benefit from visible management support and consistent application to all users, for all the products your team supports. Software management may have to justify the use of the new, more structured process to customers who are used to requesting changes informally.

The ability to track change requests to closure is one aspect of a more mature software development process. After having used a simple change management and defect tracking system for several years, I would feel very uncomfortable going back to an informal method for handling bug reports and enhancement requests.

Summary

✔ Managing bug reports and change requests is essential to controlling quality and maintenance.

✔ A consistent philosophy of how your change control process and your problem tracking system will be applied helps to define and reinforce the culture of your software engineering group.

✔ A PTS facilitates two-way communication by providing a standard tool for your users to supply application feedback, and by routing support staff responses directly back to the customer.

✔ Summary reports from the data in your PTS will show how responsive your support staff is to program failures, enhancement requests, and requests for user assistance. Use this historical data to see where you are today, set goals for improved service levels in the future, and monitor progress toward those goals.

✔ Data from the PTS will help you make smart decisions about rebuilding troublesome modules, improving usability or user aids, and otherwise coping with those application components that generate the most problem reports.

✔ Rigorously recording the bugs found during testing, and applying the concepts of software reliability modeling to the data, will let you estimate the number of defects remaining in your code.

✔ Classifying and analyzing the types and sources of software defects will help you find ways to prevent those defects from being injected into future products.

✔ Look for opportunities to build error-handling code into your applications that will collect inside information about the program failure and e-mail a report to your support staff.

Culture Builders and Killers

Culture Builder: Use the problem tracking system for your group's internal reusable software components and utilities. This helps the developers become thoroughly familiar with the tool and the process, and it reinforces the culture of structured change management. In our group, more than fifty bug reports and change requests have been submitted for our home-grown SWCHANGE tool itself over the past five years.

Culture Builder: Have your support staff set goals for the length of time it should take to handle both the initial response and the resolution of entries in the categories bug report, enhancement request, and requests for user assistance. Monitor your progress toward these goals by generating periodic reports from your problem tracking system data. When you reach the goals, celebrate, and then select the next set of customer support goals.

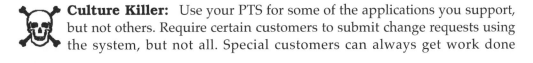

Culture Killer: Use your PTS for some of the applications you support, but not others. Require certain customers to submit change requests using the system, but not all. Special customers can always get work done through the back door. A change management system is just one more obstacle for clever users to bypass to get the changes they want made in an application.

Culture Killer: Require your developers to use your PTS for reporting bugs found during testing and in production, but never look at the data yourself. Don't bother to see how many problem reports are open at any time, or how long it takes your support staff to close them out. They will get around to the problems as soon as they can; the users can just wait their turn. The users are lucky your staff adds any enhancements at all, with your backlog of new development projects and pending bug corrections.

Culture Killer: Ship the product when scheduled, even if your own defect trends from system testing indicate that there are probably many latent bugs still lurking in there. It is more important to your group's image to be timely than to be perfect. Those defect trends always exaggerate the quality problems, anyway. You can tell from your own experience when an application is ready to go out the door.

References and Further Reading

Beizer, Boris. *Software Testing Techniques,* 2nd ed. New York: Van Nostrand Reinhold, 1990.

> Chapter 2 describes a hierarchical classification scheme for identifying software faults very precisely. The Appendix presents the complete taxonomy, along with statistics indicating the relative frequency of occurrence of each class of bug from Beizer's experience.

 Grady, Robert B. "Practical Results from Measuring Software Quality," *Communications of the ACM,* Vol. 36, No. 11 (November 1993), pp. 62-68.

> Grady describes how various kinds of defect metrics were used at Hewlett-Packard to help focus quality improvement efforts on the critical areas.

IEEE Std. 1044-1993, "IEEE Standard Classification for Software Anomalies," Los Alamitos, Calif.: IEEE Computer Society Press, 1993.

> An "anomaly" is the general term used to describe an error in a software program. This standard defines a hierarchical classification scheme for describing anomalies. Compare this classification scheme with Beizer's to see which method will better fit your needs.

 Kaner, Cem, Jack Falk, and Hung Quoc Nguyen. *Testing Computer Software,* 2nd ed. New York: Van Nostrand Reinhold, 1993.

> Chapter 6 discusses the contents and use of a problem tracking system for collecting internal bug reports from testers.

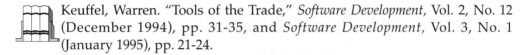 Keuffel, Warren. "Tools of the Trade," *Software Development,* Vol. 2, No. 12 (December 1994), pp. 31-35, and *Software Development,* Vol. 3, No. 1 (January 1995), pp. 21-24.

> These two columns describe the defect tracking approaches James Bach applied at Borland International. By plotting the rate of discovery of new defects versus time during testing, Bach was able to gain insight into both the quality of the product and the maturity of the development process being used for a project. Keuffel also describes some of the cultural aspects of defect tracking that Bach encountered.

Musa, John D., Anthony Iannino, and Kazuhira Okumoto. *Software Reliability: Measurement, Prediction, Application.* New York: McGraw-Hill, 1987.

> This book presents a variety of theoretical models for assessing software reliability, along with a practical guide for applying the principles of software reliability in a variety of areas. It contains some serious mathematics in the realm of reliability modeling.

Walsh, James. "Determining Software Quality," *Computer Language,* Vol. 10, No. 4 (April 1993), pp. 57-65.

> Walsh presents a case study of how reliability modeling was applied to a large C++ program to estimate the number of defects remaining in the product, based on the rate of discovery of new ones during testing. This article is easy to understand and represents an actual experience, not a theoretical model.

Chapter 16

Taking Measures to
Stay on Track

In order to keep the software process in control, you have to institute a policy of careful and effective measurement. If you don't measure, then you're left with only one reason to believe that you are still in control: hysterical optimism.

—Tom DeMarco, *Controlling Software Projects*

Military commanders in battle must cope with the "fog of war," that lack of knowledge about the disposition and activities of both their own forces and those of the enemy. Similarly, software engineers and managers must cope with the "fog of work," the lack of quantitative information about their software products, projects, and processes. The objective of software measurement is to provide managers and developers with greater insight into these three domains. Through this insight, they can take actions that will lead to high-quality products and avoid potential problems.

People working in a culture focused on software engineering excellence believe their products, projects, and processes should be open to view by both developers and managers. They agree on a concise set of measures that provide the necessary visibility into the work being done by the organization. They willingly collect the data associated with each of these measures. Much of the data is shared with the rest of the organization; it is not the exclusive property of those who did the work, those who collected the measurements, or those who analyzed them. All members of the organization seek to understand the data and apply it to their own work. Engineers are confident that the purpose of measurement is nothing other than understanding and improving the quality of work done by the organization. They are not afraid the data will be used against them at performance appraisal time.

Gerald Weinberg discusses the importance of "observation" of software development in Volume 2 of his *Quality Software Management* series [Weinberg, 1993]:

> To obtain consistent quality of our software, we must control the processes by which we produce and service that software. But we cannot consistently control a process without reliable information. Gathering such information means that we must learn how to observe. Many of the failures to manage software engineering can be traced to failures in observation.

Measurement gives us the tools to better control software projects [DeMarco, 1982]. These tools provide insight into the processes we are using, enabling us to identify improvements and to assess the effects of any changes we make in those processes. Without a consistent set of software measures, managers and developers are flying blind, making decisions based on incomplete and subjective understandings of their products and processes.

Michael Daskalantonakis of Motorola states, "Measurement is not the goal. The goal is improvement through measurement, analysis, and feedback." [Daskalantonakis, 1992]. Without having historical data from our previous projects, we cannot easily learn from them so we can do a better job in the future. Unless we collect and analyze a variety of kinds of information, we cannot know for certain whether a project is on schedule, how many defects have been found and how many might remain, how well our current processes are working, or anything else that is necessary for the effective management of software organizations and projects. Metrics allow you to provide quantitative answers to questions that ask "how many," "how much," "how long," "how big," "how bad," and "how good." A systematic measurement program is an essential component of a mature software development process and a quality-oriented software engineering culture.

The raw data you collect is not intrinsically righteous or evil, nor even informative. Insights come from observing trends over time and from comparing observed values for certain measures with the values you expect or desire. It is also helpful to compare results obtained from your own measurement program with industry averages. Chapter 3 of *Applied Software Measurement* contains extensive information about U.S. averages for software quality and productivity [Jones, 1991]. *The Software Engineer's Handbook* is another source of software industry benchmark data [Rubin, 1992]. Even a simple metrics program can provide better insight into your group's work, so you can chart a course to improved quality and productivity and track your progress toward that destination.

Why Measurement Programs Fail

Responding to the current emphasis on software measurement, all sorts of organizations are launching metrics initiatives. The sad lesson of history is that as many as 80 percent of these efforts will not succeed [Rubin, 1991]. A successful software measurement program can be defined as one in which the results are actively used by the organization for making decisions, results are communicated and accepted outside the development community, and the program lasts longer than two years [Rubin, 1991]. The following paragraphs identify several cultural and technical reasons why a measurement program may not succeed in a particular organization.

The program starts by trying to measure too many things. There are literally hundreds of measures that *could* be collected on software products, projects, and processes. A fledgling measurement program should select no more than six or seven of them at the outset. Otherwise, the team members will be overwhelmed by the tasks of collecting and interpreting the data, and the effort may collapse under its own weight.

The program starts by doing too little. At the other extreme, if you do not measure enough different aspects of your work to demonstrate some useful payback from the insights you obtain, it is difficult to justify the effort. There are no magic metrics that will tell you in a single number everything you need to know about the organization and its work. A concise set of measures in several dimensions will provide a useful profile of your group's work. Ultimately you should measure all aspects of your software-related activities (maintenance, customer support, training, and so on), not just new application development.

The wrong things are measured. If the initial set of measures does not provide information that allows the stakeholders of the metrics program to answer their questions and make better decisions, they may conclude that the effort is not worthwhile. The measures you collect should target specific organizational needs, as well as the needs of your customers. They should also connect to the business success factors of the organization. Look for measures that will help you steer your process improvement activities, by showing whether process changes are having the desired effects. Different stakeholders—managers, developers, customers—require different views into the activities being measured. One set of measures will not fit all needs. If someone asks why you are collecting a particular metric, you should have a better answer than, "It seemed like something we ought to know."

The data collected is not used. The people who are asked to measure aspects of their work will lose interest in the process if they do not see evidence that the data is being used for practical purposes. When you make effective use of metrics data, share those benefits with the team members. Management has to take the visible lead in any project-wide or organization-wide measurement activities. No one will get excited about contributing to a write-only metrics database.

The data is used to measure the performance of individuals. An excellent way to destroy the team's confidence in a metrics program is to calculate each developer's productivity as lines of code written per hour, and use the resulting distribution for determining performance appraisals and salary adjustments. If the data supplied by an individual is used against that individual, you will not get reliable data from her in the future. Some kinds of metrics data should be private to individuals, some private to projects, and some public beyond the scope of the project [Grady, 1992]. Metrics are not to be used for punishment or reward, but to learn and to adjust.

Managers expect to see benefits in too short a time. It takes time to launch a metrics program, and it takes time to collect enough data so that meaningful trends begin to emerge. When we began a work effort metrics collection program in my small group at Kodak, we correctly estimated it would take two years to see the cumulative distribution of effort in different development phases reach a steady state. However, we did not have to wait two years to learn from the preliminary trends we saw and consider what we might do differently.

It is important to remember not to jump to conclusions prematurely. Wait until you are confident the data accurately represents your organization's performance in the dimensions being measured. It is tempting to try to over-interpret individual data points, but the important insights will come from observing trends over time. We aren't conducting controlled scientific experiments, in which straightforward cause-and-effect relationships can be observed. There are often several possible explanations for any software measurement, so focus your attention on trends that persist over a period of time.

People do not measure things in the same way. A standard set of definitions for the things you are trying to measure is essential if you wish to combine data from several individuals or projects to gain broader insights. For example, the definition of a line of code is by no means standard even for a single programming language, let alone across different languages. Different tools that automate the collection of line-of-code metrics may not give the same results.

Internal consistency is extremely important. If a metrics program attempts to combine apples and oranges from different participants, you will only get fruit salad, not a meaningful big picture. Those planning the metrics program will have to create a precise definition for each measure collected. Ambiguous definitions will let every practitioner interpret them differently, a condition you want to avoid.

Inadequate resources are devoted to collecting, analyzing, and applying the data. Minimize the overhead placed on developers by using simple data collection and reporting schemes. Automate them whenever possible. Get your quality assurance people involved in selecting, defining, and analyzing the metrics. Build an infrastructure of tools and policies that will facilitate having all participants contribute the data you need from them. Integrate the collection tools with the participant's development environment whenever you can. Certain metrics, such as function points, require considerable skill and experience for accurate counting. The best solution is to have a local expert who can collect these measurements from multiple projects.

Stakeholders do not buy into the need for measurement. The person leading the metrics program will have to justify it to all of the communities affected by the program. Managers may fear that revealing the truth about their teams' behaviors and results will reflect badly on them. Sensitivity to the concerns of the participants is necessary to get the metrics program off the ground. It will help to advertise success stories of how software measurement efforts have been valuable elsewhere within your company, or in other companies. Robert Grady provides some advice on how to put your metrics sales pitch together [Grady, 1987].

Metrics Programs Don't Have to Fail

Despite the many ways a software metrics program can stumble, there have been many successes. Our group and others at Kodak have successfully implemented measurement programs of varying sophistication. Comprehensive metrics programs have been installed at other large companies, such as Hewlett-Packard [Grady, 1987; Grady, 1992] and Motorola [Daskalantonakis, 1992].

The success of every measurement program, be it a global effort across a huge corporation or a first start by a small team, depends on the involvement of every individual and on the leadership provided by managers at all levels. A metrics program needs a vision of what it hopes to accomplish; it is not just a set of forms for collecting numbers. A shared team culture directed toward building quality products is a necessary prerequisite for a meaningful measurement program. If the managers and developers are not committed to quality, you cannot expect them to take seriously any program intended to measure and track the many dimensions of software quality.

Implementing a substantial measurement program requires a supporting infrastructure to assist with collecting, storing, and reporting on the metrics data. Provide standard tools to avoid the problem of each project choosing its own local definitions for the metrics in the organization-wide set. Supply reporting and charting utilities that will let stakeholders view the information they need from the metrics database. Since software management is one of the key "customers" of the metrics program, be sure to investigate their requirements for visualizing the data.

As you begin planning a metrics program, recognize the impact that metrics will have on the software engineering culture. Plan a training program that will defuse the resistance some practitioners may exhibit when they hear the words "software metrics." Use pilot projects to resolve the uncertainties in your plan and smooth the way to a full rollout.

What to Measure

The number of aspects of your software work that you might choose to measure is so large that no group can possibly collect and interpret them all. The trick is to identify the smallest set of metrics that will enable you, as a manager or developer, to learn what you need to know to make better decisions and track progress toward your goals. Metrics can be collected and interpreted at the individual, project, or organizational level, depending on the audience and what they are trying to learn from the data.

Given the scores of things you might elect to measure about your software products, projects, and processes, how should you choose your starter set? One approach is to adopt a group recommended by a metrics expert, such as Rubin's software measurement "dashboard" with ten basic categories of metrics [Rubin, 1991]. A useful way to select your initial set is to ask yourself, "What are the objectives of my improvement efforts, and therefore of my metrics program?" From the answers, you can identify those metrics that will help you achieve your goals. For each proposed metric, ask yourself, "What will I do differently if I have this data than if I do not?" If the answer is "nothing," don't bother to collect that measure.

To launch a metrics initiative, begin with six basic types of measurements (Fig. 16.1):

Figure 16.1: A recommended starter set of software metrics.

Quality of Product: Measure defect densities in delivered software, in units of defects per thousand assembly-equivalent lines of code (described in Chapter 11), or defects per function point. Be sure to define "defect" consistently for the whole team.

Quality of Process: Count the defects that your inspection and testing processes find in interim work products. This lets you decide where to apply process improvements to reduce the number of bugs that leak into the final product.

Customer Satisfaction: Measure customer satisfaction levels through surveys or customer focus groups, to see if your products meet customer needs and achieve customer delight. Use survey responses to better understand your customers' expectations and to improve future products.

Project Status: Track project progress against the schedule, and track actual values of size, cost, and duration against your estimates. This lets you improve your estimating procedures and make more realistic forecasts of future milestones once the project is underway.

Work Effort: Track the time each developer spends on different phases of work on each project, as described in Chapter 17. This data enables you to do a better job of estimating future projects.

Product Size: Document the size of each project's work products, using lines of code, function points, number of requirements, or other measures that are appropriate for the kinds of applications your team builds.

Table 16.1 lists some of the dimensions of measurement that are pertinent in the domains of software products, projects, and processes. Just a few of the specific metrics that one could collect for each dimension are shown in the table. Most of these are historical or results measures, which tell us something about the characteristics of completed projects and systems. Few of them are predictive, enabling us to look into the crystal ball and see what is yet to come [DeMarco, 1982].

The most successful software measures are those that can be turned into "indicators" [Card, 1991]. An indicator includes some measured value, an expectation of what the value ought to be, and an analysis technique that allows us to compare the measured and expected values to determine whether any corrective action is warranted. Indicators should be understandable, field tested, economical, timely, and of high leverage.

An example of an indicator metric is source code complexity, or values derived from code attributes that can be used to help make decisions about program quality or maintainability. First, analyze the code to derive a specific complexity metric, such as the cyclomatic complexity numbers discussed in Chapter 13. Then, compare the value obtained to the acceptable range of values for that complexity measure. If the measured value is outside this tolerance range, you can decide whether to rewrite the program to bring its complexity within your preferred range or take some other corrective action.

How to Design Your Metrics Program

There are two main reasons for measuring any given aspect of software development—to help you make better decisions, and to determine whether your organization is meeting some specified goals. As described below, the goal/question/metric (GQM) paradigm provides a systematic way to go through this goal-oriented thought process [Basili, 1988].

In the GQM approach, you begin by stating your project, organizational, and process improvement goals, or by identifying areas in which you believe data will help you make correct decisions. For each goal, write a list of quantifiable questions to which you need answers to know if you are achieving the goals. The questions should suggest specific metrics that will provide the data needed to track progress toward your goals, or to give you the information you need to confidently make those difficult decisions. For each metric you select, you should be able to explain why it is important, describe a process for collecting and validating the data, and know what you are going to do with the data [IEEE, 1992].

Table 16.1.
Some Measurable Dimensions of Software Products, Projects, and Processes.

Domain	Dimension	Some Metrics
Product	Complexity	Design and code complexity (such as cyclomatic complexity, software science metrics, fan-out squared); object-oriented metrics include coupling between objects, methods/class, depth of class hierarchy, and internal and external attributes of classes [Chidamber, 1994; Lorenz, 1994]
	Maintainability	Maintainability index computed from source code metrics
	Quality	Defect density, problem reports, fault types, defect origins, customer satisfaction
	Reliability	Mean time between failures, mean time to failure, mean time to repair
	Size	Lines of code (standardized and normalized for different languages, such as assembly-equivalent source statements), other deliverable documents, function points, feature points, Bang [DeMarco, 1982]
	Usability	Ease of learning, errors made by users on tasks, time needed to perform tasks
Project	Cost	Development cost, support cost (hours/function point, dollars/function point)
	Effort	Labor hours, calendar time, work phase distribution
	Productivity	Function points delivered/month, hours of effort/functional requirement
	Stability	Changes in requirements during development, postrelease change requests, source of requirements changes
	Tracking	Schedule versus estimate, cost/earned value, percent of requirements traced into design and code
Process	Customer Support	Defect backlog, time to respond to help requests, time to resolve help requests, accuracy of responses
	Effort	Work phase distribution, maintenance/new development effort distribution
	QA Effectiveness	Defect removal efficiencies at different stages, cost of defect removal, return on investment from quality practices, bad fixes
	Reuse	Amount of reused code, designs, tests, and other artifacts
	Tools	Penetration of software tools into actual use by team members

As an example of how to apply GQM to a non-software problem, suppose the prospect of early retirement is appealing to you. Figure 16.2 shows what part of a GQM analysis for planning early retirement might look like. Without collecting accurate data, interpreting it thoroughly and honestly, and using it to answer the right questions, any decisions you make are risky. How much confidence do you have that you could plan to retire at age 50 without the sort of analysis illustrated in Fig. 16.2?

Goal: Retire by age 50.

Questions:		
1. How much money will I have saved by then?	2. What are my expenses likely to be at that time?	3. What income do I expect to have at that time?
Metrics:		
1. Current savings level	(metrics for Question 2)	(metrics for Question 3)
2. Current annual income		
3. Current annual expenses		
4. Amount I can save annually		
5. Return on my current investment portfolio		
6. Projected interest rates		

Figure 16.2: Sample goal/question/metric strategy for a goal of early retirement.

Figure 16.3 illustrates the GQM model, which begins in the upper-left corner by observing the current reality. The GQM sequence of setting goals, identifying questions, and selecting metrics prepares you to begin collecting the right information. Then you can use the knowledge you extract from the metrics data to alter those aspects of your software development process that you believe are deficient. Additional data collected after the process changes are made (that is, the new "current reality") will tell you whether the process modifications are achieving the intended results. In addition, once you begin to interpret the metrics data, you can evaluate whether you are measuring the right things, whether you have asked the right questions, and whether you have even selected the right goals. These feedback loops help you to integrate the organizational goals, pertinent questions, and relevant metrics into a package that addresses the specific needs of your organization.

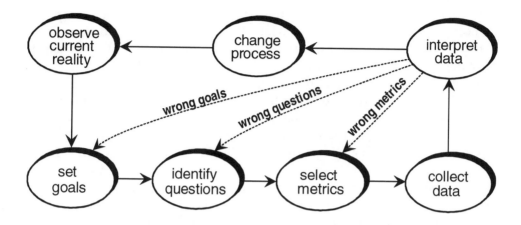

Figure 16.3: Goal/question/metric feedback model for software metrics.

Many large organizations have used the GQM approach effectively. Grady describes how GQM was used at Hewlett-Packard in Chapter 3 of *Practical Software Metrics for Project Management and Process Improvement* [Grady, 1992]. He lists the questions and supporting metrics for three of their goals: maximize customer satisfaction, minimize engineering effort and schedule, and minimize defects. Motorola applied GQM to define a set of ten charts that are used to visually depict progress over time toward their seven major goal areas [Daskalantonakis, 1992]:

1. Improve project planning

2. Increase defect containment

3. Increase software reliability

4. Decrease software defect density

5. Improve customer service

6. Reduce the cost of nonconformance

7. Increase software productivity

One large product software department at Kodak assembled a team of practitioners and managers to design its metrics strategy. They used GQM to select measures in seven important categories: product size, defect levels, product cycle time, process maturity, requirements stability, scheduling accuracy, and reuse. Only a few of the basic measures this team defined were selected for implementation in the first phase. Central to the metrics strategy this group devised is the principle of using the data to critique the process and the product, not the people in an organization.

Not everyone agrees that a top-down, management-focused program such as GQM is the best method for selecting appropriate metrics. For example, some advocate a bottom-up approach in which the inputs, outputs, and results for each software work product are measured to create understanding, which itself drives questions and enables goal setting [Hetzel, 1993]. The top-down approach characterized by GQM assumes that the metrics strategists have identified the right goals and know which questions to ask at the outset. The top-down model requires that management sell the benefits of the metrics program to the developers, who may not see the value from their point of view. However, by using a bottom-up approach, practitioners are immediately involved in directly measuring aspects of their daily work.

GQM provides a practical approach, so long as one uses the feedback mechanism illustrated in Fig. 16.3 to adjust the goals, questions, and metrics as time goes on. An important point to remember is that any metrics program has a group of stakeholders, who have different objectives and different degrees and modes of involvement in the effort. Any single perspective—management, practitioner, process improvement group—shows only part of the big picture. Whatever approach you use to define your measurement strategy and select the initial measures should be validated from these other perspectives to make sure your program is serving all of its stakeholders appropriately. If thoughtfully designed and implemented, your metrics program can facilitate a common cultural focus on organizational objectives. However, if it is designed to meet the needs of only one stakeholder group, the metrics effort can broaden the gulf between developers and managers, or between developers and quality assurance personnel.

Summary

- ✔ If you measure what you do, you can learn to do it better.

- ✔ Software metrics give managers and developers greater insight into their software products, projects, and processes, so they can make better decisions and track progress toward individual and organizational goals.

- ✔ Do not try to measure every dimension of your products, projects, and processes, but measure something. Even limited data can be informative, if it is accurate.

- ✔ Your plan for implementing a new metrics program must include approaches for dealing with fear of data misuse and other sources of resistance. Be prepared to sell the program to the various stakeholder groups, through presentations and training.

✔ Use the goal/question/metric approach to identify a few measures that will address your group's objectives.

✔ Never use metrics data to measure the performance of individuals. Use it to measure your processes and to see if the group is achieving its objectives.

Culture Builders and Killers

Culture Builder: Get your whole team involved in setting their improvement goals, identifying the questions that need to be answered to track progress toward the goals, and selecting the metrics that will enable the team to answer those questions. This will help gain acceptance of the value of the measurement process you put in place. In a software engineering culture, the team shares a responsibility for making the metrics program a success.

Culture Builder: The metrics effort should be an organization-wide undertaking. Require every project and individual in your group to collect and report the agreed-on metrics data. The data will provide a quantitative understanding that simply cannot be obtained by intuition. If anyone is exempted from the metrics effort (other than during a pilot program), it could suggest to the team that measurement is a tool for punishing people working on projects that are having problems.

Culture Builder: When you launch a metrics program, begin by collecting just those measures that will let you track progress toward your organizational goals. Provide some training in the area of software metrics to the entire group. Clearly state how the data will and will not be used. Explain how the information you are requesting will help address the issues faced by individual engineers, projects, and the organization as a whole. You will get better buy-in to a metrics effort if the participants perceive enough value from it to justify the labor involved with collecting the data.

Culture Killer: A member of your team suggests to you that the team could benefit from a metrics program. Don't give him any encouragement. If he wants to collect some personal data, that's fine, but you don't really have the time to decide what a metrics program ought to contain, how to get it started, and what you would do with the data if you had it. Besides, if you decide to support his suggestion, you will have to try to sell it to the rest of the group, and you know how they hate to do anything except write code. It is much easier just to exhort them all to do a better job, rather than trying to explain a formal measurement activity in a way they will accept.

References and Further Reading

Basili, Victor R., and H. Dieter Rombach. "The TAME Project: Towards Improvement-Oriented Software Environments," *IEEE Transactions on Software Engineering*, Vol. 14, No. 6 (June 1988), pp. 758-73.

> This paper illustrates the application of Basili's goal/question/metric approach to a specific software problem.

Card, David N. "What Makes a Software Measure Successful?" *American Programmer*, Vol. 4, No. 9 (September 1991), pp. 2-8.

> Card describes several code, design, and project progress "indicators," which can be used to help developers decide what actions need to be taken on a software project.

Chidamber, Shyam R., and Chris F. Kemerer. "A Metrics Suite for Object-Oriented Design," *IEEE Transactions on Software Engineering*, Vol. 20, No. 6 (June 1994), pp. 476-93.

> These authors describe six basic metrics that are applicable to object-oriented software development: weighted methods per class; depth of inheritance tree; number of children; coupling between objects; number of methods that could be executed in response to receiving a message; and lack of cohesion in methods.

Daskalantonakis, Michael K. "A Practical View of Software Measurement and Implementation Experiences Within Motorola," *IEEE Transactions on Software Engineering*, Vol. 18, No. 11 (November 1992), pp. 998-1010.

> Daskalantonakis presents a fine case study of metrics applied on a large scale in a company that is highly focused on software engineering excellence, including the application of GQM.

DeMarco, Tom. *Controlling Software Projects*. Englewood Cliffs, N.J.: Yourdon Press/Prentice-Hall, 1982.

> DeMarco describes a modeling approach to system design, management, and measurement. He introduces the Bang metric for quantifying system size from a set of structured analysis models.

Grady, Robert B. *Practical Software Metrics for Project Management and Process Improvement*. Englewood Cliffs, N.J.: PTR Prentice-Hall, 1992.

> Grady describes both the tactical application of software metrics to project management and their strategic application to process improvement at

Hewlett-Packard. He discusses software metrics etiqu
between public and private data. Many examples of
projects are included.

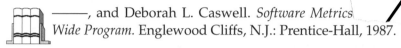

————, and Deborah L. Caswell. *Software Metrics*
Wide Program. Englewood Cliffs, N.J.: Prentice-Hall, 1987.

Grady and Caswell reveal the internal workings of Hewlett-Packard's software metrics program. They describe how H-P's metrics program was initiated, sold to management and staff, and applied throughout the company. Some
of the data collected during the first few years of the program is included.

Hetzel, Bill. *Making Software Measurement Work.* Wellesley, Mass.: QED
Publishing Group, 1993.

Hetzel distinguishes measurement for managers from those measurement
activities that can and should be carried out by practitioners throughout the
software development life cycle. He presents a fresh angle on software metrics,
while thoroughly covering the measurement of products, projects, and
processes in a persuasive and conversational style.

IEEE Std. 1061-1992, "IEEE Standard for a Software Quality Metrics
Methodology," Los Alamitos, Calif.: IEEE Computer Society Press, 1992.

This standard defines a systematic methodology for establishing quality attributes for a project, selecting metrics that represent the various quality factors
associated with each attribute, and setting target values for each metric.

Jones, Capers. *Applied Software Measurement.* New York: McGraw-Hill,
1991.

Chapter 4 describes the mechanics of establishing a multi-dimensional baseline of data around a software organization's products and projects. Ways to
measure software quality and user satisfaction are addressed in Chapter 5.

————. *Assessment and Control of Software Risks.* Englewood Cliffs, N.J.: PTR
Prentice-Hall, 1994.

Jones states that inaccurate metrics, particularly line of code metrics, constitute
the single most serious risk factor (of sixty described in this book) facing software development today. I am skeptical whether this is really the case.
Chapter 20 describes the risk area of "Inaccurate Metrics," while Chapter 28
addresses "Inadequate Measurement."

Lorenz, Mark, and Jeff Kidd. *Object-Oriented Software Metrics.* Englewood Cliffs, N.J.: PTR Prentice-Hall, 1994.

> Lorenz and Kidd describe several dozen project and design metrics for object-oriented systems. Project metrics cover application size, staffing size, and scheduling. Design metrics address the size, inheritance, and internals of methods, and the size, inheritance, internals, and externals of classes.

Rubin, Howard. "Measuring 'Rigor' and Putting Measurement into Action," *American Programmer,* Vol. 4, No. 9 (September 1991), pp. 9-23.

> Rubin provides data on the failure rate of software measurement programs over the period 1980 to 1990, and he describes his "dashboard" of ten metrics categories that every organization should collect.

———, Bob Marose, Gonzalo Verdago, and Margaret L. Johnson. *The Software Engineer's Benchmark Handbook.* Phoenix, Ariz.: Applied Computer Research, 1992.

> This is a compendium of standards and benchmark data on application development quality and productivity, collected from hundreds of sources.

 Weinberg, Gerald M. *Quality Software Management, Volume 2: First-Order Measurement.* New York: Dorset House Publishing, 1993.

> Weinberg describes a four-step model for "observation" of the software development process and products. He addresses the basic measures that every organization should collect to consistently build quality software, as well as ways to create a culture that supports such measurement.

Chapter 17

Case Study: Measurement in a Small Software Group

Programmers regard themselves as artists. As such, they consider keeping accurate records of their handiwork on par with washing ash trays.

—Otis Port, *Business Week*

Metrics programs in small software groups don't always begin with a systematic analysis of organizational goals and a supporting measurement methodology. One of our small teams at Kodak began its metrics program with a simple desire to better understand how team members were spending their development and maintenance effort on projects. Measurement of our work effort distribution over time provided process understanding, impetus for process change, and opportunities for improving our project estimating ability. Later, we became more interested in quantifying code quality, so we explored ways to apply source code analyzer tools. This chapter takes a look at our long-term work effort measurement program, and it describes how source code metrics analysis can be used to estimate the maintainability of program modules.

Software Work Effort Metrics

When I first became a software manager, one of our team goals was to minimize the amount of effort we devoted to maintenance, so we could spend more time developing new applications for our internal Kodak customers. Another goal was to develop improved project estimating capabilities. A third goal was to evolve toward a more sophisticated development process that would improve both our software quality and our productivity. Some of the questions we wished to answer to help us achieve these, and other, goals were

1. How much more time would we have for new development if we did not have to spend any time on maintenance?

2. How much does it cost us each year to adapt our software portfolio to work with new versions of compilers, databases, operating systems, and other applications?

3. Which of the applications we support require us to spend the most time providing assistance to users? Exactly how much time is that?

4. What fraction of our development time do we spend on testing?

5. Do we feel our developers are devoting enough effort to software design?

6. Are our attempts to improve software quality reducing the time we must spend correcting bugs in released products?

7. Can we derive useful correlations between our project development effort and some measure of system size or functionality?

8. What is the average number of effective project hours per week for our staff members?

9. How many different projects did each of our developers work on last year?

This goal-oriented questioning process led us to conclude that a work effort metrics program would help us understand how we are doing our work, the diversity of work that we perform, and how our work effort distribution changes over time. Any kind of productivity metric also requires that one know how much effort went into creating a product. Historical measurements of productivity are necessary if you wish to prepare accurate estimates for future projects.

Since 1990, our group has recorded the time we spend in different work phases on all new development and maintenance projects. By tracking trends in the distribution of these activities, we have improved our understanding of how we develop software. We have used the data to set quantitative improvement goals, identify leveraging opportunities that can increase productivity, and develop heuristics to assist with estimating new projects. Our database now represents more than 70,000 staff hours of work for one group; several other Kodak software groups are also using this system. Collecting, analyzing, and applying work profile and work distribution metrics has become a valuable component of our software engineering culture.

We classify work effort into one of six development and four maintenance phases. The development phases are: preliminary activities and project planning, requirements specification, design, implementation, testing, and writing documentation. The maintenance categories are: adaptive, corrective (fixing bugs), perfective (adding enhancements), and user support. We use another category for capturing the time spent on routine execution of certain programs, such as generating monthly management reports from an information system (including the metrics database itself).

The following paragraphs describe the activities that are recorded in each of these ten work effort phases. Some tasks cannot be neatly compartmentalized, so we established conventions to enable all team members to report similar activities in a consistent way. For example, working on a user interface prototype could logically be attributed to requirements specification (if the purpose of the prototype is to elicit requirements), to design (if the purpose is to explore possible solutions), or to implementation (if the prototype is in the process of evolving into the final product).

Preliminary Activities and Project Planning. This category includes: time spent defining the scope of a project, establishing the team and project champions, and so on, prior to gathering requirements; time spent on estimating, planning, and tracking activities throughout the project's duration; training specifically required for the project (not general software engineering training—this is not captured in the metrics database); and time spent evaluating and selecting tools, computers, and operating systems for a specific project.

Requirements Specification. Specification effort includes: working with customers to define the functions that must be contained in the system (including interviews, surveys, JAD workshops, and so on); writing and inspecting the software requirements specification document; doing any necessary rework as a result of these inspections; and creating and evaluating prototypes intended to more completely specify the requirements of the system.

Design. The design category is used to capture time spent: defining system architecture; creating and inspecting high-level design models (such as data flow diagrams, entity-relationship diagrams, and dialog maps); low-level program design activities; designing user interface screens, algorithms, data structures, file formats, database schemas, and object classes; doing any necessary rework as a result of design inspections; and creating and evaluating prototypes intended to determine whether the proposed system design is correct.

Implementation. This category includes: coding a program; inspecting the source code; doing any necessary rework as a result of these inspections; writing unit-level, internal module documentation; creating database tables, user interface screens, data files, or other artifacts that are part of the final system; and correcting defects found during testing, but prior to delivery of the system.

Testing. Aspects of testing effort that we measure include: writing and executing unit tests in a disciplined and systematic way, as well as informal, ad hoc testing of the program; writing and inspecting software quality assurance plans and test plans; doing any necessary rework as a result of these inspections; writing and executing user interface or other system tests; acquiring or building automated test drivers and associated test data files; engaging in systematic alpha or beta testing; and documenting the results of formal test executions.

We do *not* count the effort spent fixing bugs found by testing in the testing category, because this rework is really a part of the implementation effort. If the implementation (and requirements specifications, and designs) had been done correctly in the first place, rework would not be required. Our testing phase is defined as activities to find errors, not to correct them. This distinction encourages our engineers to logically separate the testing and debugging activities.

Writing Documentation. A separate category was established to capture time devoted to writing user aids (on-line help displays, user guides, reference manuals, tutorials, training materials), writing system documentation (that is, external to the programs themselves), and writing reports or giving presentations on the project.

Adaptive Maintenance. This maintenance category encompasses time spent making changes in software to cope with a new computing environment, such as a different operating system, a new version of a compiler or database management system, a modified third-party library, or changes in an external system to which this application interfaces.

Defect Correction. Defect correction is defined as making a feature in an existing software system work correctly, when it does not work correctly at present. The feature was always there; it just doesn't do what it is supposed to.

Enhancement. Enhancement includes adding an unanticipated new capability to a program and modifying an existing capability to satisfy a user request for improvement.

User Support. We include several aspects of customer assistance in this category: answering questions about how to use an application; helping users work around bugs or missing features; looking at a user's data to explain why the program is behaving as it is; helping a user move data produced by one application into another application; and delivering training to users.

The allocation of work effort to one of the six new software development categories has some cultural and behavioral implications, as well. For example, we split out unit testing from the implementation (coding) phase. This is to encourage developers to perform unit testing as a discrete, structured, and systematic activity, rather than following a code-a-little, test-a-little hacking approach. Measurement is a way to draw sharper distinctions between activities, providing visibility into what you are really doing, so you can decide if you ought to do something different.

The use of these work effort phases does not necessarily imply that a waterfall software development life cycle (SDLC) is being used for every project. Most software work can be classified into one of these ten categories, regardless of the SDLC being used. The main difference between one SDLC and another is the sequence in which the activities are carried out. For example, in an incremental development model, you do a little specification, design, implementation, and testing for the first increment, followed by another such sequence for the next increment.

We do not report time based on what phase the project as a whole is considered to be in. The classification depends strictly on the type of work being performed. Tasks like project planning and testing can span nearly the full duration of a project, at levels of intensity that vary over time. Figure 17.1 illustrates the distribution of different work categories over time for one of our larger projects. This distribution provides a profile of the life cycle activities on the entire project, so you can take corrective actions where necessary. For example, Fig. 17.1 shows that no time was devoted to testing on this project until after implementation began, around month 13. This indicates that test planning was not performed as early in the development cycle as it should have been—an improvement opportunity for the next project. You can also see how much calendar time was spent in each development category, which will help you plan staffing profiles for future similar projects. These are examples of how metrics data can provide a manager with better insight into the way a project is being conducted.

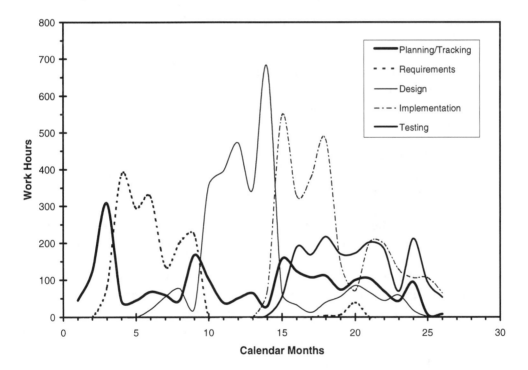

Figure 17.1: Work effort distribution over time for one software project.

Using six categories for capturing new development work is a very simple way to classify work effort. Software Productivity Research, Inc., developed a list of twenty-five "cost accumulator" categories for software projects [Jones, 1991]. Military software, management information systems (MIS), and systems software projects perform various subsets of these task types. MIS projects typically only perform twelve of these activities, and most of these are accommodated by the six work categories for new development that we used at Kodak. All testing categories are combined in our scheme, as are all design activities.

The six-category classification scheme we used for new development work adequately answered the initial questions that drove the design of our metrics program. In retrospect, however, finer granularity would have been desirable for some parts of our work effort metrics. For example, as we became more interested in measuring our total cost of quality, we realized we were not explicitly capturing internal rework, one of our major opportunities for improving productivity. The feedback aspect of the goal/question/metric approach (as described in Chapter 16) led us to conclude that it would be informative to make several changes in the categories we used:

- Add installation and training as a separate category in new development.

- Split the single testing phase at least into unit and system testing.

- Capture internal rework in separate categories, rather than lumping it into the phase in which the product being reworked was created (requirements, design, implementation), so we could get a better handle on the cost of quality.

- Capture software review time as a separate category (or as part of testing), instead of reporting it as part of the phase in which the product being reviewed was created.

We expect each of our team members to keep daily records of the time spent on each project activity, to a resolution of one-half hour. For accuracy, work time must be recorded as the work is done (daily), rather than trying to reconstruct it from memory at the end of the week or month. Time spent working at home or outside normal working hours must be captured as well. The objective is not to add up to forty hours per week, but to understand how much labor we actually invest in each project.

DeMarco and Lister suggest that the appropriate measure of effective work time is *uninterrupted* hours [DeMarco, 1987]. Frequent interruptions break up the state of flow that is so conducive to productive work. This perspective addresses the *quality* of the time increments, which is a different issue from the *quantity* of time, however badly fragmented, that is devoted to a project. Both measures can be important. Total time tells you how much work effort (cost) went into building a product. Uninterrupted hours gives you an indication of the quality of your work environment and how productive you can realistically expect people to be in that environment.

Our team members record only the time they spend on software project activities. We do not capture the time spent in hallway conversations, meetings that are not associated with a particular project, vacation, general training activities, or any of the many other ways that time evaporates [Perry, 1994]. (Some people do wish to record this sort of time for their own information, so we provide a "non-software activity" category they can use for this purpose.) This distinction represents a significant difference between a true work effort measurement program and an accounting process masquerading as a metrics program. Corporate accounting systems typically must account for exactly forty hours per week, regardless of how much time is actually spent on project work. We contend that our approach provides a more accurate assessment of the actual labor invested in a project.

Overtime must be counted to truly document how much effort went into an application, even if the unpaid overtime did not directly affect the project's dollar cost. (Chronic, institutionalized overtime incurs indirect costs by burning out staff members, reducing their productivity through exhaustion, and leading to excessive staff turnover. Is it worth it?) Similarly, we really should count other hidden costs, such as the time devoted to the project by customer representatives and other non-software people. Our team does not capture this effort; however, we do record the time spent on a project by group members who are not assigned to the project team, such as when an engineer reviews code written for a project other than his own.

Until an application is officially released, we report work time only in the six new development phases. Time spent finding or correcting bugs or adding new features is counted as testing or implementation until the application goes into production. Similarly, maintenance work on a released system is not subdivided into the six development categories unless we are using a different project name for a major enhancement effort.

For systems that are developed incrementally, we classify the time spent working on a released increment as maintenance, while time spent on an unreleased increment is classified as development. This released-unreleased demarcation avoids the complexity of slicing every enhancement into tiny chunks of specification, design, and so on. We do distinguish between the planned implementation of new features and the unanticipated enhancements that are requested by users. The goal is to really understand the distribution of our work effort between maintenance and new development. Therefore, we want to know how much unanticipated work we are doing on systems that we thought were completed.

The raw metrics data is stored in a simple relational database on a shared computer. To minimize the number of rows in the database, team members enter their work summaries weekly, using a simple on-line form. All of the hours spent that week on the same phase of the same project are totaled and reported as a single entry in the main table of this database. A second table is used to decode the work phase codes, while a third links the team member's login ID to his name and the name of the group to which he belongs. The process of recording and reporting work activities is not unduly burdensome: group members spend an average of only ten minutes per week on these steps.

Some concerns have been raised about the temptation for team members to report inaccurate data in an attempt to look better to management. However, the metrics reporting seems to be a self-controlling process. If someone reports fewer hours than he really worked, to increase his apparent productivity, the question arises as to where the remaining hours in the week went. Conversely, if more hours are reported than were actually worked, one's productivity would appear to be lower than it really is. In practice, the integrity of our team members has superseded any inclinations to distort the data.

Whether a manager even sees this data for an individual is up to the group to decide when you establish your metrics program. If individual work effort data is strictly private, with only group summaries being available to management, each team member is fully responsible for reporting his data regularly and accurately. Your culture will determine the degree of privacy required for a sustainable metrics program. Achieving a state of honest software measurement is only possible in a culture in which team members know the data they report will not be used as a weapon against them. Instead, measurement is a tool to help you understand the way the group works and to steer it to where it ought to be.

Most of our team members view the metrics effort not as a write-only database, into which data goes, never to be seen again, but as a repository of useful information. We wrote a simple reporting function to let group members generate a variety of summary reports; anyone can generate summary reports for an individual project or for the entire team. Engineers can browse through their own raw data, but to protect the privacy of individuals, team members cannot view data belonging to someone else. Our metrics system has three main reporting options, as follows:

1. We can generate a summary distribution of work effort subtotaled by phase over all projects worked on during a specified time frame, for an individual or for the group as a whole.

2. We can generate a summary distribution of work effort subtotaled by phase over the duration of a particular project, for an individual or for the group as a whole.

3. We can list the hours and percentage of total time spent on each project during a given time period, for an individual or for the group as a whole.

We generate summaries from the first reporting option on a quarterly basis, adding the data from the most recent three months to the historical quarterly summaries to show how the phase distributions are evolving. These quarterly reports are shared with the entire team and with management, so we *all* have a better understanding of how our group is building software. The reports also help us to identify problem areas and provide us with an opportunity to think about what we ought to be doing differently. Figure 17.2 illustrates the second reporting option. The third option is useful for identifying the myriad small activities that siphon time from one's principal assignment, but if each of your developers spends all of his time on a single project, this view of the information won't tell you anything new.

```
                    Phase Summary of All Work on SOME_APP
                    (for entire duration of project to date)


                                     Overall   Development  Maintenance
              Phase            Hours  Percent     Percent      Percent
              -------          -----  -------   -----------  -----------

    Adaptive Maintenance       144.5   11.9                     69.6
    Bug Correction              27.5    2.3                     13.3
    Design                     156.5   12.9       15.6
    Enhancement                 20.0    1.7                      9.6
    Implementation             369.5   30.5       36.9
    Preliminaries/Planning      46.5    3.8        4.6
    Specification              105.5    8.7       10.5
    Testing                    185.5   15.3       18.5
    User Support                15.5    1.3                      7.5
    Writing Documentation      139.0   11.5       13.9

    Total Hours:              1210.0                1002.5       207.5

    Percent of Total:                  100.0         82.9        17.1
```

Figure 17.2: Sample work effort distribution report for one project.

Trends and Applications

Collecting data for a few people over a short period of time provides a view of the group's work effort distribution that may not accurately represent long-term trends. Our group's composition and activities changed over time as we merged with other groups and absorbed their historical baggage of older, high-maintenance systems. Another complication was that the target moves (at least, it should, if the group is pursuing continuous process improvement). Consider these factors when you interpret long-term trends, since no single explanation will account for all of the work effort changes you observe. It can be tempting to over-interpret the data, but remember that not every glitch in any set of metrics data is necessarily significant. The long-term trend is more important than any one data point.

We chose to use our metrics data as a driving force for change. Consequently, the distribution of work for our group back in 1990 looks quite different from that for the years since. Figure 17.3 shows the distribution of our development work over a span of five years, with the total development time for each year normalized to 100 percent, as if no maintenance work had been performed.

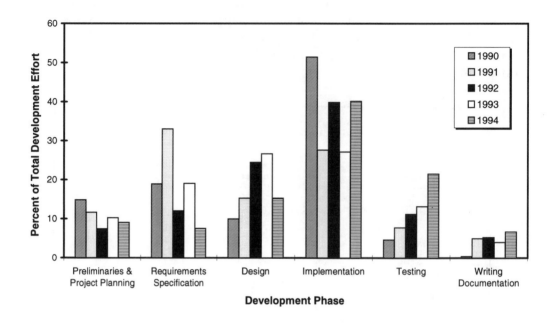

*Figure 17.3: New development work effort distribution
for one software group, by year.*

The figure shows several notable trends. For example, design and testing efforts increased from 1990 through 1993. This was not an accident. After collecting data for two years, the group felt our products would benefit from increasing the relative effort in these two areas. We set, and met, a goal for 1992 of increasing both design and testing effort by 50 percent over their cumulative 1990-91 values. The continued growth in 1993 suggests that the behavioral changes we adopted to achieve our initial goals had become instilled in our routine activities. Such trends in the distribution of new development work effort over time provide a quantitative depiction of a software process change.

The fraction of time devoted to implementation decreased from the 1990 value, as more effort was focused on the up-front activities of requirements specification and design. A corresponding decrease in defect correction confirms that we are building better software with the help of better requirements, better designs, and more testing.

The requirements specification and implementation categories reveal complementary trends, with one being high when the other is low. In a small group, with just a few projects underway, such relationships are to be expected. The work distributions of a larger organization working on many projects will not be so heavily influenced by the ebb and flow of individual projects. The drop in requirements specification effort in 1994 could be a warning signal that we need to pay more attention to this activity. Or, it could just be because several projects were in an implementation-intensive stage that year. Anomalies in the trend data should raise a flag and stimulate some investigation into the cause for the unexpected shift. This is one of the major benefits of the metrics effort.

An initial downward trend in preliminaries and project planning was reversed in 1993, when we began to concentrate more on formal project management. Again, process evolution will affect the trends in your work effort distributions.

Plotting the long-term trends in our four maintenance work effort categories provides similar insights into how well we have managed those activities. In particular, changes in the fraction of our total software work that is devoted to defect correction tell us how effective the quality improvement methods we implemented for new development work have been.

The primary value of these metrics charts is to help you identify your major improvement opportunities. Without quantitative data, you are always guessing where to focus your energies for the greatest impact. If you want to know how large your maintenance burden—or anything else—truly is, you'll have to measure it yourself.

Metrics-Based Project Estimation

Estimating the duration and cost of new software projects is a major challenge for most software organizations. Many available estimating tools rely on models such as the COnstructive COst MOdel, or COCOMO [Boehm, 1981]. COCOMO is derived from a sample of sixty-three projects executed in the 1960s and 1970s. How accurately will such models predict *your* organization's delivery capability in the 1990s?

Estimating work effort requires that you know the quantity of software to be written, which is itself difficult to estimate. COCOMO is based on the projected lines of code in the final product, which is not easy to predict early in the project. Finding some comparable historical projects on which to base your estimates will help you estimate lines of code for a new project. Metrics relating to the amount of functionality contained in a system are more meaningful early predictors of software size. Such functional metrics include function points, feature points (which extend function point concepts to deal with system and scientific software [Jones, 1991]), and DeMarco's Bang metric [DeMarco, 1982]. Functional metrics can be estimated from user requirements, screen mockups, or structured analysis models, which typically are available early in the project life cycle.

The most reliable estimates are those based on your group's previous performance on similar projects, adjusted for staff capabilities, new technology learning curves, and so on [DeMarco, 1982]. If you wish to use any published cost estimating model, you must adjust it for your own environment of people, projects, and processes for it to be a useful predictor.

Our team approached metrics-based estimating by exploring the relationship between the number of requirements in the software requirements specification and the number of post-specification work hours needed to deliver the system. This effort includes all project time classified as design, implementation, testing,

and writing documentation. We have been writing requirements specification documents in a similar fashion for several years. Preliminary versions of the SRS can
be generated early in the project's life cycle, which made the SRS attractive as a
starting point for preparing estimates. We believed the requirements count (at the
fairly fine granularity of our SRS documents) should be an approximate indicator
of system size. While this is true for our group, it may not pertain to the kind of
applications you build, or to the way you write your requirements documents.

We examined SRS documents from eight completed projects for consistency of
style. We applied a simple plus-or-minus 50 percent factor to the raw count of
functional requirements for documents that contained requirements written in
especially complex or simple styles. These documents represented a range of tiny
to medium sized projects, including information systems, utilities, reusable components, and real-time process control systems.

Figure 17.4 depicts the correlation between the number of post-specification
development hours and the adjusted number of functional requirements for the
eight projects (shown as circles). A linear regression fit to the data gives a slope of
5.6, which is the average number of hours required to design, implement, test, and
document one requirement for the projects in this sample. To be sure, some system
requirements can be implemented in minutes, while others may take days, so this
average figure of 5.6 is only useful when applied to a collection of requirements.

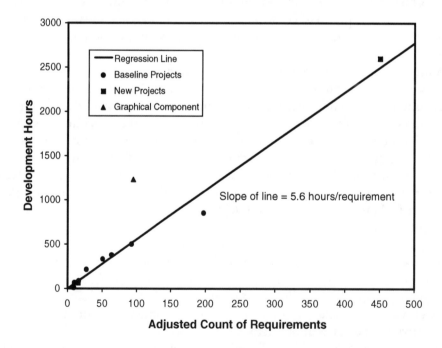

Figure 17.4: Development time as a function of number of requirements.

There is always the concern that a relationship this linear is a fluke. Two new project data points were added since the original study was done (depicted by the squares in Fig. 17.4). These new points fell very close to the original line, without any adjustments in the requirements count. Thus, we conclude that in our little world, this correlation is the best available predictor of the effort required to deliver a system similar to those we have built in the past. We must continue to add data points from new projects to test the validity of this simple model and to understand deviations from it. As your software process evolves, the oldest information in your historical database will become a less relevant predictor of future results.

The next step in building our estimation algorithm was to translate an estimate of total work hours into calendar time. The metrics database again showed its value, indicating that each team member reported an average of 31 hours of effective project time per work week in 1993 (up from 26 hours in 1990). Consequently, the estimated number of work hours for a new project should be divided by 31, not by 40, to estimate the calendar weeks of labor required per staff member. You must apply further adjustments for absences, work on other activities, and so on to the resulting number of weeks. This model now forms the starting point for our new project work estimates.

Not all of the projects that we estimated using the relationship in Fig. 17.4 adhered to the regression line. We had to adjust the initial predictions to account for unusual characteristics of a particular system. For example, a reusable graphics software component (depicted by the triangle in Fig. 17.4) required nearly twice the estimated work time, largely because we performed much more extensive testing than we had on older, self-contained applications. Software components that are intended to be reused can consume several times the design and verification efforts of a stand-alone application of comparable size. Portability was another critical attribute of this graphics program, so we had to devote extra design and implementation effort to achieve this objective and deliver it on two platforms.

I certainly do not recommend that you use this specific, simplified model for preparing your own project estimates unless you validate it with your own historical data. However, if you begin to accumulate a database of project effort and size, you will find that your ability to predict the future will improve. It is comforting to have an established estimating algorithm available when you are asked to project the effort and schedule for an upcoming application, rather than simply pulling numbers out of the air and hoping you can meet them.

With an estimation model in hand, you are also in a better position to push back against unrealistic management-imposed goals for delivery dates, which are rarely based on any kind of formal estimating procedure. A "goal" is the date someone wants to have the product completed; an "estimate" is the date you believe it will actually be delivered. Often, they are not the same.

Lessons from Work Effort Metrics

During the past several years, our team has found that the collection and analysis of software work effort metrics provides multiple benefits. The investment we made in collecting this data was relatively modest: a simple shared database, some simple input screens and reporting functions, the ten minutes each team member spends on data collection per week, and a few minutes to generate reports periodically. Team members derive value from the summary data for project planning, estimation of tasks, describing their work activities to management, and identifying personal improvement opportunities, such as activities to which they ought to devote more time.

The metrics data provides a quantitative understanding of certain aspects of the group's development process, as well as a way to monitor the evolution of the process over time. As one team member said, "It has been enlightening to compare where you *think* you spend your time with where you *really* spend your time." By tracking the time spent on various activities, we can have fact-based discussions about problem areas, rather than arguments founded on incomplete recollections and fragmentary knowledge. The metrics data helps us cope with staff turnover, by revealing exactly which projects were being worked on, and at what level of effort, by someone who leaves the group.

Most importantly, we are now able to confidently answer each of the questions posed at the beginning of this chapter. While we still are not able to control every aspect of our software development activities, we have much clearer insight into them than we ever did before.

Predicting Maintainability with Metrics

Work effort metrics are an example of historical metrics—they provide a look at what has happened in the past so we can learn from it and try to improve. It would be ever more useful to have some predictive metrics to give us a glimpse of the future (at some confidence level), from which we can make decisions and take appropriate actions. For example, our group is interested in the anticipated maintainability of new applications we write, since we have a continuing goal of controlling maintenance effort. Wouldn't it be great if we could identify the shaky modules in a new system early enough to do something about them?

One approach used to quantify maintainability is described by Don Coleman and collaborators [Coleman, 1994]. Coleman derived several different models in an attempt to calculate a maintainability index (MI) that would reliably predict which modules in a large system were more likely to pose maintenance problems. One model uses four metrics readily obtained from a source code analyzer tool, such as those described in Chapter 13. The MI is calculated using an equation that incorporates dimensions of code size, complexity, and comment density.

The MIs computed in this way for several hundred modules in a large system at Hewlett-Packard correlated well with subjective or other semi-quantitative assessments of maintainability. Combine these objective indicators of maintainability with subjective assessments of code clarity and comment quality obtained from peer reviews to pick out those modules that are in the greatest need of improvement. Improving these modules prior to delivery might protect the original programmers from enraged future maintainers seeking vengeance for the crummy code they inherited.

One of the project teams in our organization is applying this model to calculate MIs for the modules in a medium-sized system. Our intent with this study is to record the number of faults identified in each module over time and the effort required to correct each fault, to see if we can establish correlations with the predicted maintainabilities. If so, we can have some confidence in a new tool for providing an early warning signal about problem software components: a useful predictor metric. Then we can use calculated maintainability indexes to identify modules we should inspect and test thoroughly, or actually rebuild.

To focus the culture on quality, remember that you're measuring maintainability to reduce the risk of future problems by understanding what actions you can take *now* to improve the product. Your goal is not to reach some desired numerical target but to use accurate measurements to help you make informed decisions about how best to invest your resources. The prospect of using easily obtained code metrics to identify shaky modules provides another example of how measurement can help us control our software projects, products, and processes.

Summary

✔ Use the data you collect; don't just let it sit in a database someplace. People should be able to see the connection between the data they report and its application. Provide tools so the team members can generate reports and graphs from the data.

✔ Measuring work effort is not very difficult, and it can tell you a lot about your software development processes and their improvement opportunities.

✔ Use measurements to quantify your maintenance effort, to look for the right knobs to turn so that you can keep the maintenance dragon under control.

✔ Collect a historical base of productivity data, so you can make more accurate estimates of the effort needed for future projects.

✔ It takes time to collect enough data to observe long-term trends, so begin a measurement program now.

Culture Builders and Killers

Culture Builder: Your staff will be more motivated to collect the requested measurements if they see tangible benefits from having them available, so share summaries of the group's metrics data with the entire team periodically. Explain how you are using it for assessing progress, making decisions, and communicating with upper management. Discuss the trends revealed by the data with the team. Obtain their input into how to interpret the trends and how to apply the insights thus revealed to further improve the group's software development processes.

Culture Builder: Make your metrics database available to every member of the team. Encourage them to review their own data periodically to look for lessons and improvement opportunities. Individuals should be able to see their own data, accumulated data for any project, and accumulated data for the whole group. However, no team member should be able to see the data for another individual.

Culture Killer: Find a metrics tool that estimates how many errors are likely to be found in a given module, and stop testing when you have found exactly that many. It's not necessary to tailor the algorithms used for this prediction for your own environment; whatever defaults the metrics tool vendor selected will be fine.

Culture Killer: Your company uses an accounting system to bill your internal customer departments for forty hours of project work per staff member each week. You learn that some of your developers have set up a little database to record the actual time they spend on each project every week, for some mysterious reason. You should put an end to this nonsense right away. There is no point in using two systems to do the same measurements; the accounting system is the only project measurement activity your team members need to use.

References and Further Reading

Boehm, Barry W. *Software Engineering Economics.* Englewood Cliffs, N.J.: Prentice-Hall, 1981.

> Boehm describes the COnstructive COst MOdel (COCOMO) for predicting project schedule and effort from the estimated number of source statements in the final system. While the model provided good fits to the basis data, there are two major concerns. First, to what extent can you tweak various parameters to make the model relevant for the kinds of work done by your own team? And second, how accurately can you estimate lines of code in a product early in the development cycle?

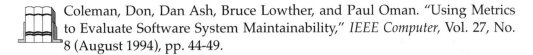 Coleman, Don, Dan Ash, Bruce Lowther, and Paul Oman. "Using Metrics to Evaluate Software System Maintainability," *IEEE Computer*, Vol. 27, No. 8 (August 1994), pp. 44-49.

These authors explored five models for quantifying module or system maintainability from software metrics. Their data suggests that a value calculated from metrics that are easily obtained from source code can identify those modules that are likely to be more difficult to maintain.

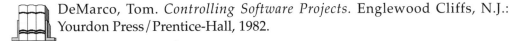 DeMarco, Tom. *Controlling Software Projects.* Englewood Cliffs, N.J.: Yourdon Press/Prentice-Hall, 1982.

Extensive sections of this book are devoted to software cost models and to various aspects of software quality. Chapter 16 identifies nearly thirty correction factors that can be incorporated into cost models.

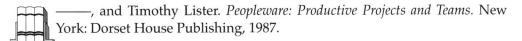 ———, and Timothy Lister. *Peopleware: Productive Projects and Teams.* New York: Dorset House Publishing, 1987.

DeMarco and Lister explain the importance of working in an environment in which interruptions can be controlled. Effective work comes from the focused, single-minded mental state called flow. Anything that interrupts the state of flow causes a big productivity hit. An honest work effort tracking program should look at the ratio of uninterrupted hours to body-present hours, rather than counting little snippets of time as if they are all equally useful for working effectively.

Jones, Capers. *Applied Software Measurement.* New York: McGraw-Hill, 1991.

Jones describes many aspects of measuring software work effort, work volume, productivity, and quality.

Perry, Dewayne E., Nancy A. Staudenmayer, and Lawrence G. Votta. "People, Organizations, and Process Improvement," *IEEE Software*, Vol. 11, No. 4 (July 1994), pp. 36-45.

These authors describe a study in which detailed recording of how developers spend their time revealed the many daily activities that siphon time away from design and coding. Self-reported times in a daily diary did not exactly agree with those captured by an independent observer.

Chapter 18

If It Makes Sense, Do It

*A foolish consistency is the hobgoblin of little minds, adored
by little statesmen and philosophers and divines.*

—Ralph Waldo Emerson

The greater the ignorance the greater the dogmatism.

—Sir William Osler

Books and articles on software development methodologies abound. Organizations that are attempting to improve their processes sometimes make the mistake of adopting some published methodology lock, stock, and barrel. This can be a recipe for wasted time and money, frustration, and a feeling that effective process change is not possible in your team. Overstuffed methodologies that clash with your culture and fail to meet your business needs quickly turn into shelfware.

Every methodology has good ideas and silly ideas, in varying proportions. You should become familiar with the various development methodologies that have been published so you can select the most appropriate ideas for your project needs. Combine the best features you can identify from the many choices: structured analysis and design, object-oriented development, iterative prototyping, evolutionary delivery, information engineering, and a host of in-house and custom-built alternatives. No one will arrest you for synthesizing your own methodology from bits and pieces of these others.

Once your group incorporates a new technique or tool into its culture, move on to the next set of good ideas. Look for approaches that will address specific shortcomings in your group's current development practices, as identified through the assessment methods discussed in Chapter 9. If you find that a method you tried (*really* tried!) does not add value, don't attempt to force-fit it into the way your group works. As your culture, projects, and technologies evolve over time, you may wish to revisit these rejected methods, just as you periodically revisit and tune your current methods, to see if the time is right to blend them into your development process.

Process improvement efforts are more likely to succeed when the culture permits experimentation and backing out of failed experiments. Remember our Kodak group's experience with our first CASE tool, which we nicknamed PaleoTool? The experiment was only a limited success, so we returned four of the five copies of PaleoTool we had purchased. However, we didn't give up on CASE, and once we selected more appropriate tools, we got a lot of mileage from them.

People who perceive that a risk of failure is acceptable are more willing to explore new ways to do their work. If, however, the methods are imposed from on high, without regard to how well they work on *your* problems in *your* environment, you can expect rough sailing ahead. Encourage your team members to share their frustrations and failures with new methodologies, as well as their successes, at team meetings. Project postmortems of what went well and what could have gone better will help you select the best approaches for the next project.

Our Kodak research software groups elected not to adopt any one methodological dogma. Instead, we routinely carry out those analysis and design activities that we have learned by experience will help us produce better systems for our customers. We adhere to this simple philosophy: No Dogma.

The "No Dogma" philosophy extends beyond how you apply specific software development methodologies in your group. Any aspect of software effort can lead you into the trap of doing work by the numbers, just because someone wrote down "The Rules." In this book, we have explored many techniques that can improve the quality and effectiveness of your organization's software work. Rather than following any of these recommendations religiously, apply them in the context of your company's goals. Table 18.1 illustrates the differences between the letter and the spirit of these practices. Any activity that helps you achieve your organizational goals is good; anything that inhibits progress toward those goals is evil.

Saying "No Dogma" is not the same as saying, "Everybody can write software any way he or she likes." A quality-oriented software engineering culture sets high standards for the way work is to be done, and team members are expected to take these standards seriously. This is a more practical approach than simply decreeing that the rules embedded in any particular book or CASE tool must be applied to every aspect of a project. Following are some examples of things not to be dogmatic about:

- executing every step in a published or purchased methodology

- collecting every metric in some author's list of "metrics you really ought to collect"

- following every part of every pertinent IEEE standard

- applying every practice defined within every key process area of the SEI's Capability Maturity Model, one CMM level at a time

Table 18.1.
Relating Software Engineering Practices to
Organizational Goals.

The goal is to...	Not to...
Understand the actual needs of your customers well enough to minimize the risk of delivering a system that does not meet those needs.	Write a perfect, complete, and frozen software requirements specification before beginning any subsequent activities.
Improve the quality, productivity, and predictability of your group's software development activities.	Be assessed at Level N of the Capability Maturity Model.
Use a framework of established standards and guidelines to ensure that work is done by your team members in a repeatable and consistent way.	Conform to every detail of some published software development standard.
Understand and achieve the required quality level for each of your products, so they meet customer needs and expectations.	Achieve a six-sigma defect level.
Collect data that will let you continuously improve your work through measurement, analysis, and feedback.	Measure everything you read about in a book on software metrics.
Obtain superior results by applying the best available software development and maintenance practices in a systematic fashion.	Follow somebody's favorite methodology to the letter.
Improve the developer's understanding of customer needs and possible system architectures by drawing multiple views of the system.	Draw a perfect set of fully validated models with a particular CASE tool.
Avoid unpleasant surprises by acquiring a thorough and honest understanding of the tasks that are required to complete a project.	Create a perfect project plan that is always current, complete, and accurate to the nearest labor hour.
Effectively apply new technical and managerial skills in one's daily work.	Send a certain number of people to some training class.
Write well-structured programs that can be understood and maintained.	Avoid using GOTO statements in all circumstances because you heard they are evil.

In contrast, here are a few of the nonnegotiable high standards you should set for your team:

- involving customers in the process of gathering and analyzing requirements

- documenting requirements in a structured and systematic fashion so they can be validated

- involving all team members in continuous improvement of the group's processes

- routinely performing quality reviews of software work products

- performing structured, repeatable, and automated testing

- acquiring training to enhance the skills of all team members

- defining and following pragmatic procedures for performing key activities that are common to your projects

- measuring multiple aspects of your work products and processes

If you were to undertake improvements in just these eight areas, you would be well on your way to increased quality and productivity in a healthier software engineering culture than your organization probably has today.

Gerald Weinberg suggests that if programmers notice that standards or rules are being enforced, most of them will follow the standards [Weinberg, 1988]. I believe that clearly communicating a high level of quality expectations for your team will induce most of them to strive to meet those expectations. This is not the same as demanding outrageous quantities of unpaid overtime to meet unrealistic schedules; this may work for a short time, but it cannot become a lifestyle. A leader who grows a culture oriented toward high quality and sensible approaches to building software nurtures a lifestyle of values that should persist after that leader moves on.

Another characteristic of a software engineering culture is that processes and behaviors are revised when they clearly are no longer appropriate. The team had agreed to certain procedures as the best known solution to their quality and productivity challenges at one point in time. As the environment evolves and projects change, the established approaches may no longer be optimal. Members of a forward-looking culture will recognize when old solutions do not fit new problems, and they will reevaluate their established processes to make necessary improvements. Rather than being forced to adhere dogmatically to obsolete methods, developers in a software engineering culture are always looking for better ways to do their work.

Carried to an extreme, you can wind up chasing every new technology in search of the magic silver bullet to cure your software woes. Or you can spend all of your time writing processes and procedures, with no time left to write software. A healthy culture finds an appropriate balance between doing and improving, without compromising its standards and principles to meet some short-term or misguided objective. This requires each member of the team to be personally committed to quality and integrity, as well as having good sense.

Summary

✔ Do what makes sense; don't resort to dogma.

✔ Become familiar with a variety of software development methodologies, so you can select those elements that will add value to your organization's work.

✔ Keep sight of the organizational goals. Do not strive to meet some standard or apply some method unless it will help you achieve those goals.

✔ Make sure your team members understand that quality is not an option but a nonnegotiable expectation.

Culture Builders and Killers

Culture Builder: Set clear, high standards for your team: Most people will rise to the challenge. They want to do quality work, so they will welcome the opportunity to work in an environment where quality is not only valued but expected. Look for local best practices that certain individuals in your team are applying, and encourage them to share their approaches with the rest of the team through technical exchanges at group meetings.

Culture Killer: Require all new development projects undertaken by your group to be performed according to the multi-volume methodology that some consultant created for your company ages ago. You paid a lot of money for that methodology, and you don't want to see the investment wasted. If the methodology worked for your company ten years ago, it should work today.

Culture Killer: Downsize, rightsize, reengineer, and outsource until your overextended in-house software group exists only to support the critical legacy systems you are still stuck with. Those programmers that remain will soon realize they are dwelling in the technological outback of software engineering. They'll transfer to another department or quit the company, and then you won't have to worry about managing those difficult software engineers any more.

References and Further Reading

Weinberg, Gerald M. *Understanding the Professional Programmer.* New York: Dorset House Publishing, 1988.

> This collection of essays about the programming profession addresses the attitudes and psychology of people who become programmers, how to survive working in a bureaucracy, and how people can learn to think and communicate more effectively.

 Yourdon, Edward. *Decline and Fall of the American Programmer.* Englewood Cliffs, N.J.: Yourdon Press/Prentice-Hall, 1992.

> Yourdon presents a comprehensive overview of contemporary software development principles, methodologies, and issues. As he points out about software methodologies, "There is no one single bullet. But taken together, perhaps a collection of small silver pellets will help to slay the werewolves of software development quality and productivity."

Part VI

What to Do on Monday

F rom the many approaches described for improving a software engineering culture, there are specific actions that managers and developers should consider taking, starting with their next day back at work. You may already be doing some of these; others may not pertain to your organization at this time. You may well have other action items to add to these lists, but those presented here can provide immediate benefits to most software teams. Even these short lists contain too many activities to initiate at once. Think of them as menus, and start with those items that will have the highest impact on your group.

A "healthy" software engineering culture includes the physical and mental health of its constituents. Repetitive motion injuries and other health problems are a growing concern for users of computers. The final chapter includes a discussion of the importance of providing a safe, healthy, and ergonomically correct work environment for anyone who spends extended periods of time at a computer workstation.

The cultural premise for Part VI is

✔ You can't change everything at once. Identify those changes that will yield the greatest benefits, and begin to implement them next Monday.

Chapter 19

Action Planning for Software Managers

Leaders communicate by giving understandable direction and by setting evident example. Leading means stating objectives in a way that is precisely understood, ensuring the commitment of individuals to those objectives, defining the methods of measurement, and then providing the impetus to get things done.

—Philip B. Crosby, *Quality Is Free*

Whenever I attend a particularly stimulating conference or read a truly great software book, I get lots of ideas, too many to implement at once. I make a list of tasks to try to accomplish when I return to the office. But when I do get back to work, the alligators that were snapping at my heels before the conference are still there. It is easy to stay mired in the swamp of day-to-day problems, losing the drive for change that the conference or book stimulated. Since I cannot implement all of these great ideas, it is tempting to let inertia take over, and go on with my daily life without trying any of them.

Resist this temptation! No one can implement all the changes they know they should. But almost any process change you are able to make, if thoughtfully selected and skillfully implemented, will lead to better results (and greater wisdom) than if you do nothing different. Don't try to change your own or your group's behaviors by revolution, but rather change it through a steady evolution toward improved practices, enhanced individual capabilities, and superior software products. Begin by identifying changes you think are both significant and feasible. When selecting action items, ask yourself these questions:

- What benefits do I expect if the change is successful?

- How might I be able to put this change into practice?

- How much effort will be required?

- Who will I have to persuade to go along with the idea?

- What is the worst that could happen if we fail?

Everyone can list dozens of reasons why he cannot change the way he does his work, at least not this week. The excuses you might hear in your role as a change agent sometimes require translation to understand the hidden message. "I haven't got time now—maybe later" might really mean, "Not now, not ever." An appropriate response would then be, "Let's look at your current priorities and commitments to see if we can free up some time to try this new approach." When a team member says, "I already do something just as good as what you are recommending," he might really be saying, "I would rather not move out of my comfort zone," and you might reply, "Let's compare both methods and make sure we select the best practice available." The reaction, "I don't know how to do what you suggest" in response to a proposal to apply an improved process could also imply, "And I don't want to learn." You can defuse this resistance with an encouraging comment such as, "Let's determine what kind of training or consultant support will get us up to speed on these new techniques." Make sure you understand the underlying sources of resistance as you try to determine how best to steer your group toward an improved software engineering culture.

The leader of a small software group plays a critical role in the ability of the group to improve the way it does its work, and hence in the quality of the products it builds. Following are ten significant actions a first-level software manager can take to begin to improve his or her organization's software engineering culture through proactive leadership.

1. Examine your priorities as a software manager.

2. Make quality an unambiguous top priority.

3. Set up a technical peer review program.

4. Schedule an assessment of the team's software development practices.

5. Set group goals, and define metrics to monitor progress.

6. Assess each team member's training and career development needs.

7. Set up a recognition program.

8. Acquire books and magazines for team use.

9. Assess the team's image with managers, customers, and professional peers.

10. Evaluate the ergonomics of each team member's work place.

Action Item Menu

Examine your priorities as a software manager. Do you focus on meeting the needs of your team members, rather than on striving to please your own manager? Do your people have adequate access to your time? Do you follow through on commitments you make to those who report to you? Take a close look at your values and behaviors: Are you doing anything that could get you convicted of criminally negligent teamicide?

Consider collecting input from your team members about how you can improve your performance as a manager. I have done this several times, using different formats, such as anonymous questionnaires or a special group meeting that I did not attend. The results of these exercises always provide clear indications of things I should try to do better. A manager who is not willing to have his performance evaluated by the people he supervises has no business being a manager.

There are two reasons why someone may be reluctant to request performance input from those below him on the organization chart: He already knows what sort of feedback he is likely to get, and he doesn't want to hear it; or he doesn't care what sort of feedback he gets. Both of these attitudes are unacceptable. I have a responsibility to be the best manager I can possibly be. If this means hearing someone's opinion that I fall short in certain respects, so be it. I need to know what the group feels my improvement opportunities are, so I can decide what actions to take. Without those perspectives from the people who count, I can base my improvement efforts only on my own perceptions and the feedback I get from my supervisor or my peers, who have a very different view of my performance.

If your priority as a manager is the people you manage, you have to know where you really stand with them. You don't have to make every behavioral change your team members suggest, but you must take their recommendations seriously. If you view those you supervise as the customers of your leadership services, remember that the customer is not always right, but the customer always has a point.

Make quality an unambiguous top priority. Some managers preach the importance of software quality, provided that the quality activities do not interfere with one's daily software productivity. These managers have not accepted the ideas behind the cost of quality. Take the time to learn about cost of quality concepts so you can internalize the premise that doing the job right the first time increases overall productivity by reducing expensive rework. Make sure your team members understand your commitment to quality. Hold them to high (but not impossible) expectations. Slogans like "Six Sigma by '96" don't mean anything.

Getting each developer to understand the importance of producing quality products, measuring the quality, and continuously improving quality by applying superior processes means a great deal.

Set up a technical peer review program. Since reviews and inspections of software products have the highest impact of any single software quality practice (with a return on investment of up to 15 to 1, according to Capers Jones), start a peer review process in your group. This can range from a buddy system in which two developers exchange work products for individual peer deskchecks, to a formal and documented inspection procedure, whatever seems most appropriate for your current culture. Arrange training for inspection participants, and rely on the guidelines from Chapter 12 to help make inspections become an effective contributor to your quality improvement activities.

Schedule an assessment of the team's software development practices. As we saw in Chapter 9, you can use a variety of assessment techniques to gain insight into the way your team builds software and to reveal shortcomings in the present approach. Select one of these assessment methods, and use it to identify several major improvement opportunities. A formal assessment is not always necessary; much can be accomplished in informal group brainstorming sessions. The goal is to have the team reach consensus on the areas where improvement energy should be expended. Areas that are likely to make it onto your initial list of problem areas include requirements engineering and management, configuration management, development guidelines, project planning and management, and change control.

Choose up to three areas for initial action planning, and make substantial progress on them before you attack others. A process improvement effort that tries to go in too many directions at once can stall because people are spread too thinly and progress is made too slowly. Assemble small teams of people to work on solutions for each of these areas, applying a sequence of assess-plan-do-verify in the context of a formal mini-project. Make it clear that you expect all team members to spend a certain percentage of their time (five percent is a good target) on individual and group improvement activities. Adjust project schedules to free up the necessary time and demonstrate your commitment to continuous improvement.

Set group goals, and define metrics to monitor progress. The assessment process will help the group select specific goals. Identify the questions you will have to answer to know if you are meeting each goal. Then, choose some metrics that will give you the information you need to answer those questions. This application of GQM (goal/question/metric) is a straightforward way to establish a measurement program in your group, as Chapter 16 described.

The goals you pursue should encompass elements of your products, projects, and processes. They could be in the areas of product quality and customer satisfaction, delivery schedules, improved processes, new technologies to deploy, or anything else that is necessary for your group to survive and prosper. Keep the goals visible to the team members throughout the year, and share the metrics data with them to track progress toward the goals. Reaching these goals is a team achievement. However, the manager provides the nurturing environment in which goals are taken seriously and have a positive impact on the team's application development and support effectiveness.

Assess each team member's training and career development needs. Perform a skills assessment for each member of your team. Compare each individual's proficiencies in different skill areas with his personal objectives and with the needs of the organization. Define training needs and schedules for each individual, selecting from the many training sources described in Chapter 4 or from other sources of training available to your organization. Plan to have each training experience result in effective technology transfer to the student's daily work. Learn about the career objectives of each member of your team, so you can give individuals responsibilities that will help them grow toward their goals. Use the skills portfolio information you collect to identify gaps between the organization's needs and available resources. This gap analysis will be useful when you are selecting candidates to fill new or vacant positions.

Set up a recognition program. Determine the sorts of recognition and rewards that your team members would find to be meaningful; refer back to Chapter 3 for ideas. Make recognition events for accomplishments large and small a standard component of your team culture. Practice the implicit recognition of showing sincere interest in the work being done by each member of your team and doing all you can to remove obstacles to their effectiveness.

Acquire books and magazines for team use. Have group members select several technical periodicals to which they would like subscriptions. Set up a circulation process to make sure that everyone who is interested can see the magazines before they become obsolete. Circulate software engineering reading lists or book catalogs to the members of your group. Buy the books they indicate they would like to read, and encourage the team to set up a book discussion group. For yourself, begin with *Peopleware* by Tom DeMarco and Timothy Lister. Seek out books on project management, people management, and leadership; the books in Gerald Weinberg's *Quality Software Management* series provide a good start.

Assess the team's image with managers, customers, and professional peers. Application development groups become convenient whipping boys in a troubled company. Assess the reputation your group has with its managers, its customers, its customers' managers, and other development organizations. Enhance your group's image by improving your communications with these other stakeholders. Strive to build partnerships instead of adversarial or competitive relationships. Keep your customers informed of your activities through periodic newsletters and progress reports. Educate your managers to better understand the development methods you espouse and to make them appreciate the importance of investing in process improvements. Send team members to participate in professional conferences, to share your group's experiences and bring back the best available practices to leverage throughout your company.

Evaluate the ergonomics of each team member's work place. All people who use a computer workstation for a living have a right to a hazard-free work environment. Unfortunately, thousands of computer users suffer from an assortment of ailments that are induced or aggravated by long hours at the keyboard.

You have a responsibility to ensure that your team members have the equipment they need to work safely and comfortably. See Chapter 20 for more details.

Summary

✔ You can't change everything at once. Identify those changes that will yield the greatest benefits, and begin to implement them next Monday.

✔ Select some initial improvement initiatives from among the top ten action areas listed for software managers. Focus your energies on just a few of those until you have made some good progress, then move on to the next area.

✔ The first-line software manager plays a key role in creating a software engineering culture. Lead your team to a way of life that combines a devotion to quality, a commitment to producing superior software products for your customers, collaborative teamwork, and fun on the job.

References and Further Reading

DeMarco, Tom, and Timothy Lister. *Peopleware: Productive Projects and Teams.* New York: Dorset House Publishing, 1987.

> *Peopleware* should be on every manager's desk, because it provides invaluable insights into attracting and managing good people, the office environment, and growing productive teams.

Weinberg, Gerald M. *Quality Software Management, Volume 1: Systems Thinking.* New York: Dorset House Publishing, 1992. *Quality Software Management, Volume 2: First-Order Measurement.* New York: Dorset House Publishing, 1993. *Quality Software Management, Volume 3: Congruent Action.* New York: Dorset House Publishing, 1994.

> Weinberg's series focuses on helping people become high-quality, effective software managers.

Chapter 20

Action Planning for Software Engineers

A journey of a thousand miles must begin with a single step.

—Lao-tzu

While much of the work of creating a software engineering culture falls to the first-line manager, every member of a software group is responsible for contributing to the growth of the culture. This contribution comes from personal behaviors that lead to ever-increasing quality in each individual's work products, as well as to effective team interactions on both project work and improvement activities. Below are ten actions all software practitioners should consider taking when they go back to work. As with the suggestions for managers, you cannot expect to do all these things at once, so pick out the most worthwhile and give them a sincere try.

1. Learn and use at least one improved quality practice this week.

2. Set up a peer review for one current work product.

3. Identify three skill areas for improvement.

4. Select software magazines and books to read.

5. Get in the habit of iterative design before coding.

6. Apply effective structured testing techniques.

7. Begin tracking your project time daily, by work category.

8. Look for opportunities to reuse existing software and to create reusable work products.

9. Learn how to do a better job of planning and estimating tasks.

10. Examine your work environment for ergonomic problems.

Action Item Menu

Learn and use at least one improved quality practice this week. The customer/supplier process model for software (see Fig. 11.3) was based on the premise that the quality of the products created by any step in the development process is limited by the quality of the raw materials (specifications, code, documentation, and so on) supplied to that step. Each person working on a software project is responsible for ensuring that the quality of the products he or she creates is sufficient to meet the overall project goals. It is not the responsibility of the quality assurance department, the testers, or the customers to find the errors in your work products: It is *your* responsibility, with a little help from your friends through peer reviews. The project leader and department manager are responsible for providing you with the time, training, and resources you need to perform the practices that result in quality software. But it's up to you to learn what those practices are and to apply them effectively in your daily work.

Begin your contribution to your group's software engineering culture by making a personal commitment that you will bring quality—in its many dimensions—to the forefront of the work that you do. Select one of the many techniques discussed in this book, learn about it, and apply it to your own work—this week! The other suggestions in this chapter support improved quality at the individual practitioner level, so you may want to select your new quality practice from among these options.

Set up a peer review for one current work product. Programmers often have difficulty convincing themselves to give their work products to a group of their peers for evaluation. However, once you have experienced the many benefits of a healthy peer review process, you won't feel entirely comfortable with your work *unless* someone else has looked it over. Asking your colleagues to search for defects in your designs and code requires that you set your ego aside in the quest for quality. It isn't easy, and your ego may regain control quickly if your early review experiences leave you feeling personally assaulted.

Two approaches can ease the transition into the routine use of reviews. First, you can pair up with a peer you trust personally and respect professionally, and exchange materials for individual deskchecks. For a more aggressive approach, acquire some training in formal inspection procedures and give them a try. Formal team inspections always find more errors than informal individual deskchecks, but any kind of peer review is better than blindly trusting your own work. Reviews are most likely to succeed in a culture characterized by openness, mutual respect, and a common focus on quality. If you don't work in such a culture now, begin to set the example of egoless programming for your teammates by asking some of them to review one of your work products—this week!

Identify three skill areas for improvement. The field of software engineering is so extensive that we cannot all expect to be fully proficient generalists, able to adroitly perform every task associated with the construction of a complex application. Think of the areas where you would benefit from additional knowledge, and work with your supervisor to define an appropriate learning sequence to address them. For each new project, set a personal goal of one or two areas you intend to improve on, relative to your performance on previous projects. As you internalize the new techniques you learn, they will establish your baseline for future work. Then, you can select different areas to tackle when the next project comes along.

Select software magazines and books to read. When we are hustling to meet looming deadlines at work, wishing we had more time to spend with our families, and wondering when we will get the lawn mowed, reading a computer magazine gets a pretty low priority. However, being a professional engineer means devoting some of your precious free time to self-education. Begin by identifying three or four technical publications in your field of interest and follow them regularly. Also, set a goal of reading at least four work-related books a year, including some that explore ways to work more effectively and enrich your life, in addition to the technical books. *The 7 Habits of Highly Effective People* is a good example of the nontechnical category [Covey, 1989]. Chart your course toward increased knowledge by picking out two software books from the many I have cited. Buy copies at a bookstore or borrow from a library and start reading—this week!

Get in the habit of iterative design before coding. Few of us went into the field of software engineering because we like to draw models of systems. We selected this profession because we think it is fun to write programs that make computers do interesting and useful things. Nonetheless, as professionals we have a responsibility to build the best applications we can for the customers who are paying our salaries. Rather than glossing over the design of your next program, think it through carefully and document it before you begin generating code. Draw some pictures, and draw them again if your first try isn't as good as you know you can do.

If you conclude that drawing pictures *is* a useful way to help you design programs, consider buying a simple CASE tool for your PC or Macintosh to help you draw effective models that depict different views of a software system. Acquire the discipline to spend some careful thought on creative designs before you write the program. You are going to perform analysis and design in some fashion on every project; my recommendation is to do it formally, documenting your analysis of the problem domain and the design decisions that you make during the construction process. The alternative is to write the program, then spend a lot of time trying to make it right.

Apply effective structured testing techniques. Many programmers do their testing in a way that reminds me of a song from *The Music Man*. These new lyrics fit the tune; see if you can hum along:

> Code a little, test a little
> Code a little, test a little
> CODE, CODE, CODE
> Test a lot, test a little more

Learn how to perform unit, integration, and system testing in a structured, systematic, and repeatable fashion. Set quantitative goals for test coverage of source code and requirements. Learn to use code analyzer tools to identify complex modules and testing tools to measure the coverage provided by your test suite. Keep records of the defects found by different kinds of testing. Examine each defect to understand how it got into the program, why it was not found earlier, and how you might prevent defects like it in the future. Record the tests you perform so you can execute them again, without having to spend time reinventing good tests.

Begin tracking your project time daily, by work category. Start using a daily calendar planner to record how you spend your time, as discussed in Chapter 17. You can set up a simple spreadsheet to accumulate your personal data, if your department does not already use a centralized database for work effort metrics. Look at the patterns that emerge from several weeks of data to decide if you are spending your time where you thought you were, or where you think you should be. You may also find the data helpful in assessing whether you can take on additional responsibility when asked. Show your boss a summary of your recent project activities, and ask what she would like you to stop doing to be able to work on this new assignment. In a software engineering culture, activities and commitments are negotiated as priorities change over time.

Look for opportunities to reuse existing software and to create reusable work products. The single most powerful way to increase your productivity is to use an existing solution to solve a new problem. Even if we cannot attain the paradise of widespread and automated reuse through comprehensive component libraries, designs, and test cases, we can all find opportunities to leverage software investments that have already been made. The most productive programmer I know has built an extensive collection of robust reusable libraries to exploit for every new project.

Train yourself to resist the temptation to write original programs if you can assemble comparable functionality from existing pieces. Fight the "not-invented-here" syndrome we use to convince ourselves that we can do the job better than anyone else we know, and build your own suite of reusable libraries only when nothing else is available. Validate the libraries thoroughly, and share them with others (who might be willing to share theirs with you). Our group created an on-line catalog of reusable software components we had written, with on-line descriptions and a searchable index. Now we look in the catalog for an existing solution before taking the time to build something new.

Look for opportunities to create potentially reusable objects when you are building a new application, so that you can further leverage your work in the future. Yes, it is more work to create a robust reusable module than to hack out some custom code, but you only have to reuse it a few times to recoup your investment. Watch out for the trap of having the reusable component grow into a complete project unto itself, unless that's a conscious decision or you play the role of component builder on your team.

Learn how to do a better job of planning and estimating tasks. Software people are notoriously poor at estimating the effort required to accomplish a task. We generally do it off the cuff, with only a cursory appreciation of the real extent of the project. Effective project planning involves picking up all the rocks you can find and looking beneath them for work to be done. Unless we really dig under all those rocks, we will forever be encountering new tasks we had not thought about, but which are necessary to complete the project.

The only way to get better at estimating is to keep records of your software size and schedule estimates, compare them with the actual values, and adjust your estimating heuristics accordingly. Break any nontrivial task into a hierarchy of subtasks—a work breakdown structure—until each subtask represents no more than a few days of work, according to your best guess. Sequence the subtasks, find the critical path (with the help of a project management tool, if there are more than just a few tasks), factor in unavailable time (vacations, weekends, holidays, other responsibilities), and then generate an estimated duration for the overall project. Think of the time you spend learning how to generate more realistic estimates as an investment in becoming a more capable project leader.

Examine your work environment for ergonomic problems. Picture in your mind Jack, the stereotypical programmer: reclining back in an office chair, keyboard in his lap, wrists perched on the edge of the keyboard, hands cocked up at an angle, eyes focused permanently on the monitor, can of cola within easy reach. Jack maintains this posture for ten hours a day, then he goes home. He dials in to the Internet or an on-line service for a few hours, and then hits the sack. Jack repeats this routine five or six days per week, year after year. But then Jack's wrists begin to hurt. His neck is sore. His eyes are red and burning. His back aches. His shoulders are stiff (especially on the mouse-hand side). And he wonders why?

Even though you might not work exactly like Jack, software developers in general are at great risk from the hazards of repetitive motion disorders and other painful conditions caused by poor work habits and ergonomics. The next time you sit down to work, take a few minutes to compare your environment and habits with those described in the next section. Physical ailments from poorly laid out computer workstations and bad habits are serious stuff. Don't wait until you have permanent pain to start looking for causes and cures.

Building a Healthy Workplace

A software engineering culture is more than just the work you do, the way you do it, and the people with whom you do it. It also includes the place where you work. The physical surroundings (noise, lighting, privacy) and your equipment (workstation, peripherals, furniture) have a huge impact on the balance of pleasure and stress associated with your job. One component of a healthy culture is the emphasis it places on healthy computing. All group members should be aware of the health risks of extended computer use, and management must be willing to pay for items that will let everyone work comfortably and efficiently.

Many intense computer users suffer from wrist and forearm pain. Referred to as repetitive strain (or stress) injuries (RSI), repetitive motion injuries, or cumulative trauma disorders, this sort of pain is caused or exacerbated by extended hours of working with keyboard and mouse, often in an ergonomically appalling environment. The best-known form of RSI is carpal tunnel syndrome (CTS), but RSI can appear in various forms in the hands, arms, shoulders, and neck. RSI can reduce productivity, make work an ordeal, and affect the sufferer's life outside the office.

These disorders are not to be taken lightly. They are much harder to cure than to prevent. A relatively simple surgical procedure provides relief to many CTS sufferers, but no one wants to have surgery that can be avoided. Severe cases of RSI make it impossible for the victim to perform routine activities. I know software developers in their early thirties who have been forced to give up sports and hobbies they enjoy because their arms hurt so much from typing all day at work.

Anyone who spends extended periods of time working at a computer should learn about repetitive strain injuries and how to prevent them, as well as the myriad other health problems that can occur as a result of using computer workstations. *Zap!* [Sellers, 1994] and *Healthy Computing* [Harwin, 1992] are two books that address the health risks posed by extended computer usage. Every professional computer user and manager should study such books to find ways to correct problems in the workplace before they cause lasting injury.

The science of ergonomics addresses workplace design factors that are intended to maximize productivity by minimizing operator fatigue and discomfort. For computer users, such factors include lighting, chair height and angles, monitor position, table height, posture, keyboard position, mouse location, and so on. I cringe when I see people working with computers in awkward configurations that require them to

- stretch to reach the mouse,

- use several mouse movements to move the pointer because the mouse pad area is so tiny,

- bend their wrists to reach a keyboard that is too high,

- tilt their head to see a monitor at the wrong height (particularly if they wear bifocal eyeglasses),

- squint because of glare on the monitor screen, or

- keep their head rotated to view a monitor positioned at an angle from the keyboard.

A normal desk or office table is too high for safe and comfortable keyboarding. It forces your elbows and wrists into positions that can aggravate repetitive motion disorders. Tables specifically intended for computer use are two or three inches lower than normal desks. The type of chair you use is also important. Select one that allows you to adjust its seat height, seat back height and angle, and armrests. An adjustable footrest is necessary if you cannot place your feet comfortably on the floor while sitting at your workstation. Figure 20.1 illustrates Kodak's recommended distances and angles for the components of a computer workplace.

Take a close look at the safety of your workplace. See if you should change furniture, layouts, or lighting. Get an ergonomics or human factors expert to watch you work and point out problems with hardware, furniture, posture, or habits of which you are not even aware. Take regular breaks from the keyboard: stand up, stretch your arms, relax your eyes, and walk around for a few minutes. If your shoulder bothers you, try replacing your mouse with a different pointing device, such as a trackball. Voice recognition software can remove some of the burden from your hands and arms, as can a more naturally sculpted keyboard. Don't ignore those nagging pains at the end of the day; check them out, and do something about them.

Part of a software engineering culture is knowing that our managers care about our personal well-being. The responsible employer provides the right equipment to let employees work safely, comfortably, and productively. Every individual shares a responsibility with the organization to take actions to ensure we can look forward to coming to work, rather than dreading the physical or emotional pain we know we will feel at the end of the day. Do your part by educating yourself about safe, healthy computing, and demand nothing less from your employer.

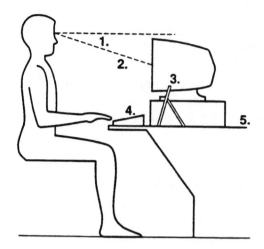

1. Viewing angle: 15°–25° below horizontal eye level
2. Viewing distance: 12"–32"
3. Copyholder: up to 20° tilt away from operator
4. Adjustable keyboard platform 25"–30" above floor
5. Adjustable display platform 3"–13" above work surface

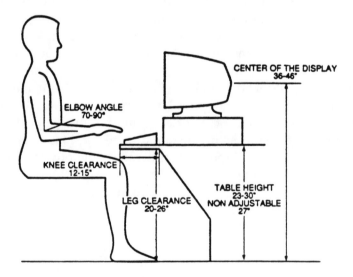

Figure 20.1: Recommended configurations of a safe computer work environment (courtesy of Corporate Ergonomics, Eastman Kodak Company).

Summary

✔ You can't change everything at once. Identify those changes that will yield the greatest benefits, and begin to implement them next Monday.

✔ Select some initial improvement initiatives from among the top ten action areas listed for software engineers. Focus your energies on just a few of those until you have established a foothold, then move on to the next area.

✔ Read a book about healthy computing. Examine your workplace and work habits to see if you should make some changes to avoid computer-induced health problems. If your employer is more concerned about saving a few hundred dollars than about providing you with a safe and productive work environment, consider looking for a more enlightened employer.

References and Further Reading

Covey, Steven R. *The 7 Habits of Highly Effective People.* New York: Fireside, 1989.

Covey presents a principle-centered approach for solving personal and professional problems. The seven habits he discusses are: (1) be proactive; (2) begin with the end in mind; (3) put first things first; (4) think win/win; (5) seek first to understand, then to be understood; (6) synergize with others; and (7) renew the physical, mental, spiritual, and social/emotional dimensions of your nature. Habit 3, "put first things first," will help anyone balance scarce time against excessive demands for it in an effective fashion.

Harwin, Ronald, and Colin Haynes. *Healthy Computing.* New York: AMACOM, 1992.

Harwin and Haynes describe computer-related health problems and how they can be minimized. Chapters address eye problems, headaches, and repetitive stress injuries. The book presents ways to avoid health problems through exercise, proper nutrition, controlling stress, and properly configuring your desk and chair.

 Sellers, Don. *Zap!* Berkeley, Calif.: Peachpit Press, 1994.

Subtitled "How Your Computer Can Hurt You—And What You Can Do About It," this book addresses many computer-related injuries, such as eyestrain, headaches, back and neck pain, and pain in the shoulders and arms. The author also discusses other ergonomic factors, including lighting, monitors, desks and chairs, keyboards and mice, radiation, and office air. The book contains much advice about how to minimize the risk of health problems from these and other sources. It includes an extensive list of sources for healthy computing equipment, as well as pointers to publications containing additional information about occupational hazards and workplace ergonomics. Every member of your organization who spends significant periods of time at a computer should have a copy of this book.

Epilogue

An organization's characteristic culture comes into being through the behaviors and interactions of people who work together. Much of the culture that results is formed spontaneously. However, an enlightened and skillful manager can steer his or her team's culture toward preferred actions and values that will stimulate superior performance and build a more favorable working environment. A culture that emphasizes quality in software engineering is better positioned to cope with the many challenges that face the software development business today and into the foreseeable future.

Quality is the responsibility of every individual in the organization: engineers, managers, testers, process improvement leaders, support staff, and all the others. A defect that slips through your quality control filters is bound to cause a headache down the road for a coworker, a customer, or both. Every member of the organization should be committed to quality, which means they need to acquire the attitudes, values, technical competencies, and people skills discussed in this book.

The first-line manager carries the lion's share of the burden of creating a software engineering culture. Through the manager's words and actions, principles and techniques that lead to software excellence can be nurtured and promoted. Alternatively, he or she can stifle grass roots efforts by the practitioners to improve the way work is done in the group. Managers are responsible for doing more than completing the project on time and on budget. They must

- ✔ lead the evolution of their technical staff into a cohesive team that shares a commitment to excellence in software development,

- ✔ encourage personal and professional growth through continual learning experiences,

✔ foster an environment of collaborative teamwork,

✔ promote and reward the use of superior software engineering practices,

✔ build a devotion to continuous improvement of the engineering processes that are used in the group,

✔ demonstrate unflagging integrity and professionalism in their interactions with their employees and managers,

✔ actively improve their own people management and communication skills, and

✔ learn how to properly balance the needs of their customers, their company, their team members, and themselves.

It's a big job. Good luck!

Appendix A

Sources for Continued Software Learning

The tables on the following pages list various resources for professional education. These addresses and details were current at the time of this printing, but may change periodically.

Table A.1.
Some Suppliers of Software Training Seminars.

Training Supplier	Some Course Offerings
Clarity Learning 319 Littleton Road, Suite 201 P.O. Box 761 Westford, MA 01886 phone: (508) 692-0950	• C and C++ programming • programming Microsoft Windows™ environment • UNIX fundamentals • programming the X Window System and Motif • object-oriented analysis
Digital Consulting, Inc. 204 Andover Street Andover, MA 01810 phone: (508) 470-3880	• client/server architecture and implementation • object-oriented analysis and design • business process reengineering • database technologies • groupware
Learning Tree International 1805 Library Street Reston, VA 22090-9919 phone: (703) 709-9019	• software development and management skills • networking, telecommunications, Novell NetWare • programming in various languages and operating systems • relational databases • client/server computing
Quality Assurance Institute Suite 350 7575 Dr. Phillips Blvd. Orlando, FL 32819-7273 phone: (407) 363-1111	• information technology quality assurance • systems testing • building an effective measurement program • process management • quality-based business information modeling
Software Engineering Institute Carnegie Mellon University Pittsburgh, PA 15213-3890 phone: (412) 268-3296	• profit through software process improvement • software quality and productivity improvement • software risk management • managing software development with metrics
Software Quality Engineering 3000-2 Hartley Road Jacksonville, FL 32257 phone: (904) 268-8639	• software testing; test management and automation • writing testable requirements • client/server and object-oriented testing • software measurement • technical reviews and inspections
Technology Exchange Company One Jacob Way Reading, MA 01867 phone: (800) 662-4282	• programming in various languages and operating systems • database design and implementation • object-oriented software development • software quality assurance, project management • requirements analysis and specifications

Table A.2.
Some Software Development and Quality Conferences.

Conference	Description
International Conference on Software Quality American Society for Quality Control 611 East Wisconsin Avenue P.O. Box 3005 Milwaukee, WI 53201-3005 phone: (414) 272-8575	This annual conference covers the full spectrum of software quality topics. A recent ICSQ conference included tracks on metrics, the CMM and ISO 9000, quality techniques, software practices, and process assessment methods.
National Conference on Software Testing and International IT Quality Conference Quality Assurance Institute Suite 350 7575 Dr. Phillips Blvd. Orlando, FL 32819-7273 phone: (407) 363-1111	These two annual conferences feature presentations by practitioners in the fields of testing, inspections, quality assurance, and process improvement. The emphasis is on real-life experiences with applying these techniques in corporate, commercial, or government software development organizations.
Software Development Miller Freeman Inc. 600 Harrison Street San Francisco, CA 94107 phone: (415) 905-2200	Presented in California in winter and on the East Coast in autumn, this event fuses multiple conferences on software development and management. Over 200 presentations on some twenty tracks cover nearly every software domain.
Software Engineering Process Group Conference (SEPG) Software Engineering Institute Carnegie Mellon University Pittsburgh, PA 15213-3890 phone: (412) 268-7388	The SEPG conference focuses on practical applications of software process improvement. Tutorials and presentations address aspects of the CMM in practice, and other aspects of process improvement work in many companies.
Software Quality Week Software Research, Inc. 625 Third Street San Francisco, CA 94107-1997 phone: (415) 957-1441	This large conference that addresses advances in client/server technologies, software test technology, quality control, the software test process, managing OO integration, software safety, and test automation.
Software Testing Analysis & Review (STAR) and Applications of Software Measurement (ASM) Software Quality Engineering 3000-2 Hartley Road Jacksonville, FL 32257 phone: (904) 268-8639	These conferences are both held annually, as is a European version of STAR called EuroSTAR. STAR features several tracks of real-world experiences with testing and other aspects of software quality practices. ASM is touted as the largest practitioner-oriented conference in the field of software metrics.
Software World USA Digital Consulting, Inc. 204 Andover Street Andover, MA 01810 phone: (508) 470-3880	Over 75 sessions are presented in this large conference. Recent topics included software management, client/server development, component-based development, GUI development, and C++ development.

Table A.3.
Some Software Engineering and Software Quality Periodicals.

Magazine	Description
American Programmer Cutter Information Corp. 37 Broadway, Suite 1 Arlington, MA 02174-5552 phone: (617) 648-8702	This is one of several high-quality (and expensive) periodicals edited by Ed Yourdon. Each monthly issue contains several well-written articles on a contemporary and significant theme in software development, not just programming.
Communications of the ACM Association for Computing Machinery 1515 Broadway New York, NY 10036-5701 phone: (212) 869-7440	*CACM* is the monthly publication that comes with your membership in the ACM. The articles span the breadth of the computing field. Each issue of *CACM* contains several articles on a common theme. They are of high quality and generally easy to read.
IEEE Computer IEEE Computer Society Publications Office 10662 Los Vasqueros Circle P.O. Box 3014 Los Alamitos, CA 90720-1314 phone: (714) 821-8380	Members of the IEEE Computer Society get *IEEE Computer* automatically. It is a monthly journal with well-written articles covering a wide range of topics in computing, although issues devoted to software engineering are infrequent.
IEEE Software IEEE Computer Society Publications Office 10662 Los Vasqueros Circle P.O. Box 3014 Los Alamitos, CA 90720-1314 phone: (714) 821-8380	*IEEE Software* contains a wealth of excellent feature articles and columns. Although it has some academic flavor, the articles are more useful than those in some of the other IEEE technical publications.
The Journal of the Quality Assurance Institute Quality Assurance Institute Suite 350 7575 Dr. Phillips Blvd. Orlando, FL 32819-7273 phone: (407) 363-1111	This quarterly publication contains articles on a variety of software quality topics. Subscriptions are free for members of the Quality Assurance Institute, and they can be purchased separately by nonmembers.
Software Development Miller Freeman Inc. 600 Harrison Street San Francisco, CA 94107 phone: (415) 905-2200	Through feature articles, columns, and product reviews, *Software Development* covers several practical application development topics each month. The writing style is more conversational than academic.
Software Process Improvement Forum Research Access, Inc. 800 Vinial Street Pittsburgh, PA 15212 phone: (412) 321-2992	This is a bimonthly magazine targeted at readers who are engaged in software process improvement efforts. It covers topics in process maturity, the SEI Capability Maturity Model, appraisal methods, and available tools, training courses, conferences, and workshops.
Software QA Software Quality Engineering 3000-2 Hartley Road Jacksonville, FL 32257 phone: (904) 268-8639	Dedicated to improving software quality, *Software QA* contains articles and columns on testing, process improvement, and the role of quality assurance in the development process.

Table A.4.
Sources of Information about Testing Tools.

Source	Description
Software Technology Support Center STSC Customer Service Office Ogden ALC/TISE 7278 Fourth Street Hill AFB, UT 84056-5209 phone: (801) 777-7703	The *Software Test Technologies Report* presents condensed descriptions of several hundred testing and static analysis tools. It is available at no charge.
"Annual Tools Catalog," *Software QA*, vol. 2, no. 3 (1995), pp. 19-38.	A large number of commercially available software testing tools are profiled in this article.
Software Quality Engineering 3000-2 Hartley Road Jacksonville, FL 32257 phone: (904) 268-8639	The 250-page *Testing Tools Reference Guide* contains profiles of hundreds of commercially available software testing and evaluation tools.
Ovum Ltd. 1 Mortimer Street London, W1N 7RH England phone: +44 71 255 2670	Ovum Ltd. publishes detailed evaluations and comparisons of more than 25 automated testing tools. This guide is both extensive and expensive.

Table A.5.
Sources of Information about CASE Tools.

Source	Description
Software Technology Support Center STSC Customer Service Office Ogden ALC/TISE 7278 Fourth Street Hill AFB, UT 84056-5209 phone: (801) 777-7703	*Requirements Analysis and Design Technology Report* provides a list of product characteristics and short descriptions for over one hundred upper-CASE tools. It is available at no charge.
Ovum Ltd. 1 Mortimer Street London, W1N 7RH England phone: +44 71 255 2670	Ovum Ltd. publishes comprehensive evaluations of many kinds of software tools, including CASE products. Their current CASE evaluation covers more than thirty-five products (over 700 pages). This guide is quite expensive.
Applied Computer Research, Inc. P.O. Box 82266 Phoenix, AZ 85071-2266 phone: (602) 995-5929	The 500-page *Guide to Software Productivity Aids* describes hundreds of tools that support every aspect of application development and maintenance. Tools are identified by the life cycle phases they support, and they are classified into sixty-six categories.

Contact Information for Selected Resources

Applied Computer Research, Inc.
P.O. Box 82266
Phoenix, AZ 85071-2266
phone: (602) 995-5929

The International Function Point Users Group (IFPUG)
Blendonview Office Park
5008-28 Pine Creek Drive
Westerville, OH 43081-4899
phone: (614) 895-7130

National Technological University
700 Centre Avenue
Fort Collins, CO 80526-1842
phone: (970) 495-6400

SET Laboratories, Inc.
P.O. Box 868
Mulino, OR 97042
phone: (503) 829-7123

Software Engineering Institute
Carnegie Mellon University
Pittsburgh, PA 15213-3890
phone: (412) 268-5800

Bibliography

Ambler, Scott. "Use Case Scenario Testing," *Software Development,* Vol. 3, No. 7 (July 1995), pp. 53-61.

Bach, James. "Enough About Process: What We Need Are Heroes," *IEEE Software,* Vol. 12, No. 2 (March 1995), pp. 96-98.

———. "The Immaturity of the CMM," *American Programmer,* Vol. 7, No. 9 (September 1994), pp. 13-18.

Bankes, Kirk. "Ford Systems Inspection Experiences," *Proceedings of the 1994 International IT Quality Conference.* Orlando, Fla.: Quality Assurance Institute, 1994, pp. 3-83 to 3-114.

Basili, Victor R., and H. Dieter Rombach. "The TAME Project: Towards Improvement-Oriented Software Environments," *IEEE Transactions on Software Engineering,* Vol. 14, No. 6 (June 1988), pp. 758-73.

Beizer, Boris. *Software Testing Techniques,* 2nd ed. New York: Van Nostrand Reinhold, 1990.

Bergin, Thomas J. *Computer-Aided Software Engineering: Issues and Trends for the 1990s and Beyond.* Harrisburg, Penn.: Idea Group Publishing, 1993.

Binder, Robert. "Software Process Improvement: A Case Study," *Software Development,* Vol. 2, No. 1 (January 1994), pp. 59-70.

Boddie, John. "Growing Better Managers by Doing Nothing," *American Programmer,* Vol. 8, No. 1 (January 1995), pp. 21-27.

Boehm, Barry W. *Software Engineering Economics.* Englewood Cliffs, N.J.: Prentice-Hall, 1981.

Bollinger, Terry B., and Clement McGowan. "A Critical Look at Software Capability Evaluations," *IEEE Software,* Vol. 8, No. 4 (July 1991), pp. 25-41.

Brooks, Frederick P., Jr. *The Mythical Man-Month: Essays on Software Engineering,* 20th anniv. ed. Reading, Mass.: Addison-Wesley, 1995.

———. "No Silver Bullet: Essence and Accidents of Software Engineering," *Computer,* Vol. 20, No. 4 (April 1987), pp. 10–19. Reprinted in *Software State-of-the-Art: Selected Essays,* edited by Tom DeMarco and Timothy Lister (New York: Dorset House Publishing, 1990), pp. 14-29.

Card, David N. "What Makes a Software Measure Successful?" *American Programmer,* Vol. 4, No. 9 (September 1991), pp. 2-8.

Carnegie Mellon University/Software Engineering Institute. *The Capability Maturity Model: Guidelines for Improving the Software Process.* Reading, Mass.: Addison-Wesley, 1995.

Chidamber, Shyam R., and Chris F. Kemerer. "A Metrics Suite for Object-Oriented Design," *IEEE Transactions on Software Engineering,* Vol. 20, No. 6 (June 1994), pp. 476-93.

Cohen, Rich, and Warren Keuffel. "Pull Together," *Computer Language,* Vol. 8, No. 8 (August 1991), pp. 36-44.

Coleman, Don, Dan Ash, Bruce Lowther, and Paul Oman. "Using Metrics to Evaluate Software System Maintainability," *IEEE Computer,* Vol. 27, No. 8 (August 1994), pp. 44-49.

Constantine, Larry L. "Design for Usability" and "UI to Fit the Uses: Essential Use Case Modeling," *Software Development '94 Proceedings.* San Francisco: Miller Freeman, 1994.

———. "Leading Your Team—Wherever It Goes," *Software Development,* Vol. 3, No. 1 (January 1995), pp. 26-34.

———. "Work Organization: Paradigms for Project Management and Organization," *Communications of the ACM,* Vol. 36, No. 10 (October 1993), pp. 35-43.

Cornell, John L., and Linda Shafer. *Structured Rapid Prototyping: An Evolutionary Approach to Software Development.* Englewood Cliffs, N.J.: Yourdon Press/Prentice-Hall, 1989.

Covey, Steven R. *The 7 Habits of Highly Effective People.* New York: Fireside, 1989.

Crosby, Philip B. *Quality Is Free.* New York: McGraw-Hill, 1979.

Curtis, Bill. "A Mature View of the CMM," *American Programmer,* Vol. 7, No. 9 (September 1994), pp. 19-28.

———, William E. Hefley, Sally Miller, Michael Konrad, and Sandra Bond. "Increasing Software Talent," *American Programmer,* Vol. 7, No. 12 (December 1994), pp. 13-20.

Daskalantonakis, Michael K. "Achieving Higher SEI Levels," *IEEE Software,* Vol. 11, No. 4 (July 1994), pp. 17-24.

———. "A Practical View of Software Measurement and Implementation Experiences Within Motorola," *IEEE Transactions on Software Engineering,* Vol. 18, No. 11 (November 1992), pp. 998-1010.

Davis, Alan M. *Software Requirements: Objects, Functions, and States.* Englewood Cliffs, N.J.: PTR Prentice-Hall, 1993.

DeGrace, Peter, and Leslie Hulet Stahl. *The Olduvai Imperative: CASE and the State of Software Engineering Practice.* Englewood Cliffs, N.J.: Yourdon Press/Prentice-Hall, 1993.

DeMarco, Tom. *Controlling Software Projects.* Englewood Cliffs, N.J.: Yourdon Press/Prentice-Hall, 1982.

———, and Timothy Lister. *Peopleware: Productive Projects and Teams.* New York: Dorset House Publishing, 1987.

———, eds. *Software State-of-the-Art: Selected Papers.* New York: Dorset House Publishing, 1990.

Deeprose, Donna. *How to Recognize and Reward Employees.* New York: AMACOM, 1994.

Deutsch, Michael S., and Ronald R. Willis. *Software Quality Engineering: A Total Technical and Management Approach.* Englewood Cliffs, N.J.: Prentice-Hall, 1988.

Dion, Raymond. "Process Improvement and the Corporate Balance Sheet," *IEEE Software*, Vol. 10, No. 4 (July 1993), pp. 28-35.

Dixon, Robert L. *Winning with CASE: Managing Modern Software Development.* New York: McGraw-Hill, 1992.

Dreger, J. Brian. *Function Point Analysis.* Englewood Cliffs, N.J.: Prentice-Hall, 1989.

Ebenau, Robert G., and Susan H. Strauss. *Software Inspection Process.* New York: McGraw-Hill, 1994.

Fagan, Michael E. "Advances in Software Inspections," *IEEE Transactions on Software Engineering,* Vol. 12, No. 7 (July 1986), pp. 744-51.

———. "Design and Code Inspections to Reduce Errors in Program Development," *IBM Systems Journal,* Vol. 15, No. 3 (March 1976), pp. 182-211.

Fenton, Norman E. *Software Metrics: A Rigorous Approach.* London: Chapman & Hall, 1991.

Freedman, Daniel P., and Gerald M. Weinberg. *Handbook of Walkthroughs, Inspections, and Technical Reviews,* 3rd ed. New York: Dorset House Publishing, 1990.

Gause, Donald C., and Gerald M. Weinberg. *Exploring Requirements: Quality Before Design.* New York: Dorset House Publishing, 1989.

Gianturco, Mark D. "Testing Techniques for Quality Software," *Software Development,* Vol. 2, No. 8 (August 1994), pp. 45-61.

Gilb, Tom. *Principles of Software Engineering Management.* Wokingham, England: Addison-Wesley, 1988.

———, and Dorothy Graham. *Software Inspection.* Reading, Mass.: Addison-Wesley, 1993.

Glass, Robert L. *Building Quality Software.* Englewood Cliffs, N.J.: Prentice-Hall, 1992.

Goodman, Paul. *Practical Implementation of Software Metrics.* London: McGraw-Hill, 1993.

Grady, Robert B. "Practical Results from Measuring Software Quality," *Communications of the ACM,* Vol. 36, No. 11 (November 1993), pp. 62-68.

————. *Practical Software Metrics for Project Management and Process Improvement.* Englewood Cliffs, N.J.: PTR Prentice-Hall, 1992.

————, and Deborah L. Caswell. *Software Metrics: Establishing a Company-Wide Program.* Englewood Cliffs, N.J.: Prentice-Hall, 1987.

Grady, Robert B., and Tom Van Slack. "Key Lessons in Achieving Widespread Inspection Use," *IEEE Software,* Vol. 11, No. 4 (July 1994), pp. 46-57.

Harwin, Ronald, and Colin Haynes. *Healthy Computing.* New York: AMACOM, 1992.

Herbsleb, James, David Zubrow, Jane Siegel, James Rozum, and Anita Carleton. "Software Process Improvement: State of the Payoff," *American Programmer,* Vol. 7, No. 9 (September 1994), pp. 2-12.

Hetzel, Bill. *Making Software Measurement Work.* Wellesley, Mass.: QED Publishing Group, 1993.

Hughes, Cary T., and Jon D. Clark. "The Stages of CASE Usage," *Datamation* (February 1, 1990), pp. 41-44.

Humphrey, Watts S. *A Discipline for Software Engineering.* Reading, Mass.: Addison-Wesley, 1995.

————. *Managing the Software Process.* Reading, Mass.: Addison-Wesley, 1989.

IEEE Software Engineering Standards Collection, 1994 ed. Los Alamitos, Calif.: IEEE Computer Society Press, 1994 (IEEE product number SH94213).

IEEE Std. 610.12-1990, "IEEE Standard Glossary of Software Engineering Terminology." Los Alamitos, Calif.: IEEE Computer Society Press, 1990.

IEEE Std. 830-1993, "IEEE Recommended Practice for Software Requirements Specifications." Los Alamitos, Calif.: IEEE Computer Society Press, 1993.

IEEE Std. 1044-1993, "IEEE Standard Classification for Software Anomalies," Los Alamitos, Calif.: IEEE Computer Society Press, 1993.

IEEE Std. 1061-1992, "IEEE Standard for a Software Quality Metrics Methodology," Los Alamitos, Calif.: IEEE Computer Society Press, 1992.

Ince, Darrel. *ISO 9001 and Software Quality Assurance.* New York: McGraw-Hill, 1994.

Jacobson, I., M. Christerson, P. Jonsson, and G. Overgaard. *Object-Oriented Software Engineering: A Use Case Driven Approach*. Reading, Mass.: Addison-Wesley, 1992.

Johnson, Mark. "Dr. Boris Beizer on Software Testing: An Interview. Part 1," *The Software QA Quarterly*, Vol. 1, No. 2 (Spring 1994), pp. 7-13; "Part 2" (Summer 1994), pp. 41-45.

Jones, Capers. *Applied Software Measurement*. New York: McGraw-Hill, 1991.

———. *Assessment and Control of Software Risks*. Englewood Cliffs, N.J.: PTR Prentice-Hall, 1994.

———. "Gaps in SEI Programs," *Software Development*, Vol. 3, No. 3 (March 1995), pp. 41-48.

Kaner, Cem. "Software Negligence and Testing Coverage," *The Software QA Quarterly*, Vol. 2, No. 2 (1995), pp. 18-26.

———, Jack Falk, and Hung Quoc Nguyen. *Testing Computer Software*, 2nd ed. New York: Van Nostrand Reinhold, 1993.

Karten, Naomi. *Managing Expectations*. New York: Dorset House Publishing, 1994.

Keil, Mark, and Erran Carmel. "Customer-Developer Links in Software Development," *Communications of the ACM*, Vol. 38, No. 5 (May 1995), pp. 33-44.

Keuffel, Warren. "Tools of the Trade," *Software Development*, Vol. 2, No. 12 (December 1994), pp. 31-35, and *Software Development*, Vol. 3, No. 1 (January 1995), pp. 21-24.

Layman, Beth. "ISO 9000 Standards and Existing Quality Models: How They Relate," *American Programmer*, Vol. 7, No. 2 (February 1994), pp. 9-15.

Lorenz, Mark, and Jeff Kidd. *Object-Oriented Software Metrics*. Englewood Cliffs, N.J.: PTR Prentice-Hall, 1994.

Maguire, Steve. *Debugging the Development Process*. Redmond, Wash.: Microsoft Press, 1994.

McCabe, Thomas J. *Structured Testing: A Software Testing Methodology Using the Cyclomatic Complexity Metric*. National Bureau of Standards Special Publication 500-99, 1982.

McConnell, Steve. *Code Complete*. Redmond, Wash.: Microsoft Press, 1993.

Mosley, Daniel J. *The Handbook of MIS Application Software Testing.* Englewood Cliffs, N.J.: Yourdon Press/Prentice-Hall, 1993.

Musa, John D., Anthony Iannino, and Kazuhira Okumoto. *Software Reliability: Measurement, Prediction, Application.* New York: McGraw-Hill, 1987.

Myers, Glenford J. *The Art of Software Testing.* New York: John Wiley & Sons, 1979.

———. *Software Reliability.* New York: John Wiley & Sons, 1976.

Nielsen, Jakob, and Robert L. Mack, eds. *Usability Inspection Methods.* New York: John Wiley & Sons, 1994.

Page-Jones, Meilir. "The CASE Manifesto," *Computer Language,* Vol. 10, No. 6 (June 1993), pp. 39-52.

———. "Managing in the Object-Oriented Environment," *Proceedings of the Fourth International Teamworkers Conference,* Cadre Technologies, Inc., 1991.

Paulk, Mark C., Bill Curtis, Mary Beth Chrissis, and Charles V. Weber. "Capability Maturity Model, Version 1.1," *IEEE Software,* Vol. 10, No. 4 (July 1993), pp. 18-27.

Perry, Dewayne E., Nancy A. Staudenmayer, and Lawrence G. Votta. "People, Organizations, and Process Improvement," *IEEE Software,* Vol. 11, No. 4 (July 1994), pp. 36-45.

Perry, William E. *Quality Assurance for Information Systems: Methods, Tools, and Techniques.* Wellesley, Mass.: QED Information Sciences, 1991.

Pfleeger, Shari Lawrence. "Lessons Learned in Building a Corporate Metrics Program," *IEEE Software,* Vol. 10, No. 3 (May 1993), pp. 67-74.

Pressman, Roger S. *Making Software Engineering Happen.* Englewood Cliffs, N.J.: Prentice-Hall, 1988.

———. *Software Engineering: A Practitioner's Approach,* 3rd ed. New York: McGraw-Hill, 1992.

Raynor, Darrel A. "Team Training for Successful Projects: Using a Skills Matrix for Planning," *American Programmer,* Vol. 8, No. 1 (January 1995), pp. 11-14.

Rettig, Marc. "Prototyping for Tiny Fingers," *Communications of the ACM,* Vol. 37, No. 4 (April 1994), pp. 21-27.

Robertson, James, and Suzanne Robertson. *Complete Systems Analysis: The Workbook, the Textbook, the Answers.* New York: Dorset House Publishing, 1994.

Roetzheim, William. *Developing Software to Government Standards.* Englewood Cliffs, N.J.: Prentice-Hall, 1991.

Rubin, Howard. "Measuring 'Rigor' and Putting Measurement into Action," *American Programmer,* Vol. 4, No. 9 (September 1991), pp. 9-23.

———, Bob Marose, Gonzalo Verdago, and Margaret L. Johnson. *The Software Engineer's Benchmark Handbook.* Phoenix, Ariz.: Applied Computer Research, 1992.

Saiedian, Hossein, and Richard Kuzara. "SEI Capability Maturity Model's Impact on Contractors," *IEEE Computer,* Vol. 28, No. 1 (January 1995), pp. 16-26.

Sellers, Don. *Zap!* Berkeley, Calif.: Peachpit Press, 1994.

Sharon, David, and Rodney Bell. "Tools That Bind: Creating Integrated Environments," *IEEE Software,* Vol. 12, No. 2 (March 1995), pp. 78-85.

Spurr, Kathy, and Paul Lazell, eds. *CASE on Trial.* Chichester, England: John Wiley & Sons, 1990.

Szmyt, Peter. "Get Over the Software-Centered Wall," *Software Development,* Vol. 2, No. 11 (November 1994), pp. 49-59.

Thayer, Richard H., and Merlin Dorfman, eds. *System and Software Requirements Engineering.* Los Alamitos, Calif.: IEEE Computer Society Press, 1990.

Tripp, Leonard, ed. *Survey of Existing and In-Progress Software Engineering Standards* (1993) and *Master Plan for Software Engineering Standards* (1993).

Walsh, James. "Determining Software Quality," *Computer Language,* Vol. 10, No. 4 (April 1993), pp. 57-65.

Weeks, Kevin D. "Glass-Box Testing," *The C Users Journal,* Vol. 10, No. 10 (October 1992), pp. 47-54.

Weinberg, Gerald M. *The Psychology of Computer Programming.* New York: Van Nostrand Reinhold, 1971.

———. *Quality Software Management, Volume 1: Systems Thinking.* New York: Dorset House Publishing, 1992.

———. *Quality Software Management, Volume 2: First-Order Measurement.* New York: Dorset House Publishing, 1993.

———. *Quality Software Management, Volume 3: Congruent Action.* New York: Dorset House Publishing, 1994.

———. *Quality Software Management, Volume 4: Anticipating Change.* New York: Dorset House Publishing, 1996.

———. *Understanding the Professional Programmer.* New York: Dorset House Publishing, 1988.

Weller, Edward F. "Lessons from Three Years of Inspection Data," *IEEE Software,* Vol. 10, No. 5 (September 1993), pp. 38-45, and "Using Metrics to Manage Software Projects," *IEEE Software,* Vol. 11, No. 5 (September 1994), pp. 27-33.

Whitaker, Ken. *Managing Software Maniacs.* New York: John Wiley & Sons, 1994.

Wiegers, Karl E. "Creating a Software Engineering Culture," *Software Development,* Vol. 2, No. 7 (July 1994), pp. 59-66.

———. "Effective Quality Practices in a Small Software Group," *The Software QA Quarterly,* Vol. 1, No. 2 (Spring 1994), pp. 14-26.

———. "Implementing Software Engineering in a Small Software Group," *Computer Language,* Vol. 10, No. 6 (June 1993), pp. 55-64.

———. "Improving Quality through Software Inspections," *Software Development,* Vol. 3, No. 4 (April 1995), pp. 55-64.

———. "Lessons from Software Work Effort Metrics," *Software Development,* Vol. 2, No. 10 (October 1994), pp. 36-47.

———. "In Search of Excellent Requirements," *Journal of the Quality Assurance Institute,* Vol. 9, No. 1 (January 1995), pp. 23-32.

Wilson, James D. "Methodology Mania: Which One Fits Best?" *Journal of the Quality Assurance Institute,* Vol. 7, No. 2 (April 1993), pp. 18-22.

Wirth, N. "A Plea for Lean Software," *IEEE Computer,* Vol. 28, No. 2 (February 1995), pp. 64-68.

Wood, Jane, and Denise Silver. *Joint Application Design.* New York: John Wiley & Sons, 1989.

Yeager, Chuck, and Leo Janos. *Yeager.* New York: Bantam Books, 1985.

Yourdon, Edward, ed. *American Programmer.* Arlington, Mass.: Cutter Information Corp., published monthly.

———. *Decline and Fall of the American Programmer.* Englewood Cliffs, N.J.: Yourdon Press/Prentice-Hall, 1992.

———. *Rise and Resurrection of the American Programmer.* Englewood Cliffs, N.J.: Yourdon Press/Prentice-Hall, 1996.

Author Index

Subject Index

Reviewers' Comments and Praise for
CREATING A SOFTWARE ENGINEERING CULTURE
by Karl E. Wiegers

ISBN: 0-932633-33-1   Copyright ©1996   384 pages, hardcover

"Karl Wiegers' new book has a good chance of joining the select few books that top 100,000 copies and become standard references for the software engineering world. What Karl's book has in common with the classic software engineering books are these four factors:

- It starts a new theme of important research or goes beyond its competitors.
- It covers important and practical topics dealing with day-to-day problems.
- It is well written and easy to read.
- It includes real data rather than just the author's opinions.

What sets Karl's book apart from the other treatments is that it deals with how real people react to changes, to mandates, to new methods, and to both success and failure in their work.

. . . not just a theoretical discussion of how software engineering is supposed to work, but rather some informed observations of how things really do work in an actual company that wants to improve software. . . .

. . . a graceful writing style, clear illustrations, and a very extensive set of bibliographic references. . . . a welcome addition to the software engineering literature."

—Capers Jones, Chairman, Software Productivity Research, Inc.

"I give it Four Stars! A book in which both managers and technicians can find practical guidance in their common quest for a more productive, healthier, and happier software development organization."

—Tim Lister, Principal, Atlantic Systems Guild

". . . an insightful description of a healthy software engineering culture. His culture builder and culture killer tips present good commonsense advice to both software developers and managers on how to evolve a professional culture. . . . a very readable book."

—Bill Curtis, Co-Founder and Chief Scientist, TeraQuest

DORSET HOUSE PUBLISHING CO., INC.
353 West 12th Street   New York, NY 10014   USA
1-800-DH-BOOKS   (1-800-342-6657)   212-620-4053   fax: 212-727-1044
dhpubco@aol.com   http://imasof.com/dh